THE ORIGIN AND EVOLUTION OF RELIGION

BY

ALBERT CHURCHWARD
M.D., M.R.C.P., Etc.

Published 2000
The Book Tree
Escondido, CA

LONDON: GEORGE ALLEN & UNWIN LTD.
RUSKIN HOUSE, 40 MUSEUM STREET, W.C. 1

First published by George Allen & Unwin Ltd, London, 1924.

Printed on Acid-Free Paper

The Origin and Evolution of Religion
ISBN 1-58509-078-6

©2000
THE BOOK TREE
All Rights Reserved

Published by
**The Book Tree
Post Office Box 724
Escondido, CA 92033**

We provide fascinating and educational products to help awaken the public to new ideas and information that would not be available otherwise. We carry over 1100 Books, Booklets, Audio, Video, and other products on Alchemy, Alternative Medicine, Ancient America, Ancient Astronauts, Ancient Civilizations, Ancient Mysteries, Ancient Religion and Worship, Angels, Anthropology, Anti-Gravity, Archaeology, Area 51, Assyria, Astrology, Atlantis, Babylonia, Townsend Brown, Christianity, Cold Fusion, Colloidal Silver, Comparative Religions, Crop Circles, The Dead Sea Scrolls, Early History, Electromagnetics, Electro-Gravity, Egypt, Electromagnetic Smog, Michael Faraday, Fatima, The Fed, Fluoride, Free Energy, Freemasonry, Global Manipulation, The Gnostics, God, Gravity, The Great Pyramid, Gyroscopic Anti-Gravity, Healing Electromagnetics, Health Issues, Hinduism, HIV, Human Origins, Jehovah, Jesus, Jordan Maxwell, John Keely, Lemuria, Lost Cities, Lost Continents, Magick, Masonry, Mercury Poisoning, Metaphysics, Mythology, Occultism, Paganism, Pesticide Pollution, Personal Growth, The Philadelphia Experiement, Philosophy, Powerlines, Prophecy, Psychic Research, Pyramids, Rare Books, Religion, Religious Controversy, Roswell, Walter Russell, Scalar Waves, SDI, John Searle, Secret Societies, Sex Worship, Sitchin Studies, Smart Cards, Joseph Smith, Solar Power, Sovereignty, Space Travel, Spirituality, Stonehenge, Sumeria, Sun Myths, Symbolism, Tachyon Fields, Templars, Tesla, Theology, Time Travel, The Treasury, UFOs, Underground Bases, World Control, The World Grid, Zero Point Energy, and much more. Call **1 (800) 700-TREE** for our *FREE BOOK TREE CATALOG* or visit our website at www.thebooktree.com for more information.

CONTENTS

	PAGE
LIST OF FIGURES IN THE TEXT	xi
LIST OF PLATES	xiii

CHAPTER I

DEFINITIONS OF RELIGION. THE DAWN OF RELIGIOUS IDEAS . . 1

    1. Propitiation of Elemental Powers.
    2. Propitiation of Ancestral Spirits.
    3. Propitiation of a Great Spirit.

All of which first originated amongst Primitive Man—The Pygmies: the first humans evolved in Africa—The reason for Ancestral Worship, Propitiation, and Sacrifices—All Pretotemic, arising in these three primary forms.

CHAPTER II

THE RELIGIOUS CULT OF THE TOTEMIC PEOPLE 14

Totemic Sociology and Ceremonies, reasons for, first brought into being by the Nilotic Negroes—Totem, its origin, derivation, and signification explained—The Primitive Eucharist—Origin of the Mystery of the Resurrection and Doctrine of Soul-making—Origin of the Ka Statue, a type of eternal duration—Origin of the Mystery of passing through the Underworld—Beliefs in Ancestral Spirits, the reason and proofs of same.

CHAPTER III

MAGIC AND FETISHISM 36

Magic and Fetishism defined and explained—Totemic Ceremonies performed for increase of food, and those of religious nature: Tree-Worship, Sun-Worship, Phallic Worship, Serpent-Worship defined and explained.

CHAPTER IV

HERO CULT AND MYTHOLOGY 47

The Mythology—The Sacred Signs which were evolved by the Nilotic Negroes—The commencement of Hero Cult, Set, Horus and Shu, as the three Primary Heroes, found in many countries —Set the first Primary God of the Southern Hemisphere; various types of Set; ceremonies still in existence connected with the primary Myths—Shu type of the God of the Equinox.

CONTENTS

CHAPTER V

SACRED SYMBOLS 67

Primary forms of the Dual God—Set as Primary God and his Cult widespread—Signs and Symbols associated with Set and Horus—The great Serpent of Evil traced to Hero-Cult Nilotic Negroes—List of zootype types—The custom of burning incense and making libations, and their meaning.

CHAPTER VI

THE STELLAR CULT 86

Its origin and world-wide distribution—Horus God of the North, the Primary God—Horus as the great Fish—The Assyrian-American and Christian types—Various depictions of the Great Mother.

CHAPTER VII

THE STELLAR CULT (*continued*) 117

Depiction of Spirit landing at the Stellar Mount of Glory—Portrayal of Great Mother in various countries and forms—The birthplace at the Pole—Children born of the Great Mother—Uranographic representations—"Brothers of Horus" found in many countries under various types—The Deluge Myths.

CHAPTER VIII

THE STELLAR CULT (*continued*) 135

Reference to the Crucified Horus on the North and South Poles in "Arcana of Freemasonry," p. 41—Various portrayals of Horus and Set in different countries.

CHAPTER IX

THE GREAT PYRAMID OF GHIZEH 145

Its Origin and Builders—Its description and Symbolical meaning—The difference between Stellar Cult and Solar Cult Temples—The Temples of Jerusalem.

CHAPTER X

DIFFERENT PHASES OF THE STELLAR CULT 173

Distinguishing characteristics of Stellar Cult Temples—Temples of the Axe and their decipherment and orientation—Horus of the Double Horizon or Dual Power—Mexican and Indian portrayals of Horus—The Winged Disk and its meaning—Horus Behutet and the Cult of Atem—The Serpent type of Horus as Tem—The Tower of Babel and its explanation—Signs, Symbols and Ideographs used during the Stellar Cult and their explanation—Proofs of Stellar Cult having been carried to most parts of the world—The original division of Egypt into Nomes and proof of its type being carried to the Pacific Isles.

CHAPTER XI

THE LUNAR CULT 194

The change of types and time, as reckoned by the Lunar Orb and description of the same—The proofs of the Lunar Cult having been carried to many lands—The Moon God Aah-Tehuti and the Great Mother Hathor amongst the Papyrus reeds.

CHAPTER XII

THE SOLAR CULT 212

The reason for changing the Cult and the reckoning of time—The different imagery arising from bringing on part of the Stellar and Lunar Cults into the Solar—Tem and Tum brought on in the early Solar as Atum-Iu and Atum-Ra—Mexican portrayals—The Fatherhood first recognized—The foundation of Monotheism—Professor Maspero's opinion—The Sphinx: its origin, its Symbolical meaning, and Mexican portrayal—The doctrine of the incarnation and resurrection—The different imagery of the Double Horus or Horus of the Double Power, explanation of the Mystery—Horus as the "All-one" and Mexican portrayal of the same—Horus as the two Lions—The Chaldean, Babylonian and Assyrian, and Mexican portrayal of Horus.

CHAPTER XIII

THE SOLAR CULT (*continued*) 238

The Mystery of Har-Makhu—Explanation of the different imagery—The Cult of Ptah—The Cult of Amen—The making of Amenta and explanation of same—Iu-em-Hetep and Dr. Wallis Budge's opinion—The Mexican portrayal of the same, also Mexican portrayal of the making of Amenta—Depiction of Shu—Mexican Gutemala and Peruvian—Osiris as the God in Mummy form in Amenta—How this Cult was brought on into the Christian—The difference between the Pyramid portrayal and the Amenta—Proof of the Totemic Mysteries survived as Eschatological—The Egyptian depiction of the passage of the Spirit and Soul to the Paradise as the North Celestial Pole—Ptah-Seker-Ausar, the Triune God of the Resurrection—The Ritual of Ancient Egypt commonly called the Book of the Dead—The Nesi-Khonsu Book of the Dead—Amsu-Horus—The ten great Mysteries—The reason for the Mummy type.

CONTENTS

CHAPTER XIV

THE JEWS AND ISRAELITES 291

Manetho's statement with regard to Moses—The people of Ysiraal and the Exodus—The Books of Genesis, Exodus, and Joshua—The Laws of Moses—Clement of Alexandria's statement—The Pentateuch, its origin—The Creation, the fiction and truth—Traditions among the nations of Antiquity—The Semetic derived from the Egyptian originally—The Elohim are the Ari—The Garden of Eden —The passage of the Red Sea and the Exodus.

CHAPTER XV

BABYLONIAN CULT 328

CHAPTER XVI

BUDDHISM 330

The first Buddha—The system of Buddhism in Thibet—The Hindu Golden City of the Gods—Buddha in China—Explanation of Buddhism and Hindu Beliefs—Khonds of Orissa—The Buddhist and Brahmins—The Cult of Tem carried to India.

CHAPTER XVII

THE DRUIDS 346

Remarks on the Religion of the Druids.

CHAPTER XVIII

MOHAMMEDISM 355

Remarks on Mohammed and his Religion.

CHAPTER XIX

CULT OF CHRISTIANITY 362

First establishment of the Religion of the Cross—The name of the Bible—Historical opinions—The sacred books of the Hebrew and Egyptian-gnostic writings—The early Christian Fathers and their writings—The writings of Paul—The dogmas of Christianity introduced—*Pistis Sophia*: the Ritual of Ancient Egypt and Christian doctrines compared—The Resurrection—Revelation and its origin—John and Taht Aan—The question of an Historical Jesus and the Devil on the Mount in the wilderness.

CHAPTER XX

CONCLUSION 404
GLOSSARY 411
INDEX 413

LIST OF FIGURES IN THE TEXT

FIG.		PAGE
1.	A KA IMAGE FOUND AT EASTER ISLAND	30
2.	THE "DUAL GOD" OF BABYLON—MEXICAN AND EASTER ISLAND	49
3.	BIRD REPRESENTING "GREAT MOTHER" WITH EGG, FOUND AT EASTER ISLAND	59
4.	BIRD REPRESENTING "GREAT MOTHER" WITH GOLDEN EGG, FOUND AMONGST MAYA RUINS	61
5.	SEB AND NUT SLEEPING IN EACH OTHER'S ARMS	62
6.	STARRY HEAVENS OF NIGHT UPRAISED BY SHU	63
7.	HORUS OF THE INUNDATION, STELLAR PORTRAYAL	64
8.	PRIMARY DEPICTION OF ANUBIS, AS JACKAL	74
9.	EGYPTIAN PRIEST BURNING INCENSE AND POURING LIBATIONS	80
10.	MEXICAN DEPICTION OF GREAT MOTHER IN DUAL FORM	99
11.	MEXICAN DEPICTION OF HORUS CONTENDING WITH SET FOR WATER	106
12.	MEXICAN DEPICTION OF APAP HAVING SWALLOWED ALL THE WATER AND HORUS TRYING TO MAKE HIM DISGORGE IT	107
13.	APT THE GREAT MOTHER GIVING BIRTH TO HER SON HORUS	110
13A.	MEXICAN DEPICTION OF HORUS AS GOD OF AM-KHEMEN	112
14.	RANNUT, THE SERPENT GODDESS MOTHER, SUCKLING HORUS	113
15.	A SOUL ASCENDING THE LADDER TO THE MOUNT OF GLORY	117
16.	THE GREAT MOTHER APT AND HAUNCH	118
17.	CONSTELLATION OF THE HIPPOPOTAMUS AND THIGH	122
18.	SCOTTISH SYMBOL OF HORUS OF THE DOUBLE HORIZON	124
19.	SCOTTISH SYMBOLS OF THE GREAT MOTHER APT GIVING BIRTH TO HER SON HORUS	125
20.	VARIOUS FORMS OF SWASTIKA FOUND IN ASIA BY DR. DRUMMOND OF CEYLON	126
21.	SYMBOLS FOUND IN MEXICO	127
22.	THREE DEER HEADS	127
23.	SYMBOLS OF THE DIVINE CIRCLES	133
24.	THE GODDESS SESHETA	140
25.	HETEP. SUMMIT OF GREAT PYRAMID	155
26.	HORUS AS THE NATZAR AND DOUBLE HORIZON	176
27.	CHALDEAN WINGED DISKS	180
28.	"WINGED DISKS" AND NATZAR FROM SCOTLAND	182
29.	FOUR JACKALS, TYPES OF FOUR GREAT SPIRITS	183

LIST OF FIGURES IN THE TEXT

FIG.		PAGE
30.	THE IBIS OR HEBI WITH THE GODDESS MAÂT	202
31.	THE DOG-HEADED APE	203
32.	CHÁNGES IN THE EQUINOXES	219
33.	DIAGRAMATIC PORTRAYAL	220
34.	EGYPTIAN SIGNS OF THE ZODIAC	221
35.	THE EATER OF THE ASS	222
36.	MEXICAN PORTRAYAL OF PTAH PIERCING APAP	225
37.	HAR-URAS AN IMPUBESCENT CHILD	229
38.	MAYA PORTRAYAL OF ATUM-IU	234
39.	BES-HORUS WITH EGYPTIAN HARP	236
40.	BES-HORUS	246
41.	MAYA DEPICTION OF KHNUM FORMING MAN FROM CLAY	248
42.	THE TWO TATT PILLARS	249
43.	RAISING OF THE TATT CROSS IN AMENTA	251
44.	MEXICAN DEPICTION OF PTAH FORMING AMENTA	257
45.	MEXICAN DEPICTION OF PTAH OPENING AND CLOSING AMENTA	259
46.	MEXICAN PORTRAYAL OF INSTRUMENTS FOR THE OPENING AND CLOSING OF AMENTA	260
47.	SHU, THE KNEELER	261
48.	SHU, FROM PERU	264
49.	MEXICAN DEPICTION OF AMSU-HORUS	286
50.	HINDU GODDESS MAYA	341
51.	MAKARAS	344
52.	THE MAKARAS OF VARUNA	345
53.	THE GREAT CAT	390

LIST OF PLATES

PLATE		FACING PAGE
I.	SHU UPRAISING THE HEAVENS, I.E. NUT THE SKY FROM SEB, I.E. THE EARTH	63
II.	SET AND HORUS POURING OUT LIFE OVER SETI I.	72
III.	MEXICAN DEPICTION OF THE SUBMERGENCE OF SET IN THE SOUTH AND ELEVATION OF HORUS IN THE NORTH AS "GOD OF THE NORTH AND SOUTH"	73
IV.	THE GOD SET REPRESENTED AS FIGHTING	80
V.	HORUS-BEHUTET, OR THE ELDER HORUS	81
VI.	A TYPE OF HERU-UR	88
VII.	SOLAR TYPE OF HORUS ISSUING FROM THE WATER	96
VIII.	SEBEK-HORUS AS THE GREAT FISH	97
IX.	HORUS HAVING BOUND THE BLACK BOAR OF SET IS SPEARING HIM	104
X.	PORTRAYALS OF ZOOTYPES OF GREAT MOTHER FROM SOUTH AFRICA	105
XI.	PORTRAYALS OF ZOOTYPES FROM GUATEMALA	108
XII.	SEKHET-BAST AS THE GREAT MOTHER	109
XIII.	MERSEKERT AS THE GREAT MOTHER SUCKLING HORUS	112
XIV.	ISIS AS THE GREAT MOTHER SUCKLING HORUS IN THE PAPYRUS SWAMP	113
XV.	NUT, THE MOTHER OF THE GODS	120
XVI.	BIRTHPLACE OF HORUS IN SOTHIS	121
XVII.	SYMBOLS OF THE DIVISION OF HEAVEN	128
XVIII.	THE FOUR GREAT SPIRITS	129
XIX.	SYMBOLIC PLATE	160
XX.	THE THIRTY-SIXTH PAGE OF THE DRESDEN MAYA CODEX	161
XXI.	PHOTOGRAPH OF A TEMPLE IN INDIA	176
XXII.	DOOR OF THE TEMPLE	177
XXIII.	INDIAN REPRESENTATION OF HORUS AS SAVIOUR BY FOOD AND WATER	178
XXIV.	HORUS AS NAPRIT	178
XXV.	CHALDEAN DEPICTION OF HORUS	179
XXVI.	MEXICAN DEPICTION OF HORUS	184
XXVII.	ASSYRIAN WINGED DISK	185

LIST OF PLATES

PLATE		FACING PAGE
XXVIII.	EGYPTIAN WINGED DISK	185
XXIX.	THE URÆUS SERPENT OF EGYPT	196
XXX.	THE GODDESS HATHOR WITH HORUS (ZOOTYPE)	196
XXXI.	THE GODDESS HATHOR IN HUMAN FORM	196
XXXII.	HATHOR AMONGST THE PAPYRUS REEDS	196
XXXIII.	THE GODDESS MEH-URIT	197
XXXIV.	STATUE FOUND IN THE TEMPLE OF KHONSU AT KARNAK	197
XXXV.	THE DUAL GOD KENSU STANDING UPON TWO CROCODILES (LUNAR DEPICTION)	200
XXXVI.	HERU-SMA-TAURI	200
XXXVII.	AÃH-TEHUTI	200
XXXVIII.	AÃH-TEHUTI IN LUNAR ARK	201
XXXIX.	TEHUTI OR THOTH	208
XL.	THE GODDESS MAÃT	208
XLI.	THE GODDESS SATI IN HUMAN FORM	208
XLII.	SEB, THE ERPÃ OF THE GODS	209
XLIII.	THE GOD TEMU IN HUMAN FORM	216
XLIV.	THE GOD TEM SEATED IN HIS BOAT	217
XLV.	HORUS STANDING ON TWO CROCODILES, SOLAR TYPE	224
XLVI.	HERU-PA-KHART	225
XLVII.	THE GREAT SPHINX OF EGYPT	232
XLVIII.	THE GREAT SPHINX OF THE MÃYA (MEXICAN)	232
XLIX.	INDIAN PORTRAYAL OF HORUS WITH LUTE	233
L.	HORUS AS THE GOD OF GAMES AND MUSIC (MEXICAN TYPOLOGY)	233
LI.	PTAH FASHIONING THE EGG OF THE WORLD	240
LII.	KHNUM FASHIONING MAN FROM EARTH	241
LIII.	PTAH-TANEN	248
LIV.	PILLAR OF PTAH	249
LV.	THE CREATION OF HEAVEN—BY "SHU"	264
LVI.	"SHU" UPLIFTING THE HEAVENS	264
LVII.	"SHU" FROM GUATEMALA	264
LVIII.	MEXICAN DEPICTION OF SHU DIVIDING THE NORTH FROM THE SOUTH, GIVING THE NORTH TO HORUS AND THE SOUTH TO SET	265
LIX.	MEXICAN DEPICTION OF FIGHT BETWEEN HORUS AND SET	264
LX.	ANUBIS, ANUP OR AP-UAT	268
LXI.	I. MEXICAN DEPICTION OF SET ATTACKING HORUS IN THE PAPYRUS SWAMP	272
	II. EGYPTIAN PORTRAYAL	272
	III. MEXICAN DEPICTION OF FIGHT BETWEEN HORUS AND SET	272
LXII.	MEXICAN DEPICTION OF HORUS AS "CLEAVER OF THE WAY"—GOD OF THE AXE	273

LIST OF PLATES

XV

PLATE   FACING PAGE

LXIII.–LXIV   THE SPIRIT OF THE DECEASED AND HIS WIFE BEFORE THE SYCAMORE OF NUT RECEIVING THE BREAD AND WATER OF LIFE IN PARADISE 308

LXV.   MEXICAN DEPICTION OF THE TREE OF NUT OR THE TREE OF HEAVEN 312

LXVI.   HUNIMAN AND SHIVA 336

LXVII.   KRISHNA 337

LXVIII.   THE STORY OF THE ANNUNICIATION 337

HIEROGLYPHICS IN THE TEXT

PAGES 9, 15, 39, 65, 70, 86, 93, 95, 106, 118, 121, 128, 133, 156, 158, 177, 179, 201, 202, 207, 245, 252, 254, 258, 267, 303, 332, 342, 348, 353, 354, 363, 366.

I Dedicate

THIS WORK TO ALL HUMANITY
WHO WISH TO LEARN AND KNOW
THE TRUTH

INTRODUCTION

Other than Sir James Frazer (*The Golden Bough*), Albert Churchward is the only person to have written such an extensive and monumental work on religion. It is called monumental because he attempts to encompass the evolution of religious ideas that have taken place over millions of years. This inevitably results in having to explore human evolution, not only in a religious sense, but physically and psychologically as well. To explore these areas successfully, as Churchward has done here, is truly a monumental achievement.

The very first humans appeared in Africa, which also resulted in this being the birthplace of religious ideas, according to Churchward. These first humans engaged primarily in the worship of elemental powers, then progressed into ancestor worship, then finally began to recognize what we could term a "Great Spirit." These forms of worship clearly became more sophisticated as time went on.

Some of our earliest mythological stories are brought to light in this fascinating work, including stories of Resurrection, journeys to the underworld, and the first hero stories. Also explored are the meanings and true origins of sun worship, tree worship, phallic worship, and serpent worship.

Churchward covers Egypt in great depth because many original religious concepts started here. He even includes a complete chapter on the Great Pyramid at Giza, with views on who built it, why it was constructed, and its symbolic meaning.

Major cults of the sun, moon, and stars played important roles in our religious development. We then "graduated" into our more modern systems, as explained by Churchward, with interesting sections on Judaism, Buddhism, Babylonian religion, Druidism, Mohammedism, and Christianity. Some of the information is absolutely amazing concerning the belief origins of these major systems—these last chapters alone are worth the entire cost of the book. This information is simply not available elsewhere.

Churchward closes the book with something we should all take to heart—our religious "evolution" is definitely not over. Many of us think that it is, and that we have reached a "final truth" with whatever religion we hold dearest to. Nothing could be further from the truth. In looking at the big picture, Churchward points out that although we've reached a higher step, another needed one awaits us.

Paul Tice

ORIGIN AND EVOLUTION OF RELIGION

CHAPTER I

DEFINITIONS OF RELIGION. THE DAWN OF RELIGIOUS IDEAS

THE first Thought and Question is: What is Religion?

There are many definitions as well as different phases, and it would be as well to begin with a few examples:

1. "A belief binding the spiritual nature of man to a Superhuman Being on Whom he is conscious that he is dependent; also the practice that springs out of the recognition of such relation, including the personal life and experience, the doctrine, the duties, and the rites founded on it."—*Standard Dictionary*.

2. "Religion is man's belief in a Being mightier than himself and inaccessible to his senses, but not indifferent to his sentiments and actions with the feelings and practice which flow from such a belief."—*Standard Dictionary*.

Writers hitherto have given the different phases, or forms, under a classification which omits the true interpretation of the origin and evolution of religion.

They commence with the Anthropological as: (1) Animism, or Polydæmonism. (2) Polytheism embracing Therianthropism. (3) Nomistic religions, as Brahminism, Confucianism, Zoroastrianism. (4) Individualistic religions, as Buddhism, Mohammedanism, and Christianity.

They also class them Philosophically: (1) Antitheistic, embracing Atheism, Agnosticism, Pantheism, Nature religions and Animism.

(2) Theistic, embracing Polytheism and Monotheism, or Theism proper, including Theism, Mohammedanism, Judaism, and Christianity, etc. It is my task to try and show that all these various forms, and the different phases of religion, originated from three sources, and that as man advanced in evolution so his religious ideas became more and more developed upon a higher plane; all was at first depicted in Sign Language because primitive man had not the words to express his ideas otherwise.

Nothing short of the remotest beginnings could sufficiently instruct us concerning the origin of religious rites, dogmas, and doctrines that still dominate the minds of men without being understood.

One has to go back and study the *mental evolution* that has taken place in the human race *pari passu with the physical*, and show that the mode in which primitive man attained expression, in terms of external phenomena, by a process as purely scientific as the origin, was simply nature governed by the Periodic Laws; then we can understand why mankind should come to worship a divine being alleged to divide all things into three as a mode of representing its own triune nature.

The earliest forms of religion can only be found when we study the Anthropological Ethnology of earliest man.

The Offering Propitiation to the elemental powers was the first origin of religion—by the Pygmies, first of the human race, born in Africa.

The earliest mode of worship recognizable was of three kinds: (1) *Propitiation of the Superhuman Powers*. The power was of necessity elemental, a power that was objectified by means of the living type; and of necessity the object of propitiation, invocation, and solicitation was the power itself, and not the types by which it was imaged in the language of Signs. If we use the term "worship," it was the propitiation of the power in the thunder or storm, not the thunder or storm itself. Primitive man had observed the various powers and attributes of the forces of nature—water flowing, trees growing, darkness, light, thunder, storms, etc.—and from these powers of nature man would imbibe his Spiritual ideas, and so lay the primary foundation of the later myths. Each at first was given, and recognized by, a Sign and Symbol; afterwards a name would be attached to or connected with each power or attribute—one greater than all would become "The One" Great Power or Spirit, and others would become attached as attributes or powers of The One.

(2) *The propitiation of the Spirits of the Ancestors*, which has been called Ancestral worship.

This was the dawn of true religion, because:

Religion proper commences with and must include the idea or desire for another life. The belief in another life is founded on the Resurrection of the Spirit. The belief in the resurrection of the Spirit was founded upon the faculties of abnormal seership, which led to Ancestor Worship in all lands at one time. It was a worship, or propitiation, of the Ancestor Spirits, not the body Corpus which died and disintegrated, but the human soul emerging alive, in the likeness of the man, out of the body of dead matter. The Corpus could not, and never did, come back, or make its appearance again in any form but the "Spiritual body" of pure Corpuscles which arose out of the dead body, and was visible to seers. It was for this reason that man was so sure of an after life, and upon this religion was founded. If man had not seen any ghosts, there never would have been any religion. Unfortunately, the present "wise men" have made a great mistake, which primitive man did not. The later homo has mixed up the "elemental powers" with the "human Ancestors." The former never had been men or women, the latter had; and this is where the Hindu, Christian, and others have gone wrong in their doctrines, not knowing the true gnosis or origin of these religious doctrines. There could be no transmigration of Souls from elemental powers which were not nor ever had been human.

The "Anima" signifies one of the seven elemental souls, but does not comprehend the group.

The Animistic nature powers were typified: the Ancestral spirits are personalized.

The elemental powers are commonly a group of seven, but spiritualism has no experience or knowledge of seven human spirits that visit earth together, or traverse the planetary chain of seven worlds.

In Animism, mediums could not interview the serpent, bull, or turtle of eternity in spirit form; on the contrary, the Animistic powers have had to be objectified and made apparent by means of these totemic types.

Thus in Animism there are no spirits—that is, no spirits which appear as the doubles of the dead or phantasms of the living.

Thus when the Zulus say: "There are Amatonga or Ancestral spirits who are snakes and who come back to visit the living in the guise of reptiles," they are speaking in sign language. Both the monkey and the snake had been totemic types, not only of the human brotherhood, but also of the elemental powers or souls. Thus there was an elemental soul of the snake totem and the Ancestral spirits of that same totem, and the snake remained a representative of both, to the confounding of the Animistic soul with the Ancestral spirit at a later stage.

But those who kept fast hold of the true doctrine, always and everywhere insisted that their Ancestral spirits did not return to earth in the guise of monkeys, snakes, lions, crocodiles, or any other of the totemic Zootypes, but in the human likeness.

They did not mistake the "souls" of one category for "spirits" in the other, because they knew the difference. The Egyptians always made it clear betwixt the superhuman powers, and the Manes, or the "Gods" and the "Glorified"—and that can be followed all over the world. Thus the human soul never was "conceived as a bird," but may be *imaged as a bird*, according to the primitive system of representation. The Golden Hawk, for instance, was a bird which typified the sun that soared aloft as Horus in the heavens, and the same bird in the eschatology was then applied to the human soul in its resurrection from the body. Hence the hawk is a confirmed image, not the portrait of a human soul. The feathered Angel was never yet seen by clairvoyant vision, and is not a result of revelation.

We know how they originated, why they were so represented, and how they came into the Syrian and Mohammedan Doctrines and Christian eschatology. They are the human-headed birds that were compounded and portrayed for souls in Egypt, and carried out thence into Babylonia, Judea, Greece, Rome, and other lands.

Thus in the Koran (Sura XXXV) it is said that God maketh the angels His messengers and that they are furnished with two, or three, or four pairs of wings, according to their rank and importance; the archangel Gabriel is said to have been seen by Mohammed the Prophet with six hundred pairs of wings. The duties of the angels, according to the Mohammedans, were of various kinds. Thus nineteen angels are appointed to take charge of hell fire (Sura LXXIV); eight are set apart to support God's Throne on the Day of Judgment (Sura LXIX); several tear the souls of the wicked from their bodies with violence, and several take the souls of the righteous from their bodies with gentleness and kindness (Sura LXXIX); two angels are ordered to accompany every man on earth, the one to write down his good actions and the other his evil deeds, and they will appear with him at the Day of Judgment, the one to lead him before the Judge, and the other to bear witness either for or against him (Sura L). Mohammedan Theologists declare that the angels are created of a simple substance of light, and that they are endowed with life and speech and reason; they are incapable of sin, they have no carnal desire, they do not propagate their species, and they are not moved by the passion of wrath and anger; their obedience is absolute. Some are said to have the form of animals. Four are Archangels, viz. Michael, Gabriel, Azrael, and Israfel; they possess special powers, and special duties are assigned to them.

If we turn to the older Syrian system of angels, we

find them divided into nine classes and three orders—upper, middle, and lower. The upper order is composed of Cherubin, Seraphim, and Thrones; the middle order of Lords, Powers, and Rulers; and the lower order of Principalities, Archangels, and Angels. The Archangels in this system are described as " a swift operative action," which has dominion over every living thing except man, and the Angels are a motion which has spiritual knowledge of everything that is on earth and in heaven.

With the Hebrews, they were grouped into ten classes, i.e. the Erelim, the Jshim, the Bene Elohim, the Malachim, the Hashmalim, the Tarshishim, the Shishanim, the Cherubim, the Ophannim, and the Seraphim. Amongst these were divided all the duties connected with the ordering of the heavens and the earth, and they, according to their position and importance, become the interpreters of the Will of the Deity.

As I shall endeavour to show, *these were the elemental powers divinized* by the *Egyptians*, and the true gnosis was perverted, after the esoteric meaning had been lost.

(3) *The third was propitiation, invocation, and worship of a Great Spirit whom they could not define.*

Thus we find that the origin of spirits and religion is threefold.

First, elemental powers were propitiated; secondly, Ancestors were invoked and propitiated, and, thirdly, propitiation, invocation, and worship were made to the Great Spirit.

The Gods and Goddesses of the oldest races were developed from the superhuman nature powers which originated with and from the earth, as the universal Great Mother, and not from the Ancestral human Spirits. The one is always and universally differentiated from the other.

The supposed transmigration of human souls, of turtles, or of other Zootypes was impossible when as yet there was no human soul descreted. Those who believe that primitive man fancied he had a separate soul which he could hide for safety in a tree, a stone, or an egg are but speculative theorists who have never mastered the language of the primitive signs. The soul which transmigrates was pre-human, elemental, and totemic: a soul that was divisible according to its parts and elemental powers, but common to life in general in all its forms, in earth and water, air and tree, to man and reptile, fish, bird, and beast.

Primitive man has been portrayed in modern times as if he were a philosophic Theorist. He has been charged with imagining all sorts of things which never existed; as *if that* were the origin of his Spirit and his Gods; whereas the beginning was with the elemental powers. These were external to himself. There was no need to imagine them. They *were*, and with this cognition his Theology began. However primitive, they neither had not pretended to have the power of taking the human soul out of the body when in peril, and depositing it for safety in a tree or stone, nor any other Totemic type. Such a delusion belongs to the second childhood of the human race rather than to the first.

Now we cannot get back *further* in the origin of religion, its meanings, and true interpretation than the Pygmies, for the Pygmy was the first human in evolution from the Anthropoid Ape. Here then we find the origin and dawn of all religion and religious ideas.

With the Pygmy the elements of life themselves are the objects of recognition, and the elemental powers were and are propitiated. This was the beginning which preceded the Zootype, and which was expressed in Sign Language; it preceded Mythology and Totemism. The Pygmies are pre-totemic, and there are no legends or folk-lore tales connected with them; they possess no magic, but they do possess religious ideas.

These Pygmies are upon the lowest step in the ascent of man. They were the first humans, and, although still found in many parts of the world, their Motherland on earth is Africa. In no other country do we find even any trace of the connecting links (Bushman and Masaba

Negro) with the Nilotic Negro who developed religious ideas in the next stage of evolution.

So closely were the facts of nature observed and registered by the Egyptians that the earliest divine men in their Mythology are portrayed as Pygmies, and the earliest form of the Human Mother was depicted with the characteristic of the Pygmy woman.

The Great Mother was not depicted *as a woman* until the later part of the Lunar Cult, and then only as " part of a woman."[1]

The Divine man was not portrayed as a man until the Solar Cult. All Gods and Goddesses and the Powers of Nature before the late Lunar and early Solar Cults were imaged by Zootypes in one form or another.

Thus we see how erroneous are the terms: Animism, Polydæmonism, Polytheism, Therianthropism, and all that these terms imply, when used to express the true conceptions of primitive man, because from the first the Pygmy recognizes:

1. *The One Great Spirit* Whom he cannot define or see, but to Whom he *erects a primitive altar and makes offerings, supplications, and invocations*, and invents a Sign or Symbol to depict or image Him objectively.

2. *He propitiates* the Spirits of the departed by erecting little houses wherein he places food, because he can see *them* and knows that they exist; not that he believes *his former friends* will eat the actual material food, but that *the Spirit of the food* will be consumed by them and will satisfy their wants, and thus they will leave him in peace.

3. *He propitiates the Elemental Powers or Spirits*, but he does not believe that these are human, or ever had been human, neither does he believe that they are demons in the present-day acceptation of the term. He recognizes them as a force or power—either for good or ill—and during the pre-totemic period of human evolution he had not as yet imaged them by one or other of the Zootype

---

[1] I have dealt with this point at greater length in my " Origin and Evolution of the Human Race."

forms. These forms the later Nilotic Negro brought into existence to establish the distinction one from the other. He had no *words to do so at that time*, nor any other means to visualize and distinguish these elemental powers but by Sign Language, which would best convey to his mind the force or meaning.

The Pygmies imaged by a Sign or Symbol " The One Great Spirit " whom they cannot define by name, not having seen Him; it is portrayed thus ✻ and is their most sacred Sign or Symbol—just three sticks crossed.

This primary Sign or Symbol, fashioned in the beginning by the African Pygmies to represent " The One Great Spirit," has been carried on by the various cults during human evolution, down to the present-day Cross of the Christian Doctrines; it always represented the *One Great One*. Sometimes it was varied in form or shape by the pre-totemic people who left Africa, e.g. by a spear, or, as among the Veddas, by an arrow; but nevertheless it was the Pygmies' Sacred Symbol from the beginning.

The Spirits of the elements of air, fire, water, earth, trees, etc., were in a sense Ancestral, though not Ancestral Spirits. The one was pre-human, the others are originally Human.

The most essential part of religion assuredly originated in the worship of Ancestral Spirits. These must have been the Spirits of human origin discriminated from the Animistic Spirit or elemental powers, as the *raison d'être* of the worship. The first fear and dread of the destroying powers was followed at a later stage of development by the natural affection for the Mothers and children, who were universally propitiated as the Ancestral Spirits, the Spirits of the departed who demonstrate the continuity of existence hereafter by reappearing to the living in phenomenal apparition; but they never appeared in Totemic or Zootype forms.

All Ancestor worshippers have been Spiritualists in the modern sense; they have had evidence by practical demonstration that the so-called dead are still the living, in a rarer but not less real form. Their belief in a personal continuity has ever been firmly based on phenomenal facts, not merely ideas or dreams.

Herbert Spencer could find no origin for the idea of an after-life, save the conclusion which the savage draws from the notion suggested by dreams (Spencer, "Facts and Comments," p. 210). But whatsoever dreams the savage had, they would become familiar in the course of time. He would learn that dreams had no power to externalize themselves in apparitions, had there been no ghosts or visible Spirits of the dead. He would also learn readily enough, and the lesson would be perpetually repeated, that however great his success, when hunting in his dreams of the night, there was no game caught when he awoke in the morning. Clearly no reliance could be placed on dreams for establishing the ghost, any more than on the result of other dreams. Moreover, the same savage that is assumed to have relied on dreams for a false belief also reports that he sees the Spirits of the dead by abnormal vision, and has the means of communicating with them. But all the credulity of all the savages that ever existed cannot compete or be compared with the credulity involved in this belief or assumption that the ghost itself, together with the customs, the ceremonies, the religions, rites of invocation, and propitiation, the priceless offerings, the countless testimonies to the veritability of abnormal vision, the universal practices for inducing that vision for the purpose of communicating with Spiritual intelligences, had no other than a subjective basis and a false belief that the dream-shadow was the sole reality. Can one conceive anything more fatal to the mode or belief of evolution as a mode of nature's teaching than this assumption, that man has universally been the victim of an illusion derived from a baseless delusion? If primitive men were the victims of a delusion which has been continued for thousands of years in defiance of all experience and observation, what guidance or trust could there be in evolution; or how are we to distinguish between the false product and the true, if men dreamed the ghost into being when there was no ghost, and founded the whole body of his religious beliefs and customs on that which never existed? Primitive man was not a hundredth part so likely to be the victim of hallucination or diseased subjectivity as the modern. Eternal Nature is not hallucinative; it is the scene of continuous education in primal or rudimentary and constantly recurring realities. His elemental spirits or forces were real and not the result of hallucination; why not his Ancestral Spirits? African Spiritualism, which might be voluminously illustrated, culminated in the Egyptian Mysteries. The Mystery teachers were so far advanced as phenomenal spiritualists, and record so little about it in any direct manner, that it has taken one who owns to have a profound experience of the phenomena many years to attain the true Knowledge of the Spiritual Laws of the Universe and Spiritual World as set forth in the eschatology of the Ritual, and which is proved by the Periodic Laws of the Corpuscles.

The Christian Cult is the only one Religion in the world that was based upon the corpse instead of the Resurrection of the Spirit. In no other Religion is continuity in Spirit made dependent on the Resurrection of the earthly body (Origen's teachings).

The Christians mistook the risen Mummy in Amenta for the corpse that was buried on Earth, whereas all other religions were founded on the rising again in the Spirit from the corpse as it was imaged in the Resurrection of Amsu-Horus transforming from the Mummy Osiris, and by the human soul emerging alive from the body of dead matter. There is no instance recorded in all the experience of Spiritualists, ancient or modern, of the corpse coming back from the Tomb. The so-called worship of Ancestors depends entirely on the Ancestors being considered living, conscious, acting, and recipient Spirits, and not as the corpses mouldering in the earth. This furnishes the sole reason for all the sacrificial offerings, the life, the blood, the food, the choicest and costliest offerings that could be given to the dead. Those whom we call *dead* were the veritable *living* in superhuman form, possessing superhuman powers. Clairvoyance was " the vision and the faculty divine," the " beatific vision " of all the early races, which a few possess at the present day. It was sought for and cultivated, prized and protected, as the most precious of all human gifts.

Both the pre-totemic and Totemic people had learnt by experience how to communicate with their loved ones who had departed this earthly life; yet they never mourned them nor wept for them, but rejoiced at the time of death because they knew that they lived again. Their " Underworld " was founded upon the facts that they had ascertained from their departed, and the smallest details are left recorded as to what the Spiritual body of the departed had to undergo before entering the " Final Paradise." Only those who had attained that Great End were permitted to return and visualize themselves to their friends. The Materialists of the present day can never obtain that gnosis, because they have never tried to learn, and therefore will ever remain in dark and dense ignorance of the subject which is most material to their future existence; but it is none the less true, notwithstanding their unbelief or ignorance of the true gnosis. This is set forth in the Book of Everlasting Life, the oldest in the world.

In studying the beginnings, our first lesson is to learn something of the Symbolic Language of Animals, as primitive man did, and to understand what it is they say as Zootypes.

Primitive Language is still extant in divers forms. It is extant in the so-called dead language of the Hieroglyphics, the Ideographs and Pictographs, in the figures of Tattu, in the portraiture of the Nature Powers, which came to be divinized at length in the human likeness of the Gods and Goddesses of Mythology; and in that language of the folk-fables still made use of by the pre-totemic people in which the Jackal, the Dog, the Lion, the Crane, the White Vulture, and other beasts and birds kept on talking as they did in the beginning, and continue more or less to say in human speech what they once said in the primitive Symbolism; that is, they fulfil the same characters in the Marchen that were first founded in the Mythos.

Actuality was earlier than Typology, and the elements of life themselves, as the objects of recognition were earlier than the Zootypes, as, for instance, Earth, Air, Wind, Water, Rain, Vegetables, etc., which became Totems without being, as it were, first in types of Mythology.

Thus we find all pre-totemic people:

1. Worshipped and made offerings to " The One Great Spirit," Whom they could not define but portrayed in Sign Language by a Symbol.

2. They believed in the Spirits of their Ancestors because they could see the Corpuscular body after it was dead; and they propitiated and made offerings in order that the Spirit of their Ancestors should do no harm to the living humans.

3. They believed in the Elemental Powers, or Spirits, and propitiated them, not as demons, but as powers or forces of Nature. These are the three primary forms of religion *proving* pre-totemic man's religious beliefs, and the foundation and beginning of all Religion and Religious beliefs in the world.

CHAPTER II

RELIGIOUS CULT OF THE TOTEMIC PEOPLES

THE next stage of Religion and Religious ideas was evolved by the Nilotic Negroes. We find as man advanced up the ladder in evolution, so his Religious ideas progressed and advanced to a higher plane.

All humans in the pre-totemic stage were in the state of a gregarious horde with its general promiscuity.

The earliest form of human society was brought into existence by the Nilotic Negro under what may be termed Totemic Sociology, which in one phase distinguishes it from the pre-totemic people.

For reasons unnecessary to be dilated upon in this book, they first divided themselves into two halves, or tribes; afterwards these divided again into four; later a further subdivision took place into eight, and then further subdivisions, each tribe having its own distinguishing Totem. It became necessary to distinguish the blood relationship of these various tribes—the one from the other, as the Father of a child was never known—because all Women, of, say, A tribe, were common to men of B tribe, and vice versa, only the Mother blood could be traced. To ascertain this and keep it true they introduced " Totems " and performed Sacred Ceremonies called Totemic Ceremonies. Whilst some of the Nilotic Negroes carried out the primitive wisdom from the same central birthplace in Africa (at the head of the Nile and around the Great Lakes), to the islands of the Southern Seas and other parts of the world, and were fossilized during long ages of isolation, those that remained carried it down the Nile to take living root and grow, flourish and expand as their Mythology and Astro-Mythology,

ORIGIN AND EVOLUTION OF RELIGION 15

finally ending in the development by evolution in the Eschatology of Ancient Egypt.

Totemism has been variously described. Sir James Frazer calls it "both a religious and social system," a description with which I entirely agree.

The name Totem is not, however, in my judgment, derived from an Ojibway (Chippeway) word, as he states ("Totemism," p. 1), but from the Egyptian ⟨hieroglyph⟩ Tem-t.

The hieroglyphic is the figure of a total composed of two halves.

The Egyptian Tem or Tem-t has various applications in Egyptian.

It signifies Man, Mankind, Mortals, also to unite, to be entire, or perfect; it is the name for those who are created persons, as in making young men and young women in Totemic Ceremonies. Also it is a Total and to be totalled. It is the figure of totalling a number into a whole which commences with a two-fold unity.

To understand this definition, take the case of two different classes of one clan or class; the whole clan or tribe we will call A. This is subdivided into A and B. All A can marry all B, or all B can marry all A, but A must not marry A nor B marry B. These again can be (and are in some cases) re-divided again as regards their children and come under either C or D, and these again into two other sub-classes. Yet all are totalled into the one tribe.

It is also a place name, as well as a personal name for the social unit or division of persons.

Among the Nilotic Negroes the Totem first represented two phases—primarily it was given to the girl when she was made a woman, as her badge or banner by which she, as the Mother, and all her children would be known; and, secondly, it included that of food districts, and the special food of certain districts was represented by the Totem of the family or Tribe. *The Totem was first eaten by members of the group* as their own special food; later this was altered, and the Totemic food was only very sparingly eaten by the Tribe with that Totem; it became Tabu, or *sacred*, to them. The Tribe was appointed its preserver and cultivator and was named after it.

The Totem primarily, then, was given to a girl when she became pubescent, as her badge or banner, by which she and all her children were always known. Thus, if her Totem was a Lizard, all her children would be Lizards, or, if a Crocodile, all her children would be young Crocodiles; and when we read in books, as we do, of women bringing forth Snakes, Crocodiles, or any other Zootype, we know that the Totem of the Mother was a Snake or Crocodile, or some other Zootype which was the name of her Totem, and her children obviously were named accordingly. The Totem, then, represented the Maternal Ancestor, the Mother who gave herself up for food to the tribe, and was eaten absolutely alive after she had ceased to bear children, because she should never die, but always be alive. *This was the primitive Eucharist, and was the foundation of all such rites. " The body and blood" were veritably eaten whilst alive, and no morsel, however small, was allowed to remain uneaten.* It was a sacred feast to be equally partaken of by each member of the tribe. This custom has now died out in most parts of the world, if not all, inhabited by the Nilotic Negroes, and *her Totemic Zootype is eaten sacramentally* once a year in place of the human Mother. It is very important to remember this as it is the origin of one of the principal doctrines of the Christian Cult, and it can be traced all through the different Cults in evolution to the present time in its various phases. She, the Mother of the Tribe, was afterwards represented as the Mythical Great Mother in Egypt, as the Goddess Hathor in the Tree, the Suckler as Rerit the Sow; the Nurse as Rannut the Serpent, and the enceinte Mother as Apt, who was translated into fleshly form for eating as the Totemic Cow, i.e. when the elemental powers became divinized.

In Totemism, the Mother and Motherhood, the Sister and Sisterhood, the Brother and Brotherhood, the girl who transformed at puberty, the Mother who was eaten as a sacrifice, the two women who were Ancestresses, were all of them human, all of them actual, in the domain of natural fact. But when the same characters have been continued in Mythology, they are superhuman. The Mother and Motherhoods, the Sister and Sisterhoods, the Brother and Brotherhoods, have been divinized. The realities of Totemism have supplied the types to Mythology as Goddesses and Gods who wear the heads and skins of beasts, to denote their character. The Mother, as human in Totemism, was known by her Totem as the Water-Cow, and this became the type of the Great Mother in Mythology. *But it is the Type* that was continued, not the Human Mother. The Mother as first person in the human family was the first person in Totemic Sociology. Hence came the Great Mother in Mythology who was fashioned in the Matriarchal mould, but with this difference : it is the Human Mother underneath the mask in Totemism. It *is not the* Human Mother who was divinized as the Great Provider in Mythology. Thus the Mother was human in the mask of Totemism and is superhuman in the mask of Mythology. The human Mother might be represented by, or as, the Totemic Cow, Serpent, Frog, or Vulture, nevertheless they were not Human Mothers who were divinized in these same likenesses, as the Egyptian Goddesses Isis, Rannut, Hekat and Neith. But the Human Mother who was eaten alive at the sacramental meal did supply a type of the superhuman Mother in external nature, who also gave herself as a voluntary sacrifice for human food and sustenance ; the Mother of life in death who furnished the first eucharist which was eaten in the religious Mysteries, the Human Mother had been an actual victim, eaten as a sacrifice. The Superhuman Mother or Goddess was eaten typically or by proxy. Hence she, who was the giver of food and life to the world, came to be eaten sacramentally and vicariously ; that is, in some Totemic victim, by whose death her sacrifice was symbolically represented. There were different types of the sacrificial victim at different stages of the eucharist. At one stage it was the Red-Calf as the type of Horus, the child; this same type was continued in the Hebrew Ritual; it was carried on under various types in different Cults, and finally into the Christians' Doctrines; but the origin of the Rite was the actual eating of the Mother of the Tribe, as a sacred and solemn sacrificial rite so that the Mother should never die, in the Totemic Mysteries established first by the Nilotic Negroes.

The object of certain sacred ceremonies associated with the Totems is to secure the increase of the animal or plant which gives its name to the Totem.

Each Totemic Group has its own ceremony, and no two are absolutely alike; but however they may differ in detail, they all have for their main object the purpose of increasing the supply of food; not food in general, but the food represented by their Totem.

Other Sacred Totemic Ceremonies are associated with what may be called the second "Creation"; that is, making the boy into a man and the girl into a woman, and may be termed religious ceremonies of the most premature form.

"The Cutting and opening" was the making of men and women; hitherto all had been a promiscuous herd, now at the inception of these Totemic Ceremonies the boy was made into a man and the girl into a woman. And this is the origin and meaning of the second creation as recorded in the Hebrew Texts.

Thus the Creation of man was mystical in one sense, and in another Totemic; i.e. pre-totemic and Totemic. —pre-human and Human.

The Totem afterwards, in its religious phase, was as much the sign of the Goddesses and Gods as it had been for the Motherhoods and Brotherhoods from whence it took its origin. The Zootype became and was the image of the superhuman power; for example, the Mother-Earth as a giver of water was imaged as a Water-Cow. Seb, the Father of Food, was imaged by the Goose that laid the eggs. The primary seven elemental powers were looked upon Mythically as children of the Great Earth-Mother, who were all born as Males; they were begetters as transformers. The two primary were twin-brothers, Set and Horus, representing as powers, Night and Day, or Darkness and Light, assigned as Set, God of the South, and Horus, God of the North. Shu was the Third, representing the breath of life, breathing force; the winds, represented at the Equinox by the Lion; and these formed the primary Trinity, or the God in a triune form, or with three attributes. The cult of the primary Mythology was founded in invocation and propitiation of the Great Mother-Earth, the giver of life and birth, of food and water, as the primary power who brought forth the seven elemental powers, called her children. Many and various Zootypes have been used by the Nilotic Negroes all over the world as representative images, by the later Lunar and Stellar Cult people who came after. The powers of nature had been represented by pre-totemic people by sign language only.

It was the Hero Cult Nilotic Negro who first represented these nature powers by means of Zootype forms. The Goddess, the old Earth-Mother and her seven children, were developed from the superhuman nature powers originating with, and from the earth, as the Universal Great Mother, *and not from Ancestral Human Spirits*. The one is universally differentiated from the other. These powers, which were called her children, were at a later stage:

In Egypt: The seven Ali.
In Phœnicea: They are the seven Elohim.
In Assyria: They are the seven forms of Lli.
In Israel: The seven Elohim, Kabirim, or Baalim.

It was these Nilotic Negroes who first used Zootypes to distinguish the human Motherhoods and Brotherhoods.

These Zootypes were re-applied to the elemental powers in their Mythology which the Hero Cult people developed and, afterwards, repeated in the constellation figures as a mode of record in the heavens in the prehistoric past during the Astro-Mythology, which followed the Mythology which can still be read by the aid of the Ancient Egyptian wisdom, but not by means of Semitic legendary lore. Thus we find that all the types of Sign Language of Mythology had first been founded in Totemism and brought on in evolution as man ascended the ladder to the present time.

It is only by studying primitive man, his thoughts and his Totemic Ceremonies, and all that these represented to his mind in Sign Language, following and tracing them through the evolution of the human race, that one can arrive at a definite and true knowledge of the origin and meaning of our present-day beliefs.

We must remember, to understand correctly, that Totemism originated in Sign Language rather than Sociology; the Sign Language originating with the pre-totemic people, the Signs being now, at the Totemic Stage, applied for use in Sociology, Mythology, and Fetishism.

Ceremonial rites were established as the means of memorizing facts in Sign Language when there were no written records of the human past. In these the Knowledge was acted, the Ritual was exhibited and kept in ever-living memory by continual repetition. The Mysteries, Totemic or Religious, were founded on the basis of action.

Thus the Sign to the Eye and the Sound to the Ear were continued, *pari passu*, in the dual development of Sign Language that was visual and vocal at the same time. The brothers and sisters were identifying themselves, not with, or as, animals, but by means of them, and by making use of them as Zootypes for their Totems.

The secrets of the most primitive form of the Myths and Symbols for thousands of years existed in *human memory* alone. In the absence of written records the oral method of communication was held all the more sacred, as *was exemplified* in the ancient Priesthood, whose ritual and gnosis depended on *living memory* for its truth, purity, and sanctity.

It was the mode of communicating from *mouth* to *ear*; it continued in all the Mysteries, and is still carried on as from the original, in the present Masonic Mysteries. The earlier religions thus had their Mysteries interpreted.

We have ours mis-interpreted.

It is these elemental Souls or Spirits, which have no sex, that have been mixed up with human souls by Hindu, Greek, Buddhist, and Pythagorean after losing the true gnosis of the Egyptian Mystery. Teaching had become lost and perverted, and mistaken for the human soul in course of transmigration through the series which were but representative of souls that were distinguished as non-human by those who understand Sign Language. No transmigration of *human* souls is involved, and this is where the translators of the Book of Enoch have erred —" The Sons of God who cohabited with the daughters of men." The translator or writer of this book mixes the seven elemental powers, which were divinized, or the Mythical Gods, with the human women, not understanding the Sign Language of the Ritual from whence this book originated. (See Genesis vi. also.)

The change of the human descent from the Mother-blood to the Father-blood is obviously commemorated in the Mysteries or ceremonial rites of the Arunta. In the operation of young-man making, two modes of cutting are performed upon the boy by which he becomes a man and a tribal Father. The first of these is commonly known as circumcision, or lartna, by the Arunta; the other ceremony of initiation, which comes later, is the rite of subincision called ariltha. The second cutting is necessary for the completion of the perfect man. With this trial test the youth becomes a man; fathership is founded, and, as certain customs show, the Motherhood is in a measure cast off at the time, or typically superseded by the Fatherhood.

Nature led the way for the opening rite performed upon the female, and therefore we conclude that this preceded the operation performed upon the men, which was a custom established like the couvade, in the course of commemorating the change from the Matriarchate to the Father-right.

When we hear Nilotic Negroes say that : " The Lizard first developed the sexes " (as stated by the Australians) and also that it was the author of marriage, we must first know or ascertain what the Lizard signifies in Sign Language. We find that, like the Serpent or Frog, it denoted the female period, and we see how it distinguished or divided the sexes and in what sense it authorized, or was the author of, Totemic marriages, because of its being a sign or symbol of feminine pubescence. It is said of the Amazula : That when old women pass away they take the form of a kind of Lizard.

The Lizard in the primitive system of Sign Language was a Zootype, the Ideographic value of which informs you that it appeared at puberty, but disappeared at the turn of life, and with the old woman went the disappearing lizard.

The Frog, which transformed from the tadpole condition, was another Ideograph of female pubescence—a type of transformation. Also it was a sign of " Myriads," and as Lunar, it would denote myriads of renewals.

The custom of " the couvade " found amongst the Iberians, Basques, Corsicans, Navarres, many African Tribes, Carabs, Tamanacs, Abipones, Dyaks of Borneo, Tupis of Brazil, West Yuman in China, Greenlanders, Indians of California, and many others, originated amongst the early inhabitants of the Stellar Cult people, or Hero-Cult in the Valley of the Nile. It is a custom typical of the transformation of the father into the child. This is demonstrated by the doctrine of Kheper who was the creator or transformer, and, although the doctrine of Kheper came into existence during the Solar Cult, in my view the custom originated during the earlier Stellar Cult in a primitive form at least, and the doctrine was carried all over the world by the later Hero Cult or earliest Stellar Cult people, which is the reason why we find it existing at the present day.

When the Arunta perform the rite of subincision, which follows that of the primary operation (circumcision) a slit is cut in the penis right down to the root. The natives have no idea of the origin of the practice,[1] but, as the practice proves, it is performed as an assertion

[1] Spencer and Gillen : "Northern Tribes of Australia," p. 263.

of manhood, and is a mode of " making the boy into a man," or " creating man." Now, at this time it was customary to cast the Motherhood aside by some significant action ; that is, when the Fathership is established in the initiation ceremony. And in the Arunta rite of subincision, the operating Mura first of all cuts out an oval-shaped piece of skin from the male member *which he flings away*. The oval shape is an emblem of the female all the world over, and this is another mode of rejecting the Mother and of attributing begettal to the Father, as it was attributed in the creation by Atum-Ra, who was both male and female. (As the one " All Parent.")

From the " cutting " of the male member now attributed to Atum-Ra, we infer that the rite of circumcision and of subincision was a mode of showing the derivation from the human Father in supersession of the Motherhood, and that in the Arunta double cutting the figure of the female was added to the member of the male ; nor is this without corroboration. In his ethnological studies (p. 180) Dr. Roth explains that in the Pitta-Pitta and cognate Boulia dialects, the term Me-Ko Ma-ro denotes the man with a vulva, which shows that the oval slit *was cut* upon the penis as a figure of the female, and a mode of assuming the Fatherhood. In the Hebrew Book of Genesis this carving of the female on the person of the male, in the second creation, has been given the legendary form of cutting out the woman from the body of the male. Adam is thus imaged as a biune parent, Atum-Ra.

But when the custom of circumcision was transferred to the time of childhood, as it had been by the Jews and Arabs, to be performed on the infant of eight days old, then the natural (i.e. according to the Totemic religious condition) loses its sense and becomes cruel in its dotage.

The Mystery of the resurrection, which was originally instituted by these Totemic Nilotic Negroes, may be seen still performed symbolically by the Arunta Tribes in the *quabarra inguriringa inkinga*, or *corroborree* of the arisen bones, which bones image the dead body, whilst the performers represent the Ulthauna, or spirits of the dead. The bones were sacredly preserved by those who were yet unable to make the mummy as a type of permanence.

Every native has to pass through certain ceremonies before he is admitted to the secrets of the tribe. The first takes place at about the age of 12 years; the final and most impressive one is probably not passed through until the native has reached the age of 30 years. These two initiations thus correspond to, or represent, the origin of those mysteries of the double Horus, or Jesus, at 12 years of age; the child Horus, or Jesus, makes his Transformation into the adult in his baptism or other kindred mysteries. Horus, or Christ, as the man of 30 years is initiated in the final mysteries of the resurrection. The long lock of childhood was worn by him until he attained the age of 12 years, when he was changed into a man. With the Arunta Tribe, the hair of the boy is for the first time tied up at the commencement of the opening ceremony of the series by which he is made a man. His long hair is equivalent to the Horus Lock. The first act of initiation in these Mysteries is that of throwing the boy up into the air. This was a primitive mode of dedication to the Ancestral purity of the Totem or the tribe, whose voice is heard in the sound of the churinga or bull-roarers whirling around.

It is said by the natives " that the voice of the Great Spirit was heard when the resounding bull-roarer spoke." The Great Spirit was supposed to descend and enter the body of the boy and to make him a man, just as in the mystery of Tattu, the soul of Horus the adult, descends upon and unites with the soul of Horus the child, or the soul of Ra, the Holy Spirit, descends upon Osiris to quicken and transform and re-erect the Mummy, where risen Horus becomes bird-headed as the adult in Spirit; the Arunta youth is given the appearance of flight to signify the change resulting from the descent of the Spirit, as the cause of transformation. When one becomes a soul in the Mysteries of the Ritual by assuming the form or image of Ra, the initiate exclaims: " Let me wheel round in whirls, let me revolve like the turning one " (Ch. 83, Rit.). The " turning one " is the sun God Kheper, whose name is identical with that of an Australian Tribe, Chepara (Kheper), as the soul of " self-originating force," which was imaged under one type by the Bennu, a bird that ascends the air and flies to a great height whilst circling round and round in spiral whorls (Ch. 85, Rit.).

The doctrine of soul-making at puberty originated amongst the Nilotic Negroes, as did many of the other Egyptian Mysteries. For example: In the Egyptian Mythology, Horus is the Blind-man, or, rather, he is the child born blind, called Horus in the Dark. He is also described as the Blind Horus in the city of the Blind. In his blindness he is typical of the emasculated sun in winter and of the human soul in death. At the place of his resurrection or re-birth there stands a tree up which he climbs to enter Spirit life. In Australia, near to the Charlotte Waters, is the tree that rose to mark the spot where a blind man died. This tree is called the Apera Okilchya; that is, the blind man's tree. In another place where a tree stands was the camp of the blind, the city of the blind, the world of the dead, in which the tree of life or dawn was rooted. Should the tree be cut down, the men near where it grows will become blind. They would be like Horus in the Dark, this being the tree of light or the dawn of eternal day. In another of their Ceremonies the Arunta perform the Mysteries of the fight between Horus and the Sebau—in a primitive phase.

The Chepara tribe of Southern Queensland also perform the great Mystery of the Kurungal, in which may be identified the baptism and re-birth by fire. The same ceremony is described in the Ritual as an exceedingly great Mystery and a type of the hidden Things in the underworld (Ch. 137A, " Ritual of Ancient Egypt ").

The most sacred ceremonial object of the Arunta is

called the Kanana. This is erected at the close of the Engwurn Mysteries. A young gum-tree, 20 feet in height, is cut down, stripped of its branches and its bark, and erected in the middle of the sacred ground. The decoration of the top was "just that of a human head." It was covered all over with human blood. The exact significance of the Kanana has been forgotten by the natives—they do not know now. They tell you it has some relation to a human being, and is regarded as common to the members of all the Totems. The Mystery is made known at the conclusion of the Engwura series of ceremonies, the last and final of the initiatory rites through which a native must pass before he becomes a fully developed member, then admitted to all the series and secrets of the tribe. This is the original of the Egyptian Ka statue which is a type of eternal duration as an image of the highest soul. To make the Kanana, so to say, the pole is humanized. It is painted with human blood and ornamented like the human head. It has but one form, and is common to all the Totems. So it is with the Egyptian Ka, the eidolon of the enduring soul. The name of the Kanana answers to the long-drawn-out form of the word "Ka" as Ka-a-a (Egyptian).

Another Ceremony performed is called the Bora, which typifies symbolically passing through the underworld. It is the primitive form of the Egyptian Amenta. "A valley of death" is portrayed on the selected ground with the form of a dead man thereon depicted. Members of the Mysteries stand in two rows, one on each side; these men are armed with spears and clubs, etc., and form an arch over the representative dead body. The initiate is conducted through this "valley of death" and has to undergo trials, etc. His conductor carries implements of power and might to ward off all dangers. As he arrives at each man, he is told, with threats of death, he cannot pass unless he gives the password. The word is given, and he is conducted through safely. It is the primitive, symbolic, and dramatic form of passing through the underworld. He is initiated into the passage of the dead to the Spirit world. It is the Totemic form of the Abyss of later Cults and Purgatory of the Roman Church.[1]

The Nilotic Negroes also believed in their Ancestral Spirits and propitiation of the same. Livingstone tells us that the natives about Lake Moere make little idols of a deceased father or mother; to them they present beer, flour, and bhang; they light a fire for the Spirits to sit round and smoke in consort with their living relatives.

This was the origin of the Egyptian Ka or image of a Spiritual self.

The Ewe-speaking natives also have their Kra or Eidolon, which existed before the birth of a child, and is precisely identical with the Egyptian Ka (Ellis: A. B., "Ewe-speaking Peoples" p. 13).

Sir Harry Johnston, in his "The Uganda Protectorate," states: "It is a common practice with the Bantu tribes for the relatives of deceased persons to carve crude little images as likenesses of the dead and set them up for worship or propitiation." Offerings are made to them in place of the later Ka of the Egyptians.

The earliest type of the departed was a body portrait, which may be found amongst these Nilotic Negroes, all over the world. Later it was the Mummy. The Ka was the Spirit likeness; but both imply the same recognition of the Ancestral Spirit which lives on after death.

The Ka-chambers in the later Egyptian Tombs were evolved from these prototypes.

Erecting a little hut for the Spirit is a recognized mode of propitiation. Lionel Decle in his "Three Years in Savage Africa" (pp. 34-6) describes his Wanyamwezi as making little huts of grass or green boughs, even when on the march, and offering them to the musimo or Spirits of their Ancestors.

All primitive races held, and still do hold, that in death the spirit rose again and lived on, and for this

[1] Photograph of this in "Signs and Symbols of Primordial Man," p. 455, 3rd ed.

reason the Ka statue was erected in the funerary chamber as it had been in the forest hut.

A black shadow of the body cast upon the ground could not demonstrate the existence of an eternal soul, neither could the hawk or serpent or any other symbol of force. But the Ka is the double of the dead. It is a figure of the ghost. The Ka was an image of the only soul of all the series that ever could be seen outside the human body. This was distinct from the soul of life in a tree, a plant, a bird, a beast or reptile, because it was an apparition of the human soul made visible in the human form. The doctrines of its propitiation are definitely stated in the rubrical directions to Chapter 144 of the Ritual. At this stage of his spiritual progress the deceased has reached the point where the mummy Osiris has transformed into the risen Horus, the divine one, who is the eighth at the head of the seven great spirits. Thus, in the Mysteries of Amenta, human Horus dies to rise again as lord of the resurrection and to manifest as the double of the dead. He is divinized in the character of the ghost, and as such he becomes the spirit medium for his father, the holy spirit his " Witness for Eternity," who is called the only begotten and anointed son. In this character the deceased is Horus in spirit, ready for the boat of Ra. An effigy of the boat was to be made for the deceased. In the instructions given it is said " a figure of the deceased is to be made " in the presence of the gods. This figure is the Ka. Oblations of flesh and blood, bread and beer, unguents and incense are to be offered ; and it is stated that this is to be done to make the spirit of the deceased to live. It is also promised that the ceremony, if faithfully performed, will give the Osiris strength among the gods, and cause his strides to increase in Amenta, earth, and heaven. Thus the Ka image to which the offerings were made was representative of the deceased who lived on in the spirit, whether groping in the netherworld, walking the earth as the ghost, or voyaging the celestial water in the boat of Ra on his way to the heaven of eternity. Naturally enough, the sustenance of life was offered to feed those who were held to be the living, not the dead.

The Ka image depicted in the Egyptian must be distinguished from the Mummy. The mummy was made on purpose to preserve the physical likeness of the mortal. The mummy was a primitive form of the effigy in which the body was preserved as its own portrait, whereas the Ka was intended for a likeness of the Spirit or immortal, the likeness in which the just spirit made perfect was to see " The Father " or " God " in his glory. Both the Mummy and the Ka were represented in the Egyptian tomb, each with a chamber to itself. In the Egyptian custom, described by both Herodotus and Plutarch, it was not the dead mummy that was brought to table as a type of immortality, but the image of the Ka, which denoted what the guests would be like after death, and was therefore a cause for rejoicing. This was brought on by the gnostics, and Christianized in Rome. One of the many titles of Osiris in all his forms and places is that of " Osiris in the monstrance " (Rit., Ch. 141, Naville). In the Roman ritual the monstrance is a transparent vessel in which the host or victim is exhibited. In the latest Egyptian Cult, Osiris was the victim. The elevation of the host signifies the resurrection of the crucified god, who rose again in spirit from the corpus of the victim now represented by the host.

I reproduce (Fig. 1) a "Moai-Miro" or "Ka image," found on Easter Island.

The " Ka " Image is a primitive type of " eternal duration," representing the spirit of their ancestors. The fact that these are called " Moai-Miro " proves that they, the Easter Islanders, have retained the Egyptian belief of their forefathers, i.e. that in spirit form " the male was blended with the female " to attain the ultimate and final type of " the Ka " for eternity, because the words, or one double word, means " male and female."

Moai-Papa : Female.
Moai-Tangata : Male.
Moai-Miro : " The Ka," or blending of the two.

The Shennu Ring ○ portrayed on the back is also Egyptian and an emblem of eternity.

It is of little use to attempt to write the past history of religion and the human race if the Spiritualism proper, which is based on phenomenal and veritable facts in Nature, is left out. Hitherto this, the most important of all mental factors, has been omitted, derided, decried, or falsely explained away.

The Egyptians were profoundly well acquainted with

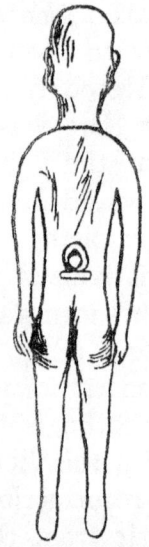

Moai-Miro or Ka image, found at Easter Island with Egyptian Shennu Ring depicted on the back —type of everlasting eternity.

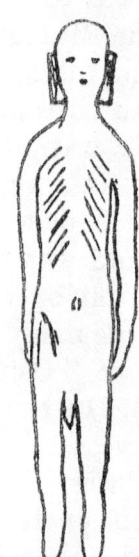

Moai-Miro or Ka, image, found at Easter Island.

FIG. 1.

those abnormal phenomena which are just re-emerging within the ken of modern science, and with the hypnotic means of inducing the conditions of trance. Their "rekhi," or wise men, the pure spirits in both worlds, were primarily those who could enter the life of trance or transform into the state of spirit, as is shown by the determinative of the name "rekhi," which is the "phœnix" of spiritual transformation.

When the Zulu King, Cetewayo, was in London, he said to a friend: "We believe in ghosts or spirits of the dead, because we see them, but we cannot see 'the Great God or Great Spirit.' "

I know some people, now living, who possess the inestimable gift of seeing and being able to converse or communicate with their departed friends, who never leave them night or day.

But these good spirits cannot speak so that one can hear them, they cannot make noises, nor can you take photographs of them. All that kind of phenomena of which most present-day Spiritualists tell you, is chicanery and humbug. Spirits are composed of pure Corpuscles in the likeness and form of their previous earthly state as humans, only much more beautiful. They cannot leave Paradise without Divine permission. They cannot visualize Themselves to anyone without Divine permission. When a person dies, his or her Spirit leaves the body matter at once. Some are permitted to enter Paradise immediately, after being judged by the Great God; others have to go through another state or trial, which the Ancient Egyptians imaged by an Ideograph, and termed Amenta, before being allowed to enter Paradise, and others never enter There. They are annihilated as Spirits, and their Corpuscular forms are returned to the ultimate Separate Corpuscles to be regrouped for some other purpose.

Some evil Spirits are allowed to remain on earth for a time, and they are always trying to influence or work some evil on poor humanity, but their ultimate end is always the same—annihilation.

The belief that deceased persons make their reappearance on the earth in human guise is universal amongst all the ancient races.

The Kareus say, that the La, or ghost, sometimes appears after death, and cannot be distinguished from the deceased person; only has a lighter form.

The Eskimo states: the soul or spirit exhibits the same form and shape as the body it belonged to, but is of a more subtle and ethereal nature.

The Tonga Islanders say that the human soul is the

finer, more aeriform, part of the body, the essence that can pass out, as does the fragrance from a flower.

The Islanders of the Antilles found that the ghosts vanish when they tried to catch them, having no apparent material substance.

The Greenland seers describe the soul as pallid, soft, and intangible when they attempted to touch them.

Huxley says: "That there are no savages without ghosts."

So we see that amongst these early people it was recognized that the ghost or Spirit of their Ancestors could, and did return to manifest itself to their friends and in a purer Corpuscular form. Of course, they did not use that terminology, because they could not comprehend what Corpuscles were; but their objective evidence confirms the fact, or rather science confirms the fact of their objective evidence.

All the Nilotic Negroes believe in a Great Spirit whom they cannot see or define, but various names are used by the different Totemic Tribes all over the world to express their ideas and beliefs.

Amongst certain tribes in Australia He is called Baiame or Daramulun, and they have different names for all his fingers, toes, limbs; these represent the different attributes they attach to him.

Amongst some tribes the women and children are taught to believe that the sound of the bull-roarer is the voice of the Great Spirit, called amongst the Arunta tribe Twanyirika, and amongst the Katish tribes Atnatu, which is an Egyptian word, in one form of its interpretation, meaning "the breath of life."

The Bushmen's Creator, or Great Spirit, whom they call "Kagan," is symbolized by a grasshopper.

Ideographs were adopted first to represent the superhuman Powers or Spirits.

The living Ideographs or Zootypes were primary, and can be traced to their original habitat or home, Africa, and to nowhere else upon the surface of the earth.

The Cow of the waters, Female Hippopotamus, thus

represented the Earth-Mother as the great bringer forth of life, before she was divinized as Apt the Goddess in human guise with the head of a Hippopotamus; so also all the talking animals, as the Hawk of Horus, the Kaf-Ape of Taht-an, the White Vulture of Neith, the Jackal of Anup, and many others were pre-extant as the talking Animals before they were delineated in a semi-human form as Gods and Goddesses or elemental powers, thus figured forth in the form of birds, beasts, reptiles, and fishes.

Animals that talk in the folk-lore tales of the Bushmen, or the Indians, or the Marchen of Europe, are still the living originals which became pictographic and ideographic in the Zootypology of Egypt, where they represent divinities—i.e. nature powers at first and deities afterwards, then ideographic, and finally the phonetics of the Egyptian Alphabet. No race of man ever yet imagined that the animals talked in human language as they are made to do in the popular Marchen.

No man is so primitive as to think that anyone was swallowed by a great fish and remained three days and three nights in the monster's belly, to be afterwards belched up on dry land alive.

They were not human beings of whom such stories were told, and therefore those who first made the Mythical representation were not capable of believing they were human.

Professor Max Muller asked how the total change of a human being or a heroine into a tree is to be explained. But Hathor in the green Sycamore, or Tefnut in the emerald sky of the Egyptian dawn, were never human beings.

The root of these things lies far beyond the Anthropomorphic representation, where the Arynists have never travelled.

The Animals and Birds, etc., were ever superhuman, therefore were adopted as Zootypes and as primary representations of the superhuman Powers of the Elements.

They were adopted as primitive Ideographs, and they

were adapted for use and consciously stamped for their representative value, not ignorantly worshipped.

The origins of mythology, symbolism, and numbers have all to be sought in the stage of gesture-language, which was the first mode of figuring an image. The most ancient Egyptian hieroglyphics are those which convey by direct representation or imitation. In a later phase these were still continued as ideographic determinatives, so that notwithstanding the development of the hieroglyphic the links are complete from the gesture-signs down to the alphabet.

The beetle, in Egypt, during the Inundation, would have been washed out of life altogether but for its Arkite cunning in making ready for the waters by rolling up its little globe, with the seed inside, and burying it in the dry earth until the Inundation subsided. How primitive man must have watched the clever creature at work; no font of letter-type employed in radiating human thought could shed a clearer light of illustration on the idea of resurrection from the earth than this living likeness of the process of transformation into the winged world. How the primitive man observed the works and ways and on-goings of the intelligence thus manifested around him; how he copied where he could, and gradually found a line of his own in the scheme of development; how he honoured these early teachers and instructors, and made their forms the pictures of the primal thoughts which they had evoked from his mind, is at length recorded in the system of hieroglyphic symbols and mythology: and the illustrated proofs are extant to this day. As an example, both the Kaffirs and Zulus, as well as the Pygmies, say that the spirits of their dead ancestors appear to them in the shape of serpents, but they are speaking only in sign language; the serpent was a type of the eternal by periodic renewal, an emblem, therefore, of immortality, and their belief that their ancestors survived in spirit was expressed by the serpent symbol. The truth can be recovered in Egypt, with whom survived the consciousness of Kam. The goddess Renen, the Gestator,

OF RELIGION

is said to receive in death the breaths (souls) of those belonging to her (Rit., Ch. 160). The serpent was one of her symbols; consequently these souls, or breaths, would enter the serpent-woman to be born again; the serpent was a type of renewal before Renen was personified in Egypt, and so we hear these primitive people talking in the same figures of speech that were made visible by Egyptian art.

This Sign Language must be studied when considering the Paleoanthropic.

CHAPTER III

MAGIC AND FETISHISM

PROFESSOR Sir James Frazer considers that all tribes have developed their religious ideas, Totems and Totemic ceremonies from their own surroundings, and that those that practise magic represent a lower intellectual status : he thinks that magic preceded religion. I do not share this view. I believe that magic is very late in comparison with religious ideas, probably by many thousand years, and that we do not meet with this evolution until the time of the Nilotic Negro ; even amongst the primitive tribes of these it is questionable if it is practised by them ; certainly none of the pre-totemic races practise it, except when they have adopted it by intercourse with the Nilotic Negroes.

I know it has been stated that " The Veddas," who are a Pygmy race, practise Magic, but—

1. These have no Totems or Totemic Ceremonies ; they have the Pygmy dances, but no history of pre-human Ancestors.

2. They believe in a Great Spirit whom they call " Kataragam " ; make offerings and propitiate.

3. They believe in the Spirits of their Ancestors, whom they propitiate, under the name of " Nac Yaku."

Also they believe in the two Heroes of the Hero Cult Nilotic Negroes, Kan de Yaka and Belindi Yaka, corresponding to Horus and Set of the Ancient Egyptians, and they believe in the Great Earth Mother, under the name Gale Yaka or Indigollac Kiriamma (Goddess of Earth or great provider of food). This shows that at some time these beliefs of the non-Hero Cult and Hero Cult Nilotic Negroes have been adopted by them, probably from association with the Tamils and Sanghalese. I do not agree that they practise Magic.

Magic is the power of influencing the Elemental Powers or Ancestral Spirits.

The phrases of great Magical efficiency in the Ritual are called: "The words that compel."

They compel the favourable action of the superhuman power to which appeal is made.

To make magic was to *act* the appeal in a language of signs which, like the words, was also intended to compel, and to act thus magically was a mode of compelling, forcing, and binding the superhuman powers.

Magic was also a mode of covenanting with the power apprehended in the elements.

The theory and practice of Magic was fundamentally based on Spiritualism. The greatest magician or sorcerer, witch or wizard, was the spirit-medium. The magical appeal made in mimetic Sign Language was addressed to superhuman powers as the operative force. The Spirit might be elemental or Ancestral, but without the one or the other there was no such thing as Magic.

Magical words are words with which to conjure and compel. Magical processes were acted with the same intent, i.e. magical incantations which accompany the Gesture sign. The appeal is made to some superhuman force; i.e. one of the elemental powers in Mythology, which become the Gods and Goddesses in the later Cults.

The beetle, Kheper, typified the self-reproducing power in nature which operates by transformation according to the Periodic Laws of evolution.

The Green Jade stones found buried with the dead was the Amulet, typifying that which was for ever green, fresh, and flourishing. In this, Sign Language tells us that an evergreen was, so to say, made permanent in stone, and buried with the dead as a type of eternal youth.

The deceased exclaims: "I am the column of green felspar" (Rit., Ch. 160), and he rejoices in the stone being so hard that it cannot be crushed or even receive a scratch, saying: " If it is safe, I am safe ; if it is uninjured, I am uninjured." The power of this Amulet was in its impenetrable hardness, which represented eternal permanence for the soul which it imaged.

The Ritual of Ancient Egypt contains many references to magic as a mode of transformation. " My mouth makes the invocation of magical charms. I pray in magical formulas. My magical power gives vigour to my flesh." The one great reason of these Nilotic Negroes for making fetish images and honouring them was that the so-called worship was a mode of laying hold upon the power which they represented. The images are a means of taking tangible possession of the powers themselves through their hostages. The devotees thus have them in their power and hold them, as it were, in captivity, to control, command, and even punish.

Wearing the fetish as a charm, a medicine, a visible symbol of power, is common with these Negro races ; the fetishes represent a helpful power. His fetishes represent power in various forms, whether drawn from the animal or human world, whether the tokens be a tooth, a claw, a skin, a bone, a stone, or any other thing. They represent a stored-up power to him and he has faith in them, and that acts as a potent mental influence. When it was known what the type or fetish signified as a representative figure, it could make no direct appeal to religious consciousness, nor evoke a feeling of reverence for itself, any more than the letters of the alphabet.

The Arunta have an emblem in their Churinga which is a very sacred fetish. This is associated with the Alcheringa spirits. When there is a battle, the churinga is supposed to endow its owner with courage. So firm is their belief in this, that if two men were fighting and one of them knew that the other carried a Churinga, whilst he did not, he would certainly lose heart, and without doubt be beaten (Spencer and Gillen).

Magic and Fetishism takes up the tale of development in Sign Language following Totemism, and this proves how erroneous is Sir James Frazer's opinion.

Fetishism does not mean a " worship," but a reverent regard for Amulets, Talismans, Mascots, Charms, and Luck tokens that were worn or otherwise employed as magical signs of protecting power.

The Amulets, Charms, and Tokens of magical power that were buried with the dead, afterwards became fetish on account of what they imagined symbolically, and Fetish Symbolism is Sign Language in one of its ideographic phases.

The fetishes acquired their sacred character, not as objects of worship, but from what they had represented in Sign Language, and the meaning still continued to be acted when the language was no longer read.

The Serpent was a symbol, or type, of periodic renewal and self-renovation, and thus the slough or skin remains a fetish to the end, the Serpent being therefore an emblem of immortality.

The Ankh-cross signified the life to come; that is the life everlasting.

The Shen-ring imaged continuity for ever in the circle of eternity.

The Egyptian word Sa, *whence the meaning of the word Magic was derived*, means aid, protection, defence, virtue, touch, soul, efficacy. In Egypt, Sa or Ka was the author or creator of the types which became fetishes (Rit., Ch. 17). Thus Fetishism was a mode of Sign Language which supplied a tangible means of laying hold of nature powers that were to some extent apprehended as superhuman without being comprehended.

We see by the Zunis that one great reason for making fetish images and honouring them was that the so-called worship was a mode of laying hold upon the powers which they represented, and this is the universal belief. It is still extant in the Church of Rome, as witnessed by the Amulets and charms, the cross, the rosary, and other fetish figures that are yet worn for protection, and are touched in time of need to establish the physical link with the invisible power with which it is desired to keep in touch.

Totemism, Magic, and Fetishism culminated in the Egyptian Mysteries, ending finally in the Eschatology from which Christian religions in the world have arisen.

In totemism, then, we find sacred Mysteries performed in various modes of Sign Language, by which the Thought, the Wish, the Want is magically expressed in act instead of, or in addition to, words. Obviously the object of these most ancient mysteries of magic is the perennial increase of food, more expressly for the animal, or plant, that gives its name to the totem of those who perform the particular rites. Spencer and Gillen (N.T.) describe a mystery of transformation in relation to the Witchetty-Grub Tribe, the Grub being an article of diet amongst these natives. With magical incantations they call upon the Grub to lay an abundance of eggs; they invite the Animals to gather from all directions, and beg them to feed on this particular feeding-ground of theirs. The men encase themselves in the structure intended to represent the chrysalis, from which the Grub emerges in re-birth, and out of this they crawl. To interpret the dumb-drama of all these Totemic Mysteries we must learn what is thought, and meant to be expressed, chiefly by what is done. Here we see the mystery of transformation is acted magically by the men of the Witchetty-Grub Totem for the production of food in the most primitive form of a prayer meeting or religious service. The Powers are solicited, the want made known by signs, especially by the sign of fasting during the performance. They shuffle forth one after another in imitation of animals newly born. Thus they enact the drama or mystery of transformation in character. It is only amongst these Totemic peoples that we can find the true origins of all our sacred Mysteries and beliefs.

The Spirit that moved upon the face of the Waters from the beginning was recognized as a force or power, not human, and this force or Spirit of the Air was divinized in Shu, the God of breathing-force, whose Zootype was a panting or roaring lion.

What has been continually miscalled *Phallic Worship* originated in the idea and symbolism of Motherhood. The Earth itself as producer of food and drink, which was the primary want of primitive man, was looked upon as the Mother of life.

The Cave in the Earth was the womb of the *Bringer-forth*, the interim symbol of the Genetrix. The Mother in Mythology is the Abode. The Sign of the female signified the place of birth.

The Cave or the Cavern in the rock was an actual place of birth for man and beast, and therefore a figure of the uterus of the Mother-earth.

In the Mysteries the stone with a hole in it was made use of as the emblem of a second or Spiritual birth. In their magical ceremonies they represent a woman by the emblematic figure of a hole in the Earth ("Arunta Tribes," by Spencer and Gillen, p. 550); also a figure of the Vulva as the Door of Life is imaged on certain of their Totems. The Esquimaux Great Mother Sinde is the earth itself as producer of life and provider of food, and is a figure of the Mother.

"Phallic-worship" began with the earth itself being represented as the Womb of Universal Life, with the female emblem for a figure of the Birthplace and Bringer-forth. Not that the emblem was necessarily human, for it might be the sign of the Hippopotamus or Sow; anything but worshipful or human. The mythical gestator was not imaged primarily as a Woman, but as a pregnant Water-Cow, size being required to emphasize the Great; i.e., enceinte Earth-Mother and her Chamber of birth.

The Cave as birthplace of the Earth-Mother was identified with the uterine abode by the emblem scrawled upon the Rock from time immemorial. This figure, called the symbol of wickedness "in all the land" by Zechariah (Chaps. 5–8), portrayed through all the world, has ever been most prominent in the primitive art of all aborigines in Africa and other countries. Not as an object of worship, nor of degradation, but as a likeness of the human abode depicted in the birthplace of the Cavernmen.

The Superhuman type of the Motherhood is portrayed in Symbolism not only as the Cave, the Gap, or the Stone, but also as the Tree, the Sow, the Water-Cow, the Crocodile, the Lioness, and many other Zootypes.

The God Seb is the Egyptian Priapus, who has sometimes been called a Phallic deity. He is the Earth-God and Father of Food, the God of Fructification associated with plants, fruits, flowers, and foliage, which are seen issuing from his body. He is the "Lord of Aliment," in whom the reproduction powers of earth are icthyphallically portrayed. But the potency represented by Seb was not human, although a human member is depicted as a type of the begetter or producer.

The Lion and phallus are elsewhere identical as Zootype and type of the Solar force, when it is said the luminous lion in its Course (the sun) is the phallus of Ra (Rit., Ch. 17), as, therefore, this was solar force, it will be obvious why this image was made in so enormous a size when carried in the processions of the Phallus (Herodotus, B. 2, 48).

Spencer and Gillen mention the custom, still extant amongst the aborigines, for the widow of a deceased person of importance to wear the phallus of her dead husband suspended around her neck for some time, even for years after his death. This custom is dominated by a religious sentiment and is a symbolical action which Egypt explains. By wearing the phallus the widow was preserving it from decaying in the earth, and in wearing it she was preserving that type of resurrection which Isis in her character of the widow sought to preserve in a typical image. In Egyptian Resurrection scenes the re-arising of the dead, or inert Osiris, is indicated by the male emblem; re-erection being one with resurrection.

It is thus the dead are raised or re-erected as Spirits, in Sign Language, and the power of rising again is imaged in the life-likeness as by the figure of Amsu-Horus.

Thus these poor natives wear the phallus of their

dead husbands as a token of his future resurrection, being the most primitive representation in living form of the prototype of the widow divinized as Isis, who consecrated the phallus of Osiris and wore it, made of wood to preserve in a typical image her belief in his resurrection.

The most exact and comprehensive title for the religion designated "phallic worship" would be the Cult of the Great Mother, taking Hathor for the type, who was the womb of life as Mother Earth, the suckler as the Cow, the giver of food, shelter, and water, as the tree, and who, in the course of time, became goddess of Love, of fecundity, and child-birth. The primitive simplicity of Hathor-worship was that of the infant at the Mother's nipples when the source of plenty was portrayed as superhuman in the likeness of the Cow. But in the later phallic Cult the type had been changed *from the Cow to the Human Mother*. The Cow was superseded in the Temples by the woman as the more alluring type of the great goddess. It is pitiful to see how the sex became the human organ of the superhuman power, offering itself as Hathor in the Asherah-tree, or as the house of God, acting the goddess as the great harlot of the Cult in its debasement and deterioration. The Great Mother was the ideal in the minds of the devotees, she whose size had been imaged by the hippopotamus, whose sexual force had been represented by Sekhet as the Lioness in heat. The Great Mother when represented in human form becomes the harlot of promiscuous intercourse who brought much revenue to the religious Temples by her capacity for performing the rite on behalf of the Great Mother, in her tree-tent, or Rock Cave, or later sanctuary. It was as representatives of the Great Mother that the Temple prostitutes attained pre-eminence in various lands, and afterwards even highly honoured as servants of the goddess. The Great Mother in the Mount was represented by such goddesses as Astarte, whose Ephebæ and Courtesans received her devotees in grottoes and caves that were hollowed out for the purpose in the Syrian hillsides. The Temple of Hathor at Serabit-el-Khadem in the Peninsula of Sinai, was based originally on a cave in the rock which was the Great Mother's earliest shrine.

The phallic festival was periodically celebrated in honour of the Great Mother, the supreme power in nature personalized as the goddess of fertility, the giver of food and drink, the celebration being in accordance with primitive usages and the promiscuous sexual intercourse of pre-totemic times.

The Asherah is a sacred simulacrum of the goddess whose desire was to be ever fecundated. And when the women of Israel set up the Asherah and wore the hangings for curtains of concealment (2 Kings xxiii. 7) they became the representatives of the Great Mother, who is denounced by the Biblical writers as the Great Harlot, but who was a most popular Mother in Israel, and was Sekhet in Egypt.

In the Biblical version, Israel is charged by Hosea with having become a prostitute by letting herself out for hire upon the Corn-floor. " Thou hast gone a whoring from thy God : thou hast loved hire upon every Corn-floor " (Ch. ix. 1). In this case the Mother-Earth as the Corn-goddess was being fertilized by human proxy in the phallic festivities, which included the rite upon the Corn-floor, as well as on the hill, under the green tree, etc. The Great Mother was the object of propitiation and appeal, pregnant with plenty, as the bringer-forth to birth and the giver of food. This was the superhuman Mother in Mythology, and not the human parent as in Totemism. This was brought on in Rome, the first types being the " Vestal Virgins," and the last the White Nuns of the Roman Christian Religion.

It is as Amsu-Horus, rising in Icthyphallic form with the sign of virility erect, which only can account for the Phallus found in the Roman Catacombs as a figure of the resurrection ; it is the typical member of Horus, whose word was thus manifested in Sign Language with pubescent power in the person of the risen Amsu.

The Totemic Ceremony, or festival of fructification,

naturally had a phallic character, as it was sexual from the first.

It was not only performed at seed-sowing and harvest, on behalf of food. Thousands of years before corn was cultivated in the name of Isis of Demeter there was a general rejoicing at the time when the youth was made into a man and the girl into a woman. This Totemic ceremony was brought on into the early Christian Church as witnessed by the festival of the Agape, and the present-day Maypole dance is a remnant of this same ceremony carried down through the ages of time.

Amongst the early Christians, the Agape was celebrated in connection with the Eucharist and was held to be a Christian Sacrament. Paul, in speaking of the love feast at Corinth as a scene of drunken revelry (1 Cor. i. 20-2), recognizes the celebration of two suppers which he is desirous of having kept apart, one for the Church and one for the house. These two are the Eucharist and the Agape. But at the time of the advent of Christianity these two festivals had assumed a different phase. Ecclesiastical writers differ as to which of the two ought to be solemnized first. But Egypt tells us which stood first in order.

At the time of the Osirian doctrine the last supper was the last night of the old year, and the Mesiu on the first night of the New Year. This duality was maintained by the Agnostics and continued by the Christians.

With so-called Tree-Worship, the Tree is a type, but the type is not necessarily an object of Worship. The forest men were dwellers in the tree or bush; the tree that gave them food and shelter grew to be an object of regard. It thus became a type of Mother-Earth as the birthplace and abode. Hence Hathor was the hut or house of Horus (Har) in the Tree.

Myth-making man did not create the Gods in his own image. Totemism was formulated by Myth-making man with types that were very opposite of human, and in the Mythology and the Anthropomorphic representations was preceded by the whole world of Totemic Zootypes.

If primitive man had projected the shadow of himself upon external nature to shape its elemental forces in his own image, then the primary representation of nature powers ought to have been Anthropomorphic; whereas the primary powers and Divinities were first represented by Zootypes.

Thus Totemic People—

1. Worshipped and made offerings to the One Great Spirit whom they could not define, but portrayed as having many attributes which they depicted by Zootypes or other forms.

2. They believed in the Spirits of their Ancestors because they could see the Corpuscular body after they were dead, and they propitiated and made offerings to these to assist them in this earthly life.

3. They believed in the elementary powers or Spirits, and portrayed them as the Great Earth Mother and her seven children, in Zootype form, all of which they propitiated.

4. They established Totems and Totemic Ceremonies with some religious beliefs and sentiment attached to them.

5. They were the first to practise Magic and, following this, Fetishism.

6. The later Totemic people were those who *founded the Mythology* and *established Hero Cult Worship*.

So far, we find that the types of man had gradually ascended in evolution, that religious ideas and beliefs had kept pace with his anatomical and physiological development, and that the Hero Cult Nilotic Negroes with their religious beliefs and Totemic Ceremonies, as they left Africa, spread over all the world. Remnants of the old exodus are yet found in isolated lands still professing, believing, and practising their religious beliefs of this prehistoric past, the primary foundation from which all others have been built.

CHAPTER IV

HERO CULT AND MYTHOLOGY

In Totemism the dual Motherhood is followed by the dual Brotherhood, represented in the primary Mythology as the Twin Brothers, Set and Horus, the first two Heroes, and followed by Shu, forming the three first Kamit Heroes—the primary Trinity.

The followers of the romantic school who hold Mythology to have been Magic, out of some general undefined feeling, or popular conviction, can only be taken as trying to read before learning the Alphabet; their deductions can only be assumed as fabulous romances, because they have never learnt the Sign Language, or touched bottom of the subject-matter. *There is assuredly nothing more unscientific and unhistorical than to deny a law of development in the religious idea as a whole.* Mythology or mythological forms of religion are not represented quite as thoughts only, but *are types* used to express certain original powers that are inherent, physical as well as spiritual.

Therefore it would be true to regard all the representations which were formed out of the original religious consciousness, by means, or by the observation of natural phenomena—*simply an evolution in primary religion.*

Propitiation of a superhuman nature power for food and drink was the most primitive form of the appeal that ultimately culminated in worship. The gods of Egypt, from the beginning, represented food and drink, not only as givers of sustenance—they were the sustenance in food and liquid. The Great Mother was the suckler, or wet-nurse. Hathor offered food in the sycamore-fig, and Isis in the persea-tree of life. Child Horus was the shoot, the branch, the calf, the lamb, or fish. Seb, god of earth, was the father of aliment. Plenty of food and water first made heaven palpable to primitive or archaic man on earth. Hence the primitive paradise was imaged as a field or garden of food. The deity Atum-Ra, who first attained the status of " Holy Spirit " in the eschatology, says of himself: " I am the food which never perishes " (Rit., Ch. 85). Horus of the inundation was constellated on his papyrus as the evercoming shoot (Plan of Denderah); he was also the giver of food as the fish, the calf, and the lamb that were made celestial types in the Astral-Mythology. The tree of life was planted in the midst of the celestial oasis. Upon this grew the fruit as food upon which the gods and glorified fed. A power of perennial renewal was perceived in nature, and this was manifested by successive births. Hence the child god of Egypt became a type of the eternal recurrence of the seasons and of the elements of life and light, which in the character of Horus was at first by food and then water. This was the eternal, ever-coming, ever-renewing spirit of youth.

Ta-Urt, the Great Mother Earth, was the first or original form of the later Isis, the first or earliest Mother in Mythology.

In the next phase of the development of the Mythology, Ta-Urt was divinized and called Apt, and depicted astronomically. She mythically brought forth seven children—two at first, Set and Horus, the twins, and then the third, Shu. These are the three Heroes of the Hero Cult Nilotic Negroes, and they play an important part in the folk-lore tales, under different types, throughout the world.

Apt is represented as male and female, both in one, and her seven children are all males, and are termed " The Bulls of their Mother," because at that time there was no fatherhood known. These Heroes were the first three Mythical Gods or divinized elemental powers.

Set, as the primary elemental power, represented Darkness; Horus, born twin with Set, represented Light.

OF RELIGION

In the Mythology they were given two Stars on high, the South and North Pole Stars. These first two elemental powers of darkness and light were the first two children born of the Great Mother.

The eternal contest betwixt the powers of light and darkness is extant in the African folk-tales; for example:

The Han (a Rabbit) Kalalu and the Dzimivi are two of the contending characters.

The Han, as in Egypt, is typical of the Good Power.

1. The Babylonian dual God, or their representation of the Egyptian Horus and Set.

2. The Mexican Ometecutle and Omecinatl. The Lords of duality.

3. Two birds representing Horus and Set of the Egyptians from Easter Island.

FIG. 2.

The Dzimivi is the Evil Power, like Apap, the Giant Ogre, the Swallower of the water or the light (see Werner: "African Folk-Lore" *Contep. Rev.*).

As a proof of my contention that this Cult was carried out of Egypt to many parts of the world, I here reproduce (Fig. 2), pictures of the "Dual God," or "God with two attributes," the first phase of the Hero Cult, and afterwards carried on into the early Stellar Cult.[1]

No. 1. The Babylonian "dual God," or their representation of the Egyptian Horus and Set.

No. 2. The Mexican Ometecutle and Omecinatl, "The Lords of duality," their representation of Horus and Set of the Egyptians.

No. 3. The "dual God" of the Easter Islanders, which is their representation of the Egyptian Horus and Set. I could reproduce many more from other countries, but the above is sufficient and critical proof of the statements I have made.

Shu, the next child of the Great Mother, represented breathing power or air, wind, etc., and was imaged by the Zootype of a roaring or panting lion, also later by a feather. These three represented the Heroes of the Hero Cult people and the Primary Trinity, and were carried throughout the world by the Hero Cult Nilotic Negroes.

In the preface of the Japanese Kojiki the beginning of the separation of Heaven and Earth is described by Yasumaro; Heaven and Earth first parted and the three Kami performed the commencement of creation. The passive and active essences then developed, and the two spirits became "The Ancestors of all Things." These are identified with Izanagi and Izanami in the Japanese system, and with the Yin and Yangi in the Chinese. The three Kami, called the Heaven-born Kami, are one with the Egyptian Set, Horus, and Shu, whilst the twin brother and sister are identical with Shu and Tefnut, who represented breathing power, or air and moisture, as the two halves of a soul of life. Shu of breathing force, and Tefnut of liquid life, the active and passive essences which blended and became the creative spirit moving on the face of the firmament. In Mythology that which has been called "Creation" begins with duplicating, by dividing; darkness was divided from light, dry land as breathing-place was divided from water. The North was divided from the

[1] I have given the Egyptian representation in "Signs and Symbols," p. 72, 2nd ed.

OF RELIGION

South and the Earth was divided from the Heaven; the same is found in the Japanese and other creations.

In Genesis, the powers of darkness and light are present when the drama opens, not as powers personified, but *as elements*. "Darkness was upon the face of the deep," and the Elohim said: "Let there be Light." Set and Horus were the first of the primal powers in an elemental phase, the black Neh being the bird of night, or Set, and the Solar Hawk of Horus the bird of day. Then was Set, as the power of darkness, on the one hand, and on the other Horus, as the Hawk of Light. These are equivalent to: "There was evening and there was morning one day." It must be noted that the Hebrew word for evening ערב is the name of the raven, the Zootype black bird of Set.

All the earth, heavens, and seas (two lakes) were considered dual. It was South and North, the wet season and the dry, and although Horus was called God of the North, and Set God of the South, the two were one God depicted with two different attributes; the primary form was dual. A trinity was not conceived until the element of air, wind, or breathing force had been divinized and imaged as a panting Lion, under the name of Shu.

Then we had the first form of a Trinity or Great Spirit with three different attributes, which were first elemental.

As the Mythology first came into existence in the old land South of the Equator, so Set was recognized as the first or Primary God, and when in their migrations North they arrived at the Equatorial regions Set and Horus became equal or the "bi-une God."

It shows that the earliest Egyptians founded their Mythology on facts that they had observed in ever-recurring phenomena of external nature and then expressed in Sign Language.

In the beginning was the void, otherwise designated the Abyss. From our sun, this earth, and other planets forming our Solar System have been thrown off as superheated vapour, gradually cooling down, ever revolving on their own axis around our Sun, in their allotted space and time. Our sun was thrown off from another sun, around which it revolves, taking 25,827 years to perform its cycle of one year. " The one Great Year of the Egyptians." (They have left records of ten great cycles at least.)

As Hero Cult developed, the types of totemism attained a uranographic setting; they were not limited to the human group.

They were no longer merely of the earth, but also represented the Mother and big-brothers in the Sky, from whom descent was claimed by the totemic group. These were the bear that lived again in future food, the serpent that renewed itself, the panes bird that never died, the turtle of eternity, and other types of superhuman powers that were constellated in the heavens.

The first of these was the Great Mother and her three sons, as we have seen imaged variously. As examples, the Ainus say they descended from the region of the bears, which was at the summit of the very lofty mountains in the North, that is at the Pole. They claim to derive their origin from the bear as their Mother and the dog as their father, which can easily be read as Astronomical Hero Cult. The She-bear took the place of the female hippopotamus, the original Great Mother in the Egyptian whose Constellation as Apt was the Great-Bear. The dog is equivalent of the earlier jackal, one of the zootypes for Set, and Set was one of the " bulls of his mother " imaged in the Little Bear and these two Constellations; the Great Bear as the Mother and the Little Bear as her children were the primary foundation of the Stellar Cult, which was a continuous development from the Hero Cult in evolution and was carried all over the world, and is extant at the present day.

Amongst the Iroquois they claim descent from the Bear and the Wolf. The primal pair here again were the Great Bear as Mother, and the Jackal, Wolf, or Prairie-dog as her son and consort.

The Navajio Indians derive their origin from the top of the divine mountain in the North, where the Pole is represented as a great reed which saved their progenitors from the waters of the deluge in the region of the Stars which never set (Mathews: "The Navajio Mythology" *American Antiquarian*, 1883). This indicates that they were a *very primitive* Stellar Cult exodus from Egypt.

The Samoans say that the first human race were a woman and her son, and in "Turner's Samoa" the same tales are told as in the original Egyptian.

The Khonds of Orissa have a divinized form of the primal pair (Early Stellar Cult) in their ancient goddess Tari-Pennu and her son Buri-Pennu, who is the representative of Horus, and not Set, as he was called "the light," which was one of the names of Horus.

The Finnic triad was named:

1. Ukko, the old one, the God of Heaven above, the Supreme One.
2. Ilmarinen, the eternal forger, god of the earth.
3. Wainamoinen, the friend of the waves.

These three were said to have established the celestial vault, fixed the gates of air, and sowed the stars in space (Kalwala, Part II, Runa XIV).

The Hawaiians had the male triad as a Trimurti named Kane, Ku, and Lone, equal in nature but distinct in attributes. Ku was surnamed Ka-Pao, the Builder or Architect.

Lono was Noho-i-ka-wai, the dweller on the water. They formed a triad as "the one who is established" (Fornander, Vol. I, p. 61).

The New Zealanders have the masculine triad as the three brothers: Mani, the "elder Mani, the tallest Mani, and the younger Mani."

The Mexicans were called the three sons of Can, first symbolized by three Deer heads, and later by three Triangles.

The Hero Cult people of South America, the Quimlaya have:

1. Abera, a creative deity = Horus.
2. Canicuba, an evil spirit = Set.
3. Debečeba, a female deity = Apt.

The New Guinea Hero Cult people have :
1. A Great Mother deity = Apt.
2. Harmuna, a good spirit = Horus.
3. A bad spirit = Set.

There is a unity of origin for all mythology, as is demonstrated by a world-wide comparison of the great primary types, and the origin of that unity, the common origin of the Mythical Genetrix and her " children " of seven elemental forces or powers lies in Egypt.

The Mythology which commenced with the Hero Cult and ended in the Astro-Mythology did not arise from a hundred different sources as frequently stated, but :

It is one as a system of representation ;

One as a mould of thought ;

One as a mode of expression ; and all its great primordial types are universal.

Mythology commenced with those whom we might term savages, Nilotic Negroes, in Africa ; it was preserved and continued by the Egyptians. But although *their* Ancestors were savages, and they continued to repeat the Myths of their savage Ancestors, they did not continue to remain savages.

The Egyptian Mythology is the oldest in the world ; it did not begin as an explanation of natural phenomena, but as a *representation* by such primitive means as were available at the time.

The earliest form of a religious Cult was founded in avocation and propitiation of the Great Earth-Mother, who was divinized in their Astro-Mythology and uranographically represented in the Great Bear, Ursa Major, with her seven elemental powers constellated in Ursa Minor, the Giver of Life and Birth, of Food and Water, as the primary provider. She was represented in Zootype form as the Water-Cow, the fruit Tree of Hathor, the Sow of Rerit, the Serpent of Rennit, who was first besought in worship as the Great Goddess, the All Mother.

The Totemic Mother was and is a live woman. There are millions of " Totemic Mothers " to-day, her " goddess representative," or "representative goddess," i.e. the Great Mother of Mythology was mythical, but the Mythical Mother was taken from the Totemic Mother as a type.

In the later Semitic legend it was said the earth was founded on the flood, as if it were afloat upon the water of the abyss. But according to the primary expression, the earth stood upon its own bottom in the water, at the fixed centre, with the tree upon the summit as a figure of food and water in vegetation. The mythical abyss of the beginning was the welling place of water underground, where life was brought to birth by the Great Mother from the womb of the Abyss. In the Ritual, this is described as the Tuat, a place of entrance and egress from the lower earth. It is a secret Deep that nobody can fathom, which sends out light in the dark, and " its offerings are eatable plants." It is the birthplace of water and vegetation, and therefore more abstractly of life.

" The bottomless pit," is a figure that was derived from this implumbed deep inside the earth itself. From this abyss the Mother Earth (as the womb of life) had brought forth her elementary progeny as the perennial renewers of food to eat, water to drink, and air to breathe.

The Tuat in the recesses of the South is identified in the hymns as the secret source of the river Nile, which is thus traced to the Lake Tanganyika. Such was the birthplace of the beginning, the birthplace of water in the beginning from which the papyrus plant rose as the primal food, so the fact is recorded in the Ritual. It is the habitat of the dragon, called " The crocodile coming out of the abyss." It is also the lair of the Apap-monster, of whom it is said by Shu : " If he who is in the water opens his mouth, I will let the earth fall into the waters well," being the South made North (Records, Vol. 4).

Dr. Elliot Smith, in his " The Evolution of the Dragon," p. 104, states that : " In Egypt we do not find the characteristic dragon and dragon story." Surely he is wrong in this statement ; it was from old Egypt that the *original*

Dragon and Dragon stories arose and were carried all over the world. He has mixed up the old evil Dragon with the dragon Crocodile Sebek, a Zootype of Horus; also another type of Horus was Tem, the Great Serpent type. Horus was the Crocodile or Great Fish who brought the waters to Egypt annually to give life and food to the people, hence a Saviour. The great dragon, Apap, was the devouring monster who drank up all the water and blasted the country with hot, burning winds and air; the fight was annual and continues.

"The Dragon Story" originated in the old dark land of Africa; it was the oldest myth of Egypt, and is represented in the earliest Stellar Astronomical Mythology, as the conflict of the two brothers, Set and Horus, as the two Dragons.

The primal mother in the Kamite representation was the bringer-forth of Set and Horus as her first two children, who were represented as having been born twins.

These, as the powers of darkness and light and drought and fertility, were a pair of combatants who fought for the supremacy until one brother overcame the other. In the different Cults they are depicted under various types and forms, one of the first being as two Dragons—Horus, the Crocodile Dragon of water, and Set, the Dragon of Drought—both of which were represented in the Astronomical Mythology. "Hydra" remains for all time as the "hellish Apap," who drank up all the water and swallowed all the light; and "Draconis" as a figure of the good Dragon; the "Horus-Crocodile," figured also as "Sebek-Horus."

When the two brothers were repeated in the Solar Mythos, as the two warring sons of Atum, or as two of the associated gods in the constituent parts and powers of Atum, or as the sons of Ptah and members of the Put Company of the Ali, the conflict was continued for the possession of the Arru-garden in Amenta. These various types have been carried all over the world from old Egypt, whence they originated; each type representing at the time of the Exodus the types adopted by the different Cults at the point of evolution they had then attained, the latest being " Cain and Abel " in the Hebrew metaphrastic rendering.

Dr. Elliot Smith in his book calls Osiris the first God of the Egyptians, and " believes that all the Gods were originally men " (pp. 30–1). But as we have seen, " these Gods " only represented types of elemental forces ; Osiris, in my view, represented the last, not the first, phase.

Osiris originated as a god in matter when the powers were elemental, but in the later theology the supreme soul in nature was configurated in a human form. Matter as human was then considered higher than matter unhumanized, and the body as human mummy (Osiris) was superior to matter in external nature. Also the spirit in human form was something beyond an elemental spirit ; hence the God as Supreme Spirit was based upon the human ghost, with matter as the mummy.

Osiris as a mummy in Amenta is what might be called the dead body of matter invested with the limbs and features of the human form, as the type to which the elemental powers had attained, first as Ptah, then as Amen in the human-featured Horus, who succeeded the earlier representations depicted by means of Zootypes. Osiris is a figure of inanimate nature, personalized as the mummy with a human form and face, whilst being also an image of matter as the physical body of the god. Resurrection in the Ritual is the coming forth to day (Peri-em-hru) whether *from* the life on earth or *to* the life attainable in the heaven of eternity. The first resurrection is, as it were, an ascension from the tomb in the nether earth by means of the secret doorway. But the coming forth (in the Osirian Cult) is *in*, *not from*, Amenta, after burial in the upper earth. The deceased had passed through the sepulchre, emerging in the lower earth. He issued from the valley of darkness and the shadow of death. Osiris had been cut to pieces in the Lunar and other phenomena by the evil Set. His limbs were gathered up and put together by his son and by his mother in Amenta, when he rose again as Horus from the dead; whatsoever had been postulated of Osiris the mummy in the mythology was repeated on behalf of the Osiris in the eschatology. The process applied to the human body first in death was afterwards applied to the god in matter, in the elements, or in the inert condition at the time of the winter solstice represented as awaiting, corpse-like, for his transformation or transubstantiation into the young body of the sun, or spirit of vegetation in the spring. The Solar God, as the sun of evening or of autumn, was the suffering, dying sun, or the dead sun buried in the nether earth. To show this, it was made a mummy, bound up in linen vesture without seam, and thus imaged in the likeness of the dead who bore the mummy form on earth, the unknown being represented by the known. The sun god, when descending to Amenta, may be said to mummify or karas his own body in becoming earth, or, as it were, fleshed in the earth of Ptah. Hence the mummy type of Ptah, or Atum and Osiris, each of whom at different stages was the solar god in mummied form when buried in Amenta. This was mythological and formed the types of the eschatology.

Professor Elliot Smith also states (p. 214): " But the Babylonians not only adopted the Egyptian conception of the power of evil as being *seven demons*, but they also seem *to have fused these seven into one*, or *rather given the real dragon seven-fold attributes*."[1] This is entirely misleading. There are no seven serpents of death, no seven evil serpents in the Egyptian, nor yet any one serpent with seven-fold attributes.

The seven Uraei, though elemental, born of matter, and of earth earthly, like their mother Rannut, are not evil powers; they are not in the same category with the Sebau of Apap or the semi-fiends of Set, which were not seven, but very numerous.

Again on p. 216, Osiris, Isis, and Set were not identified with the Pig. The many-teated Sow was an image or type

[1] Italics are mine.

of the Great Mother, as the suckler, called Rerit. The type was brought on from Totemic times and ceremonies. The later type or image was mythical, the primary Totemic was not. (The ceremonies and imagery are still practised at the present day amongst the natives of New Guinea.) The type was used as a zootype, but was not anthropomorphic. The Black Boar was one of the types, or Symbolic imagery for Set, but *never for Isis or Osiris*. *Osiris was imaged in mummy form only at first*, and *when he rises, it is as Amsu-Horus, who pierces the Black Boar Set with his spear* and puts chains upon and binds him.

BIRD, WITH EGG, FOUND ON EASTER ISLAND.
FIG. 3.

On the first of the Tablets of Creation of the Chaldeans it is written:

" At a time when neither the heavens above nor the earth below existed, then was the watery abyss; the first of seed, the mistress of the depths, the Mother of the universe. The waters clung together, no product had ever been gathered, nor was any sprout seen. Ay, the very gods had not yet come into being." i.e. when it was still Totemic.

On the third Tablet it is related how the gods are preparing for a grand contest against a monster known as Tiamat, and how the God Bel-Marduk overthrows Tiamat.

In the Tableau over the door of the East façade of the temple at Chichen; we see the same cosmogonic notions expressed, the same as in the first book of the Manava-Dharma-Sastra, in which the union of the great Mother Goddess, the God Mother of all Gods, with the son, " brings forth an egg, which becomes a form or type of the Supreme Being." The inhabitants of the islands of the Pacific entertain similar notions regarding creation.

Ellis, in his " Polynesian Researches," says : " In the Sandwich Islands there is a tradition that in the beginning there was nothing but water, when a big bird descended from on high and laid an egg in the sea. That egg burst and Hawaii came forth."

They believe that the bird is an emblem of deity : so it was. In one type it represented the great Mother of the old Egyptians, and the " egg " has been substituted for the " fish " as a type of Horus. In the Solar Cult " Ptah " issues from an " egg," another imagery.

In the Mythology it was the bird of Earth, The Great Mother, that laid the Egg, but in the Eschatology, when the egg is hatched, it is the bird of Heaven that rises from it as the Golden Hawk, a type of Horus.

The Lake of the Goose or Duck is referred to in the Ritual, Chapter 109.

The Sun was imaged as a golden Egg laid by the Duck or Goose, or Seb, the Earth.[1]

The Hill or Island standing in the Lake is the Earth, considered as a Mount.

The explorers of Easter Island found this Symbolic Symbol there, but not understanding Sign Language or the Ritual of Ancient Egypt, remained ignorant of its meaning or from whence it was derived or originated.

The bird symbol of the principal female divinity is met with in Polynesia, Japan, China, Chaldea, Greece, America, and all originated from Egypt.

It was in the region of the two great lakes and in the land of the papyrus reed that souls in the germ first emanated as the soul of life from water, and the Goddess

[1] The Zootype for Seb was a Goose. See also in " Solar Cult."

OF RELIGION 61

Uati is the African Great Mother in the bed of reeds which the Egyptians rendered mythically by means of the reed plant, as a symbol of the primeval birthplace on earth, with Horus issuing from the waters on the reed which became the lap of life, the cradle and the ark of the eternal child. This is recorded in the Ritual, Chapter 172. It was in the birthplace of the reeds, in the region of the

BIRD, WITH GOLDEN EGG, FOUND AMONGST THE
MAYA RUINS. (FROM "QUEEN MOO.")

Here the bird is represented as a Parrot.
In the Egyptian original it is a Duck
or Goose.
The fauna would be different in different
countries, but typical.

FIG 4.

reeds, that light first broke out of darkness in the beginning, in the domain of Set, and where the children of darkness and of light were born. The Mother Earth was a womb of universal life, the producer of food of various kinds, and the food was represented as her offspring. Horus, on his papyrus, imaged food in the water plant as well as the branch of a tree or in general vegetation.

Thus the doctrine of life issuing in and from the papyrus reed was first Egyptian, before it spread over other parts of the world. Naturally the earliest life thus emanating from the water was not human life; but this later would be included in the mythical representation. The origin of a saviour in the guise of a little child is thus traced to Child-Horus, who brought new life to Egypt every year as the Messu of the inundation. This was Horus in his pre-human characters—of the fish, the shoot of the papyrus, or the branch of endless years during the early Stellar Cult. In the Solar, the same image of

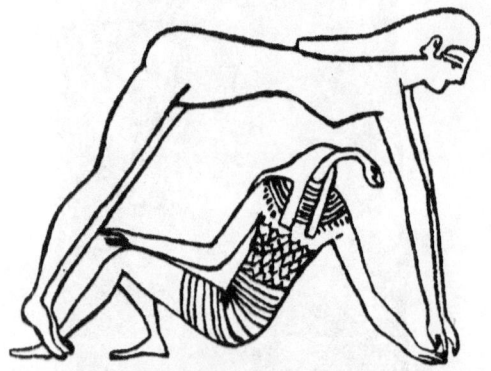

SEB AND NUT SLEEPING IN EACH OTHER'S ARMS.
FIG. 5.

Horus on the papyrus represented the young god or Solar cause of creation.

The above proves that the Egyptians possessed a very good idea of the origin of life at a very remote period, as well as "evolution," set forth later in this work.

Without doubt the contention of Set and Horus began with the conflict of darkness and light, drought and water, when these were elemental powers, and the birthplace of the twin brothers—one black and one light—was in the bed of reeds. The phase was continued in all the cults. In the Lunar, by the twins who struggled for supremacy in the dark and light halves of the moon, which yet imaged the light eye of Horus and the dark eye of Set. But the war extended to the whole of nature that was divided in halves betwixt the Set and Horus twins who

SHU UPRAISING THE HEAVENS, I.E. NUT FROM SEB, I.E. THE EARTH.
See also in Solar Cult.
PLATE I.

were the firstborn of the ancient Mother in two of her several characters.

Shu, the third Hero and third child of the old Earth Mother, comes into being at the time when the Hero Cult [1] people had arrived at the Equinox or equatorial regions, a place of no latitude, where the pole stars were to be seen upon the two horizons. The heavens signified in the old Kamite Mythology was the starry heaven of night upraised by Shu as he stood on the Mount of Earth. Nut or Nu, the Egyptian name for heaven, has the meaning and sign of "uplifting" (Plate I).

In Fig. 5 we see Nut lying in the arms of Seb (God of the Earth) at night, being uplifted by Shu in the day. There was but one point at which the heavens could be

THE STARRY HEAVEN OF NIGHT UPRAISED BY SHU.
FIG. 6.

said to rest upon the earth; that was in the region of no latitude, where the two pole stars were to be seen on the two horizons. As the Hero Cult people travelled toward the North, the heaven of the pole which touched the earth as viewed in equatoria, naturally rose up from the mount, or as mythically rendered, it was raised by Shu, who now became the third hero, and the tripartite division took the place of the dual in the heavens and the earth, Shu becoming the arbitrator of the two brothers at the equinox, giving the northern division to Horus and the Southern to Set, in the phases both Celestial and Terrestrial.

Horus of the inundation was constellated on his

[1] Hero Cult Nilotic Negroes first and Stellar Cult people after.

papyrus as the evercoming shoot, Fig. 7 (Plan: of Denderah). He was also the giver of food as the fish, the calf, and the lamb which were made celestial types in the Astral-Mythology.

Thus came a saviour to the land of Egypt as **Horus** of the inundation, Horus the shoot or natzar.

The deity Atum-Ra, who first attained the status of Holy Spirit in the later eschatology, says of himself: " I am the food which never perishes " (Rit., Ch. 85.)

The feminine type was first, because Motherhood was known before paternity could be identified under Totemic Sociology, and the Mythology was founded on this. The Tree was producer of fruit, so was the female.

HORUS OF THE INUNDATION.
FIG. 7.

The font of water was from the Mother-Earth.

The Serpent changed periodically, so did the female; thus the Fatherhood could not be discovered in heaven until recognized on earth. Therefore in the first plerome of the Gods there is no Fatherhood. The Gods are a family of seven born of the genetrix of " Gods and Man." The whole seven were born from Mother Earth, afterwards divinized as Apt, the only Mother; hence the biune parent, a twin form of " double primitive essence," and the seven elemental forces found in Egypt, were carried thence into Akkad, India, Britain, New Zealand, and other lands, and became Kronotypes in the secondary aspect and Gods in the final psychotheistic phase—the seven souls of Ra in the Solar Mythology, and the seven great Spirits in the Eschatology. Mythology exhibits a series of types as the representation of certain natural forces from which the earliest Gods and Goddesses were evolved and were finally compounded into one Deity, who assumed all their attributes as His manifestations, and therefore was typical of the Supreme Being and the God of all.

Platonists are simply metaphysical speculators. All such interpretation is finally futile that is not founded on the primary physical phenomena which are still veritable in the phenomena of nature.

Metaphysical explanations have been the curse of Mythology from the time of the Platonists up to the present. The non-evolutionist, who is likewise a metaphysician, would deal in vain with the problem of the religious origins. None but the evolutionists can go back far enough. Only the evolutionist can present the facts in their natural sequence and the true order of their development. An Egyptologist may know the monuments from first to last and yet be unacquainted with the origin and development of the Egyptian religion, because its roots must be traced back to pre-Totemic man in the vast ages of the hidden past. It is easy to assume that all the divine types are modes of manifestation of the one God, but we require to know what they signified in their pre-monumental phase, and what was their origin. It is not until we have followed through the series of Elemental, Stellar, Lunar and Solar Cults that we attain the highest phase of the various religious Cults. There is no origin of religion worth discussing apart from the primitive foundations and evolution of the same. The utterly misleading way in which the Egyptian physics were converted by Plato and his followers into Greek metaphysics makes Platonism only another name for imposture.

Thus we perceive how evolution continued as man advanced to a higher plane. First, the Pygmies believed in a Supreme or Great Spirit, whom they could not define or comprehend, but imaged or symbolized by ✷, which became a representation of the Great Spirit in Sign Language

In the next phase, the Nilotic Negroes, who believed in the same Great Spirit, attributed two primal elemental powers or spirits to Him—Light and Darkness—thus representing, or believing Him to be a Dual form, or a Dual God, i.e. God of Light and God of Darkness, as well as God of the North and God of the South, and they imaged this by symbolizing the type as two Birds, one Black, the other White. Later they added the elemental force or spirit of "Breath of Life, or Force of Wind," and symbolized or imaged this by a panting or roaring Lion. Thus the Primary Trinity, or a Great Spirit with three attributes of the elemental powers, was first portrayed, imaged as God of Darkness, God of Light and God of the Breath of Life, as well as the God of the North, God of the South, and God of the Centre. In this figure of Horus of the Double Power, we find a still further advancement, that is, He is here represented as the God of the Eastern and Western Horizons and a God of the Double Force as well as the God of the North and South. He is also represented by symbolism as the young Child, representing the spirit of life in the young shoot, or the young Fish, or Bird, or Lamb, or other types of "rebirth of Spirit life"; also as the adult man as typified by the head of Bes or Har-Ur as representing the full development of the Spirit of the Fish, or Shoot, or Tree, or Fruit, or other types. These attributes were the elemental Nature Powers or Spirits of Nature which were visible and cognisant to them, and they objectified the same by this imagery of Symbolism in Sign Language when they had not the terminology to express their ideas and beliefs otherwise.

CHAPTER V

SACRED SYMBOLS

THE Sacred Signs and Symbols which were evolved by the Nilotic Negroes must be taken into consideration in our argument to show the origin and meaning of many which have been brought on in every Cult up to the present-day Christian Doctrines.

To comprehend why these were invented and used, we have to carry ourselves back into that early state of the evolution of the human race when man had no words to express all his ideas and beliefs. He had " to think in things " which were *visible* before any *abstract* ideas were evolved in the human brain. Man observed nature in all its phases, which was ever before him visually ; *it was there objectively ;* there could be no imagination in the visible facts of nature or nature's Laws. Not possessing sufficient words, he objectified these powers by inventing signs and symbols which would best convey to his mind the powers of these elemental Spirits. Each sign or symbol typified the best image he was able to produce, objectively representing the qualities or properties, of a Spirit, or power, in nature's universe.

Naturally, the first two man would image would be Light and Darkness, Day and Night. Therefore the primary imagery of the first two Heroes representing the elementary powers of Light and Darkness, Night and Day, were represented by two birds—one white, one black—as two personal Totems representing Horus and Set. There are many other types of images for the two primary gods amongst the Hero Cult Nilotic Negroes in Africa, as well as all over the world. The next would be the force or power or Spirit of the wind and storms.

Shu, portrayed in Lion form, represented this elemental god. Then the whole seven elemental Powers were Symbolically depicted by a Sign or Symbol for each. In tracing the evolution of the primary gods we find that during the various Cults, which have ever been brought on from the original, the same types have sometimes represented different attributes, and sometimes the one attribute has been represented by many and various Signs and Symbols. But the interpretations, when correctly rendered, are identical, the variations being caused either from the different fauna found in the country to which Nilotic Negroes migrated or owing to the passing from one Cult to another during evolution; i.e. although the types have varied, the esoteric meaning attached to each has been the same. Furthermore, as man attained greater knowledge, more attributes would be added to his Great Spirit.

That Sut or Set was the primary God and chief Hero of these Nilotic Negro Hero Cult people is amply proved and borne out by the monuments as well as the Ritual.

He was the God of the South Pole or Southern Hemisphere.

How long the cult of Set lasted is impossible to say, but I should say fifty thousand years was the lowest estimate. On the oldest Monuments, although his name has been almost invariably chiselled out, we find names of Kings who have taken his name in the same manner as we afterwards find the Horus name; and although the legend of the conflict between Horus and Set is as old as the Ritual at least, it is, however, likewise a proof of Set's position having once been very different. There can be no doubt that these Hero Cult people worked out their primary Mythology South of the Equator first. Set was the firstborn of the old Earth-Mother and was, whilst South of the Equator, the Primary God, because the Southern Pole Star, one of the Symbols by which he was imaged, was in the ascendant, i.e. it was more prominently visible and higher in the heavens.

Set was called the Father of the Gods (Rit., Ch. 8)

first because he was the Primary Deity, as God of the South, secondly because he, being the firstborn of the elemental powers from his Mother Apt, represented "both parents in one person," i.e. the Bull of his Mother. In this form Set is represented or imaged as a Bull Hippopotamus who consorts with his Mother, imaged as a Female Hippopotamus.

The Totemic Zootype, in its religious phase, was as much the sign of the Goddess or the God as it had been of the Motherhood or Brotherhood. It was an image of the superhuman power.

As regards the "Slaughtering Block of the God Sept," mentioned in the Ritual, it is a question if this was made for *human* sacrifices or not (the Masai Group still offer sacrifices, but not human); at the same time, from monumental evidence still extant, there is evidence that some of the captives of war were sometimes offered as sacrifices in the earlier part of the Stellar Cult, and during the early part of Totemism; Homo was certainly Androphagi as regards his Tribal Mother. *Although Juvenal in his Satires declares that* "the Egyptians ate human flesh," there is not a particle of evidence in the Egyptian inscriptions to show that they ever did, and we have every reason to believe that the practice of Androphagi founded by the Non-Hero Cult Nilotic Negroes died out, that the human was supplanted by the Totemic Zootypes by the later Hero Cult people, and that the Zootype form of the primary eucharist was the only class of mortuary meal eaten by the Egyptians. Neither do I consider that much reliance can be placed on what the Spanish priests recorded on this point in America, for they did not understand the Cult, and they would blacken the character of the old Stellar Cult priests as much as possible to leave themselves whitewashed for all the horrors they committed in the name of Christianity.

The earliest Ta-Neter, or Holy Land of the Egyptians, was Puanta in the South, which was sacred on account of its being their primeval home—the earthly Paradise of the Hebrew legend. The field of reeds was the field of

Uat, the papyrus reed and the sources of the Nile. Hence the traditions found amongst all nations that the human race emanated from "a watered Paradise." Also Uati is a title of the Great Mother Isis, who brought forth child Horus on the lap of the papyrus flower. Uat, in Egyptian, is also the name of Lower Egypt. Uat is the oasis. Uat is the water and the wet fresh evergreen. Uat is the papyrus reed and the most ancient name in Kamite Mythology. When the Hero Cult people left their original Paradise in the South, they travelled North through desert sands and trouble until they came to Egypt; here it was that Paradise was regained, and so they depicted it uranographically as the Mount of Heaven in the North with the Eye of Horus (North Pole Star) on the Mount, The Great God of All, a type of the Eternal.

Set, as primary Judge, was imaged in one phase by the Jackal, the Jackal being a Zootype for the Judge amongst the Egyptians. Also the Eye on the Mount, or the dot ⊙ within the centre of the circle was a type of Anup. The earliest law of Heaven was given on the Mount, because the Mount was an image of the Pole, and Anup (the Jackal) administered the law as the Judge.

That the dual type was thus portrayed is proved by the planisphere of Denderah, where the two Poles are represented by two Jackals as well as the two Eyes.

The Pole Star is an emblem of stability, a seat or throne of the Power which is the highest God, which was

First, Set-Anup of the Southern Hemisphere, and

Secondly, Horus in Egypt of the Northern Hemisphere.

This was carried out of Egypt under the terminology of

Bar-a-Pa-Bar by the Syrians,
Sydik in Phœnicia,
Anu in Babylonia,
Baal of the Hebrews,
Ueucteoll of the Mexicans,
Tai-yih of the Chinese,
Avather or Zivo in Mesopotamia,
Ame-ro-Yoko-Tachi-Kami in Japan,

and various other names in other parts of the world during the Stellar Cult.

Two Pillars or Poles were used sometimes to depict the North and South divisions of heaven, and symbolized as the two supports.

The two poles still survive amongst the descendants of the original Nilotic Negroes, in many parts of the world, as for example amongst the Arunta of Central Australia. These people have no North Pole Star, or Northern division of Heaven, but they still continue to carry the two Symbolic Poles about with them, which they erect wherever they go, as a sign of locality or encampment. See my "Origin and Evolution of Freemasonry."

Another phase was when Horus pursued Set and Set went in a hole in the ground *called the Devil's hole*, and Horus put a pole over him; he thus became hidden. For further information on this Symbol, see "Signs and Symbols of Primordial Man," 2nd edition.

It is Set whose sign is changed for that of Osiris in the letters of the Father of the Great Rameses, and two other Kings of that dynasty; it is the same God, with his ordinary monumental name, Nubi (in *Nubian*), who is pouring out life and power over the King. In Plate II we see Horus and Set pouring out life over Seti.

Dr. Budge's "Gods of the Egyptians" (Vol. II, p. 248) shows the equal divinity of these two Gods at one time, as Set and Horus, as two brothers (Chief Heroes) reigning together. His hieroglyphic figure of a Giraffe, or Okepi, is the Nubian Primary God Set, and with Anup added the translation is "The Lord of the Southern Hemisphere," as witnessed in the monuments of Karnak and Medinel Habu. The first figure to remark in Plate II is Horus (Amun-Khem) to whom the King is sacrificing and doing homage, while Horus is pouring out life and power upon him. The fact that we find Set *here* as one of the great Gods is a proof that he was considered and looked upon at the earliest period of their Mythology as, at least, a brother to Horus, and that now Horus was primary.

The myth had shifted or changed places. The domain of Paradise of the South with Set as God of the South, had shifted to the Paradise of the North, with Horus as God of the North. It is probable that the primary part of the Mythos was first evolved at the Lakes at the head of the Nile, South of the Equator, when the Southern Pole Star was most prominently visible, and that the primary Cult of Set continued *pari passu* with that of Horus for thousands of years.

How far they had worked out their Mythology in the Southern Hemisphere before they came North it is at present quite impossible to say; they had, however, made considerable advancement, which was afterwards absorbed and blended with the Horus Cult when he became the primary God of the Pole Star North, which he did as they left the Equator Lands behind them. The different names of Set taken by Kings, which we find on the oldest monuments, prove this; on some the Set name has been obliterated and the name of Horus, and later of Osiris, substituted.

That the Cult of Set was still practised by some of the Tribes is also shown from the "Totems of the Nomes." We also find that during the earlier part of the Stellar Cult, Temples were built and dedicated to Set, not only in Egypt, but in many parts of the world, wherever the earlier exodus had settled. Set was the El Shadda of the Hebrews and Phœnicians.

The apparent internal connection which we find on the monuments and in the Ritual can be understood and explained critically in the manner above set forth: the points of resemblance in the oldest types and monuments indicate a general amalgamation of the attributes in the order which had been first worked out in the Southern Hemisphere and brought on to that of the Northern, in the type of Horus, Lord of the Northern Heavens.

The Pyramid Text also shows the change from Set to Horus and the appropriating of all Set's previous attributes to Horus.

Drawn by K. Watkins.
SET AND HORUS POURING OUT LIFE OVER SETI I.

PLATE II.

Drawn by K. Watkins.

The Mexican depiction of the Submergence of Set in the South and elevation of Horus as " God of the North and South " from the Torano MS.

PLATE III.

[To face p. 73.

In the Pyramid Text and in the Text of Unas, we meet the change as Heru-Sept, who is mentioned in connection with Ra-Tem, Thoth, Horus of Tat, and the Star, Nekhehk.

The Hero Cult gradually evolved into the Stellar Cult when all the elementary powers were divinized. Although the Cult of Horus commenced after the Nilotic Negroes had left the South of the Equator regions behind them on their way North, the Cult of Set continued for many thousands of years, as we find from monumental evidence. Many of the oldest Temples were dedicated to Set; their orientation was South, and they were always built in a circular form, differing from the Horus Cult where the orientation was North. The Chinese have these two typical Temples at the present day, one of which is consecrated to Heaven, built in a circular form, a Temple of Set (see " Origin and Evolution of the Human Race," p. 368), the other is built in the form of a square and consecrated to the Earth, and is a " Horus Temple."

Set, in another phase, was God of the dead or abode of the dead. This was founded on the fact that, as the Nilotic Negroes began to travel the 3,700 miles to the North, they would gradually lose sight of the Southern Pole Star, and all the Uranographic images they had configurated with it in the nightly heavens. Their celestial primal Paradise was situated in the heavens at the South Pole; the primal Paradise on Earth was situated in the reedlands around the Great Lake Tanganyika.

Thus, in Astronomical Mythology, begun here by these Hero Cult people, do we find the origin of the " fall and deluge."

There would be a gradual sinking down in the waters of space, called a deluge—a lost Paradise—and the symbol of the God Set went down to the nether world and henceforth would represent the Power or King of Darkness.

The Ritual describes the ways of darkness in the entrance of the Tuat as the tunnels of Set, which show that a way to the nether world *was made by Set when his Star and the primal paradise went down with him in the abyss*, which was from the beginning situated in the South where the Egyptians figuratively localized the Tuat, or entrance to the underworld, which also was the place of egress for the life that came into the world by water from the recesses of the south. It is certain that in one phase they imaged Set as going down South to some sort of underworld, and thus he became the representative of the power of darkness.

In the Eschatology he is phased as Ap-Uat, or the Jackal, as the conductor of souls, the opener of ways, the seer in the dark. The two forms of the Jackal, that of the South and North, now become " The guide of the

Drawn by K. Watkins.
PRIMARY TYPE OF THE JACKAL ANUBIS FROM THEBES.
FIG. 8.

Southern ways," or the " nether-world," and " as the opener of the Northern ways to the summit of the Mount," the North Pole or Paradise of the North, with Horus as God of that Paradise. The scene had now shifted from South to North, and all the attributes which had belonged to Set were transferred to Horus; the two Gods were really one; the Ritual proves this when it mentions " The two Horuses." It was the one God who had changed his abode in the South and gone to the North. In other words, the Nilotic Negroes had transferred their Paradise from South to North as represented by their Astro-Mythology. But it was the one God all the time.

Different types were now given in which Set is depicted as ever warring against Horus—one was Zootype form, and later another assumed the Anthropomorphic.

Darkness being the primordial condition, the earliest type in Mythical representation was Apap, the Serpent reptile, the devouring reptile, all mouth, the prototype of all evil in external nature, which rose up by night from the Abyss and coiled around the Mount of Earth as the Swallower of the Light, who in another phase drank up all the Water as the fiery dragon of drought. The voice of the Monster was the Thunder which shook the firmament (Rit., Ch. 29). Other powers born of the void were likewise elemental with an aspect inimical to Man. In the Ritual these are called the Sami or demons of darkness, or the wicked Sebau, who for ever rose in revolt against the powers that wrought for good.

Set, as Typhon, was considered an evil power, a sort of Devil of Darkness, and the conflict between him and Horus was a struggle between light and darkness, taking place in the twilight of evening and morning or in the mid-winter season or at the Equinoxes. Plutarch tells us how the evil Set or Typhon was humiliated and insulted by the Egyptians at certain festivals when they abused red-haired men because Set was red haired (Ch. 30). To explain the Egyptian symbolism, Set, the treacherous opponent of Horus, was the Egyptian Judas. He betrayed his brother to his enemies, the Sebau. He was of red complexion, but the complexion and the red hair of Set were not derived from any human origin. Set was painted red or sandy as representing the desert; he was the original devil in the wilderness, the cause of drought, darkness, and the creator of thirst. In the beginning was the void, otherwise designated the abyss, the dwelling-place of Set, and one of his imagery symbols was a stone. Maspero ("Dawn of Civilisation," p. 133) states: "Set was the Spirit of the Mountain stone and sand, the red and arid ground, as distinguished from the moist, black soil of the valley. He was cruel and treacherous, always ready to shrivel up the harvest with his burning breath,

and to smother Egypt beneath a shroud of shifting sand."
A bronze statuette of the Twentieth Dynasty, a drawing of which I give (Plate IV) shows Set as having the body of a man with an animal head, wearing the crown of the South and in a fighting attitude.

Maspero states: "At the time of the Osirian Cult ("Dawn of Civilisation," p. 200), which was very late, Set still possessed his half of Egypt, and his primitive brotherly relation to the Celestial Horus remained unbroken, either on account of their sharing one temple, as at Nubit, or because they worshipped as one in two neighbouring nomes, as, for example, at Oxyrrhynchos and at Heracleopolis Magna.

"Certain small districts persisted in this double worship down to the latest times. It was, after all, a mark of fidelity to the oldest traditions of the race."

The Gods and Goddesses of Ancient Egypt were at first portrayed as Superhuman Powers by means of Superhuman human types. Primitive man did not create the Gods in his own image, or at first of any sex.

The Three Primary Divinities, or Heroes, Set, Sebek (Horus), and Shu, were represented in the likeness of the Hippopotamus, or the Okapi, the Crocodile, and the Hawk, and the roaring Lion and Feather, whilst other later divinized elemental powers were Hapi imaged as an Ape, Anup as a Jackal, Ptah as a Beetle, Taht as an Ibis, later as the Kaf-Ape, Seb as a Goose. So it was with the Goddesses. They are likenesses of powers that were superhuman, not human. Hence Apt was imaged as a Water-Cow. The Cow of Waters represented the Earth-Mother as the great bringer forth of life before she was divinized as Apt, the Goddess in human guise with the head of a Hippopotamus, Hekt as a Frog, Tufnut as a Lioness, Serk as a Scorpion, Rannut as a Serpent, Hathor as a Fruit Tree, Neith as a White Vulture, and a hundred others.

The Mother in Mythology, who gave birth to the Polemic annually, and who is confused at times with the human Mother, is Mother Earth, who in one type is represented by the Snake as the Renewal of vegetation, or the Goddess Rannut.

We have seen that the Hero Cult Nilotic Negroes first evolved two chief Heroes, later a third, from the old Earth-Mother, all of whom they divinized. That South of the Equator, Set was Primary Deity; at the Equator, Set and Horus were equal; but that as they came North, Horus became primary. The Art of smelting iron and other ores had been discovered by these people, and Horus was the chief deity of the clans; therefore the Hammer or Axe was assigned as His Symbol, and he was styled " God of the Hammer," or " Great Blacksmith " and " God of the Axe." This is one of the Symbols that has continued to be used to typify the " Great God " through all the Cults up to the Christian.

These Hero Cult Nilotic Negroes came up from the South, drove out the Masaba and Non-Hero Cult inhabitants, and established themselves there in pre-dynastic times. At first there were three different Totemic Tribes who settled here in Egypt, and very soon four others came, making seven in all, each with a separate and distinct Totem of their Motherhood. They settled down according to their Totemic Law into seven different districts or Nomes; and each Totemic Clan or Tribe was given a part. There is distinct evidence that one of the clans, and that the *first one to settle here*, brought on the Cult of Set with them from the South, and that the second were the followers of Horus Behutet, or the Great Blacksmith.

These Nilotic Negroes had formed a secret and sacred Society, *which still exists amongst Hero Cult Nilotic Negroes at the present day.* They invented Signs and Passwords for their working members. Primitive Religious Ceremonies were established and performed with sacred Signs, Symbols, and Words amongst the Priesthood, only known to themselves. There were some Signs and Passwords in common, but the Priesthood and religious sect was quite distinct and separate. These were the men who came North and founded the second Nome with Edfu as the Centre or

Capital, and were the "Followers of Horus-Behutet," called "The Great Blacksmith," their deified God (Plate V).

The Priests all had to be initiated into their sacred Mysteries and Rites, and were a distinct class by themselves. *Those Nilotic Hero Cult Tribes at the present day possess most of the secret Mysteries of Horus of Edfu, also sometimes called Heru-ur or the Elder Horus, and in one phase or imagery symbolized by the Hawk.* The Tradition amongst the Masai still existing at the present day is " that Horus came down from Heaven in the form of a man," but was not a Human Man, but a Spirit.

All these people, Nilotic Hero Cult Negroes, were Paleolithic, the Fathers of the Stellar Cult people, who were Neolithic and were evolved from them. They were indigenous to these regions, and instead of *coming from the East, some of them went there*, following their predecessors, the Non-Hero Cult people. The Proto Semetics, as Dr. Wallis Budge calls them, were the early Stellar Cult people, who left Egypt after the Hero Cult Nilotic Negroes, and followed them to many lands.

During the whole of the Neolithic Period, Stellar Cult was practised; Hero Cult was during the Paleolithic Age; Lunar Cult followed Stellar, and Solar after Lunar.

Egypt was divided up by these early Stellar and Hero Cult Nilotic Negroes with a Totem or Badge for each Tribe, which originated with the original Mother of the Tribe as her Totem. These Totems were of Zootype form, but they were never worshipped. All the Totems of the Tribes, representing the Elemental Powers and a great many others, were brought on to represent the Gods and Goddesses in their Mythology and Astro-Mythology types. But there was no such thing as Serpent-Worship, Tree Worship or Animal Worship. In the Mythology which arose out of Totemism, the Mother and Child are represented in the Tree and Branch. The Tree being a type of the Abode, the Roof-Tree, the Mother of Food and Drink, the Giver of Life and Shelter, the Wet Nurse in the dew of rain, the producer of her Offspring as the branch and promise of Periodic continuity. Was it the Tree then that was worshipped, or the Giver of Food and Shelter in the Tree? Dr. Wallis Budge states, that they worshipped the "Apis-Bull," and designates this "Apis-worship." But the Apis carries the Solar Disc betwixt its Horns. This also is being saluted. Which, then, is the object of worship? There are two objects of religious regard, but neither is the object of adoration. That is the God in Spirit, who was represented as the Soul of life in the Sun and in the Tree, also by the fecundating Bull.

In Egypt the Totems of the tribal system had been continued in the towns and cities which bore the same name of the Zoological types.

The Hero Cult developed into the Stellar Cult, and that development took place along the valleys of the Nile, which I will term Old Egypt. The reason why we find these types all over the world is because they went out from Old Egypt and carried all their Religion, Arts, and Cults, which had been evolved up to date, with them.

Neither were there a large number of Gods worshipped. There was only "one Great God," from the first to the last, under whatever terminology or imagery He was depicted.

The different Iconographic or Zootype figures found portrayed on temples and stones in ruined cities in many lands were Zootypes, engraved or painted by these old Stellar Cult people to depict their so-called Gods and Goddesses, and were the imagery of the *attributes of the* one Great God, the *divinized elemental powers*. For they had no language at this time to express their mental ideas, nor could they portray the human form as a superhuman power; all they could do and did was to use this Sign Language.

Men who first employed signs had not attained the art which supplies an ideal representation of natural facts; they directly represented their meaning in visible forms, but the Sign enters a second phase as the representatives of ideas when they become ideographic and metaphorical, which they did during the Stellar Cult.

80 THE ORIGIN AND EVOLUTION

The very numerous remains of Ancient Temples in Central and South America, in the Caroline Islands, and also in Asia, prove how thickly populated these countries must have been during the Stellar Cult period, and that

Drawn by K Watkins.

EGYPTIAN PRIEST BURNING INCENSE AND POURING LIBATIONS.

FIG. 9.

the portrayal of all the Religious Cults were identically the same, and could only have emanated from one centre.[1]

[1] For further illustrations of Old Signs and Symbols and their significant meaning, I must refer my readers to my former books, "Origin and Evolution of Freemasonry," "Signs and Symbols of

Drawn by K. Watkins.

THE GOD SET REPRESENTED AS FIGHTING.

PLATE IV.

[To face p. 80.

HORUS-BEHUTET—THE ELDER HORUS, OR HORUS IN THE TREE.

Here seen with a Spear in right hand instead of the usual Axe or Hammer and Ank ot Life in left hand. Head of Hawk with Disk and Uraei.

PLATE V.

I cannot agree with the explanation of the custom of burning incense and making libations in religious ceremonies given by Professor Tory ("Introduction of the History of Religion," p. 486). He states that "when burnt before the deity," it is " to be regarded as food, though in course of time, when the recollection of the primitive character was lost, a conventional significance was attached to the act of burning. A more refined period demanded more refined food for the gods, such as ambrosia and nectar, but these were finally given up."

Professor G. Elliott Smith, F.R.S. (on incense and libations in the "Evolution of the Dragon," p. 31) states : " I do not think that anyone who conscientiously and without bias examines the evidence relating to incense-burning, the arbitrary details of the ritual and the peculiar circumstance under which it is practised in different countries, can refuse to admit that so artificial a custom must have been dispersed throughout the world from some one centre where it was devised," and (on p. 33), " that the original object of the offerings of libations was for the purpose of animating the statue of the deceased, and so enabling him to continue the existence which had merely been interrupted by the incident of death." " In course of time, however, as definite gods gradually materialized and came to be represented by statues, they also had to be vitalized by offerings of water from time to time. Thus the pouring out of libations came to be an act of worship of the deity ; the reduced use of water for anointing the corpse or the statue was merely a specific application of the general principles of biology which was then current." Also (p. 36) " the idea of divinity of the incense-tree was a result of, and not the reason for, the practice of incense-burning. As one of the means by which resurrection was attained, incense became a giver of divinity, and by a

Primordial Man," "Arcana of Freemasonry," and " Origin and Evolution of the Human Race," wherein I have given many further illustrations and proofs not included in this work, but which prove critically my contention.

simple process of rationalization the tree which produced the divine substance became a god." As I have already tried to prove, propitiation and offerings were first made by the little Pygmies, both to the elemental Powers and their Ancestral Spirits. What did they offer? Naturally, whatever they had themselves, and something they valued. Their first idea would be that what was good food for them would naturally be appreciated by the spirit of their former chiefs and friends. To the elemental Powers they would offer something valuable, such as a Club, an Arrow, or stone Axe; at that time there were no statues. The Ka image was first (rudely) fashioned by the Nilotic Negroes, and they still do this in whatever part of the world found. It is an image made to portray, or represent, the Spiritual body of Man, to which they offered food and drink, as a propitiation, in the first place, to do them no harm; later it became a custom of love and affection and supplication to assist them in their daily lives and wants. The primitive practices of offering food and drink to the dead, more especially to the Soul of Life in Blood, were based upon the postulate that the so-called dead were living still in Spirit form. Obviously enough the sustenance of life was offered to feed the life of those who were held to be living because seen to be existing in the likeness that was represented by the human figure of the Spirit-Ka.

The Ka image is the double of the dead. It is a figure of the ghost. It was, and is, an image of the only soul or spirit that could be seen outside the human body.

The gods and goddesses representing the seven elemental powers, and imaged at first by Zootypes, never could appear as ghosts, although called "The Glorious Ones" and "The Seven Great Spirits" (in distinction to the Ancestral Spirits who were called the Glorified). They had never been humans and never could be. Thus the Ka-Spirit was, and is, entirely distinct from the soul or Spirit of Life in a tree, a plant, a bird, a beast, or a reptile, which may image either one or other of the seven Great Spirits. It was to the apparition of the human soul visible in human form that the offerings were made to the representation of the deceased, who lived on in Spirit form ; the food of life was offered to feed the life of those who were held to be the living, not the dead.

In the Ritual it is commanded that four measures of blood shall be offered to the Spirit or Ka image of the deceased.

The doctrine is identical with that of the races who gashed and gored their bodies to feed the spirits of the departed with their blood because the blood was the life and because it was the life they desiderated for their dead.

In the same rubrical directions it is ordered that incense shall be burned in the presence of the Ka image as an offering to the Spirit. In Sign Language incense represents the breath of life, and this *was one that another element of life, besides the blood*, should be offered to the deceased, " to make the perfect spirit live."

The Egyptian Ka is portrayed in their drawings as a spiritual likeness of the body, to identify it with the soul of which it is the " so-called double," the soul, that is, which has the power to duplicate itself in escaping death " from the body of dead matter," and to reappear in a rarer or Corpuscular form than that of the mortal, as the soul or spirit outside the body, to be seen in apparition or by the vision of seers.

The Ka was propitiated, that is, saluted with oblations, as a divine ideal. The Kamite equivalent for eternal life is the permanent personality which was imaged by or in the Ka. As a sacrifice of " blood," the Tribal Mother was the " first sacrificial victim " ; the soul in the spirit of blood which should not die was the reason for her being eaten alive ; she was the primary eucharist, and was the original of all " blood and body " offerings, which have been carried down through all the Cults to the Christians.

Present-day Christians offer " flowers and wreaths " to the spirits of their dear ones as tokens of love and affection, but the practice fundamentally has been the same through all ages.

"Tree Worship" was the propitiation of a power in nature that was represented by the tree and by the vegetation that was given for food; and although votive offerings were hung upon its branches, the tree itself was not the object of the offerings but the power personified in Nut or Hathor, the Great Mother, as giver in the tree. This custom has been carried down to the Roman Church of to-day, where votive offerings are placed on the *image of the Virgin Mother* in their churches.

The tree was never thought of as a "God," although the spirit of the giver in the tree was *imaged by a goddess*, as a type of the Great Mother. Waitz tells the story of a Negro who was making an offering of food to a tree when a bystander remarked that "a tree did not eat food." The Negro replies: "Oh, the tree is not fetish; the fetish is a spirit and invisible, but he has descended into this tree; certainly he cannot devour our bodily food, but he enjoys the spiritual part, and leaves behind the bodily part, which we can see." The above, therefore, is not "worship," neither was the tree looked upon as "God" or "become a God," as assumed. The tree was not the object of religious regard. There was a spirit or power of nature that manifested in the tree.

In like manner "earth worship" was the propitiation of the power in nature that was worshipped as the Great Mother, the bringer-forth and nurse of life, "The Only One," who was the producer of plenty.

Many have asserted that there was no prayer connected with the lower forms of the human race and lower forms of religion. Such an assertion can only be determined by Sign Language rather than words. Let me try to point out that such statements are erroneous. Two hands of a person clasped together are equivalent to a spoken prayer.

In the Ritual, the speaker says of the God Osiris (Ch. 28) "His Branch is of prayer, by means of which I have made myself like Him."

The word used for Branch is Teru, and this word signifies to adore, invoke, and pray. Thus the strewing of branches of the birch in Ancient British graves was a symbol of prayer. It is the same language and the same sign when the Australian Aborigines approach the camp of strangers with a green bough in their hands as a sign of amity equivalent to a prayer for peace and goodwill.

Acting Sign Language is a practical mode of praying and asking for what is wanted by portraying instead of saying. A green branch of a symbolic tree is dipped in water and sprinkled on the earth as a prayer for rain.

The Australian Diererie solicit the Good Spirit by bleeding two of their Mediums or divinely-inspired men, supposed to be persons of influence with the Moora-Moora, or Good Spirit, who will take heed of their suffering and send down rain. " The Customs of the Native Tribes of South Australia" (p. 276, G. Gason), should be compared with 1 Kings xviii, when the Priests of Baal (Set) cut and slash their flesh with knives and lances and limp around the Altar with their bleeding wounds as a mode of invoking heaven for rain.

Such customs were universal from the time of the first primitive man; he was praying and supplicating in the dumb drama of Sign Language for the water or the food that was fervently desired.

In these Totemic Ceremonies performed for food or water, we find the most primitive form of prayer-meeting or religious service; the powers, elemental, ancestral, and the Great Spirit, were solicited, and wants made known by Signs, emphasized by the sign of fasting during the performances.

CHAPTER VI

STELLAR CULT

THE Stellar Cult was not a new Cult, but a continuation and further development of the Hero Cult and the Mythology, which originated amongst the Nilotic Negro Hero Cult people.

The Great Spirit and Great God of the North was the same as the Great Spirit and God of the South, as stated in the Ritual, "the two were One." It was the primary form of representing a biune God, i.e. a great God possessing two attributes, and with Shu added, a triune God.

As already stated, the followers of Horus-Behutet came up from the South and established themselves at Edfu. They were the Mesinu or the Mesenti 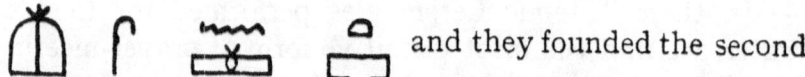 and they founded the second nome in Egypt. The first nome was established by the followers of Set. Many followers of the Cult of Set remained true to that name and Cult until quite late, and travelled to many countries, including Asia and South America, after having founded the first nome in old Egypt.

Dr. Wallis Budge, in his "Book of the Dead," states "that the Heru-seshu, or *followers of Horus*" are a class of mythological beings or divine-gods, who already in the Pyramid Text are supposed to recite prayers on behalf of the deceased and to assist Horus and Set in "opening his mouth" (or coming forth in Spirit form from the Mummy).

Dr. Budge has here mixed up the seven divinized spirits, the primary elemental powers, brothers of Horus, and Set in the Stellar Cult, also followers and his children in the Solar Cult, the astronomical Stellar Cult gods, or spirits, which were never human, with the true human "followers of Horus," the Mesinu or Mesenti, who came up from the South with their Hero Cult, and founded Ancient Egypt, with Horus-Behutet as their god; *these were the human followers of Horus*, and were not mythological. The brothers, servants, or followers, *as the Seshu of Horus* were seven in number, and were never human, only mythical astronomical characters, which is proved by the Ritual, the book which contains the divine words that bring about the resurrection to the glory of eternal life. It is the book of the mysteries in which the revelation was dramatically enacted. In his form of the Divine Son on earth, Horus, as the Word, gives voice to the decrees which his Father has spoken in heaven. In his form of the divine son, Horus executes those decrees, and Aan is the recorder of the decrees for human use.

It is announced in the opening chapter of the Ritual that Ra, the holy spirit, "issued the mandate which Taht-Aan, or Aan, hath executed (Ch. 1, Renouf). This was the revelation made by the Father in Heaven as testifier to Horus, the son, who is the "word made truth" in the Books of Aan.

The revelation of Taht-Aan in the Ritual begins with the resurrection, or coming forth in spirit form from the life on earth, and in the Solar Cult from the lower earth or Amenta.

It is the same opening in the Book of Revelation. "Ra issued the command to Aan that he should effect the triumph of Horus against his adversaries, and the command is what Aan hath executed in writing the Ritual."

The Revelation of John is termed "The Revelation of Jesus Christ, which God gave to him to show unto his servants; and he sent and signified it by his angel unto his servant John, who bore witness of the Word of God and the testimony of Jesus Christ of all things that he saw" (Rev. i. 1, 2).

Jesus is accompanied by the seven great spirits, whose place is before the Throne of God. As Egyptian, these were the seven servants, or followers, or "seshu of Horus."

Thus "the Revelation of Jesus Christ" was given to John by God the Father "to show unto his servants," the first of whom are "the seven spirits" which are before the Throne." This is similar to the Revelation of Horus that was given him by Ra to be written down by Aan, or Taht-Aan, the scribe of the gods. Therefore John the divine seer in the isle of Patmos is the Christian form of Aan upon the Stellar Mount of Glory in the isle of flame.

Not only are the "seven seshu of Horus" given to Jesus as his servants, or followers, in Revelation; they are also grouped around him in their various characters by name. (1) The seven spirits of God. (2) The seven as spirits of fire. (3) The seven as stars. (4) The seven as eyes. (5) The seven as golden lampstands. (6) The seven as seven ruling powers, as heads of the dragon (Apt). (7) The seven as the seven angels of the seven churches.

Thus we see that the "followers of Horus" were "spiritual" and "human"; they were imaged into two continuatories, spiritual and human; i.e the Human were the Mesinu or Mesenti Nilotic Negroes with "Hero Cult," who came up from the South having Horus-Behutet as their god or chief Hero. When the Stellar Cult was fully established, the seven elemental powers, born of the Old Mother Earth, Ta-Urt, were given stars on high and became reborn as divinized elemental powers, as children of Apt, who were the brothers or followers of Horus in the Astronomical Mythology, which the old Egyptian Urshi formulated symbolically to teach the Eschatology. Dr. Wallis Budge has mixed up the two characters; he has confounded the mythological with the human, or I might add more truthfully, he has not recognized "the human followers of Horus" at all, but attributed them to an influx of some foreign element. The Ritual gives the type in the Solar representation, but the types and imagery were brought on from the

A TYPE OF HERU-UR.

The Elder Horus with the Crown of the South only. He holds the Hare-headed Sceptre in his right hand and Ank of Life in his left. He sits on the Square as seat of divine judgment. The two disks on his head and two uræi. Lord of the North and South.

PLATE VI.

[To face p. 83.

Stellar and Lunar, which were pre-Solar. Taht-Aan of the Lunar was Aan of the Stellar, and the mythical followers, or brothers, of Horus, were originally Stellar Astronomical characters, or imagery, quite distinct from the "human followers of Horus."

Menetho states that the Hero Cult lasted in Egypt for 24,000 years before the Stellar Cult was evolved; but time must always be allowed for overlapping. The fight between Horus and Set and the Sebu, or evil elements, was continuous, periodic, and mythical, but there is distinct evidence on the monuments that the *followers of Horus and those of the prior cult of Set* fought many battles which were actual fights in the domain of fact, and therefore not mythical.

The mixing up of these, the one with the other, has confounded many translators who are unacquainted with Sign Language and the Mythology. Although we find remains of the Temples of the Cult of Set in Africa, Asia, and South America, it was only by, and through, the further evolution of the Horus Cult that religion was evolved to a higher plane, and it is through all the phases of the portrayal of Horus that we must study their thoughts and beliefs expressed in Sign Language; this gives us the key to the knowledge of the development of religion in the Human race. It was the followers of Horus, now called the Mesinu, the descendants of the earlier Mesenti, who by imaging in Zootype forms and then uranographically representing, and thus for ever registering His different attributes, could express themselves and keep the records of the past.

The whole of the human form was imaged during the Solar Cult, and replaced entirely the Zootypes which had hitherto been employed to represent the Gods and Goddesses and elemental powers; but this was a gradually acquired art as is shown by the pictures and statues still extant, i.e. with Zootype head and human body. The Zootype head was used to distinguish which attribute, or deified elemental power, was assigned to the God, as is portrayed here in this picture of Heru-ur or the Elder Horus (Plate VI). The Eagle head is one of the imaged types of Horus. It is here superimposed upon the body to depict the properties attributed to that Zootype. It is the same symbolism as found in the Christian Cult, where St. John is imaged symbolically by the Eagle.

Before the Stellar Cult there was no record of time except night and day, the wet season and the dry.

They formulated time by continuous observation and registration of the changes that took place in the recession of the seven Pole Stars or Ursa Minor, " The Stars which never set," and by observing Ursa Major and other constellations through ages of time.

How accurately they had worked out their Astronomical and Mathematical knowledge, and to what a high state they had attained (which has never been surpassed, if equalled), is proved by the records they have left written in stone, i.e. the Great Pyramid. The Sacred doctrines were *first written during Stellar Cult*, and in Sign Language ; emphasized in the old Hieroglyphics, and known only to the old Her-Seshta, or Urshi, or Watchers, or Mystery Teachers, of whom there were seven classes. The Urshi, or Watchers, were the first humans to reckon and register human time. *All the Stellar Cult people wrote in Glyphs only.* Alphabetical linear writing was not invented until the Solar Cult.

The Creation exoterically described in the Semitic legends of the beginning *was not cosmogonical.* It was Uranography, not Cosmography.

Uranography is Sign Language constellated in the Stars. That which has been called " chaos " in the legends of creation was a condition in which there was neither law nor order, time nor name, nor means of representing natural phenomena, because there had been no mode of expression. But things existed even when they had no name or record before Mythology, and the Mythical representation did depend upon the elements or nature force being already extant, to be named or to be constellated and to become pictoral for the purpose of the Mystery Teachers.

The History of Horus is depicted in the heavens as upon the wall of some vast picture gallery. It was the subject of subjects in the Astronomical or Stellar Cult.

Har-Ur, or Horus the elder, was represented also as the child in the Mythos. His title of Repa will identify the child born to be King, as that signifies the Heir-Apparent, or the Prince, who was predestined to become the King.

The Elder Horus was the mother's child who was born but not begotten.

In the Maori[1] tale of Ko-Ka-Ko the boy is called the bastard. Horus was called the bastard, also in the Jews' legend Jesus is called the Mainzer or bastard.

Horus on his papyrus, a pedestal, Uat, as a Vulture, is an early form for Horus as the son of Neith (imaged by a bird). Horus as the Golden Hawk standing on the column with cestus was the child of Hathor in Lunar Cult, the Hathor who gave birth to the blue-eyed golden Horus as her child, her golden hawk or golden calf. Horus the child, or shoot on the papyrus, or on his mother's lap, is representative of the resurrection and renewal of life for another year. Horus came to Egypt as a Saviour of the people from the dreaded drought. He came invested with "The Power of the Southern Lakes," to drown the dragon in the inundation. In the Ritual, Chapter 64, it says of him, "I am the inundation." In one phase He is the Saviour as the bringer of water, in another He is the child of Light. He also treads the serpent of darkness under foot, as the renewer of light. In Ritual, Chapter 64, it says: "I who know the Depths is my name I give to spiritual things. Millions and billions are the measure of things. I am *the Inundation. Rising from the Great Water is my name.* I am yesterday, the morning, the Light at its birth the second time. My transformations are made of Tum or Kheper. I have departed from the shrine" (Solar).

When Horus came by water as Ichthus the fish, who gave himself for food, he swam the deluge of the inundation

[1] The Maories were Nilotic Negro Hero Cult people.

when as yet there was no boat built, or ark; but when the Ark is built, Argo is constellated as the Ark of Horus. This is portrayed in the planisphere with the child on board and the devouring Apap coiling round it seeking to destroy the child, the infant Saviour of the World, who brings the food and water as the lord of life.

In the Stellar Cult, the constellation representing Hydra represented the Apap reptile. It is figured in the waters of the Southern Heavens, and is that fearsome monster which in various legends drank up all the water. In the Solar Cult, Apap, the enemy of Ra, is the blind, devouring darkness.

But as the adversary of the Elder Horus, he of the inundation, Apap or Hydra is the dragon of drought. Drought in the land of Egypt was "the curse," and the evil dragon as its deadly image was the primitive type of physical, not moral, evil.

The first uranographic portrayal of Paradise was a Stellar enclosure round the pole of Set in the Southern Heavens, which was followed later, when the followers of Horus came North, by the configurating of the circumpolar Paradise in the Northern Heavens by the Astronomers when they reached the land of Egypt from the South.

The South was the scene of the so-called "Creation," or, as it signifies in Egyptian, "of the first time," and it is stated in the inscription of Tahtmes on the stele of the Sphinx, "The first time goes back to the days and domain of Set." Set, who is traditionally "the inventor of astronomy" and who as such had created the pillars of the Pole Star. The domain of Set was south of the Equator.

The first portrayal in their astronomical mythology was to depict their Paradise on Earth in the land of the Lakes, uranographically in the Southern Heavens.

Earth, as the mother of life and giver of water, was portrayed in the abyss as a great Fish emaning water from its mouth; the primary water, or the wet nurse of Mythology, was on earth, imaged as the Lake Tanganyika. She was now constellated in the Heavens as the Southern

Fish, as the producer of life and sustenance from water in the unfathomable abyss of the firmament.

This is figured in the Southern Fish. The star, Fomalhaut, at the mouth of the fish, denotes the point of emergence whence the stream is seen ascending from its source beneath the constellation of Aquarius.

In the Egyptian it states : " In the beginning was the Nun. Thus saith the primordial word."

This does not mean " in the beginning " of the Heavens and Earth—that is, the creation of the world—but " in the beginning " of the uranographic representation in their astronomical mythology. The Nun is a name in Egyptian for the firmament, when imaged as " a world of water."

The Southern Fish is figured as the bringer forth of water, i.e. of the life, or of Horus the Fish from the abyss.

Ketos, the monster, represents the Mother in another character on the southern part of the celestial globe ; there the life of the world that was born of water and, imaged as Ichthus the fish, is still represented as issuing from the mouth of the Southern Fish. The word that issued from the fish's mouth is mentioned by the writer of a Hymn to Merodach in which it is said : " The holy writings of the mouth of the deep is Thine " (Sayce : " Hib. List," p. 99).

This shows the word Ichthus had then become the written word. It issued out of the mouth of the deep which was of the fish-mother or the fish's mouth.

The mystical emblem ⊂⊃ Ru is a symbol of the Fish's mouth, or entrance into life. It is the emaning mouth of the fish which gave birth to water as the life of the world and to the Saviour, who came to Egypt by water, as the fish of the inundation, down the Nile, from Lake Tanganyika.

The fish's mouth was figured in the heavens as the primordial door of entrance of life when the soul of life came to the world by water.

Although the true meaning has been suppressed by overlaying the doctrine, enough survives in the symbols to show that the child Christ in the Virgin's arms encircled by the " vesica piscis " has the same significance as had the figure in the planisphere, where the water of life is issuing from the fish's mouth and the star of annunciation is the star Fomalhaut. Only the water of life, still represented by Ichthus the fish, is personalized in later iconography by the human child as the type of eternal rejuvenescence. The oval being a co-type with the fish's mouth, the Virgin and her child are a later equivalent for the Divine Mother bringing forth her fish in the lake, piscina, or other water-type of the primordial abyss, as in the astronomical mythology.

The primordial abyss had originated as the source of water in the Earth. Water generated by the earth was that which came from the very source itself, thus visualized as wet nurse of the world. Every spring or bubbling fount of liquid life that issued from this source below was suggestive of a deep without a bottom. It was afterwards represented in the Astronomical Mythology and constellated at the very foundation of the Southern Heavens as the mystical abyss.

The first abyss was on earth in the South, represented on earth by the Great Lake as Lake Tanganyika. The Abyss of firmamental water was outside the earth in the Southern heavens. But there were two waters actually in external nature, one the water that rose up from the springs and wells of earth, portrayed as Ta-Urt or Uati, in the Mother-earth, in the abyss; the other, the water that fell in dew or rain, from heaven. The Egyptians portrayed the latter as falling from the tree of wet, which is the Egyptian tree of Nut, or of heaven as water.

Thence water from the wells was the water of earth, and the water from the trees was the water of heaven. These two types were also imaged as the Cow of Earth, Water-Cow, and the Milch-Cow of Heaven, Nut. These two types, seen in the well and tree, are universal signs of so-called " water worship " with the oldest races. The "holy well," a water hole, is commonly found beneath the sacred moisture-dropping tree, and often a stone erected as an altar underneath the tree is found. It was a place of propitiation and appeal to the elemental power for water. Offerings were made on the altar-stone, and the object of the rite is the spirit or power that sends the water from its double source, in earth and heaven, with the stone as an altar for the sacrifice.

The double source of water being thus recognized as the water of earth and the water of heaven, the type of duality was applied to the firmamental water in the astronomical mythology and constellated in the two celestial rivers of Eridanus and the Milky Way.

The former reflects the river of the inundation, that is the water of earth below, emaning from the lower Nun or Mythical Abyss in the South. The latter is the great stream of the Via Lactea. The inundation rose up in the South "at the moment when the lord of his flood is carried forth and brings to its fullness the force that is hidden within him" (Rit., Ch. 64).

We have seen how they imaged Horus in the Mythos as the Fish-man who came to Egypt with water, as the Saviour having been born from the Great Mother in the Lake Tanganyika.

Thus in the Astronomical Mythology he was at first portrayed as born of the great Southern Fish. Achern in Eridanus then became the guiding star in the South. From that the river travelled North to Orion's foot, or rather to the point at which Orion rises up as Horus of the inundation; otherwise, is brought to birth on his papyrus, as depicted in the Egyptian drawings. When the followers of Horus arrived in Egypt, the water-cow of earth was constellated in the stars of the Northern Heavens, the Milch-Cow of Heaven represented or imaged in the group now known as Cassiopœia, or the lady in the chair, which was the earlier constellation of the Haunch,

or Meskhen 𓃻 𓏏 as a figure of the birthplace when the birth was typical of life in water.

Horus as Orion in the earlier Stellar Cult was the hunter of the power of darkness with his dogs, Kyon and Prokyon.

The earliest figure of an Ark in Heaven, or on the waters of the Nun was imaged as that of Horus on his papyrus-reed who issued as the soul of life in vegetation from the Abyss of water, the cradle of Child Horus.

When the boat was built, the souls of the deceased were ferried over the waters of space in the Mythical bark which was first Stellar, next Lunar, and finally Solar.

Modern Astronomers speak of the Starry Vast as a revolving sphere, whereas the Ancient Egyptians spoke of it as the Ship of Heaven or the Bark of Eternity.

The superhuman force that hauled the system round was imaged as a mighty monster swimming the Celestial Lake, a Hippopotamus or a Crocodile, or compound of both; also as the Great Mother of revolution, as Goddess Apt depicted in the Great Bear, as the Great Mother who gave birth to the seven circumpolar gods, all brothers, and called in the Ritual " the Bulls of their Mother." In the Astronomical phase, the visible birthplace of Spirits perfected is localized in Sothis. The opener of the year and the bringer of the babe to birth on the horizon, or the Mount of Glory, and the triumph of Horus over Set, or over the Apap dragon of drought and darkness was illustrated in the Stellar Cult, when in the annual round Orion rose and the Scorpion Constellation set upon the opposite horizon.

The scene configurated in the Southern Heavens when the conqueror Orion rose up to bruise the Serpent's head, or crush the dragon under foot, is also represented in the Ritual when Apap is once more put in bonds, cut up piecemeal, and submerged in the green lake of Heaven (Ch. 39). This imagery was carried across to America, and is fully depicted in " Mexican Antiquities."

The Stars were used by the Egyptians to illustrate the Mysteries that were out of sight.

Sothis in its helical rising was not the only Star of

Drawn by K. Watkins.

HORUS ISSUING FROM THE WATERS ON THE REED, THE CRADLE, AND ARK OF THE ETERNAL CHILD. THE BIRTHPLACE OF THE REEDS.

The above is the Solar depiction, the original was Stellar (as supra).

PLATE VII.

SEBEK-HORUS (*Solar depiction*).
PLATE VIII.

[*To face p.* 97.

Annunciation at the birth of Horus the child, as Ichthus the fish. Farther South was the Star Phact, which was also a harbinger of the inundation; and still farther South, Canopus.

The pilot of the Argo at the starting point of the journey by water, which was the river Nile as the terrestrial water, and imaged uranographically by the Milky Way or White Road, accounts for the Chinese beliefs and their representation of the same as the Egyptian, because they are Stellar Cult people who originally came from Egypt during that Cult; that is why they have a Constellation in the Milky Way called " The Ship of Heaven."

The Ship of Nu is Egyptian for the Ship of Heaven.

The beginning in Heaven as on Earth was with water. Water was the first thing rendered uranographically, not created, *in the Southern hemisphere*. This when " gathered into one place " was localized as " the water," and the Egyptians had a huge southern constellation dedicated to Menat, the wet nurse, called " The Stars of the Water " (Egypt Calendar of Astronomical Observations). The " Southern Fish " and " Ketos " are both depicted in this water of the south or the abyss. Earth, the Great Mother, was imaged as the breeder of life and the bringer forth from this abysmal water in the South. She was represented in two Mythical characters. In one she was the Mother who brought forth on dry ground as the hippopotamus (or its equivalent type), in the other she was the Mother of life or water who was figured as the Southern fish low down in the deep of the Southern Heaven.

So the power of the two monsters (in the Book of Enoch) " became separated on the same day, one being in the depths of the sea and one in the desert." That is one in the water as Leviathan (the crocodile or dragon), and one as the hippopotamus on dry ground. Enoch asks the Angel to show him " the power of those monsters and how they became separated on the same day of creation, one in the depths of the sea, above the springs of waters, and one in the dry desert." It is said of the two monsters that they had been prepared by the people of God to become food. But the two monsters had represented food and drink from the first; one as the Mother of life on the earth, the other in the Waters. The question asked shows a broken ray of the repeated Mythos. The two monsters were prepared for food in the garden or enclosure of the beginning. The name of one is Behemoth, the name of the other Leviathan. Behemoth is the Egyptian Bekamut, the female hippopotamus, and Leviathan answers to the crocodile or dragon of the deep. The Rabbis repeated a true tradition when they rendered the Biblical "Behemoth," not as a plural of majesty, but as a pair of beasts. They are a pair of beasts in the Mythology of Egypt. The female Behemoth was the original Great Mother Tekhi or Khept; the male was her son. The crocodile also, as Zootype, was both male and female. For his purpose, however, Enoch makes Leviathan a male monster and Behemoth female. Of course the type is or may be differentiated by the sex. The two monsters in the Egyptian starry scheme are both female, as two forms of the Great Mother who was the hippopotamus in her fore part and the crocodile behind, or the crocodile in the South and the hippopotamus in the North. Thus the hippopotamus and crocodile, which were natural on the Nile, had become two huge indefinite monsters of legendary lore in the Book of Enoch, and the two survived as the types of dry and wet, for land and water.

They were constellated as the Southern Fish and Ketos or the whale; but the whale has been substituted for the hippopotamus by the Euphrateans or the Greeks. The Southern Fish on the celestial globe is portrayed as the act of emaning a stream of water from its mouth, whereas the monster Ketos is depicted as the breather out of the water, the two being representative of the earth as the Mother of life in the water called the abyss. In the Set and Horus mythos the first two children of the ancient Mother represented the condition of wet and dry. They were born Twins because the conditions were co-extant in earth and water. In the course of time every day that was dry desiccative or of the desert was ascribed to Set, whereas the products of water were assigned to Horus. Hence the two monsters were continued as types of the twins. The Hippopotamus of earth as male was given to Set. The Crocodile of water was given to Horus to typify the fish as food of the inundation. (The Stellar Cult people carried these types all over the world, and as proof I here reproduce them as portrayed in Mexico, Fig. 10.) (Other places see later.)

In no land or literature has the Mythical mode of representation been perverted and reduced to more fatal

Mexican symbolism of the Great Mother in a dual form as the Great Fish—one breathing in the water and one out of the water. (From "Mexican Antiquities.")

Drawn by K. Watkins.

Fig. 10.

foolishness than in some of the Hebrew legends, such as that of Jonah and the great fish, which in the mythology is connected with the origin of the fish-man who was born of a fish-mother, identifiable with the constellation of the Southern fish and Horus of the inundation, and brought on as types, as Horus of the Double Power. The most ancient type of the fish was female, as a representation of the great Mother-Earth in the water.

This, as Egyptian, was the Crocodile. She was

the suckler of Crocodiles in the inundation. She was the bringer forth as the great Fish or Crocodile in the Astronomical-Mythology. One of her children was the Crocodile-headed Sebek who made the passage of the Nun by night, typified as the Child Horus in Solar Mythos. The fish-man was at first the Crocodile of Egypt, next the Crocodile-headed figure of Horus who is called " the Crocodile God in the form of a man " (Rit., Ch. 88).

The conversion of the crocodile god in the Nun to the fish-man of Babylonia was thus made : Jonah is a form of the fish-man in the Babylonian story (which is neither Mythology nor Eschatology), and is therefore a figure of both the Stellar and Solar God who made the passage of the waters as Horus the Crocodile, or as Ea the fish-man of Nineveh. Birth, or rebirth, from the great fish in the Lower Nun, is one of the oldest traditions of the race. It was represented in the Mysteries and constellated in the heavens as a means of Memorial in Sign Language.

The Astronomical Cult of Egypt passed into Akkad and Babylonia with the exodus of the Stellar Cult race, some of whom were termed the Cushite "black-heads," to become the wisdom of the Chaldees and the Persian magi in after ages.

The earliest Mother who conceived as a Virgin in Mythology was the Virgin Neith, imaged by the White Vulture in the Stellar Cult. In Lunar Cult it was Hathor, imaged by the sacred Heifer. The human only comes in when the mythos is related as history, when the woman took the place of the Vulture, the Heifer, or other zootype of virginity, i.e. when the type was humanized and Horus imaged as a child; and when the doctrine of incarnation, or the incorporation of a Spirit of life in matter had entered the human sphere. When the type of the Great Mother and her youngling had been changed from the totemic zootype to the anthrotype, and the Goddess was imaged as a woman, a child becomes the figure of a superhuman power that was ever coming, ever manifesting in natural phenomena. Then the youthful God was naturally born as a child. Thus the Mystical virgin and child in human guise was a result of doctrinal development, and the doctrine itself could not be understood without a knowledge of the primary phase.

In the Christian doctrines the Vulture is represented by the Pelican as having pierced her own thigh to give her blood to her young for nourishment (a fine specimen of this symbolism is the lectern in St. Saviour's Church, Reading). It represents, in Sign Language, the earliest soul considered to be human, being born of the Mother-blood. The Soul that was made flesh in the child Horus, who was born of the Mother-blood, and as such was distinguished from the earlier elemental powers, otherwise the six Totemic pre-human souls.

The origin of a Saviour in the guise of a little child is traceable to child Horus, who brought new life to Egypt every year as the Messu of the inundation.

This was Horus in His pre-solar and pre-human character as Ichthus the fish, the shoot of papyrus, or the branch of endless years. In a later stage the image of Horus on His papyrus represented the young God as Solar cause of Creation. But in the primitive phase it was a soul of life or of food ascending from the water of vegetation.

A spring of water welling from abysmal depths of earth that furnished food in the papyrus reed and other edible plants, is the earliest form in which the source of life was figured by the Kamite Mystery Teachers.

This is recorded in the Ritual (Ch. 172). It was in the birthplace of the reeds and of the reed people in the region of the reeds that light first broke out of darkness in the beginning in the domain of Set, and where the twin children of darkness and light were born. The Mother Earth, as womb of universal life, was the producer of food in various kinds, and the food was represented as her offspring. The Japanese have the same doctrine because they were an exodus from Egypt at the time of the Stellar Cult. Some of the American-Indians have still retained the same tradition.

Horus as the "Fish-man" was depicted zoomorphically during the Stellar Cult; it was as the "Fish" that he came with the inundation from the inner African Lakes down the Nile to give life and food to the people whose land was parched and dry; as a type he became the Saviour of Life, the supplier of food and plenty. Thus Sebek-Horus, the son of Neith, who is represented as the Great Fish, is the Crocodile, which was applied to Horus as a figure of force, and is portrayed as a constellation of enormous magnitude uranographically, and is truly the Great Fish of Horus-Sebek that was first of all a figure of the inundation constellation in the Stellar Cult.

In the Solar Cult, in His capacity of the Solar God, the Crocodile in Egypt, being a prototype of the Mythical Dragon, *is not the evil Dragon*, but the Solar Dragon, known in relation to Sebek of the Stellar Cult as *the Dragon of Life*, and re-applied in the Solar Cult as the Power of God which crossed the waters as a primary type of Horus of the Double Horizon.

In this Stellar Cult it was the Fish God who came from the South to the North in the inundation, to bring water, food, and life to Egypt as the Saviour of the Country from drought and disease. The type of Horus as a Fish God has been carried into many countries wherever these people went, and has been brought down into the Christian Doctrines as "Ichthus the Fish." But wherever you find this depiction, under whatever terminology or imagery, it all represents the original Horus of the Stellar Cult.

Horus-Sebek (Plate VIII) was the earliest Fish-man known to Mythology. He calls himself "the fish in the form of a man." (Other illustrated types will be found portrayed in "Origin and Evolution of Freemasonry.")

This is how the Saviour could be represented as Ichthus the Fish. Neith of Sais was supposed to be a goddess without a consort, and in the Pyramid Text Sebek is called her son; she is also represented suckling two crocodiles.

The fabled "war in heaven" began with the contending elements that strove with each other for supremacy, whether as light and darkness, water and drought, or food and famine, health, or disease. Horus of the inundation came by water as the deliverer when the land was suffering from the dragon of drought. The picture was constellated in the Southern Heavens.

Horus the victor was represented by Orion rising from the river and wielding the insignia of his sovereignty. His weapon is the Club of the Masai (commonly called the club of Herakles in Greece). It was the whip of ruling power as the Egyptian khu. He rises from Eridanus as the conqueror of the hydra-headed-dragon that is overwhelmed beneath the waters when the drought was put an end to by the lord of life with the water for his weapon. Here is a motive for the war betwixt the dragon and infant who was born to universal rule or predestined to be King. Horus also came as conqueror of the dragon of darkness.

It is of importance to know that the evil reptile, Apap, represented drought, famine, disease, and death. This was the mortal enemy of man which drank up all the water in the world; hence the battle for the water. Everywhere the warfare of the hero with the monster is for water as well as for light, because the monster is representative of drought as well as darkness. At first it was the water reptile in the African lake, then the devil snake Apap drinks up the water of the Nile.

In Australia the type was the monstrous frog that drinks up the water. It is also the chimerical malignant wild beast that is slain by Gilgames. Later it became the sea monster of the Greek Mythology. However, all originally came out of Egypt as Sebek-Horus or the Great Fish of the inundation, and Apap as constellated in Hydra the enormous reptile, imaged in the celestial waters of the Southern Heavens.

The hero of light who pierced the Serpent of drought as the dragon of darkness was also represented as the Golden Hawk (later Eagle), and at Hermopolis the Egyptians showed the figure of a hippopotamus upon which a hawk stood fighting with a serpent (Plutarch on "Isis and Osiris," p. 50). The Hippopotamus was a zootype of the Mother Earth in the waters of space; the hawk and serpent fighting on her back portrayed the war of light and darkness, which had been fought from the beginning, the war that was a primary subject figured in Astronomical Mythology. The Hawk represented Horus who was the bruiser of the Serpent's head.

Thus the same conflict that was portrayed at Hermopolis may be seen in the constellation of Serpentarius as a uranographic picture depicted in the planisphere.

In various countries the Monster of the Dark was represented by an animal entirely black.

This in Egypt was the Black Boar of Set. Plate IX.

When the Timarese are direfully suffering from lack of rain they offer up a black pig as a sacrifice. The black pig was slain, just as Apap was pierced, because it imaged the dark power that once withheld the waters of day, and now denies the rain or the Water of Life. In Sumatra it is the black cat that typifies the inimical power which withholds the rain.

What these customs signified according to the wisdom of Egypt has the same significant interpretation when found in other countries. In each case the representative of the dark and evil power was slain or thrown into the water as a propitiation to the beneficent power which gave rain and light. Slaying the type of drought was a means of fighting against the power of evil and making an appeal to the Good Spirit. It was a primitive mode of casting out Satan, the Adversary, in practical Sign Language.

We know that the universal Monster as the Evil reptile of the Dark, for ever warring with the Light, who also, as the fiery Dragon of Drought, drinks the water which is the life of vegetation, is variously represented by primitive man in different countries, but it has one and the same meaning and interpretation, the original being the Egyptian Apap carried out of Egypt, and represented by different fauna only. For example, amongst the Australian aborigines, the Andaman Islanders, and the red men (some Nilotic Negroes), it is a gigantic Frog which drinks up all the waters in the world. Here

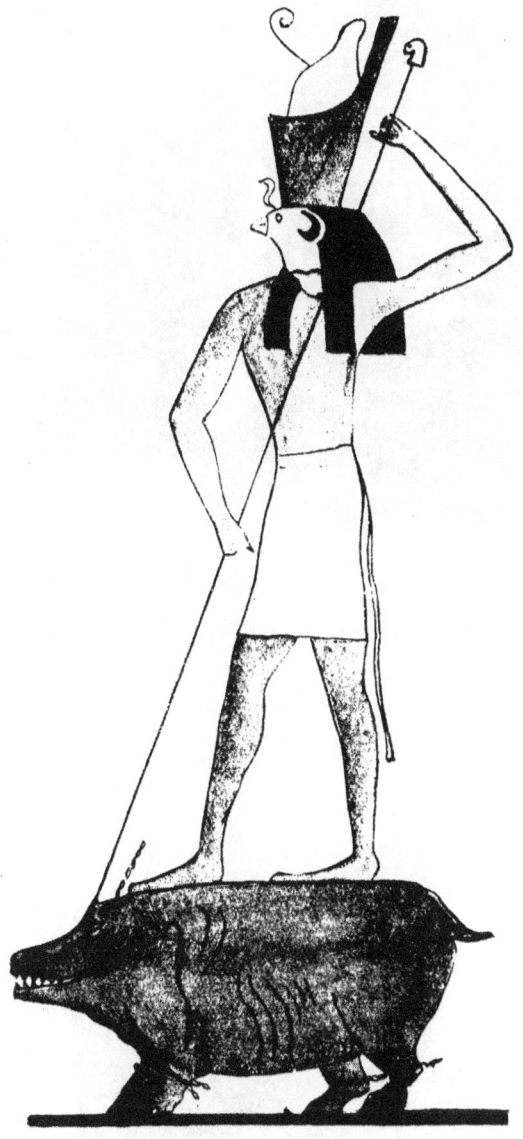

BLACK BOAR OF SET

Horus having bound him, is depicted spearing him.

PLATE IX.

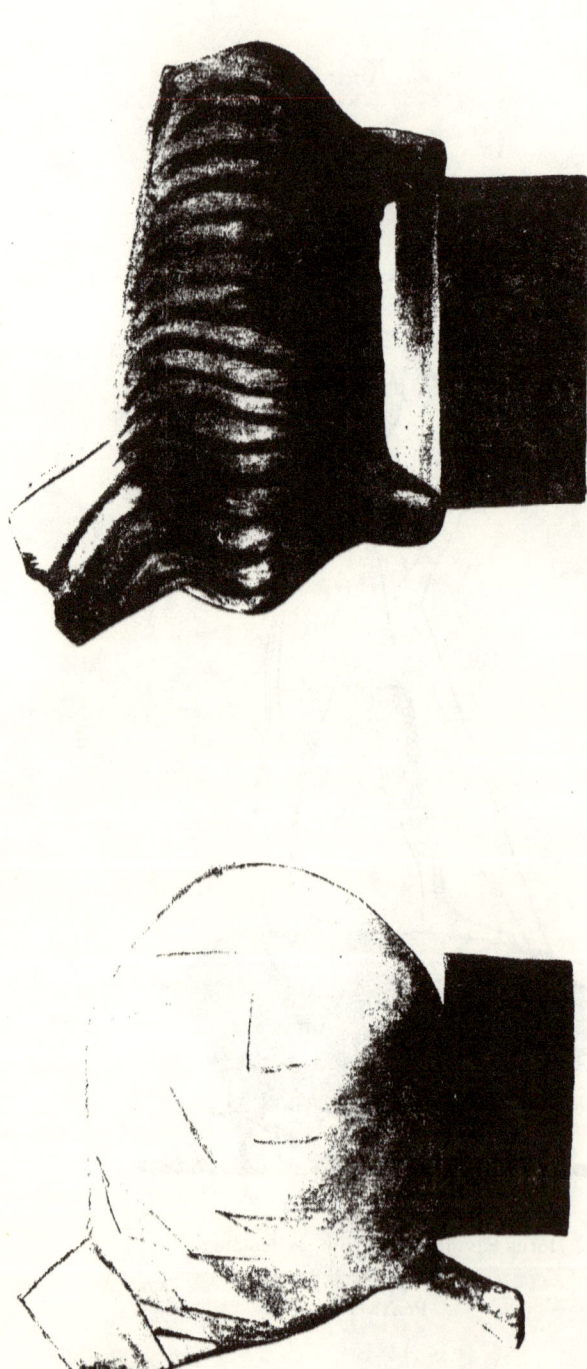

Drawn by K. Watkins, from Photograph sent me by Secretary of Bulawayo Museum.

TYPES OF THE GREAT MOTHER FOUND IN SOUTH AFRICA, NOW IN MUSEUM IN BULAWAYO.

PLATE X.

the Frog represents the part of the Apap Monster that swallows the waters at sundown and is pierced and cut in pieces, coil by coil, to set them flowing freely at the return of day either by the Hawk or the Cat, or by Horus the anthropomorphic hero. In the Andaman version of the conflict between the bird of Light and the Devil of Darkness the waters are drunk up by and withheld by a big Toad. An Iroquois or Huron form of this mythical representation also shows the devouring Monster as a gigantic Frog. The Aborigines of Lake Tyers have the same representation.

I give a representation of the Mexican, which typifies it by a Hellish Snake.

These pictures are taken from the Codex Torano MS. and proves how the old Stellar Cult doctrines were carried out of Egypt into many parts of the world, including America.

Fig. 11 portrays Horus the Egyptian God imaged as an Elephant (which was a very early type carried out of Egypt into Asia, and thence across to America). He is depicted as pouring water (rain) out of a water jug to fertilize the earth.

Set, as the great evil Serpent Apap, is trying to drink it up, but Horus stands on him; his foot crushes down his head and thus prevents him doing so.

The Glyphs read: "Ta" A-ha-u Heb Kanaan Cib Lam-a-ti-. Translated: Horus of the two lands or double earth turns abundant water to fertilize the land (and is standing on the Head of Apap to prevent its being swallowed up).

Fig. 12.—The lower picture depicts the Great Apap as having swallowed the water and light, and Horus as the Elephant God is fighting to make him disgorge it.

The Indian Nâga, the beneficent God or King identified with the Cobra, is the same as the Egyptian Uræus Deity as representing Horus. Horus and Set contending for the mount: I have given the Mexican, depicted in "Signs and Symbols."

Stellar Mythos in its lowest and highest forms was

106 THE ORIGIN AND EVOLUTION

brought to America, North and South, by people who originally came from Egypt.

What does this show?

Stellar Mythos, being much older than Solar Mythos, it follows that all the civilization of North, Central, and South America was originated by people who believed in and practised Stellar Mythos, a cult identical with the

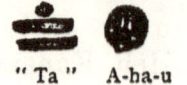

" Ta "   A-ha-u   Heb   Kanaan   Cib   Lamat

Drawn by K. Watkins.

THE MAYA GOD CHACIC, HORUS OF EGYPT AND TLALOC OF THE MEXICANS.

Samin (Asima as the Samaritans called him) is the Phœnician name of Horus as " the pourer down of rain."

FIG. 11.

Stellar Mythos of the Egyptians; identical also with that of which traces are found in the ancient ruins in the Caroline and other islands, and which we find practised to the present day among certain peoples of Asia.

Signs and symbols discovered on the remains of many an ancient city undoubtedly substantiate the contention that, prior to the advent of the Lunar and Solar Cults, the practice of Stellar Mythos was universal, and to a great extent homogeneous, throughout Asia, as well as North, Central and South America, and Africa. Moreover, in civilized Europe remains are still left to us which prove that this Cult was also in vogue here before the Lunar and Solar Cults, and that these people of the old Stellar Mythos attained to a comparatively high state of civilization.

The Elephant in Asia took the place of the hippo-

The Great Apap having swallowed the water and light, Horus as the Elephant God is fighting to make him disgorge it.

Fig. 12.

potamus type of puissance and power, but it has the same name of Abu in Egyptian as the Rhinoceros, which interchanges with the hippopotamus as an image of Set as male, and the *Great Mother as female*. In Egypt the two types are interchangeable; in Egypt the Elephant also became a type of Horus.

The Rhinoceros and Hippopotamus, or Water Horse,

were both types of the Great Mother in Africa, as well as the Frog Heket. I give here photographs of the two figures and the two types, remains of this depiction found in South Africa, and now in the museum in Bulawayo in Rhodesia (Plate X). I also reproduce (Plate XI) two figures of the Great Mother found in Guatemala, which show how widespread this old Stellar Cult was. In these depictions we have two types—first, the Great Mother with a basket of food on her back, the offering of food and water as is seen in the depiction of the earlier type of Rannut. In this case the " fauna " has been changed to the head of a Tapir, in place of the Hippopotamus (the latter animal not being a denizen of Guatemala), but the necklace with which she is adorned proves this to be the *female* Zootype, therefore the Mother, and not the Son.

The other depiction is that of the Frog, the Great Mother Heket. This is critical proof of their being representations of the Egyptian original.

The river Nile was traced back by the Egyptians to its double source, Lake Victoria and Lake Tanganyika. This, in later times, was localized at Elephantine, but was not so originally. In the Stellar Cult the Nile was known to issue from the two great Lakes which were the South source of the river according to the Ritual.

The Soul of Life, as a source of drink, was apprehended in the element of water, seen also in the plant and figured in the Fish. The superhuman type was divinized in Horus.

The Soul of Life, as a source of breath, was apprehended in the breeze and imaged as the panting Lion.

The superhuman type was divinized in Shu.

A Soul of food was apprehended in the earth and represented by the goose that laid the egg.

The superhuman type was divinized in Seb.

Thus we have Horus as Ichthus the fish, and Horus the Mother's child who came by water.

A power of yearly renewal was perceived in nature; hence the Child-god of Egypt became a type of the eternal, periodically renewing the elements of life and light by birth in time and season.

Drawn by Watkins.

TYPES OF THE GREAT MOTHER FOUND IN GUATEMALA; COMPARE WITH THOSE IN BULAWAYO.

PLATE XI

SEKHET-BAST.
One form of the Great Mother of the South.
PLATE XII.

To those who travelled Northwards through the Valley of the Nile there was an actual subsidence and submergence of a human fore-world in the South. This was a matter of latitude determinable by the stars that sank in the Abyss, the natural fact.

The Abyss became the graves, as it were, of some lost world which had been once real on earth.

That fore-world of the South was reproduced by the followers of Horus in the North, where they raised their circumpolar paradise to portray for all time some features of their old primordial home. The Southern Pole Star sank into the blind Abyss together with their old terrestrial home. This, in a later legend, would become a fall from Heaven, or submergence, or a deluge as the fact was figured in the Astronomical Mythology.

Hence we find the legend of the lost paradise, the primal pair as man and cow, the twin brothers, the fall from heaven, the deluge and other stories as indigenous products at the centre of the old dark land.

The field of the Papyrus reeds, the old primeval home, and the primal Paradise of the human race in the South, was configurated at the summit of the Northern Hemisphere, and the old Earth Mother, Uati or Ta-Urt, the Water-Cow, was now divinized under the name of Apt, as the birthplace in the reeds, and Nut was imaged as the Milch Cow to represent rebirth in Heaven.

This was the Great Mother of revolutions who was constellated as the primum mobile, the Goddess Apt depicted in the Great Bear as the procreant womb of life, the Mother and Nurse of universal life.[1]

Seven powers were born of her imaged by different types, all brothers, and called the Bulls of their Mother in one phase. These were the seven elemental powers brought on and now divinized, and were figuratively grouped in a bark that voyaged round the Pole, or as Ursa Minor, with seven souls or glorious ones on board, seen in the seven Stars that never set, a primary type of the eternal.

[1] See " Signs and Symbols," p. 459.

These seven Pole Stars represent the seven Khuti, who were the rulers in the Celestial heptanomis.

They were imaged in one type as the seven Eyes in consequence of the eye being a figure of a circle.

The type is presented in Joshua in the Book of Zechariah in the shape of seven eyes upon one stone. "Behold the stone I have set before Joshua upon one stone are seven eyes." These are the seven eyes of the Lord, also the seven Lamps, the same as in the Book of Revelation (Zec. iii. 9; iv. 1, 12). Hence the seven eyes of the Lord in the blue stone of the firmament.

These were represented by the Golden Candlestick or one with seven branches in the Hebrew text.

The submergence of the seven Pole Stars, as each one

THE GREAT MOTHER APT GIVING BIRTH TO HER SON HORUS.
FIG. 13.

gave place to the next in the cycle of procession, involves the same number of "deluges," which culminated in "The Great Deluge of All," when the seventh had finished its cycle; not the destruction of the world, but to recommence the cycle again. This is the reason why you find in all lands and amongst all people where the Stellar Cult travelled, the story of the deluge. The deluge of this world was a myth founded on the above by people not knowing Sign Language.

In Egypt the Totemism of the Tribal system had been continued in the towns and cities which bore the names of the zoological types, such as the Lion, Dog, Hawk, Fish, Hippopotamus, Crocodile, etc. There was a mapping out of Egyptian localities, according to the celestial Nomes and scenery described in the inscription of Khnumhept. The earlier Stellar Cult people took all this imagery with them wherever they went, that had been evolved up to the date of the exodus at the time of leaving Egypt. With the Ancient Arab tribes the stars were their Totems. Jupiter was the star of the Jodam and the Skehm tribes; Mercury of the Asad tribe; Sirius of the Kais tribe; Canopus of the Tay tribe; and others recognized constellations as Totemic types.

The God of Sabaoth of the Hebrews is the Deity of the seven Pole Stars, i.e. Ursa Minor. The Deity that was primary Set of the Egyptians, and later Horus, took his place. Set was the El Shadda of the Phœnicians and Hebrews.

The Japanese people themselves were originally divided into eight primary classes corresponding to the original eight Stellar Cult gods, or the prototypes of the primary seven elemental powers plus "the One," i.e. $7 + 1 = 8$. The evidence for this is that the Japanese have a different personal pronoun for various classes of person, each class being compelled to use their own, and not another. There are eight personal pronouns of the second person peculiar to servants, pupils, and children. These told which "thou" or pronoun applicable was intended as one of a class, and therefore proves a continuation of the Totemic mode of naming and distinguishing by the group only.

Eight classes of the personal pronouns answer to the eight totems of the Kamilaroi.

The Chinese have twelve signs that are Totemic in the celestial heavens, which represent "twelve houses" of the later Stellar Cult. They have also retained the Symbolism of the "seven primal powers," and the "seven plus one = the eighth as the highest," but much Solar Cult was introduced later.

The time taken for the procession, or rather recession, of the Pole Stars is 25,827 years. It was called one Great Year or one Great Day.

The seven Pole Stars were also imaged to represent the seven Stellar Gods with Horus as the Chief, making eight.

Fig. 13A is the Mexican glyph for Horus as chief of the seven—as the eight—that is Horus as God of the Am-Khemen Paradise at the North.

In the Stellar Cult there are four types, at least, of the Great Mother Earth, which had originated in the Southern Paradise, that were brought on and imaged by the Great Bear constellation and deified.

One of the primary types for the Great Mother Earth

Fig. 13A.

originating in the South was Mut; we have her in one character as bringing forth Set, as Muten-Set or Mut-Seten. Another was Sebek, the Great Mother Crocodile. Proof of this is found in the Ritual. In Chapter 164 there are some ancient names which are said to have been uttered in the language of the Nashi (or Masai), the Anti or the people of Ta-Kenset (or Nubia). In this the Great Mother is saluted as the supreme being, "The Only One," by the name of Sekhet-Bast (Plate XII), she who was "uncreated by the gods," and "who is mightier than the gods." "To her the eight Stellar gods offer words of adoration."

This shows that part of the Ritual had originated in the South, and was brought on by the pre-Dynastic Egyptians. Another type originating in the South was the

Drawn by K. Watkins

MERSEKERT SUCKLING HORUS.

A type of Hathor in the Lunar Cult.

PLATE XIII.

The Great Mother Isis in the Papyrus Swamps suckling Horus.
Solar Imagery.
Plate XIV.

Great Mother Kep, afterwards divinized and called Rannut, and imaged as the Serpent, as mother of food and periodic renewal.

I here reproduce Rannut, the Lady of Aat—"The Serpent Goddess Mother" in later form (Fig. 14).

Drawn by K. Watkins.

RANNUT THE SERPENT GODDESS SUCKLING HER INFANT, TEM, HERE PORTRAYED AS A CHILD IN THE PLACE OF THE EARLIER STELLAR CULT SYMBOL OF A SERPENT—TEM-HORUS OR HORUS AS TEM.

She wears the crown of the two feathers—South and North.
From Papyrus found in Upper Egypt.

FIG. 14.

In the primitive form she is shown in "Origin and Evolution of the Human Race," p. 158.

In this form she is depicted as suckling Horus the young child. This is the earliest type of the portrayal of the Virgin Mary and Jesus. I call attention to this particularly because, this being the original, it is interesting to trace the different depictions through the various Cults to the present day as further proof.

Also I reproduce Mersekert suckling Horus (Plate XIII). This was a Lunar type of Hathor (as shown), but earlier under the name of Ätet it represented Stellar type. I also reproduce the Great Mother Isis suckling Horus in the Papyrus swamps. This is a Solar type (Plate XIV).

The little child has taken the place of the young shoot Natzar, or the forms of life which have a periodic renewal from Mother Earth. It is only by comprehending Sign Language that we can understand how the ancient wisdom was perverted after the original exodus of the Stellar Cult people who settled in other lands, and how their descendants, having forgotten the original sacred wisdom of Egypt, so altered the original that very little was left. By converting beneficial into evil types, they left poor humanity to wallow in a mire of ignorance and false doctrines which in the end destroyed their countries.[1]

In Babylonia the Tree of Life was changed into the Tree of Death. The Serpent in the Tree that offers fruit for food as the Great Mother Rannut, the giver of food, representing a type of Mother Earth, was transformed into the evil serpent that " brought death into the world and all our woe," but which had originated as a beneficent figure in the Kamite representation of external nature.

The transmogrifying of Tiamat, the Mother of all and suckler of the seven elemental powers, into the dragon of evil might be followed on other lines of descent, as the conflict of Bel-Merodach and the dragon.

---

[1] Other types of the Great Mother illustrated in my other works are :—

 1. The Goddess Sebek-Nit Suckling Horus (Stellar), see in " Signs and Symbols," page 123.
 2. " The Mexican portrayal of Isis Suckling Horus," p. 122.
 3. " The Christian Madonna and Child," p. 126.
 4. " Indian Representative in Origin and Evolution of the Human Race," p. 335.

Which prove how evolution of religion continued, and also how this was carried out of Egypt to other countries, the types of each Cult succeeding one another.

In the Egyptian representation Apap the dragon of drought is drowned in the waters by Horus of the inundation, whose weapon therefore is the water-flood.

In warring with Tiamat the deluge is "the mighty weapon," wielded by Bel. "Bel launched the deluge, his mighty weapon against Tiamat inundating her covering," or drowning the dragon of drought.

Thus Tiamat is destroyed by Bel with the deluge, when Apap was drowned by Horus in the inundation.

This shows how the Great Mother Tiamat, the suckler, as the giver of water had been converted into the evil dragon. This is portrayed in the Egyptian picture of Rannut "The Serpent Goddess," depicted as the Mother of food, there shown as suckling Horus the young child. She is portrayed both as the Mother of Life, as the human Mother, as well as the Mother of Life, the giver of food and fruits of the earth or trees, in Serpent form (see "Origin and Evolution of the Human Race," p. 150).

In the Hebrew legend it is the woman Eve who offers the fruit of the Tree of Knowledge, and it was in this phase of the Serpent (as the Great Mother of food and renewal of life), that the Biblical legend of the fall of man in the Garden of Eden originated. The Hebrews who wrote this part of Genesis were unable to read the old Sign Language, and thus interpreted the esoteric meaning of the Ritual, perverted it, making an exoteric rendering.

In other versions, especially the Greek, the fruit is offered to the man by a serpent in the Tree. The Serpent was a type of the Great Mother Kep, afterwards divinized as the Goddess Rannut; but whether portrayed in the shape of a Serpent or in the human form (which latter was not until the Solar Cult came into existence), she was the primordial giver of food as fruit from the Tree.

The Serpent, the Crocodile, or Dragon, the Hippopotamus, the Sow, the Cow, the Lioness, all met as one in Kep, the earliest Mother of Life.

The primal Mother in the Egyptian representation was the bringer forth of Set and Horus, as the first two children, who were born twins, and were the Bulls of their Mother.

These as the powers of Darkness and Light, or drought and fertility, were a pair of combatants who fought for the supremacy until one brother slew the other.

This is one of the primary legends that became universal, but it had only one origin.

Set and Horus were perhaps millions of years earlier than the Solar Cult of Atum-Ra practised at On, or Annu, but there they were fathered on Atum-Ra, and continued as his sons.

Set and Horus offer an instructive instance of evolution in Mythology. They were born sons of the first Great Mother, as two of the primordial powers, the twin powers of Light and Darkness. But in the recast of their theology the Priests of Annu brought them on as the warring sons of Atum-Ra, who fought each other " up and down the garden " until one of them was slain.

CHAPTER VII

STELLAR CULT

The Her-Seshta had now brought on their old Paradise in the South and with Egypt added, figured it uranographically in the Northern Heavens.

An Egypt of the Heavens was figured within the Circle of the Great Bear. This was the land of Khept as a celestial locality. In the centre was the Tree of Life planted on the Mount—otherwise the Tree of the Pole.

There was a male Hippopotamus among the Circumpolar Constellations, and this as the Bull of his Mother represented Set, the son of Apt, the Water-Cow (see

The landing-place for Spirits with the tree of the Pole in the Constellation of the Hippopotamus. The hawk is a spirit ascending to the Mount of Glory ⌂ is the hieroglyphic for land amidst the water. The 8888 (eight disks) proves it to be the Paradise of Am-Khemen that was raised by Shu. The Hippopotamus in the Tree proves it to be the Pole in the Hippopotamus Constellation (Set).

FIG. 15.

"Calendar of Astil: Observations" "Trans : Soc. of Bib. Arch.," Vol. III, pp. 400–21) here reproduced.

It is a drawing which was copied by Lepisus (Lepisus, "Auswald," p. 23). The Hippopotamus is figured in the Tree, which here, as elsewhere, proves it to be the pole : the Tree and the Ladder, both of which are types of the ascent.

The Hawk that mounts the Ladder is a soul ascending

to the mount of glory in the country of the Tree. And the hieroglyphic, here depicted ▦ is a sign of land amidst the waters, the land for which the Hawk is bound, which, as the eight disks show 8888 was the Paradise of Am-Khemen; that is, the Paradise at the Pole of the eight Stellar Gods, the 7 + 1.

The hieroglyphic Khept is a symbol of birthplace. This is the Thigh, the Haunch, or Meskhen of the old Mother Khept, figured within the Circle of the Great Bear or Apt.

The Egyptian nome of the Haunch was the nome of the birthplace in Khept, Khebt or Egypt (Khept

MOTHER APT AND HAUNCH.
FIG. 16.

being a name of Egypt and Khepti a plural for the double-land, i.e. Upper and Lower Egypt).

The Circle of the Great Bear was divided into South and North, as double Egypt—Upper and Lower, and the two halves were described as the domains of Set and Horus—who were the first two children of the ancient Great Mother who had seven offspring altogether.

The seven Egyptian Nomes first formed, or founded, in Egypt, were then imaged within the Circle of the Great Bear by the seven Pole Stars of Ursa Minor, or Little Bear; afterwards these Nomes were increased in number.

Amongst the Nomes of Lower Egypt we find that these were:—

1. The Nome of the Prince of Annu, the Nome of the Prince of Lower Egypt.
2. The Nome of Supti (Set).
3. The Nome of Sam-hutit (Horus).
4. The Nome of Sebek.
5. The Nome of Shu.
6. The Nome of Hapi.
7. The Nome of the Haunch or Meskhen.

The seven rulers of the Astronomers attained the status of divine Princes in the Celestial Heptanomes.

In the seventeenth chapter of the Ritual we find that these were represented by the Little Bear Stars, thus:—

1. In the Dragon.
2. One in the Lesser Bear.
3. One in Kephus.
4. One in Cygnus.
5. One in Lyra.
6. One in Corona Borealis.
7. One in Herakles.

When the Anthrotype had succeeded the Zootype, we find that Egypt was figured as a female lying on her back with her feet to the North (and her hands raised to Heaven) pointing in the direction of the Great Bear Constellation. This was the Motherland in the likeness of the human Mother, who had taken the place of the Water-Cow of Tanganyika, an image of the birthplace and abode being thus obviously continued.

The "Thigh" was figured both in the South and in the North "to signify the birthplace," and the birth of water.

In the South the water was the river Nile, and in the North this was figured as the Milky Way.

These are the two waters of earth and heaven proceeding from the Cow that was the Water-Cow of Tekhi, or Ta-Urt in the earth, and the Milch Cow of Nut in the heaven. Two different types of the Great Mother are imaged as Ta-Urt or the Earth Mother in one character, as Apt the Water-Cow of Heaven and Nut the Mother of Heaven as the Milch Cow.

A Temple at Denderah has the Constellation of the Hippopotamus and the Thigh for the centre of the zodiac, which although made during the Solar Cult, very late, depicts the "original Stellar Cult portrayal" very distinctly, i.e. "The Leg of Nut" the "Milch Cow of Heaven" and "Sustainer of the Pole" (see Fig. 17). Although it is here called, in the Solar Cult, the "Leg of Ptah," yet Ptah was never depicted or portrayed as a Cow, although he was as a Leg, or Sustainer of the Pole, in human form during the Solar Cult. The Thigh, Leg, and Hoof show it to be the Cow, and it was a type simply brought on from the Stellar to the Solar. In the Ritual, Chapter 98, is an address to "The Leg of the Northern Sky," and it is there said: "in that most conspicuous and inaccessible stream," which Renouf identifies as the Constellation with Cassiopœia, and that the "stream" is the Milky Way. Here is a proof of the identification that the Leg was originally portrayed in Sign Language as the "Leg of Nut," the Mother Goddess at the pole, who gave forth the milk of heaven depicted by the "Via Lacta" or Milky Way. The "Mesken" also being portrayed at the top of the Thigh, i.e. the birthplace.

When the goddess pours out a libation from her vase, or two divine personages from two vases, on the water-plant, or a shoot of palm, the signification is the same as when the wet nurse Sebek-Nit suckles Horus as a child, or Neith, the Crocodile, as a Calf.

According to the most primitive imagery in Egypt, the waters of the inundation issued from the Mother Earth, as the Water-Cow, the Waterer, in the primordial abyss or water source.

But when the Sky was looked to as a source of water, heaven was represented as the Milch Cow, or Nut, and the river flowing from its highest source was imaged by the Milky Way.

Nut, the Mother of the Gods.
Plate XV

[To face p. 120.

Drawn by K. Watkins.

| The Cow Sothis as the Great Mother of New-Birth in zootype form with Star between her horns. | Horus on his Pedestal of Papyrus as the Golden Eagle or Hawk. | The Bark of Orion—with Horus beckoning to his followers, with the Hare-headed Sceptre in his hand, and the Crown of the South on his head. |

In Records, Vol. IV, it states "that his Shau (a celestial body) may shine in the Stars of Orion on the bosom of Heaven."

PLATE XVI.

Thenceforth there were two Cows. The Cow of Earth was the Water-Cow, and the Milch Cow was the Cow of Heaven.

The Water-Cow of Earth was constellated in the Stars of the Great Bear, and the Milch Cow of Heaven in the constellation of the Haunch, or Meskhen, within the circle of the Little Bear. The leg of Nut is a figure of the Pole. In the Pyramid text it is called " the leg (Uarit) of the Akhimu-Saku, " the Stars that never set," the eternals, as a type of stability.

Nut was the Stellar form of this imagery.

Hathor was the Lunar form and

Isis was the Solar.

The Nile was figuratively represented as being replenished from the abyss of source configurated as the fish's-mouth ⬭ There was but one abyss, whether this was indicated by the fish's-mouth, or other images, such as the dugs of Apt, the female breast of Hapi-Mu, or the multi-mammæ of the suckler Menat.

At the time when the inundation had run dry in Egypt the February rains were recommencing in the equatorial regions. The Lakes began to fill, and the water of the Nile to rise and rush towards Egypt. The new flood only reached the delta just in time to save the country from drought and sterility.

" Krater " was the urn or water-pot of the inundation uranographically.

This in the South was now overflowing, the Southern Fish having emaned it from her mouth at the time that the tail of the Great Bear pointed South.

But when the tail of the Great Bear pointed North the urn would be empty and the Dragon of Drought would be in the ascendant.

We see from a Theban tomb the Great Mother, who in one form is a Crocodile, has just given birth to her child Horus, Har-Ur, as the young Crocodile poised on end in front of her. It is the picture of the young child who was brought forth annually from the water by the Mother, she who was constellated as the Female

Crocodile, or Hippopotamus, at the Northern plainsphere, as the Great Mother Apt.

In Fig. 16 the portrayal (Egyptian) of the Haunch or Meskhen part of the Great Mother, situated within the circle of the " Akhimu-Saku " or the Stars that never set, i.e. Ursa Minor, that being the birthplace in the

Drawn by K. Watkins.

CONSTELLATION OF THE HIPPOPOTAMUS AND THIGH FROM THE CENTRE OF THE ZODIAC AT DENDERAH, PORTRAYING THE LEG OF NUT AS THE SUSTAINER OF THE POLE.

In the Pyramid Text it is called the Urait Akhemu-Saku. The leg of the stars that never set; the eternal as a type of stability.

FIG. 17.

Northern Celestial Paradise, so we have the typology of the birthplace on Earth and the re-birthplace in Heaven.

I have given two depictions of the above, one found in Mexico and one from the Lower Amazon, on p. 323 in the " Origin and Evolution of the Human Race." All those pictures are a critical proof of the Stellar Cult of the Egyptians being widely spread and practised in these countries and carried there by exodus of the Stellar Cult people.

The constellation of the female Hippopotamus or Great Bear was also the mother of the time circle.

It was a clock on account of its wheeling round the pole once every 24 hours.

It was also a clock of the four quarters in the circle of the year, as witnessed by the saying of the Chinese:—

When the tail of the Great Bear points to the East, it is Spring.

When it points to the South, it is Summer.

When it points to the West, it is Autumn.

When it points to the North, it is Winter.

In Egypt when the Great Bear pointed to the South, or astronomically when the constellation had attained its southernmost elongation, it was the time of the inundation, the birthday of the year, also called the birthday of the world.

In the oldest table of the months found at Edfu, the goddess Tekhi is the opener of the year.

The word Tekhi signifies a supply of water or liquid, or to supply with drink, and the goddess Tekhi is the opener of the year with the inundation.

Now the birthplace of the inundation, when the Great Bear pointed to it in the southern quarter, was a point for ever fixed by these old Urshi, in the regions of the waters of the South.

The point did not retrocede.

Their time, therefore, was accurate, but when the place of birth as Lunar and Solar was shifted to the vernal equinox, the equinox receded and the birthplace went with it from zodiacal sign to zodiacal sign, and the time of the Moon and Sun parted company with the time of the Bears and the inundation for a cycle of 25,827 years.

The birthplace of Horus (of the waters) had been in the South at the season of the year when the tail of the Great Bear denoted the birthplace in that quarter of the

Heavens, and the Great Mother presided over the birth of the child, the Crocodile, or the Papyrus shoot. The Stellar Cult Egyptians commemorated the birthday of the world, that is of the age, the cycle, the beginning of time, when Horus rose up in the Papyrus from the waters—that was the birthday of Horus of the inundation.

But in the Solar Cult the birthplace was shifted, and the point was determined by the position of the vernal equinox as it travelled from sign to sign, from the Fishes to the Waterer, from the Bull to the Ram. But in each of the Cults it was the old genetrix who presided over

HORUS OF THE DOUBLE HORIZON.
FIG. 18.

the birth of Horus on this great birthday that was commemorated in Egypt as the birthday of creation. It was an unparalleled meeting-place.

Thus the Egyptian Sacred Year is that of the inundation and the Bear.

Its opening coincided roughly with the summer solstice (when the solstice had been recognized with the Sun in the Lion Sign in the Solar Cult).

The foundation of Ancestor worship is made apparent in the Book of the Dead, when the spirit of the dead asks that he may behold the form of his Father and Mother (Cl. 52–110); also in the "Records of the Past," Vol. IV, pp. 131, 134: "Thou wilt have power to resume the form which thou hadst upon Earth."

The Great Mother under the name of Apt may also

be identified in the Ritual, Chapter 143, as Apt of Nubia who had a shrine on the way North to Khept, or Khebt, or Egypt.

On a stele among the Egyptian monuments at Dorpat is written : " Make adoration to Apt of the dum-palms to the lady of two lands" ("Proc. Soc. Bib. Arch.," p. 152, 1894).

Here appears the old First Mother under the name of Apt as goddess of the Mamma-tree, that is the dum-palm which in Egypt is a native of the South. This proves that as the Mother of two lands she was primary goddess.

In "Arcana of Freemasonry" and "Signs and

PICTISH SYMBOLS AT VITRIFIED FORT, ANWORTH, SCOTLAND, SHOWING GREAT MOTHER GIVING BIRTH TO HER SON.

FIG. 19.

Symbols" I have reproduced many signs and symbols found throughout the world, depicting the two, three, and four elemental powers, called the Great Spirits, and children of the Mythical Great Mother, all in various forms with different attributes given to each. Through the kindness of Dr. Drummond, of Ceylon, I am able to give further proof of Stellar Cult in Asia. The symbols here marked 1, 2, 3, 4 in Plate XVII, were found in old temples in Asia.

No. 1 is an ideograph of Set and Horus, or the God of darkness and the God of Light, found on a temple wall in Japan.

No. 2 represents Set, Horus, and Shu, found in a temple in China.

No. 3 is an ideograph for Set and Horus, found in a temple in the Malay States.

No. 4 is one from an old temple in Ceylon, depicting the four primary powers or Spirits.

No. 5 is the so-called Swastika of which there are many forms. It represents the four divisions of heaven, also the four brothers of Horus.

These Symbols are interesting, proving how the divisions of heaven took place in the evolution of the Stellar Cult religion, and how these were carried throughout the world by the Stellar Cult people.

No. 2 was brought on in the Roman Catholic religion as a symbol representing the Trinity, which dates about A.D. 100–200. But it was an Egyptian Symbol for the same, 300,000 years at least, before that date. Variants

FIG. 20.

of the above are found depicted on the walls of old temples in many countries, as shown here, on Fig. 20.

I have entered fully into the Swastika, of which these are some of the primary forms, in " Arcana of Freemasonry " and " Signs and Symbols of Primordial Man," and it is not necessary to reproduce the same again in this work.

The three brothers with one female, as an Egyptian group, are representatives of the Great Mother and her first three sons, or elemental power, the powers represented by the imagery of the Water-Cow, the Crocodile and Lioness; the Mother being indicated in Sign Language by the pregnant womb.

The Japanese have the same group, consisting of three (out of seven or the eighth) Kami, with their sister Izanani. The three Kami called the " All-alone-born-Kami," our Stellar Trinity, were gods of the beginning, and are connected with the sister in the raising up of heaven (Satow: "Pure Shinto," p. 67. Chamberlain: "Kojiki," p. 19).

The Mexicans also had the same representation, and in one form depicted them as the three triangles here shown (Fig. 21c), also as Three Deer Heads (Fig. 22).

They also had the later imagery of Heaven in four

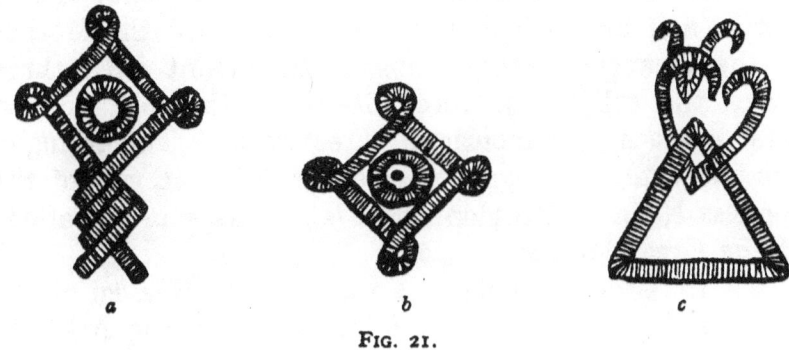

Fig. 21.

quarters, or a square, the ideograph of which is here given (Fig. 21b).

Fig. 21a was found on the north façade of the north wing of the ancient temple of "Can" or "Horus as the fish," a dedication to the seven brothers of Horus, as represented by the seven pole stars, called the

Three Deer Heads.
Fig. 22.

Fisher. Mexican depiction of Heaven as a Square with Paradise of Am-Khemen in the Centre or at the Pole.

This Symbol (Fig. 21a) represents the earth as four square. It is shaped as a square, divided into four parts marked with lines measured with cords, and suspended from the heavens by a cord to each of its four corners and its four sides.

When the Christian divinity of a triune nature is portrayed with a triangular aureole upon His head, that figure relegates the deity once more to the phenomena in which a god of the triangle had originated. The god of the triangle was of a threefold nature in the trinity of Set, Horus, and Shu, which three were one with the Mother in the Heaven of the triangle, the mount with three peaks, the ecliptic in three divisions, the year in the three seasons, the month in three weeks. The triangle, like the oval, is a figure of the female, as it was of the goddess Nana in Babylonia; it is an image of the abode of the Great Mother.

In the story of Gilgames we find the Heaven of the triangle depicted in the building of Erech the Ark-City on the summit of " the new Heaven that was divided into three parts "; " One measure for the circuit of the city, one measure for the boundary of the Temple of Nantur, the house of Ishtar; three measures together for the divisions of Erech " (Records, Vol. V, pp. 7, 148–9). This imagery was carried out of Egypt by the old Stellar Cult people into Babylonia.

Another depiction *was imaged* as two double triangles ⋈ ⋈ surrounded by four Urœi, i.e. the Khui Land of the Spirits; it was a very early portrayal at the time of the house of Horus, or Heaven, being symbolized by a Triangle. The triangle of the uranographic depiction of the Stellar Cult people △ is the equilateral triangle ▽ of Horus, or the Great God of the North, formed uranographically by Arcturus as the Apex, Spica and Denebola as the base. No. 2 is the triangle of Horus with apex downwards ▽ formed by the Pole Star Vega and Arcturus in the Constellation of Lyra. In No. 3 we have the two depictions: First, the Pole Star as the apex with a Cygni

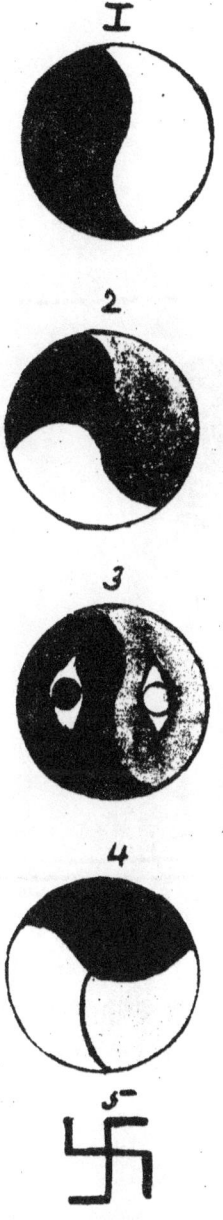

Symbols of the division of Heaven, representing Horus and Set and Horus, Set and Shu with Swastika of the four quarters.

Plate XVII.

Drawn by K. Watkins.

HĀPI MESTHA TUAMUTEF KABHESNUF

THE FOUR GREAT SPIRITS.

The four brothers of Horus in the Stellar Cult were added to the primary three to make the seven great spirits.

PLATE XVIII.

and Vega as the base; second, taking a Cygni as the apex, with B Cygnus and Vega as the base, we have the triangle of Horus in another form.

In the fourth portrayal we have the Stellar formation depicted as the Square, at present called the Great Square of Pegasus. (I am indebted to Mr. H. Richmond for these drawings, which are the present uranographic portrayals; these change in the course of the One Great Year, but at the end of a cycle of time they are as portrayed here.)

In the next phase it was represented as a Square or four divisions with four brothers to support the four corners or four parts. Thus we have the three Primary in the Triangle and now four added in the Square. These were the seven Great Spirits of Heaven and Earth as the primary portrayal of the Egyptians.

There are four Great Spirits at the four corners of the Mount of Heaven, i.e. at the four cardinal points, as supports, or protectors (Plate XVIII).

The first division into four quarters was symbolized by a man, and then by the crossing of two men, as is proved by the Symbols found depicted in the Tomb of Nagada (Fig. 59, " Arcana of Freemasonry "). This was the origin of the Swastika (a Sacred Symbol used through various Cults) and proves that this Sacred Symbol represents the Four Quarters. This is the reason why we find Four Cardinal Points in the Stellar as well as in the Solar, each Cult using the same Symbol.

The *seven* Khuti or elemental Great Spirits in the Stellar Cult had become in one phase the Lords of rule devoid of wrong, and living for eternity.

That was a Spirit perfected under the type of stars that never set (Rit., Ch. 72).

Polaris was chief of all the heavenly host, on account of being fixed in the centre, as a type of stability and uprightness. The characteristics and qualities assigned to the divinity were first seen in the steadfastness of the Pole.

The Stars in Ursa Minor were circumpolar.

These showed the seven in a group who never could be drowned by the deluge of darkness.

Not so the Stars of the Great Bear, the seven that were not Circumpolar Stars. Of these:

About 5,000 years before the present era there was but one, the Star Dubhe in Ursa Minor that was circumpolar or non-setting (Lockyer: "Dawn of Astronomy," p. 42).

Perhaps this will account for a statement made to an Englishman who met one of the old Priests of Mosel in Mesopotamia and who, in answer to some questions, told him that Satan or the Devil had been reigning for 5,000 years and would do so for another 5,000 years, but then would give place to Ira who was a good God (*Daily Mail*, July 1920). But this man was speaking in Uranographic Sign Language, which the Englishman could not understand and had probably never heard of.

The changing of the Pole Stars occurs about once every 3,690 years.

This is alluded to by Theopompus, who tells us that according to the Magi "one of the gods shall conquer, the other be conquered, alternately, for 3,000 years; for another 3,000 years they shall fight, war, and undo the works of the other, but in the end Hades will fail, and men will be happy, neither requiring food, nor constructing shelter, whilst the god who has contrived all this is quiet and resting himself for a time" (Plutarch: of "Isis and Osiris," Ch. 47). The conflict is identical with the battle of Set and Horus on the grand scale of the Great Year.

Three thousand in round numbers is a point in precession equivalent to a change from one Pole Star to another in the station of the Pole. Diodorus relates (1, 28, 29) the Egyptians claimed to have taught the science of Astronomy to the Babylonians, and declared that Belus and his subjects were a colony from Egypt. Belus (the first Bel) being identified with Bar, Set. This means that the colonizing of Babylonia from Egypt was during the reign of Set, or at least in the time of the primordial pole star, when the Pole Star was previously in the Lesser Bear or the male Hippopotamus.

The Book of Enoch says, previously to the Nouchian deluge, Noah saw that the earth became inclined and destruction approached. Then he lifted up his feet and went to the ends of the earth, to the dwelling of his great grandfather Enoch (Ch. 64). The " Ends of the Earth " was an expression for the two Poles, the dwelling of Enoch being equivalent to that of Set or El Shadda at the Southern Pole.

The most profoundly important of all deluges was that which took place at the subsidence and submergence of the Pole and the changing of the Pole Star, the Star that fell from Heaven, according to the Astronomical Cult.

When the deluge occurred at the Celestial Pole, the type of stability and fixed foothold on the land was whelmed beneath the firmamental waters, was lost or drowned and another took its place. It is related by the Miztec Indians that " in the day of obscurity and darkness the gods built a palace which was a masterpiece of skill, and made their abode upon the summit of a mountain. The rock was called ' the Place of Heaven.' It was the primary dwelling of the gods. The children of the gods planted a garden with fruit trees. But it is the old, universal tale : then came a deluge ; the happy garden was submerged and many sons and daughters of the gods were washed away " (Bancroft : " Native Races," Vol. III, p. 71).

After the Assyrian deluge, the tree was re-planted in the circle or enclosure, and to re-plant the tree was to re-establish the Pole in the new station ; the tree or wood that was to be eternal. Noah planted the tree which in his case was the vine. In the Book of Enoch it is said the portion of Noah (in time) has ascended up to God, and now " the angels shall labour at the trees " (or tree) and the " seed of life shall arise from it." This is a replanting of the tree as a Symbol of the Pole.

The typical seven were grouped in the Lesser Bear, as an object picture with something out of sight. Anup as Horus, or El-Elyon as God or the highest seated at the Pole, was thus imaged as the great Law-Giver, and added to the 7, made the 8th, 7 + 1.

In all the Stellar Cult the Pole Star is an emblem of stability, a seat, or throne, of the power which is the highest god, *pro tem.* as was Anup-Horus in Egypt.

Sydik in Phœnicia.

Anu of Babylonia.

Tai-yik in China.

Avathor or Zivo in Mesopotamia, etc., and others in different countries.

The Pole Star was a type of the eternal because apparently beyond the region of time and change.

The earliest law in heaven was given on the Mount of Glory because the Mount was an image of the Pole. It was administered by the Judge, first by Set in the South, secondly by Horus in the North, and the Jackal was the Zootype image used in each case, because the Jackal was a Zootype of the Judge.

It was not the Mount that was the divinity but the Power that dwelt upon it, as the deity called by the Japanese Ame-no-Foko-Tachi-Kam (The God Eternal Stand), i.e. the Egyptian Horus.

The power of stability fixed as the centre of the universe was the typical eternal.

The Jackal is also a type, not a divinity, and a type may be variously applied, as was the Jackal as Ap-Uat, the opener or guide of the way, the seer and crier in the dark. It was the dog of Set and of Sothis as well as the Anup of Horus, so Anup-Horus became the great Judge in Heaven and the seven Khuti are his ministers, his executioners upon the judgment day.

They are termed the seven "arms of the balance on the night when the eye is fixed," i.e. the Eye of the Judge who saw through the dark (Rit., Ch. 61).

The Eye of Heaven that judges the Wicked is the name of a Chinese Constellation; and the God Anup-Horus was the judge whose eye was the Pole Star in the North, originally Set or El-Shaddi in the South.

He was the seer in the dark, and the Jackal was His Zootype, which was followed later by the dog as a Symbol of Polaris.

Whatsoever the seven Khuti were, as individual stars, they were also, later in the Solar Cult, configurated as a group in Ursa Minor and called the followers of the coffin of Osiris, which was imaged in the Great Bear.

The forms and pictures figured in the planispheres are not merely mythical; they are also celestial illustrations for the eschatology of the Egyptian Ritual in the oldest religion in the world.

A temple at Denderah, built during the Solar Cult, has a circular zodiac depicted on its ceiling, where the

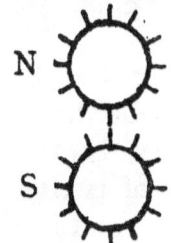

SYMBOLS OF THE DIVINE CIRCLES OF 12, IN THE STELLAR CULT, AND REPRESENTING TWO DIVISIONS OF HEAVEN, NORTH AND SOUTH.
FIG. 23.

constellation of the Jackal is located at the Pole, i.e. in Ursa Minor.

The seven stars in Ursa Minor make a very good Jackal with pendant tail as generally represented by the Egyptians (see Fig. 29).

The divine circle of twelve was first established in the Stellar Cult, and was given the Twelve Thrones or Houses, with separate and distinct banners for each, i.e. represented by different Zootypes. These are the twelve who had their thrones as rulers (æons), the twelve great Spirits, with Horus-Khuti, Lord of the Spirits in the Heaven of Eternity.

In the papyrus of Ani and of Nunefer we see depicted the Judges in the Maat as twelve in number, sitting on Twelve Thrones. The earthly representation was two circles, one North and one South, divided into twelve divisions each. This was pre-Solar, therefore **prezodiacal.**

The original characters were Stellar, and carried out of Egypt by the Stellar Cult people, afterwards represented in the Solar Cult as the Banners of the twelve tribes of Israel (originally Totemic).

The names of the Egyptian originals in the Solar Cult were:

1. Set.	2. Horus.	3. Shu.
4. Hapi.	5. Ap-Uat.	6. Kabhsenuf.
7. Amsta.	8. Anup.	9. Ptah.
10. Atum.	11. Sau.	12. Hu.

Horus was teacher of the Lesser Mysteries in His first advent, and teacher of the Greater Mysteries in His second advent. The four brothers of Horus were four out of this divine circle of twelve which was first established in the Stellar Cult, and in the Ritual, Chapter 30, they are referred to "as being on the side Lord of Horus," i.e. with him in his youth or earthly career. This refers to the resurrection (see "Origin and Evolution of the Human Race," pp. 278, 279).

CHAPTER VIII

STELLAR CULT

WE find that the gnosis of the birth of the babe, the adult man, and the Crucifixion and Resurrection first arose during the Stellar Cult. The tradition amongst these people was that "He came to this earth in the form of a Man, but was not a Man," and the same tradition exists still amongst some Nilotic Negro Tribes at the present time.

The various representations of the Egyptian Horus as the God of the Axe,[1] God of the Double Horizon, and so on, found in various parts of America, and notably his representation as the crucified victim [1] found at the ruins at Copan, Guatemala, Central America, show that the origin of all the religious cults found in America are traceable back to the Egyptians, and that various exodes from Egypt must have brought these Cults there.

To gain a true conception of "The Origins" we must follow the Symbolism of our ancient forefathers as they depicted their ideas and beliefs through the vast ages of time during the Stellar Cult, which lasted about 300,000 years.

In Egypt alone we cannot now obtain all the evidence. There are many in Asia, and some in South America, who cling to the old Stellar Cult doctrines and faith, and have never been destroyed but still exist, and from them, and from the pre-Dynastic remains and the Ritual, we can now reconstruct the past.

Other evidences of more recent finds are to be seen in the countries to which the Stellar Cult people migrated and where they formed great nations, all written in the

[1] For illustrations, see "The Arcana of Freemasonry."

old Sign Language, also proved by recent finds in South Africa.

As each Cult succeeded the previous one, the first object would be to destroy, as far as possible, all traces of the former, or at least all that could not be brought on or amalgamated into the new Cult. That has ever been the case with all religious Cults in the past history of the world; more especially was it so with the Solar Cult people and the Mahommedans.

The primeval home and original " Paradise on Earth " was situated around the Lake of Tanganyika, and not in Asia, as hitherto taught.

The word Tanganyika is African, and means " Tanga " the Thigh, and " nyika " the water, the whole signifies the Lake of the Thigh or Haunch. In Sign Language this denoted the birthplace which was imaged by the Hippopotamus, the Great Mother Sow, or Cow, of the water.

In the Stellar Cult the followers of Horus had brought this imagery on from the South, and now transferred it to the northern heavens, representing it uranographically by the Great Bear Constellation and called part of this Constellation the " Mesken," as the womb of life or birthplace at the summit of the pole, i.e. a re-birth in Heaven symbolically.[1]

In Egypt the north celestial pole was variously imaged as a mountain summit, an island in the deep, a mound of earth, a papyrus plant or lotus in the water of immensity, a tree, a pole or pillar or pyramid, and other types of the Apex of Heaven.

In Equatoria there was neither pole nor pole star fixed on high in the Celestial north.

On the other hand, there were two Pole Stars visible upon the two horizons—North and South—and these, according to imagery, were represented by two Jackals, two Lions, two Trees, two Pillars of the firmament or by the two Eyes of the two Watchers; these were " the pair of eyes " or Merti in their Astronomical Mythology. But the first representation were the two Pillars.

[1] " The Mesken " is really a separate constellation. See Fig. 16.

In the Ritual it (Tanganyika) is called the Lake of Equipoise, as well as the Lake of the Thigh and the primary earthly prototype.

Thus the old Her-Seshta, with the aid of their uranographs, registered the birthplace of Horus in the fields of the papyrus plant, the reed-bed in Uthlanga, where the black and white twins of darkness and light were born; the birthplace of the water flowing from its secret sources in the land of the Two Lakes (Victoria Nyanza and Tanganyika, called the Lake of Equipoise and the Lake of the Thigh). Recent discoveries prove that at one time the Lake of Tanganyika flowed north into the Nile and not west as now.

In Astronomy, Apta was the Mount of Earth as a figure of the Equator, whereas the summit of the Circumpolar Paradise was the Mount of Heaven as the figure of the Pole.

There were four different images of Paradise traceable in the Egyptian.

First was the primary "Paradise of Earth," the original Earthly Paradise of the Bible, situated in the papyrus field of reeds in the South, around Lake Tanganyika, and there imaged in the Southern Heavens.

The second was the Heavenly Paradise situated in the waters of space at the North, the Circumpolar Paradise of Am-Khemen, which was mythically upraised by Anhur —a form of Shu—and supported by the four pillars represented by the four brothers of Horus, who were the four divinized elemental Powers born of the Great Mother, and first imaged as Hapi, Tuamutf, Kabhsenuf and Amsta—later as Lion, Ox, Eagle, and Man, and in the Christian Doctrines by St. Matthew, St. Mark, St. Luke, and St. John.

This was the Paradise of the seven Stellar Gods with Horus as Chief, making eight.

The third was the mythical Paradise of Atum in the garden of Amenta—this may be figured as Egyptian.

The fourth phase was the final Paradise as taught in the eschatology and figured as the Mount of Glory, for the Spirits of the just made perfect, in the Heaven of Eternity, situated at the North (one hundred trillions of miles North surrounded by Ba metal, with one entrance only which is guarded by two Glorified Spirits and provisioned for Eternity).

The Stellar Cult Paradise was the first that was rendered uranographically, and was the final Paradise of all Cults.

The so-called " wisdom of the ancients " was Egyptian when the elemental powers were represented first as characters in mythology. It was Egyptian when the primeval mythology was rendered astronomically, and later in the phase of eschatology.

The Mysteries were a dramatic mode of communicating the secrets of primitive knowledge in Sign Language when this had been extended to the Astronomical Mythology, and the Egyptian Urshi or Astronomers were known by the title of " Mystery teachers of the heavens."

A later theology has wrought havoc with the beginnings previously evolved and naturally rendered, and we have consequently been egregiously misled and systematically duped by Semitic perversions.

In Babylonia the Great Mother as the Crocodile, type of water, has been confounded with the Apap reptile of evil and made to spawn the evil powers in the darkness of later ignorance. We can watch the change in a Babylonian version of the Mythos.

The seven nature forces here originated as seven evil powers; they were " rebellious spirits," and " workers of calamity " that were " born in the lower part of heaven," or the firmamental deep (" War of the Seven Evil Spirits ": Records, Vol. V, also Vol. IX, p. 143)..

They are called " the forces of the deep," for ever rising in rebellion. In truth, they are one with the Sebau of the Ritual, who were the progeny of Apap, which have been confounded with the " seven " elemental spirits who were not originally evil.

The beneficent great Mother Earth who had been imaged by the sloughing serpent as a type of renewal and rejuvenescence was transmogrified into the serpent of theology, the very devil in female guise, the author of evil that was ultimately represented as a woman, who became the mother of the human race, and who doomed her offspring to eternal torment ere she gave them birth in time. The Hebrews follow the Babylonians in confusing the Uræus—serpent of life with the serpent of death. The primal curse was brought into the world by Apap the reptile of drought, dearth and darkness, plague and disease; but the evil serpent began and ended in physical phenomena. Apap never was a spiritual type, and was never divinized, not even as a devil.

The beneficent serpent Rannut represents the mother of life, the giver of food or fruits of the earth or the tree. She is portrayed as the Mother both in the form of a Serpent, and also as the human Mother. But the good and evil have been badly mixed together in the Hebrew version of the Babylonian perversion of the Egyptian wisdom.

In the Great Year of precession there are seven stations of the celestial pole. The pole changes, and its position is approximately determined by another central Star about each 3,689 years.

Seven times in the Great Year the Pole Station was uranographically raised aloft as a landmark amid the firmamental waters in the shape of an island, or a mound, a tree, a pillar, a horn, or pyramid. Whichever the type, it was repeated seven times in the circuit of precession to form the compound and collective figure of the celestial heptonomis so that the heaven rested, or was raised, at last, upon the seven mountains, or seven mounds, seven isles, seven giants, seven caves, seven trees, seven pillars, or other seven figures of the all-sustaining poles. Seven golden circles emerged from out the watery vast, or wisdom reared the seven pillars of her house; the heavens were borne upon the backs of seven giants, or the eternal city was built upon the seven hills.

It would take one Great Year, 25,827 years, to build the heptonomis on the support of the seven Poles. These were added one by one, and figured collectively as seven sustaining powers of the heavens, such as seven hippopotami, seven crocodiles, seven bears, seven mountains,

Drawn by K. Watkins.
THE GODDESS SESHETA. THE STELLAR FOUNDRESS OF THE POLE.
She was the layer of the foundations, which are seven in number, as figured by her "Seven horns on a pole."
FIG. 24.

seven trees, or a tree with seven branches, a serpent with seven heads, seven pillars, seven giants, seven cyclops with polaris for a single eye, and lastly there were seven divinities called the "Lords of Eternity."

The seven periods in precession corresponded to seven stations of the pole. The foundress was imaged as Sesheta with seven horns (Fig. 24) in the human type.

How accurately these old Stellar Cult Urshi had worked out their Astronomical and Mathematical knowledge, and to what a high state they had attained (which in these two branches of science has never yet been equalled) is proved by the record they have left portrayed in stone, namely, " The Great Pyramid," the " Ritual of Ancient Egypt " written in stone.

In America, as I have shown in " The Origin and Evolution of the Human Race," we find remains of all the different Cults of the human race precisely similar to the Ancient Egyptians, and the evolution in the same order, the Pygmies pre-Totemic, Totemic, Non-Hero Cult, Hero Cult, Stellar, Lunar, and Solar Cults, with the Egyptian eschatology, all brought there by many waves of exodes from the old Mother Land. The earliest Stellar Cult people arrived there from Egypt via Asia. They crossed from the northern part of Asia to the West Coast of North America and travelled south and east, and finally extended from the Pacific to the Atlantic, and from north to south of the Continent of America. These were the Ancient Toltec Race. Those of the Cult of Set arrived first, followed by those of the Cult of Horus. The Solar Cult people came after and landed at Yucatan and went south.

The Great Pyramid of Cholula and all the Stellar Cult temples and buildings were erected by these old people, who originally came from Egypt and brought all the Egyptian wisdom with them. The starting point of their migration mythically is from " the mythical one tree hill of the Pole." In their picture writings both mount and tree are combined as one figure.

In the Boturini and Gamelli Careri copies the Mount of Earth is portrayed with the tree upon the summit.

The tree on the mount (a teacallis) is very rudely represented in the Aztec writings as the starting point of the migrations by water, from the mount in the beginnings. From this point, also, the seven Toltecs commenced their wanderings in a boat like the seven Hohgates, the seven Ali, the seven Kabri and other forms of the celestial heptanomis.

The organization of the Toltec and Aztec Priesthood was based on that of the Ancient Egyptians, i.e. they distinguished between high and subordinate priests.

The High Priest was called Uijo-tao, " Great Seer " amongst the Zapotecs and Quetzalcoatl amongst the Mexicans, in memory of the Priest God Toltan of the Toltecs, who was Horus as God of the Pole Stars North, or the Heaven of Am-Khemen.

They distinguished between Set and Horus (both Cults existing here) by the names Quetzalcoatl Talaloc Tlamacazpui and Quetzalcoatl Totec Tlamacacazqui. These were their two chief deities. Animals, birds, and prisoners of war were sacrificed. Many other names are found in America of Horus and Set, as, for example, Ometecutli and Omecuiatl, and others which I have given in this book. They expressed God as " God without end and without beginning. The uncreated Lord who has no beginning and no end. God who created all things and was himself uncreated." The names found here on stone and in the old ancient manuscripts which have been preserved are many for the same and one God, just as we find amongst the Ancient Egyptians; that is, different names for different attributes.

Coqui means Lord, Leader, King.

Tâo and Zoo are adjectives meaning great, and with the prefix Pitâs, Bitoo, the Great One.

Zoo also denotes strong, powerful.

Ni and pi are prefixes, the first, " he who is," and, second, " animate beings."

Cilla, morning: te-cilla in the morning.

Zee means bright, glorious, etc.

Ati-zee equals pure spirit, or glorious and pure bright ones.

This short note may enable my readers better to understand the names found and depicted in America, where the name and attribute are combined in one glyph, thus not only including the name of the god, but also the attributes attached to that name. The writings of the old Stellar Cult people here, as in all other places, were in glyphs only; whilst the Mayas and Incas, who were Solar Cult people, used the *Hieratic* writings *of the Egyptians slightly altered*, or partially glyphs.

In studying these ancient remains and manuscripts we must be particular to differentiate the Stellar from the Solar Cults; remains of both are found in some parts, but the Ancient Toltecs, Mexicans, and Zapotecs were Stellar Cult, whilst the Mayas and Incas were Solar. The old Stellar Cult Mother Ta-Urt, or Apt, was called Huichaana, i.e. creator, the maker of men and of fishes by water (as an element). Her first child's name here was Xolatl, and his twin brother Quetzalcoatl; these are Set and Horus of the Egyptians.

Tepeolotlec was another name for Set as the god of darkness and the underworld and the mountain wilderness (as known to the Mextecs and Zapotecs).

Pije-Tao and Pij-Zoo represents the Egyptian Shu as the breath of life, the great wind, the great strong living spirit of air.

Tlauizcalpan Tecutli called Pelle-Nij by the Zapotecs also Citlalpol, "The Great Morning Star," and Lord of Dawn was the Egyptian Horus. Another Zapotec name for him was Xipe, "the flayed one."

He was known to the Mexicans also under the name of Macuil-Xochitl as the deity of luck in gaming or as the representative of the Egyptian Horus of the Lyre. He has, as here represented, a dark brother called Ixtlilton, "the Little Black Face," which is Set. Pitao-Cozobi, "The god of Harvests," represents Horus as God of Corn or food. Pitao-Pezelao represents Set as God of the Underworld.

Cocijo represents Horus as god of rain or water of life amongst the Zapotecs.

Amongst the Zapotecs all the types found are typical of the old Stellar Cult, i.e. The Mother Goddess Ta-Urt or Apt (Tepeyollotl) with her three first-born, Set, Horus, and Shu, in various characters.

The Aztec Cycle of 52 years has a fine rendering of the serpent symbol in relation to the number 13.

(The Aztec time was one of 13 days = a week = 13 Signs and 28 weeks a year of 364 days, the same as 13 months of 28 days or 52 weeks of seven days—Phœnix period of 500 years being one week or seven days in one Great Year.)

The Serpent surrounds the circle of signs with its tail in its mouth, the total image of a cycle. At every 13 years there is a loop or kink made in its body, showing 13 years tied up according to the system of Quipu.

Five hundred years assigned to Enoch is one week in the Great Year, and 52 of these would make the one Great Year of the Aztecs.

(The primary time was taken from " the menstruating," 13 times a year, in periods of 28 days.)

In the Mexican tradition we have the Vulture as Polaris; in other words, 14,000 years ago Polaris was the star Vega in the Constellation known as Lyra, also 25,827 years before that, or the multiple of the same time-cycles previously.

Vega denotes the falling one, and as Vulture cadens it was " the falling Vulture " (the Arabic name signifies the falling Eagle An-naz-al-waki). This can be identified in the Ritual (Ch. 149, II aat, line 81) as the lake of the leg and a cootype with the tree of the lake on which the glorified spirits alight in the form of birds, and there is a chapter in the Ritual for assuming the form of a vulture and perching on the leg, a landing place equivalent to the Pole. " I am the divine Vulture, who is on the leg, or the Pole Star." Thus showing the Egyptian origin and " The Polaris " at the time of their exodus from Egypt.

CHAPTER IX

THE GREAT PYRAMID OF GHIZEH AND OTHER TEMPLES. THE GRANDEST AND GREATEST RELIGIOUS TEMPLE EVER BUILT

MUCH has been written on the Great Pyramid by various authors and scientific men.

It is the most perfect Temple that has ever been built, or ever will be built. It was built to teach the seven Astro Stellar Cult Mysteries in symbolism and applied Eschatologically—also to record and register time and measurement.

The name of the Great Pyramid was "Khuti," which denotes the seven Lights, or Glorious Ones; it also signifies as Heru-Khuti, the Light, a symbolic representation in stone of Horus the Light of the World and all his doctrines—the doctrines and divine message given to man at this early period to read and learn what he must do and what he has to pass through to attain triumph over darkness (ignorance), so that his Soul and Spirit, after this life, may find everlasting rest and happiness in the presence of the Divine God of Light, and obtain a full knowledge of all things.

This Pyramid was built by the old Stellar Cult people of Egypt, the followers of Horus called the Mesinu, who were the descendants of the earlier Mesenti, or followers of Horus Behutet. The proof of this is still extant.

It is stated on a parchment found in a brick wall in the foundations of Denderah at the time of King Pepi: "The Great Pyramid was built by the followers of Horus"; the Stellar Cult people were the followers of Horus in the same sense as the Christians are the followers of Christ.

It was built by the old Her-Seshta, or the wise men of Egypt, when they had worked out their Astro-Mythology and the seven Mysteries. The Architect who drew the plans was Nu-er-nub-Ari, " The Keeper of the Secrets." He was the Prince and High Priest of the Nome of " The Gazelle " of Egypt. The Great Pyramid is the Ritual of the seven Mysteries written in stone in " Sign Language," to be read accurately by anyone who can read and understand this Sign Language. " It is an Altar to the Lord in the midst of the land of Egypt."

The Arab traditions affirm that the Great Pyramid was a " star-temple " and a treasury of knowledge, built to preserve the records of all the profoundest sciences —the hidden wisdom and the means of keeping chronology from the beginning to the end of time. The Arabs were originally Stellar Cult people. The Ritual shows that a knowledge of the hidden facts of the Celestial Allegory concerning time was preserved in the Egyptian Cults for making the safe passage through all the trial scenes in death or in the Judgment Hall, the earliest guides in the darkness of night having survived as types of guidance through the dark of death (and the salvation of the deceased depended on his having the facts treasured up in memory).

Herodotus states " that ' Khufu ' (who has been erroneously stated to be the builder by many) lived and reigned in Egypt *during the Solar Cult*, but that *Khufu was not the builder*."

Manetho, who was a High Priest of Egypt and " kept the Records of Egypt," states that the Great Pyramid was built at " the end of the reign of ' The Gods and Heroes,' and that it was built by the followers of Horus." Moreover, he states that the Gods and Heroes were not Human, nor ever had been Human.

Here is a clear statement that the Stellar Cult people were the builders of the Great Pyramid, because these followed and were evolved from the Hero Cult people, who were Nilotic Negroes, and who came up from the South and settled in Egypt which they divided into seven Nomes, with a Totem for each; the Masai and Allied tribes are living types of these. According to Manetho this Hero Cult, or the Cult of the Gods and Heroes, lasted 16,000 years before the Stellar Cult was evolved.

The Great Pyramid was built in the "Nome of the Haunch"; this was not done without reason.

"The Haunch" is the birthplace, and in the Stellar Cult the earthly nome was portrayed astronomically by a group of stars, situated in the Northern Heavens called in the Egyptian "the Meskhen," or the birthplace in the Celestial Heavens. The whole Astronomical depiction is Symbolical: First of "the birth of time," as no time was kept or known before the Great Pyramid was built, except night and day, seed-time and harvest, the wet season and the dry. By observing the revolution of the Stars of the Great Bear, Ursa Major (representing by imagery the great Mother Apt who was the divinized form of the old Earth Mother Ta-Urt), revolving around the Pole Stars of the Little Bear—Ursa Minor, and the precession, or rather recession of the Ursa Minor through ages of time, the birth of human time was first recorded and written down for the knowledge of future generations of humanity—the Lunar or Solar time had not yet been established. Also the Meskhen was the Astronomical birthplace of the seven elemental Spirits who were divinized as gods with Horus as Chief.

As a proof to what a high state these old Urshi had attained in Astronomy and Mathematics, as well as Religious Conceptions, I will quote measurements and observations made recently by Colonel A. O. Green, formerly commanding the Royal Engineers in Egypt, which agree accurately with what I published in 1910 in "Signs and Symbols of Primordial Man."

Colonel Green states: "They had an absolute knowledge of the figure of the earth—an oblate spheroid flattened at the Poles, and that the Pyramid stands at the centre of the land surface of the Globe. It is truly oriented to the four cardinal points of the Heavens with

an accuracy unattainable in any building in these day
and the great circle, coinciding with the centre line
the ascending and descending passages and Grand Galle
must, at the date of the building, have coincided with tl
Stellar conjunction which can only recur once evei
25,827 years" (i.e. beginning of their One Great Yea
or One Great Day), or the number of years taken for tl
recession of the seven Pole Stars to perform their Cycl
and also the number of years in the precession of tl
Equinoxes. "The Old Stellar Cult Urshi used f
carrying out all measurements, both of space and tim
two units. The Pyramid inch, which is equal to 1·0
British inches and the old sacred Cubit of 25 Pyram
inches or 25·025 British inches, which is the same leng
as the cubit employed in the construction of the Tabernac
and the Ark of the Covenant (the Jews, who were
Solar Cult people, took this with them when they le
Egypt) and is exactly one twenty millionth of the Earth
Polar Axis of rotation."

The following facts Colonel Green also confirmed:
"The length of one side of Pyramid $\frac{9,131,055}{25} = 365\cdot24$
the exact number of days and fractions in tl
year.

"The two diagonals of the base added together are with
a fraction of the number of years in the recession of tl
seven Pole Stars, or the precession of the Equinox
25,826·5 years"—which is One Great Year or One Gre
Day of their Ritual.

"The height of the Pyramid multiplied by 1
(1,000 millions) equals the distance of the Sun or 91,837,3
miles, which is apparently the mean of all the measuremen
that Astronomers have arrived at after numerous expec
tions to observe the transit of Venus, and is probab
the true distance. The estimated weight of the Pyram
is just one billionth the estimated weight of the Earl
roughly 6,000,000 tons." Colonel Green gives "the tir
of building from these observations as 2170 B.C."

But he must go back many thousand years befc

this; as I read the evidence, it was built during the Astronomical, or Stellar Cult.

The Solar Cult lasted about 100,000 years and the Lunar before this for about 50,000 years.

The Stellar Cult was anterior to these, and lasted at least 300,000 years; how much longer it is impossible to say, but from remains found of the Stellar Cult people in Pliocene Strata formations they were in existence at least 600,000 years ago.

If we take the length of the Great Year as 25,827 and divide the total into seven equal parts this gives 3,689 years as the time for the pole star to rest in each of the seven signs, which was recorded by successive Priests as they watched through the great tube, year after year.

The last " great deluge of all " is the subject of the story told to Solon by the priests of Sais. Of this, and the conflagration that was caused by the fall of Phacthon, they sagely said: " This takes the form of a myth, *but in reality it signifies a declination of the bodies moving round the earth in the heavens.*" The astronomers knew that the deluge was mythical, and the myth was astronomical.

Plato's account of what the priests of Egypt said to Solon will approximately give the *date of the last " great deluge of all "* as having occurred about 9,000 years before that time—i.e. about 9600 B.C. or approximately *eleven thousand six hundred years ago.* That date was given by the Egyptian priests with particular precision. They said that the city of Sais had been founded 8,000 years before the time when Solon was in Egypt. After carefully examining their sacred registers, they told him that the city of Sais was 8,000 years old, and that it was founded 1,000 years after the cataclysm called " the great deluge of all." That is when Polaris was in Herakles or Man, or the *last of the seven pole stars submerged* to recommence another Great Year.

In 11600 B.C. the Pole was represented by the

last of the seven Pole Stars in the Constellation of the Man.

Thus the myth of the destruction of the human race was founded upon the astronomical base. All the previous deluges were the destruction of the totemic tortoises, jackals, vultures, swans and apes, crocodiles and hippopotami, that is when one or other of the pole stars representing one of these zootypes submerged and gave place to the next in precession; but the seventh and last represented "the Man," so all these men were mythically destroyed when the submergence of this Pole Star took place: to recommence again another Great Year.

The human birthplace was localized according to the different stations of the pole, which were seven in number. There were seven countries, seven nomes, or seven cities determined by the Pole Stars. Each race claims a particular place for a starting point in the migration from the mount, or the tree, or some other type, which enables one to trace back the time they left the old land of Kam. The seven Pole Stars themselves did not form one Constellation. In whatever part of the world we discover the tradition of the seven founders, and seven stations of the pole, it involves at least one bygone "Great Year" in the circle of precession. The Pole Star being a star that did not set in the course of the Great Year there would be seven of these which never set, and they became in one phase the lords of eternity, the seven watchers, the seven glorious ones called the Khuti, the seven judges, the seven lights on one stand (the pole), or the candlestick with seven branches, and various other types; thus the seven servants (seshu) Khuti, Uræus-gods, saluting apes or angels, spirits, or lamps of fire, are depicted round the throne of God according to the mystery of the seven stars in Revelation, *but it was not until the time of the Solar Cult (at the time of Ptah) that the seventh Pole Star was imaged as "the Man" in Polaris.*

Earth had been imagined as a pregnant hippopotamus, or sow, or as the suckler, or as the goose which laid eggs for food, and in other forms, but not until the image of man had been adopted as a type of divinity, in place of the totemic zootype, could men have traced their descent from man in the mythology. This occurred during the Solar Cult when the hippopotamus of Set, the crocodile of Sebek, the lion of Shu, the ibis of Taht, the beetle of Ptah were followed by the human likeness that was perfected and divinized in Atum, or the original Adam, and the birthland of man on high was then figured astronomically as the island, or nome of earth, which was a station of the Pole in the Constellation of Herakles, or the Man. When this—the seventh—sank down in space to give place to another Pole Star it was the great deluge which caused the destruction *of mankind*. Thus instead of the races that were imaged by pre-human and totemic types it was now " the men " who were drowned in the last great deluge of all, when the Pole Star in the Man or Herakles went under. It is stated in the Chimalpopoca MS. that the Creator produced his works in successive epochs, man being made from the dust of the earth on the *seventh day*. Here again man is created, or comes into existence, in the last of the seven periods, whatsoever the length of time or significance assigned to the cycle, which is one day in the book of Genesis, and 3,689 years in the astronomical mythology. In all the versions of the seven creations that of man was last. And this was so in the Egyptian when the island of man as the last of the celestial seven stations was formulated in the heptanomis at this point of a new creation at the time of Atum.

During the whole of the Stellar and Lunar Cults there was no *Herakles the Man imaged, or depicted*—only zootype forms. Thus *the last of the seven Pole Stars in precession forming the last Great Year lost its place as Polaris* 11,600 *years ago*, and it will be about 14,227 years more before it resumes its place in precession as Polaris. There are records extant left by the Stellar Cult people of *ten great years; no record of time could be made until the great Pyramid was built* and the Priests had carefully recorded the time accurately in the precession of the seven Pole Stars—by observation year after year, as seen and noted through the great tube which was built to observe and record the time. It would have been impossible to obtain accuracy otherwise.

Therefore it must have been built at least 269,870 years ago. This may be difficult for some people to believe but " Records of the Past " prove it.

It would take one Great Year, 25,827 years, for these old Urshi observers and recorders to build the heptanomis on the support of the seven poles, islands, or mountains. These were observed through the great tube in precession; they were added one by one and figured collectively as seven sustaining powers of the heavens, such as seven Hippopotami, seven Crocodiles, seven Bears, seven Mountains, seven Poles, seven trees or a tree with seven branches, a serpent with seven heads, seven giants, seven cyclops with Polaris for a single eye, and lastly they were seven divinities called the Lords of Eternity. Thus the seven periods in precession correspond to seven stations of the Pole.

The seven isles of the blessed were also known as seven forms of the oasis. The Lords of Thinis and Abydos bore the title of Masters of the Oasis (Brugsch). Thus the ruler of the Pole Star would be lord on an oasis, or later paradise. The Altar Mound was also an image of the pole. Periodically the Mexicans sacrificed seven batches of children on seven hills which served for altars. The Hebrews offered seven bulls and seven rams on seven altars. The Assyrian Lu-Masi were represented by seven rams of sacrifice. Blood was sprinkled seven times as an oblation. And the reason of this was because the powers or gods propitiated thus were seven in number, and these powers of seven were represented as rulers, watchers, giants, masters, ali, elohim, or lords of eternity, in the seven pole stars of the great period in precession. The seven stones set up at Stonehenge and elsewhere represent the seven stations of the pole stars in the circuit of precession or the circle of Sidi. Under one title Stonehenge was called the circle of Sidi, or the circle of seven, or the Akhemu-Seku, or never-setting Stars.

The whole of the building of the Great Pyramid is the Ritual portrayed in Stone of the seven Primal Mysteries, the depiction of the Astronomical Stellar Cult Religion, not the later Lunar Cult, or still later Solar Cult (which consisted of twelve Mysteries and the passage of Amenta).

The Great Pyramid is a Sign or Symbol of seven, comprising as it does the square and triangle in one figure; also it is an artificial figure of the Mount as the means of the ascent to Heaven. The Sun, Moon, and seven Stars are frequently grouped together on the Assyrian monuments; and among the Chinese we have the same grouping called the Sun, Moon, and seven Stars, the nine Lights of Heaven.

The same grouping is observed in the nine Pyramids of the Mexicans—one for the Sun, one for the Moon, and seven small ones for the seven Stars.

These were all carried out from Egypt by the exodus of the Stellar Cult people. The three Pyramids of Gizah answer to those of the Sun, Moon, and seven Stars found elsewhere in whatever part of the world—the origin being Egyptian. In the Great Pyramid is portrayed the whole architecture of the heavens, courses, and times of the heavenly bodies, the seasons of the year, days of the year and Great Year, time, measurements, and distance of the Sun and Moon and their time of revolution, as well as the Pole Stars. Ancient writers state that the whole of the Great Pyramid, on its outer surface, was at one time covered with Hieroglyphics.

The explanation of all was known only to the old Her-Seshta or Mystery Teachers, of whom there were seven classes.

Brugsch gives these classes as follows:

" The first represented the divine Child from Heaven.

" The second, the Mystery teachers of the Heavens.

" The third, the Mystery teachers of the Lands Celestial and Terrestrial.

" The fourth, the Mystery teachers of the Deep.

"The fifth, the Mystery teachers of the Sacred Word.

"The sixth, the Mystery teachers of the Sacred Language.

"The seventh the Mystery teachers of 'The Final' as the Son of God the Father in Heaven, the fulfiller of both the first and the second advent, the first in the life on earth, the second in Spirit; the first as utterer of 'parables' or 'sayings,' the second as expounder of the Greater Mysteries."

By knowing the secrets we can discover how the planets move in their different orbits and mathematically demonstrate their various revolutions and predict hundreds of years in advance when and where a given or certain Star shall, or will, appear in the heavens.

The different degrees or Mysteries were performed to teach the Postulate by representation dramatically what the manes had to pass through, or undergo, from the time of the death of the body (Earthly) to the final resurrection of the Soul, or Spirit, and its glorification in the Eternal Paradise which is situated in the North, or Heaven of Am-Khemen.

The Solar Cult twelve Mysteries were somewhat differently dramatized.

Thus it was taught as if in the passage of death the Egyptian could look upon a future figured in the Starry Heavens. As it was with Horus so it would be with him. The way had been mapped out, the guiding stars were visible. His bier of new-birth would be seen in the Mesken of the Mother. He rose again in Spirit as the babe of Sothis. "He joined the Company of Holy Sahus" in Orion with the pilot Horus at the look-out of the bark. He saw the golden islands, a heaven of perpetual peace to which the Pole was the eternal morning post. In a sense there was no Horus or Orion in the heavens either figured or named until the type was constellated by the Urshi. But the group of Stars was always there. The final ceremony was on the summit of the Pyramid representing Paradise.

The sides or walls of the Great Pyramid are not

carried up to the apex, or point to which all ascending lines converge, as in other Pyramids, the Great Pyramid being truncated at the summit, forming a platform about twenty feet square.

Most modern writers have assumed it to have been originally carried up to a point and shaped like the others, and to have attributed the present condition to destroyers, but this was not so, as can be proved. First to destroy " the apex " over thirty feet high, a solid mass of masonry firmly cemented, at an elevation of upwards four hundred feet from the ground, would require a most accomplished engineer, to say the least. Then we have evidence ex-

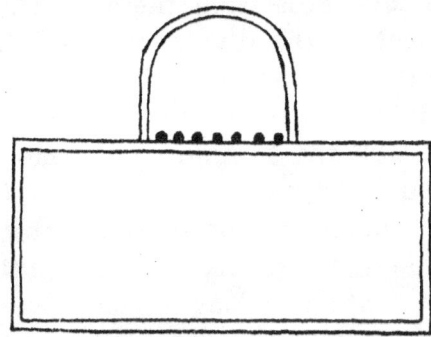

SUMMIT OF GREAT PYRAMID, CENTRAL TRANSVERSE SECTION, WHICH IS THE HIEROGLYPHIC FOR "HETEP."

FIG. 25.

tending back for two thousand years that it was the same as now, and that is before the destruction of the casing stones had begun. Abdallatif, a historian of the twelfth century, tells us that at the top the Great Pyramid ended in a platform. Diodorus, fifty years B.C., describes the building as "tapering up as far as the summit, which makes each of its six sides cubits."

Perhaps the best proof is the objective evidence one sees in the summit of the building itself, which shows no destruction of any kind, but a flat surface with some huge blocks arranged in the figure of an Amsu Cross. On the highest of these stones are sculptured a number of holes forming a square figure consisting of seven ranks of seven holes, each forming a "Hetep" or "sacrifical table of offerings."

The word Hetep (Hieroglyphic ⌂) has various meanings of rest, peace, plenty, of all which were to be realized in Hetep. The earliest spelling of the word was Hept—which also signifies the number seven, representing Paradise in seven divisions, a figure of the Celestial heptanomis, the work in seven parts being computed as a work of seven days; and Hept the place of rest was transformed into the seventh day of rest by the Hebrew legends.

Hetep was the garden of the blessed dead. The great object is "to take possession there." The manes says: "I take my rest in the divine domain. There is given to me the plenty which belongeth to the 'Kau' and the Glorified." Hetep therefore here is a symbolic figure of the Paradise on the summit of the Mount, which has been completed in seven "great days." One ideograph of Hetep, the mount of glory, is a table heaped with provisions as the sign of plenty. In the mythical rendering it is a table-mountain. That is the table of the Stellar God Horus which was the table-land upon the summit of Mount Hetep, the mount of peace and plenty when the followers of Horus, as the spirits of the just, made perfect, gathered together at the table of the Lord for their eternal feast. Thus as the Egyptian Ritual shows "the Lord's Table" was an institution in the Stellar Cult Mysteries before the Solar and Christian Cults. The Mount or Altar in Hetep which is imaged as a pile of plenty, a table of offerings, a mountainous heap of food, is the prototype of those artificial mountains exhibited in the Christian Cult, as for example, in Naples at the public festivals. Each one brought an offering of food and drink to the feast, and Mount Hetep is an altar, heaped with oblations and offerings for a feast that was to last for ever. The Hebrew Paradise upon the summit of the Mount in the promised land was a later copy of this, having been brought on from the Solar Cult and from which the Hebrews took it. "In this mountain " says the Prophet Isaiah " shall the Lord of Hosts make unto the people a feast of fat things, a feast of wine on the lees, of fat things full of marrow : of wines on the lees well refined " (Isa. xxv. 6).

Papias, that ignoramus of a primitive Christian, also recounts how " the elders who saw John, the disciple of the Lord, related that they had heard from him how the Lord used to teach in regard to these times, and say : The days will come in which vines shall grow each having ten thousand branches, and in each branch ten thousand twigs and in each true twig ten thousand shoots, and in each of the shoots ten thousand clusters, and on every one of the clusters ten thousand grapes, and every grape when pressed will give five and twenty metretes of wine. And when any one of the saints shall lay hold of a cluster another shall cry out ' I am a better cluster ; take me : bless the Lord through me.' In like manner (the Lord declared) a grain of wheat would produce ten thousand ears, and that every ear should have ten thousand grains, and every grain would yield ten pounds (quinque bilibres) of clear, pure, fine flour, and that all the other fruit-bearing trees, and seeds and grass, would produce in similar proportions (*secundum congruentiam iis consequentem*)." And these things are borne witness to in writing by Papias, the hearer of John, and a companion of Polycarp, in his fourth book, for there were five books compiled (*syntetagmena*) by him. And he says in addition : " Now these things are credible to believers " (Irenæus B. 5 Ch. 33. 3-4 Ante-Nicene Library).

Thus we see the old Stellar Cult Priests were the first to symbolize and image Hetep the Paradise of Peace and Plenty which was afterwards depicted by the Solar Cult, in Amenta, and perverted by the Christians who had lost the gnosis and symbolism, but which still remains extant upon the summit of the mount of the greatest Temple that has ever been built. Here it was that the highest and last of the ceremonies were completed and explained to the initiate who had passed through all the others. It represented the Paradise of Spirits perfected. So from the base of the building where we find the form Neter-Kar, or Hades, or the underworld, which the manes has to pass through, his whole journey is symbolized by the passages to the very summit of the mount Hetep, or Paradise. He was thus taught the Eschatology symbolically.

Part of these mysteries have been carried down through the ages of time by those who survived, by the fraternity now known by the name of Freemasons, in a purer form than any other religious Cult, although innovations have crept in and much of the gnosis has been lost—a false Hebrew rendering or explanation being substituted for the original.

Here, then, we find the first " Lord's Table " which has been brought on, and is the original of the Christian doctrines. The Amsu Cross representing symbolically the risen Horus, or the risen Christ of the Christians, and being situated at the top of the building signifies his ascent into Paradise. The " Hetep " here, with the Cross of Amsu, represents Paradise itself at the summit of the Mount, or at the Pole, formed by the seven isles of the blessed, where the risen Saviour, Horus, had gone to await all those who would become " glorified ones." By his assistance they obtained that perfection which can be consummated only when, having passed through the tomb, they rose in spirit form to join, and are united with Him for ever in a glorious and happy eternity.

The Great Pyramid depicts symbolically the passage of the Manes from the death on earth of his material body and how he passes through Hades, or the underworld, and what he has to undergo before his final ascent to Paradise. The base of the building represents Hades, the summit Hetep or Paradise, and the passages and chambers the journey on the final and eternal voyage. When you have learned the hidden mysteries contained in the symbolism of the Great Pyramid you must arrive at the conclusion that it is the word of God written in stone, the most wonderful of all buildings as well as the oldest in the world. It contains the message and gnosis for poor humans for their salvation and way to eternal life. Herein is the origin of all our present mysteries which were later carried on in the Lunar and Solar Cults, and were perverted and the gnosis lost. But it still remains there to-day as from the first, the greatest Bible written in stone.

It is a Christian belief that life and immortality were brought to light, and death, the last enemy, was destroyed by a personal Jesus only 1,923 years ago, whereas the same revelation had been accredited to Horus, the anointed, at least 300,000 years before. Horus, as the impersonal and ideal revealer, was the Messiah in the astronomical mythology and the Son of God in the eschatology. The doctrine of immortality is so ancient in Egypt that the " Book of vivifying the Soul for Ever " was not only extant in the time of the First Dynasty but was then so old that the true tradition of interpretation was at that time already lost.

The Egyptian Horus, as revealer of immortality, was the ideal figure of a fact known to the ancient spiritualists that the soul of man, or the Manes, persisted beyond death and the dissolution of the present body. The drama of the mysteries was their *modus operandi* for teaching the fact, with Horus as typical manifestor. In this character he was set forth as the first fruits of them that slept, the only one that came forth from the mummy on earth, as the " Sahu " mummy; the only one, however, as a type, that prefigured potential continuity for all—the doctrine being founded on the ghost as the phenomenal apparition of an eternal reality. The Egyptians, who were the authors of the mysteries and mythical representation, did not pervert the meaning by an ignorant literalization of mythical matters, and had no fall of man to encounter in the Christian sense. Consequently they had no need of a Redeemer from the effects of that which had never occurred. They did not rejoice over the death of their suffering Saviour, because his agony and shame and bloody sweat were falsely supposed to rescue them from the consequence of broken laws; on the contrary, they taught that everyone created his own " Karma " here, and that the past deeds made the future fate. Horus did such or such things for the glory of his father, but not to save the souls of men from having to do them. There was no vicarious salvation or imputed righteousness. Horus was the justifier of the righteous, not of the wicked. He did not come to save sinners from taking the trouble to save themselves. He was an exemplar, a model of the divine worship, but his followers must conform to his example and do in life as he had done before they could claim any fellowship with him in death. " Except ye do these things yourselves, there is no passage, no opening of the gate to the land of life everlasting." The door of stone was closed to them and could only be opened to the true and faithful followers of Horus, the Divine Spirit.

We find depicted on stones in many countries where the Stellar Cult people migrated, remains of this old Astronomical religion which proves their perfect knowledge of the revolutions of the Starry Vast and the Laws governing these revolutions, all of which they imaged iconographically or by Signs and Symbols; and where they have not built Pyramids they have recorded the truth in the so-called " Cups and Rings " and " curious carvings " found on boulders, cist-covers, on living rock, and on standing stones throughout these islands, Europe, Asia, Africa, and other parts of the world, which hitherto have been deemed to involve insoluble problems and have been to all our learned professors an outstanding puzzle in pre-historic research. But they are easily read, and the secrets are unfolded in the Sign Language of the Astronomical, or Stellar Cult Religion of the Ancient Egyptians.

If you examine these markings carefully you will find that they can be divided into two classes:

First, the Cup and Rings in most cases are arranged in a very accurate and precise mathematical and geometrical manner (I am not including those made by the

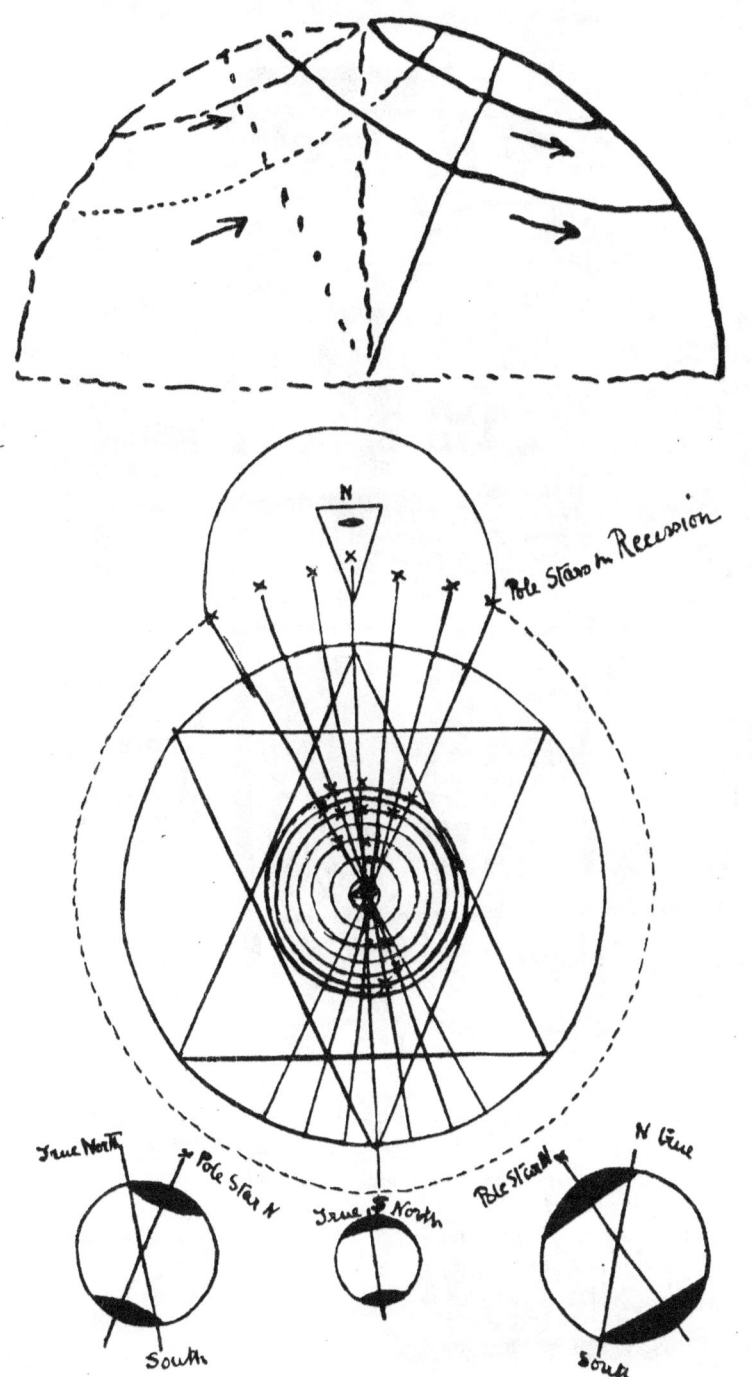

SHOWING HOW THE AXES AND THE SHIFTING OF THE POLE, ALSO RECESSION OF THE SEVEN POLES STARS, WERE MEASURED BY THE ANCIENT WISE MEN.

PLATE XIX.

From left to right:
1. Horus as *Temu*.
2. Horus as the fire god.
3. Horus of the two lands, earthly and spiritual, and god of Light.

1. Horus in Spirit.
2. Horus in Boat of Souls.
3. Horus as Hawk bruising the Serpent's head, i.e. Apap the dragon of drought.

1. Horus as god of the Axe or cleaver of the way.
2. Horus as Amsu.
3. Horus as the Great God in His House or Heaven of the four quarters.

Drawn by K. Watkins.

THE THIRTY-SIXTH PAGE OF THE DRESDEN MAYA CODEX.

PLATE XX.

Solar Cult people, but the oldest Cups and Rings and picture Stars. The Solar Cult people were just as accurate in their portrayal, but those have to be considered in a line from West to East—the Stellar must be viewed from South to North).

The common centre of lines drawn through these will point to the Pole Star North at the time they were made, not always the Magnetic North.

To obtain a right conception and knowledge of how accurately these old Urshi had worked the whole plans out you must take two triangles with the apex of one pointing North and the apex of the other South; the bases must overlap so that an accurate six-pointed Star is formed from a central eye or dot. Draw seven circles within this hexagon; now draw a straight line from the South to the North and let it continue a short distance over the apex of the triangle—to the centre of a triangle formed by continuing the lines at the apex of the triangle a short distance: the centre then represents the Pole Star North which existed when the plans were first depicted on these Pillars or Stones. The centre line will pass through those Cups and Rings that lie on that line at the time (Plate XIX). *This line corresponds to the Great Tube of the Pyramid*, and as the revolution or precession of the seven Pole Stars takes place, and at the change of each Pole Star, another line drawn from it straight through the circle will give the distance from one to the other, and a Cup or Ring or Star will mark the circle when the line cuts it, each one in precession.

Sometimes cups are found along the lines of the circle from one Ring or Star to another, which gives the time in years it has taken for its movement through space—and generally near at hand there is another stone or monolith with the Sign and Symbol depicting how far they had advanced in their division of Heaven—3, 4, 6, 8, 10, or 12. (I have given in "Signs and Symbols of Primordial Man," pp. 170-5, excellent photographs of all these, taken from Ireland.)

The three lower figures of the above will prove and

demonstrate: That the radius of the circle being 23° 28', the diameter will be nearly 47°, and thus far apart with the pivots of revolution of different periods, i.e. a Star which has been the Pole Star at one period will be 47° from the Pole at another time.

In Ritual (Ch. VII) Horus says: "I am the one who presides over the Pole of Heaven and the powers of all the gods are my powers. I am He whose names are hidden and whose abodes are mysterious for all eternity."

These were worked out on the same plan as that used for their Great Pyramid. They thus demonstrated that the Polar Axis not only rotated, but also that the Pole itself performed a circle in the Heavens around the true North or Magnetic Pole.

When we find other groupings such as three, four, or five of these Cups, Rings, or Stars detached from the main group of seven, it shows the position of the corresponding Pole Stars at the time of observation as regards the "Mesken," which stars are within the Circumpolar enclosure.

The ground plan was necessarily always laid out with the greatest care wherever these Megalithic monuments are found. The number of sections and zones is important to note as well as the number of Cups and Rings or Stars, as it is necessary to know how many divisions of Heaven had been attained. The position of the first Pole Star was of necessity accurately marked to enable the observers to reckon the time of the deluge of each of the six, and the great deluge of all—that of the seventh, as the stars changed and fell from their position in the cycle of precession. The knowledge of this was obtained by watching and marking their position through ages of time, by these old Urshi, on these boulders and temple pillars, part of which are extant at the present day.

They had divided the whole of the Heavens into North and South, and symbolized them by two Circles with twelve Pillars to represent the twelve divisions of each— and the twelve rulers or Councillors. Many hieroglyphics, pure Egyptian ideographs, etc., are also found amongst these old ruins, photographs, and decipherments, which I have given in "Signs and Symbols of Primordial Man."

These are some of the secrets of the Astronomical Cult they have left written in Stone which have been preserved to the present, waiting for the future generation to read, and showing how long and patiently these old Urshi had continued to watch from night to night and generation to generation through long ages of time, and how they migrated over the earth carrying all these old almost religious doctrines with them, forming great nations in every country.

The effect of precession is extremely striking on the Constellations near the Pole, and the changes in the apparent position of the stars would become obvious there comparatively soon.

The Ritual not only proves these Ancient Stellar Cult people to have been acquainted with the processional movements of the Pole Stars; it also gives an account of the actual changing of a Pole Star. There was a change in the position of the Maat, or Judgment Hall, which in the Stellar Cult was at the station of the Pole, and was shifted with the shifting Pole. On account of this change, Taht comes as a messenger in the Stellar-Lunar Mythos to make fast that which was afloat upon the Urnas water: to *adjust the reckoning* and to "*restore the Eye*" (Rit., Ch. 114) by making it "firm and permanent" (Ch. 116) once more for keeping time and period correctly on the scale of the Great Year. The backward motion of precession is described: "I have rescued the Atu fish from its backward course. I have done what thou hast prescribed for him" (Rit., Ch. 113).

"He has allowed for this retrograde motion in precession, and has made the eye firm, and fixed once more by means of his reckonings a guide to posterity." Also these old astronomers had measured the earth and knew it to be a globe rotating in space.

On the sarcophagus of Seti in the Sloan Museum, the Ark of Nnu may be seen. Lefebure, in his translation, says:

"The Boat is supported by Nnu, whose bust and arms only are to be seen."

The arms issue from the water and bear up the god. The entire scenes are surrounded by the waves of Nnu, which shows that these Ancient Egyptians looked upon the earth as a spherical body floating through the air.

The uranographic picture was their mode of expression. In the Ritual we find that amongst the words that are said on the day of burial to bring about "the resurrection and the glory" the deceased asks "that he may see the ship of the holy Sahus traversing the sky," that is the ark of souls represented in the Constellation of Orion. He also pleads: "Let the divine vessel, Neshemet, advance to meet me." The name of the bark is "Collector of Souls" (Rit., Ch. 58).

Safe in the ark, he crosses the waters in which the helpless souls are wrecked.

In the chapter in which the ship is sailed in the nether-world, the speaker not only sails across the waters of Nnu, for he says: "I come from the Lake of Fire and Flame, from the Field of Flame" and "he stands erect and safe" in the bark which the god is piloting on the summit of the Mount, or final resting place of the Ark (Rit., Ch. 98, Renf.), which the deceased had safely reached through fire and flood—otherwise he had arrived in Paradise after being baptised by water and fire.

The Temples of Jerusalem.

The first Temple of Jerusalem was supposed to have been built by King Solomon, and the traditions regarding it have been always of great interest to Biblical Scholars: but search history as we may for the original documents we cannot find them.

The only historical documents we have state that after the Shepherd Kings, the Hyksos, had reigned at Memphis and Lower Egypt for some years; they were driven out to the East and there founded, or built, Jerusalem 2554 B.C. in the reign of Tuthmoses.

Now these were Stellar Cult people, and if this be true

the first Temple formed or built at Jerusalem must have been that of these people, i.e. Stellar Cult. The Hebrews at first could not properly be said to have a Temple, yet they did not scruple sometimes to use the word Temple for the Tabernacle, as on the contrary they sometimes make use of " The Tabernacle of the Lord " to express " The Temple " supposed to have been built by Solomon.

The word Temple, the House of God, the place of the Most High, the Sanctuary—the Temple of the Lord, etc., are terms often synonymous in the Hebrew Text, though strictly speaking they signify very different things. The " Sanctuary " was but one part of the " Tabernacle," or Temple, and the word " Temple " does not agree with " Tabernacle " or " Tabernacle " with " Temple."

The word " Tabernacle " in Hebrew is " Obel," which word properly signifies a " tent," and the Patriarchs of old lived in " Tents " or " Tabernacles," as did Moses and his followers, and we know that all the old Stellar Cult people took their " Tents " and " Tabernacles " with them when an exodus left Egypt until they settled and formed a city, and then built their " Temples."

The authors of the Talmud and other Rabbins have never proved, nor will ever be able to prove, their suppositions, either from " Scripture " or from any authors who had ever seen " The Temple of Solomon," or had consulted those who had been supposed to have seen it. For neither the Talmudists nor Rabbins are either of antiquity or authority sufficient to convince anyone when the question is about a matter of fact, of which they could not be witnesses, neither themselves nor those whose testimony they allege, i.e. their fathers or grandfathers.

Let us set forth all the evidence we can find *that is historical*, that is extant, as proof as far as can be discovered by their most ancient documents.

The Talmud or Thalmud contains the body of the doctrine of the religion and of the morality of the Jews. They have two works that bear that name.

The first is called the Talmud of Jerusalem, and the other the Talmud of Babylon.

The first, they say, was compiled by the Rabbi Johanan, whom they state *finished it 250 years after the ruin of the Temple*, for the use of the Jews dwelling in Judea.

It is composed of two parts—the Mishna and the Gemara.

The Mishna is the work of Rabbi Judah, who compiled it about 120 years after the *destruction of the Temple by the Romans*.

About 100 years after Rabbi Johanan composed the Gemara, and these two works together make up the body of the Talmud of Jerusalem.

The Talmud of Babylon was composed by a Rabbi who was a schoolmaster, who lived at Babylon about 100 years after the Rabbi Johanan. It was not, however, finished by him, but by his disciples, according to Serrarius, Bartolocci, Trigland, and several others; also see the "Continuation of Josephus's History of the Jews," t.6.1.9. C.3.4. Edit. of Paris.

The Mishna is written in Hebrew in a very close and obscure style, and the Gemara is written in a style composed of Hebrew, Chaldee, and several terms of other languages.

The Talmud of Jerusalem and the Mishna after the Chaldee Paraphrases of Onkelos and Jonathan, are the most ancient books of doctrine the Jews have, except some Rabbinical comments or copies of sacred writings obtained from an outside origin common to themselves and the Babylonians (Lenormant).

The Jews rather make use of the Talmud of Babylon than that of Jerusalem, because it is clearer and more extensive. It abounds with a multitude of fables and myths, in many cases metaphrastically rendered, of which, however, they must entertain no doubt except they would pass for heretics. They believe the traditions contained in this book are derived from God Himself, that Moses revealed them to Aaron, to his sons, and to the Elders of Israel: that these communicated them to the Prophets and that the Prophets transmitted them to the members of the great Synagogue, who passed them from hand to hand till they came to the doctors who reduced them to the form of the Mishna and the Gemara.

Thus we see that the most celebrated Rabbins whose writings we have, did not live sooner than a few centuries before A.D. They were little conversant in the study of antiquity, and *they have no ancient documents or monuments, except the sacred writings copied from some foreign original* and that of Josephus, which can give them any true information about their supposed " first Temple of Solomon."

If the Rabbins had been satisfied with describing the Temple of Herod, which was demolished by the Romans, one might endeavour to reconcile them with Josephus, or if they have some private writings more ancient and exact than Josephus why have these not been produced ?

After collecting all the evidence extant, the *history of the Temples* is as follows :

In the year 967 B.C. Shisback, King of Egypt, having declared war against the King of Judah, took Jerusalem and sacked it. In 852 B.C. the Temple which was there was rebuilt.

In 736 B.C. Ahaz, King of Judah, having called to his assistance Tiglath-Pilnefer, King of Assyria, against the kings of Israel and Damascus who were at war with him, robbed the Temple and set up the old Stellar Cult religion which had the primary Stellar Cult Temple. Hezekiah, the son and successor of Ahaz, restored the Temple again and built the Solar Cult Temple after repairing the former Temple, but in the fourteenth year of his reign Sennacherib, King of Assyria, coming with an army into the land of Judah, Hezekiah was forced to take all the riches of the Temple and even the plates of gold that *he himself had put upon the gates of the Temple*, as tribute to the King of Assyria.

No doubt when Sennacherib had returned to his own country, Hezekiah restored the treasures of the Temple.

Manasseh, son and successor of Hezekiah, abolished the

Solar Cult and set up the old Stellar Cult, but was taken prisoner by the King of Babylon.

After his return from captivity he restored the Solar Cult.

In 584 B.C. Nebuchadnezzar took the City of Jerusalem and entirely destroyed the Temple, which remained buried in its ruins for fifty-two years, until Cyrus gave permission to the Jews to return to Jerusalem and to rebuild their Temple.

In the following year they laid the foundation of their new Temple; they had hardly been at work upon it one year when Cyrus, or his officers, being gained over by the enemies of the Jews, forbid them to go on with the work. After the death of Cyrus and Cambyses they were again forbidden by the Magian who reigned over Cambyses and whom the " Scripture " calls by the name of Artaxerxes. Under Darius, son of Hystaspes, the prohibition was removed, and the Temple was finished by Zerubbabel and dedicated four years after. Three hundred and fifty years later, by the order of Antiochus Epiphanes, the old Stellar Cult was set up and the Solar forbidden. This continued for three years; then Judas Maccabeus restored the Solar Cult once more.

One hundred years later, Herod the Great undertook to rebuild the whole Temple of Jerusalem anew in the eighteenth year of his reign. Josephus assures us that he finished it in nine and a half years, but they still continued to make additions until the beginning of the " Jewish War."

It might interest some to have the description of the Temple built by Herod, according to Josephus, who himself says he had seen it. This is the description that Josephus has left us.

" The Temple properly so called was 60 cubits high and as many broad, but there were two sides of front, like two arms and shoulderings, which advanced 20 cubits on each side: which gave in the whole front 100 cubits wide, as well as in height. The stones made use of in the building were white and hard—25 cubits long, 8 in height, and 12 in width. The front of this magnificent building resembled that of a royal palace. The two extremes of each face were lower than the middle, which middle was so extended that those which were over against the Temple, or that approached towards it at a distance, might see it though they were many furlongs from it. The gates were almost of the same height as the Temple and on the top of the gate were veils, or tapestry of several colours embellished with purple flowers. On the two sides of the doorway were two pillars, the cornices of which were adorned with branches of golden vine which hung down with their grapes and clusters, and were so well imitated that art did not at all yield to nature. Herod made very large and high galleries about the Temple, which were suitable to the magnificence of the rest of the building and exceeded in beauty and sumptuousness all of the kind that had been seen before.

" The Temple was built upon a very irregular mountain and at first there was hardly plain enough on the top of it for the site of the Temple and Altar. The rest of it was steep and sloping—so they had to build a wall and fill up space surrounding the whole mountain with a treble wall. In some places these walls were 300 cubits high and the stones used in this work some 40 cubits long, these were fastened together by iron and lead cramps. The platform on which the Temple was built was 120 paces square (a furlong).

" The entrance into the first enclosure, which was a square of a furlong on every side, was by a gate on the Eastern side, one on the South side and one on the North side, but there were four towards the West side, one of which went to the palace, another to the city and the two others into the fields. This enclosure was secured without by a very high and solid wall: and within, all round about it on the four sides, were stately porticos or galleries, sustained by columns that were so thick that hardly three men could grip them with their arms, for each of them was of the thickness of 27 feet. The number of these columns was 162. They supported a roof of cedar very well worked, and made three galleries of which the middlemost was the highest and the widest, having the width of 45 feet and the height of 100. Those on the two sides were 30 feet wide and 50 feet high. The court or area before these galleries was paved with marble of several colours, and at a little distance from the galleries was a second enclosure, formed by a handsome balustrade of stones with pillars at equal distance on which were inscriptions in Greek and Latin to give warning to strangers, and such as were unclean, not to proceed farther on pain of death.

"This enclosure had but one entrance to the East, but towards the North and South it had three at equal distances. The third enclosure, which included the Temple and the Altar of Burnt Sacrifices, was surrounded by a wall of 40 cubits high. It was square as well as the former, and the height of the wall did not appear so much without as it really was, because it was lost behind the steps by which it was surrounded and partially covered. First there were fourteen steps, upon which there was a terrace of about 10 cubits wide which went all round the enclosure. From thence there was another ascent of five steps to come to the platform of the gate, so that the wall was about 25 cubits within. The entrance into this portico was by a gate towards the East, by four towards the South, and as many towards the North. There was no gate on the West sides, but a great wall ranged all along from north to south. At the entrance of each gate within were large rooms in form of pavilions, of 30 cubits square and 40 high, each sustained by a pillar of 12 cubits or 18 feet in circumference.

"Within these enclosures were also double-covered galleries with two rows of pillars, to the East, to the North, and to the South, but there were none to the West.

"The women had a gate to themselves on the East side, and one to the South and the North, by which they passed to the place appointed for them, which was distant to that of the men.

"The Altar of Burnt Sacrifices was 15 cubits high, and 40 cubits wide every way. They went up to it by a slope without steps towards the South. At the 4 corners were so many eminences like horns, and it was built of rough stones, on which no iron was used, or tool of any metal.

"The front of the Temple, which was 100 cubits high and as many wide, was adorned with many rich spoils, which the Jews had dedicated to God as the monuments of their victories.

"The porch of the Temple was 90 cubits high and 100 in length from north to south. The door was 70 cubits high and 25 wide.

"I do not mention the Sanctum or the Sanctuary, nor the apartments that ranged along the two sides of the Temple, because these had nothing singular or different from what has been seen before.

"Within this enclosure was a wall of one cubit high, which surrounded the Temple and the Altar of Burnt Sacrifices, and which parted the priests from the rest of the Israelites. This place was not to be entered by the laity: they came as far as the wall to offer their sacrifices and offerings, but they went no farther."

As regards Vallalpandus' work, all one can say is that he might have a profound knowledge of Greek and Roman architecture, and was too much prejudiced in favour of the supposed model given to David: and thinking he could not make it too splendid, too grand, or too magnificent, therefore exhausted all the force of his imagination and genius to describe a Temple which should be the most perfect pile of buildings that was possible. But he has introduced many embellishments which are not mentioned in the Hebrew text but which ought to have been, according to the rules of architecture, of which it is supposed Solomon could not be ignorant. He has multiplied the courts and the porticos; instead of three he has described eleven in his plans. That is to say the Court of the Gentiles, or the outer Court, the Great Court, or the Court of the Israelites, and besides these nine other Courts, all surrounded with porticos, and rows of pillars. The multitude of Courts he has evidently founded upon Ezek. xlii. 3, 6, when the prophet says that the angels showed him a portico joining to a treble portico in the outward Court of the Temple. " Ubi erat porticus juncta porticui triplici."

We know that throughout Asia Minor—from Persia to Egypt, there were many small nations and tribes who still practised and professed the old Stellar Cult religion to quite a late period; in fact one tribe does to this very day. The old religion of the patriarchs was Stellar Cult. They worshipped God under the name of Baal, or El-Shaddi, sacrificed in high places, adored in groves, planted oaks, intermarried with their immediate relations, all of which was forbidden by Moses, who substituted the Solar Cult. We see also by the names mentioned of many temples in the Hebrew text that the Stellar Cult was widely believed in throughout the country, for example, the Temple of Dagon at Gaza, another at Ashdod. The Temple of Baal, the Temple of Nisroch, the Temple of Rimmon, the Temples of Chemosh and Moloch, the Temple of Nannoea, the Temple of Babylon and many others mentioned in the Hebrew text. Remains of many still exist, which proves that the first temple built at Jerusalem must have been that of the Stellar Cult people. Therefore it is not to be thought impossible that the " Temple of Jerusalem " on several occasions " changed hands " as the Stellar and Solar Cult people were always fighting for the supremacy. One may ask how long, or at what period was the old Stellar Cult overthrown and the Solar first erected ?

There is no date in history, only tradition, and this gives no account of the original Stellar Cult occupation, which we know did exist first. Excavations have disclosed that there was a period anterior to the Hebrews, and there are no authentic writings, nor does Josephus give us any information about the true form of the supposed " Solomon's Temple " at Jerusalem, but we have the description of that of Herod.

CHAPTER X

DIFFERENT PHASES OF THE STELLAR CULT

It is now necessary to take into consideration the different phases of religious beliefs, and the imagery of the various portrayals which were brought in evolution, in order to depict all the attributes which hitherto the Ancient Egyptian Stellar Cult people had associated with the great God Horus during the long period of 300,000 years, which was about the time that it lasted in Egypt.

Many different phases of this old Cult were carried out of Egypt by the numerous exodes who left their old Motherland and formed great nations in other parts of the world, some of which exist at the present time, while many small tribes are scattered over Asia and South America. No doubt much of the "true originals" became lost, and some innovations would be substituted in after years by the descendants of the original exodus. This we know is what did take place, more especially where the Lunar and Solar Cults followed the Stellar. Then again much of the Symbolism of the Stellar was carried into the Lunar and later into the Solar, and some even merged into the Christian Cult. The different phases or imagery by Zootype, or other Signs or Symbols, have been by many classed as different Cults, but that is inaccurate. They were all part of the Stellar Cult, depicting the many attributes which were gradually formulated and associated with Horus. These Signs and Symbols are found in every country where the old Stellar Cult people settled, and the portrayals on their Temple walls were all *Iconographic*, which make them *absolutely and critically distinct from the Solar*. We have seen that one of the earliest names given to Horus was "The Great Chief of the Axe," or "The Great Blacksmith" or "Chief of the Hammer," or "Great God of the Axe," and symbolized by an Axe, or Double Axe, or Hammer, as "The Cleaver of the Way" and "The God of the Double Horizon," or "Double Force." That was at first North and South. He had come up from the South and "cleaved the way" to the North. Later, when the Eastern Horizon and Western Horizon were added to the North and South by Shu, and his House "was established" in the North, he became "Cleaver of the Way" from the Western to the Eastern Horizon as "Horus of the Double Horizons," and this latter portrayal was carried on into the Lunar and later Solar phases. The original, however, was from South to North. It represented the formation of the bridge from death to everlasting life in the Eschatology. The first "Temple of the Axe" was built at Edfu, where Horus was also named "The Lord of the Forge City." The Temple at Edfu was oriented North from a point within the Little Bear Constellation, as proved by an inscription found there as follows: "I cast my face towards the course of the rising constellations, I let my glance enter the constellation of the Great Bear (the part of my time stands in the place of his house clock) I established the four corners of my Temple." This translation is by Brugsch. Dunicher reads it, "representing the division of time at his measuring instrument."

But instead of the constellation of the *Great Bear*, read it, "his eye was fixed upon the *Meskhet*" (or Mesken), which many translators supposed was the Great Bear. But the "Thigh" and "Bear" were two different constellations. The measurers of time were "the tail of the Great Bear," and the Great Year was measured by the procession of "the seven pole stars of the Lesser Bear." But for the orientation of the corners of the Temple the centre of the circle of the Great Bear must have been taken, and that point of observation was the "Mesket," or "Mesken," or "Haunch," which is a constellation *within the circle* of the Little Bear. Indeed, we have a later confirmation that this was so. When the Temple of Hathor was rebuilt at Denderah, the King tells us that "he oriented the corners and established the Temple *as it took place before*, whilst looking to the sky and directing his gaze to *the Ak* of the thigh constellation." Here the "Ak" denotes a central point, the Axis or middle of a starry group, which was the Mesken constellation as seen from a Theban Tomb. *The "Ak"* the *centre of "the haunch,"* or *"the birthplace,"* or *"chamber of birth of the cow above,"* which was copied in the Temple below, as a type of "birth on earth and rebirth in Heaven," and, as we see here, it was carried on from the old Stellar into the Lunar Cult. The Ritual positively identifies the Pole with the Leg by calling it *the leg of the seven non-setting stars*. The Hindu have the same portrayal under the name of Dhruva. All the Stellar Cult Temples were oriented thus, and many, if not all, the Lunar.

I reproduce (Plate XX) from the thirty-sixth page of the Dresden Maya Codex other portrayals of Horus. Reading from the upper figure and from left to right:

1. Horus as Temu, i.e. the Great Serpent of Good in Zootype form during the Stellar Cult.
2. Horus as Fire-God or the Red-God.
3. Horus as God of Light and God of the two lands—i.e. Earthly and Spiritual.

The second row from left to right are:
1. Horus in Spirit or Spiritual form.
2. Horus in the Boat of Souls on his way to the Celestial Northern Paradise.
3. Horus as Hawk bruising the Serpent's Head—the Great Evil Serpent, the Dragon of Drought of Egypt—i.e. Apap.

The third row from left to right are:
1. Horus as God of the Axe—the Cleaver of the Way.[1]

---

[1] The portrayal of Horus as 'God of the Axe," under different names, found in almost every country in the world, proves how widespread this old Cult was. In "Signs and Symbols," in "Arcana" and in "The

2. Horus as Amsu.

3. Horus as the Great God in His House or Heaven of the four quarters.

I reproduce, Fig. 26, two other types found in the Mediterranean Basin: (*a*) The Double Axe between the Horizons; and (*b*) Horus as the "Natzar" coming up from between the two Horizons; (*c*) the other, two trees, one at each Horizon, represents the Dual Mother with Horus as the Natzar.

It is a representative portrayal symbolical of Horus

 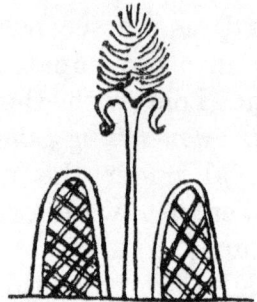 

| *a* | *b* | *c* |
| THE DOUBLE AXE BETWEEN THE TWO HORIZONS. | HORUS AS THE NATZAR BETWEEN THE HORIZON EAST. | THE DUAL MOTHER WITH HORUS OF THE DOUBLE HORIZON AS THE NATZAR. |

FIG. 26.

Behutet; also another with Horus as the Natzar between the Horizon East.

I here reproduce photographs of:

1. An Indian Temple in Simla (Plate XXI).
2. The Door of the Temple (Plate XXII).

Origin and Evolution of the Human Race," I have given numerous photographs found engraved on stones and Temples, which are still extant, and have shown that all these represent Horus of the Double Horizon of the Egyptian Cult. On page 201 of "Arcana of Freemasonry" I have produced Tepoxtecatl, God of the Axe of the Mexicans. On page 221, Con Tiesi Uracocha, God of the Axe, from Tinogasta. On page 223, The Toltec God of the Axe, from Tepozteco. This is probably one of the first ever fashioned in America, because "Tollan," another name for Horus, was brought there by the *Toltacs*, the first exodus of the Stellar Cult people to arrive in America from Egypt via Asia. On pages 198 and 199 I have given two forms of God of the Axe, namely, Ramman, God of the Axe of the Chaldeans and God of the Axe of the Susians, as well as many other forms.

PHOTOGRAPH OF TEMPLE IN INDIA.

PLATE XXI.

[*To face p* 176.

Door of the Temple.
Plate XXII.

3. The Indian portrayal of Horus as Saviour of the World by food and water (Plate XXIII).

(For all these I am much indebted to Mr. G. Reeves-Brown of Combermere House, Simla, India. The photograph was taken by W. I. Eades.)

On the door of the Temple is the portrayal of the Egyptian Horus as God of the Axe, Cleaver of the way of the Double Horizon or the Dual Power, i.e. Atum-Iu, almost identical in form as Ramman, God of the Axe of the Chaldean.[1] He is seen coming up from the underworld with one foot on the Mount of the Eastern Horizon.

In his left hand he carries a fan, the same portrayal is depicted in the design from Chama.[2] Also in the hand of Con-Tesi Uracochia, God of the Axe, from Tinogasta, denoting a new birth, or soul, or new life—Spiritual.

He is looking towards the Hammer (Horus as the Great Blacksmith). In his right hand he holds a sword sheathed, equivalent to the Axe. It is sheathed signifying that as "Cleaver of the Way" he has made the passage, has cut his way through the underworld from the Horizon West to the Horizon East; the work is finished, he is now emerging and His foot is on the Mount of the Eastern Horizon. Supporting Him on each side are his four brothers or the Spirits of the four corners with whom his fold was founded (Rit., Ch. 91).

Plate XXIII is an Indian portrayal of the Egyptian Horus as the Saviour of the World by "food and water." In his right hand he holds aloft a "bread-fruit" as an offering, equivalent to the God and Saviour as giver of life and food. In his left hand he holds the "Lotus," which is symbolical of Horus as a Saviour by water as well as by food. On his forehead is the Egyptian ideograph for His name "\|/"

He wears the Conical Hat, noticed in other Gods of the Axe, originally worn by the Ancient Egyptian Priests, a symbol typical of the Mount of Heaven, a

---

[1] Illustrated in "Arcana of Freemasonry."
[2] "Signs and Symbols of Primordial Man," p. 92.

Symbolic Pole. The "ridges" in the Hat denotes "the mode of ascent" or "type of ascent."

At Philæ, the God "Corn Spirit" is represented with stalks and ears of corn springing from its mummy—"near running water" (Plate XXIV). It is Horus represented as a bringer forth of food in the shape of Corn, a "type of the eternal manifested by renewal of food." We see by two figures discovered by Professor Marshall H. Saville at Mitta[1] how the same type was carried across to America as the Giver of Food and the Light of the World.

The Symbolism of "God of the Axe," i.e. God of the Dual Power, was carried from the Stellar into the Lunar, thence into the Solar and finally into the Christian doctrines.

At Memphis one of the names of Ptah was Great God of the Axe.

Plate XXV is a Chaldean depiction of "Horus of the Egyptians" as the "God Corn Spirit" offering food and water with the goddess Mother Nit or Neith in front. The 8-rayed Star on her bracelet identifies Him as Horus, God of the Pole, as the 8th. Nit carries the ideographic Symbol (bow and arrows) as well as a depiction of the Pole Star (8-rayed) in her right hand. In his right hand he holds the "corn spathe," in his left a "vessel of water."

CULT OF "ĀTEN" OR "DISK-WORSHIP."

One of the earliest Stellar Cult portrayals for Horus of the Double Horizon was what has been commonly called "The Cult of Āten," or "Disk-Worship." Several of our ablest Egyptologists have mistaken this so-called "Disk" for the Sun, because the Cult was revived in the Lunar and later in the Solar Mythos. Dr. Wallis Budge ("The Gods of the Egyptians," Vol. II, p. 68) states that the origin of this god (Āten) is wholly obscure, and nearly all that is known about him under the Middle Empire is that he was some small provincial form of

[1] "Signs and Symbols of Primordial Man," Fig. 36, p. 92.

HORUS OF EGYPT AS SAVIOUR BY FOOD AND WATER. (*Indian representation*).

PLATE XXIII.

HORUS AS NAPRIT.

As represented in the tomb of Seti as a man wearing two full ears of wheat or barley on his head; he is mentioned in the Hymn to the Nile. Naprit or Napit was his duplicate, her head-dress is a sheaf of corn.

The word "Naprit" means *grain*, the grain of wheat.

PLATE XXIV.

[*To face p.* 178.

Drawn by K. Watkins.

HORUS AS BRINGER OF FOOD AND WATER. (*Chaldean Depiction.*)

He is holding a spathe of corn in his right hand, and a can of water in his left. In front is " The Pole Star Goddess," Neith, with the symbolic bow and arrow.

PLATE XXV.

[*To face p. 179.*

the Sun-god, which was worshipped in one of the towns in the neighbourhood of Heliopolis. No doubt Dr. Budge has stated this because the name in the Solar Cult was written 𓇋𓏏𓈖 ☉; that is, with the Symbol of Ra ☉ as determinative, and drawn his conclusions also partly from the Hymns to Aten, as found in the Theban Recension of the Book of the Dead, which is based upon the Heliopolitan, where we find Aten mentioned by the deceased thus: "Thou O Ra shinest from the horizon of heaven, and Aten is adored when he rested (or settled) upon his mountain (i.e. the Horizon) to give life to the two lands."

Hunefer says to Ra: "Hail, Aten, thou lord of beams of light (when) thou shinest, all faces (i.e. everyone) lives." Nekht says to Ra: "O thou beautiful being, thou dost renew thyself and make thyself young again under the form of Aten. I have come before thee that I may be with thee to behold thy Aten daily. O thou who art in thine Egg, who shinest from thy Aten," etc.

These passages show that Aten was brought on into the Solar Cult at the time when the hymns, from which the above is taken, were composed.

But the "Disk" was not the Sun originally; it was an emblem of the circle made by Aten in his passage as God of the two Horizons. Aten was a very early name of Horus as god of the dual Horizons. The word Aten 𓇋𓏏𓈖 is derived from 𓇋𓏏, an ancient name for the child. Horus-Behutet is the earliest form of Aten, and is symbolically portrayed as god of " The Hut," or " Winged Disk." The Hut being a dual emblem of the divine infant and the Mother as bearer of the child. In the early Stellar Cult she is represented as the Vulture who carries him (Aten) over the intervening void of darkness (where the great Apap lay in wait to devour him) from the horizon west to the horizon east. The Vulture's Wings are an emblem of the Motherhood, and the Hut was a dual emblem of the divine infant and the mother as bearer of the child. The Cult of Áten, therefore, was a compound type of godhood in which the mother is dual with the son, who was her child on one horizon and her bull or fecundator on the other. The *glory of Áten* as the *power that is doubled on the horizon of the Resurrection was the object of regard in this religion*, not the " disk." Áten was the most ancient form of Har-Makhu god of the Double Horizon in the Solar Cult as symbolized by the Sphinx.

The recent discoveries by the late Lord Carnarvon and

CHALDEAN " WINGED DISKS "
FIG. 27.

Mr. Carter of the tomb of Tut-ank-Áten or Tut-ank-Amen make the origin of the Cult interesting. It is well known that Amen-hetep III and IV re-introduced the Áten worship for a time over a limited area of Egypt, but it had no chance of a general revival. The circle and Vulture's wings, or the " Winged Disk," found over the door of a temple at Ocosingo, near Palanque, and those found in Assyria and Japan, examples of which I have given in my books, prove how widely this phase of the old Stellar Cult had spread, i.e. the Cult of Aten, the primary portrayal of Horus of the Double Horizon.

That it was first evolved in the Stellar Cult is amply proved by the Book of the Dead of Nesi-Khonsu. It was brought on, or revived, in the Lunar, and, as we see above, from the Theban Recension and from the tomb of Tut-ank-Aten into the later Solar Cult. Many of the old forms had been revived in the later Solar Cult; for example, when the Hyksos conquered the Egyptians at Memphis they destroyed all the Solar Cult of Ptah and re-introduced the Stellar Cult. The Hyksos took this latter Cult with them when they were driven out of Egypt and founded Jerusalem. The first temples there were Stellar, and not Solar. Indeed, there was much overlapping of the various Cults of Egypt—some were revived after a long period of obscurity. At the time of the Osirian Cult (which was the latest phase of the Solar) the old and the new were practised in Egypt at the same time, which has caused Egyptologists to vary in their opinions as to the origin of these different Cults, and has taken the writer many years of research and study to unravel the order of the evolution of these Religions. We do not know yet what inscriptions have been, or will be found, in the Tomb of Tut-ank-Amen, or Aten. The fact that his name was first written as Tut-ank-Aten proves that his first belief was the Aten Cult. When the name changed to Tut-ank-Amen, he must have revived the Cult of Amen, which followed that of Ptah and was originally prior to the Osirian. The Osirian was the last phase of the Solar, and had been in existence and founded more than 30,000 years before the time of Tut-ank-Amen.

A "Winged Disk," found over the door of a Temple at Ocosingo, near Palanque, corresponded in every particular to those of Egypt. The remains of Temples here were Stellar Cult. I reproduce these Signs and Symbols of the same "Cult" found in Scotland at Vitrified Fort, Ainworth (Plates XXVII & XXVIII). Also I produce a "Winged Disk" of the Assyrians and one from Chaldea,

182   THE ORIGIN AND EVOLUTION

proving that this " Cult " was carried into these countries. Horus as a Symbolic Fish-man, or God, swam the waters, but in this earlier phase he is carried on the wings of His Mother over the void.

Serpent Type.

Another type of Horus imaged as that of the great Serpent was formulated during the Stellar Cult—not the evil or bad serpent (Apap), but the zootype form of the Child of the zootype Serpent-Mother Rannut. The Serpent brood or dragon of progeny of Rannut, a type of the Earth-goddess as the Serpent-Mother, are mentioned

"Winged Disks" and Natzar from Scotland.
Fig. 28.

in the Ritual, where they have become a subject of ancient knowledge in the Mysteries (Ch. 125). See illustrations, "Origin and Evolution of the Human Race," p. 158.

There are no seven serpents of death or seven evil serpents in Egypt, but these in Akkad and Babylonia were made the progeny of Tiamat. The Euphrateans turned the evil serpent Apap into Tiamat, the old Great Mother in the abyss of birth, where she had been supposed to have brought forth seven powers of evil and to have been herself the old serpent with seven heads. But the Akkadians and Babylonians had lost the true gnosis, likewise the Hebrews who followed them. In Egypt, happily, we find it, and Horus the son of Rannut is here imaged in zootype as the Great Serpent.

In the old temples of Egypt tame serpents were kept and suffered to coil about the sacred loaves and the consecrated bread eaten by the faithful (Bonwick : " Egypt, Bel," p. 264), and at one time a divine serpent was sacred in every Nome of Egypt. And a serpent was often carried in long mystical processions ("Proc. Soc. Bib. Arch." Nov. 1890). These were early symbols of Tem, not the

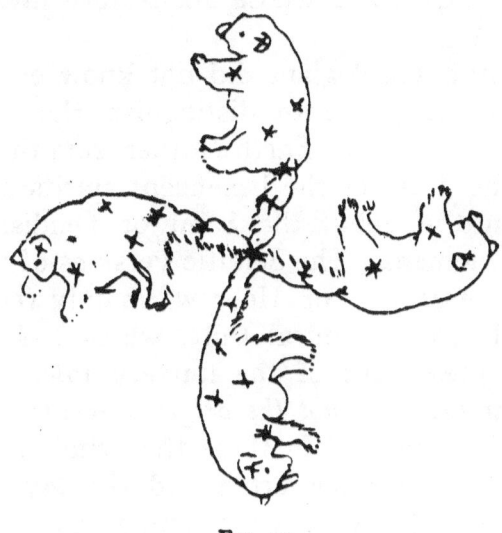

FIG. 29.

great Apapi who, when he fought with Horus for the Light and was defeated, was compelled to disgorge all that he had swallowed.

The ancient Egyptians knew that the serpent cast its skin and came forth as a new serpent, and so adopted it as a type of regeneration, or renewal of life (Spiritual).

The Serpent represented, symbolically, Horus as the God Tem as a Child, and Tmu as the adult; this type was also brought on later into the Solar Cult as Tem-Asar and Tem-Ra, but the original was Stellar Cult. The type was taken from Rannut.

But it was Horus the Great God, from the first to the last, under different types, and the doctrine from the first to the last has been fundamentally the same. The old Stellar Cult people had to use different types to depict the various attributes they associated and believed " The One Great God possessed "; they could not express their ideas and beliefs otherwise as they did not possess the terminology we now have acquired.

In the Ritual, Chapter VII, Horus says : " I am the one who presides over the Pole of Heaven, and the powers of all the Gods are my powers. I am He whose names are hidden and whose abodes are mysterious for all eternity."

The Semitic Theologians did not know enough of the ancient Sign Language to distinguish the evil serpent from the good, the great Earth-Mother from the chimerical dragon of the deep, or the beneficent spirits of elemental nature from the Sebu, the Sami or fiendish forces of external phenomena. The Semitic versions of the legends, Babylonian, Assyrian, or Hebrew, mainly reproduce the debris of the Astronomical Cult, which has often been reduced to the status of the nursery tale. *Their fatal defect is that they are not the original documents and have no first-hand authority.* In these the primitive wisdom of old Egypt has been perverted and the Mythical beginnings, which had their own meaning, have been transmogrified into what is termed " Cosmogonical Creation," as example, in the Babylonian legends of creation, the seven associate gods who are the Creators in the Egyptian Mythos, have been converted into the seven evil spirits of a later theology. And on one of the tablets (W.H. 141. 1.36.37) it is said of these seven evil spirits : " The woman from the loins of the man they bring forth." Thus the creation of woman is made to be the work of seven evil spirits, who, as the Egyptian wisdom witnesses, did not originate as wicked spirits or as powers of evil.

Lenormant held that the Chaldaic and Hebrew versions had one common origin and were not derived

The Mexican portrayal of Horus as "The Corn God" or "God of Food," called here Cinteol and in Egypt Naprit, where at Philæ he is represented with stalks and ears of corn springing from a mummy near running water. This is Horus as a type of the eternal, manifested by renewal of food in the shape of corn produced from the element of water in inundation, i.e. an ear of corn near a fall of water.

PLATE XXVI.

[To face p. 184.

Drawn by K. Watkins.

WINGED DISC OF ASSYRIA.
Representation of Horus in Circle of Disk being carried across the void.
PLATE XXVII.

Drawn by K. Watkins.

EGYPTIAN WINGED DISK
This is in the form of a Vulture holding two Flabella and two Shenni Rings.
PLATE XXVIII.

[*To face p.* 185.

OF RELIGION

from each other; he made no attempt to trace that origin to the Astronomical Egyptian Cult; that to him was a sealed and secret book. The Egyptians make no pretence of knowing anything about " Cosmical Creation." Egypt's knowledge of the beginnings was laboriously derived by the long, unceasing verification of scientific naturalists. Their astronomical knowledge did not fall from the Heavens ready made, nor was there any claim to a miraculous birth. It was gained by a long course of observation of all nature and nature's laws. Whatever they " dug and worked for " was from reality—objectively —and everything they did was for a perpetual Symbol of the Truth. However primitive the Symbolism was at first, it was all the Truth ; not like the Hebrew ancient books, which only converted the genuine into a spurious specie and passed it off on the ignorant and unsuspecting as a brand new issue direct from God.

Take another example which arose out of the Osirian Cult, a late form of the Solar, where the Hebrew Translators converted the " Symbolical and Mythical " representation into a human and literal or exotric rendering. When Osiris lay helpless and breathless in Amenta with a Corpse-like face (Rit., Ch. 74) his two wives, who are likewise his two daughters, came to cohabit with him, and raise him from the dead, or re-erect him like and as Tat. It is said of Isis: " She raised the remains of the god of the resting heart and extracted his seed to begat an heir," or make him human by reincarnation in the flesh (" Hymn to Osiris," Records, line 16, p. 102, Vol. IV, first series ; Vol. IV, p. 21, second series). The Mythos is repeated and applied to the Semitic, where Lot's two daughters are with " Child by the Father " (Gen. xix. 36), the difference being that the mythical Osiris as Father in the Mysteries of Amenta was dead, a mummy, at the time, whereas in the Semitic Lot is represented as dead drunk.

The Egyptian phrase for creation was " Of the first time," and mainly limited to the bringing forth of life. The beginning in " the first time " described in the

Ritual was with birth from the abyss, the birthplace of water within the earth. It is portrayed as " The Tuat which nobody can fathom," the place that " sent out light in the dark night," which was the birthplace of water and eatable plants (Rit., Ch. 172). Thus we have the Deep, the darkness on the face of the Deep, the light breaking out of darkness, the waters and the life springing forth from the waters in the eatable plants. Water had revealed the secret of creation in the life which came as food by water from the Mother-Earth in the unfathomable deep. The secret of water as the source of life was the primal mystery to the Egyptians, as is shown by " Kep " or " Khefa," the Mother of all living things, where the mystery was that of fertilization (by means of water) Khefa survived in Hebrew as Chavvah (Eve), but the primal pair of beings were not constellated as the human parents of the human race, but as Male and Female Hippopotamus or Behemoth and Leviathan, and later as the Greater and Lesser Bears. She as the maker of the Circle, and he as the first to plant the tree, or erect the pole, the pillar, or mount within the Circle. Job says of Behemoth he is the chief of the ways of God. . (xl. 10.)

The primal pair, as represented in the Book of Genesis by Adam and Eve, are husband and wife in a later Mythos, or Cult, i.e. the Solar.

The Tower of Babel was a Symbol of the pole which had been overthrown or shifted by the waters of the Deluge, or, in other words, it was the replacement of one Polaris for the other in precession—the hitherto reigning one's time had come to an end and the next would take its place. To build the Tower was to replace the Pole. The Tower was the Babylonian Bab-illu, which the Hebrew writer has turned into the Tower of " babble " and confusion. The story itself is founded on an Assyrian tablet in the British Museum, with this difference. In the older legend the structure was a *Mound*, whereas in the Hebrew version it is a Tower built of *bricks*. It is explained that Babylon corruptly turned to sin,

"Great and small commingled on the mound." There was a revolt against the great god Anu, "King of the Holy Mound." The rebels are described as building a stronghold, but they were confounded in their work. What they did by day was all undone by night. The supreme God gave a command to make strange their speech. "For future time the mountain," or the mound, was overthrown by Nu-nam-nir, the god of lawlessness, or no rule, and the destruction occurred, though not in the form of a deluge ("Records of the Past," Vol. VII, p. 131).

Readers must take into consideration in studying these various phases of the Stellar Cult that it lasted a very long time in Egypt, that it was a "progressive evolution of Religion." As each exodus left the old Mother-land, they could take with them only the doctrine that had been evolved up to the time of that exodus, and many were cut off from the progress which was constantly taking place in Egypt, and so would remain in a primary phase. Also the descendants of the original exodus must have forgotten in many cases the gnosis of the secret doctrines, and much substitution and innovations was the result. Then where the Lunar and Solar Cults followed; if they could not kill all the old Stellar people, as they did in Europe, they imposed some of the new doctrines, and so the whole became a mixture. This is what scientific research proves to-day. All the various types are found in some parts of the world, and can be studied; and with the help of the Ritual of Ancient Egypt and the decipherment of the Glyphs, Signs, and Symbols found all over the world, one can reconstruct the past history and the Truth of Religion.

There is ample evidence and proof that the old Stellar Cult religion of the Egyptians was carried to many and far distant lands. Fragments and the Myths found in these countries prove this. Set, as a ruler of the primal pole star, was the Arch-First in heaven, as a male.

This is the title of Tai-yih, the Chinese Great One. It is said that among all the shin, or spirits (the Japanese

Shintu gods) of the heavens, the highest one dwells in the star Tai-yih of the Constellation Draco (O'Neil: "Night of the Gods," Vol. I, pp. 513-17). One must, however, identify the deity with the definite Pole Star, as there were seven of these gods, one assigned to each pole star of Ursa Minor, and the question is which was the pole star "Seat of God" at the time. As we have seen, these were precessional, and changed every 3,600 years (about).

Draconis was the Constellation of Horus-Sebek, the crocodile dragon. Set was the first-born child of the great Mother Apt, and these two formed the primary *duad* that is sometimes called Set-Typhon, or, in Egyptian, Set-Tept or Set, and his mother as the primal pair. According to one account of the Book of Genesis, Seth, or Set, was the firstborn child of Chavval (or Eve), as he had been in Egypt.

Set was the primary ruler, the earliest representative power in heaven figured as an image of the male. He was lord as male Hippopotamus, and consort to his mother as the female.

Here we perceive that a fragment of the true tradition survived in the Biblical statement that in the time of Set (Seth) men began to call on the name of the Lord. (Gen. iv. 26.)

Set, as male, was first of the seven brothers who, in the Babylonian legend, "came as begetters." It is further proved as a fact in the texts, when it is said that "A son was born to Seth," or Set, Egyptian, who was the first form of the "father as the elder brother," with whom the fatherhood began.

It is said of Ialdabaoth that, being incensed with men because they did not worship or honour him as god and father, he being the oldest brother only, he sent forth a deluge upon them that he might destroy them all. (Irenæus, Book I, Ch. XXX, 10.)

Set, in the Ritual (Ch. 175) is proclaimed as having been the first in glory. It is said: "The powers of Set which hath departed were greater than that of all the gods."

He was looked upon as the fallen leader of the angelic host because he had been first in glory as the ruling power at the primary station of the pole. This is he that is worshipped by the Izedis in Mesopotamia, who say, " there is to be a restoration as well as a fall," which is the same representation as the primary Astronomical Stellar Cult of Egypt.

Set, as primary power of the pole (South), was first to sit upon " the mount of congregation " as the " most high " in the uttermost parts, or at the pole of heaven. Hence he was the reputed author of Astronomy. Thus when in precession the Pole Star of Set had passed away to give place to the next, he had lost his place as guide to the ways of heaven, so the legend of the fall was a fable founded on this fact in the astronomical mythology. When correctly read, " the fall of man " is resolved in the fall of Set, the light that was first uplifted at the station of the Pole.

The Great Mother Apt, who was the Mother of Set and the woman as the foundress, was charged by the Semites, the Chinese, and others, with being his instigator, unconsciously showing the great Mother (Apt) was the mover, which she was, but only as *primum mobile*, and not as the woman urging the man to his eternal misery.

In Babylon, the primal pair are shown as Ishtar and the elder Bel in relation to the mount of the Pole and the mountains of the different stations. " O lady, mistress of the mountain, goodly stronghold of the mountains, mighty lock of the mountains, queen of the land of the four rivers. O lord, the mighty mountain Bel." (Tablet S. 954, B.M., Budge, Babylonian.)

In this imagery the great Mother is called Ishtar, is mistress of the mountain, and Bel is the lord, identical with the mount itself, which imaged the pole, when Bel was the Star. In one of the Assyrian hymns this enclosure of the " lady of the eternal tree " and her comrade, is spoken of as " the park of Ishtar." Nergal the destroyer is thus addressed : " O lord, the park of Ishtar thou establishest not " (Sayce: " Hymn to Nergal," Hib. Sect), Nergal having been one of the overthrowers at the time of the Deluge. (Change of the Pole Star.)

In the Assyrian hymns to the gods it is said that the lady of the eternal tree is the comrade of the bull, the great bull, the supreme bull.

The tree is the pole, " the eternal wood," or Gas-Zida. The tree with seven branches, like the candlestick with seven lights, represents the pole as a figure of the total heptanomis, and is comparatively late.

The pair beneath the tree (a figure of the pole) are the Mother (Apt) and Son (Set) or male and female of the legend of the primal pair who fell from heaven because they failed as keepers of the tree of knowledge at the pole, because the pole changed in precession.

Wherever one travels, among Babylonians, Hindu, Red Indian, Norse, Greeks, South Americans, or Central Africans we find the same tale, all of which originated from the primary Astronomical Cult wisdom of Ancient Egypt, carried over the world by various exodes and with much of the original gnosis lost and falsified by additions beyond comprehension in many cases.

That the " Cult of Set " lasted for a long period after the " Stellar Cult of Horus " had been established is shown by writings discovered on a monument by Lepsius, which established the fact that the Hyksos Kings were worshippers of Set (2547–2288 B.C.). Therein this is confirmed by King Apepi having Set in his title (worshipper of Set), which proves the fact that although the Solar Cult had been evolved and established for a long period at Memphis, the Cult of Set was brought back, for a time, by the descendants of the old Cult, who had emigrated from Egypt thousands of years before and had not changed their religion, now returned as enemies and re-established the old Cult again in Lower Egypt. These old shepherd people were brave and vigorous, but devoid of all culture. They had gone out of Egypt at an early date and remained in the same state as the exodus of their forefathers when they left

Egypt with the old religion; whereas the Egyptians had advanced in science, civilization, and in religious evolution. This is proved by the monuments. They now returned and conquered the Egyptians, who had sunk into a state of torpid paralysis, from which Egypt never entirely recovered. Socialism and bureaucracy had destroyed them. The free and freedom-giving moral law as a basis, and intellect as the recognized highest element of the religious and civil constitution had been replaced by a senseless despotism exercised over the people by princes and priests who eventually disagreed amongst themselves, with the ever same result, that the destruction of the nation followed; this is the history of all great nations which have risen to a high state of religion and civilization; they have then been destroyed, and ever will be, as it is against the Periodic Laws of the Great God that if such Governments are set up they should never live.

Egypt began in the form of seven Nui—a most ancient Egyptian name for the nomes or boundaries.

In Polynesia, Nui, or Rapa-Nui, is the native name of Easter Island, where the colossal statues left by the old Stellar Cult race of builders have been found. Nui is also the name of a group of the Nui as islands—nomes, which are found as seven in number in the seven islands of Onoatoa. Each one of these has its own particular name, but Onoatoa embraces the whole seven.

The seven Nui islands, a group called Onoatoa, offer a parallel to the seven islands of Avaiki, with the additional fact that they have the same name as the most ancient nomes of Egypt, which were seven in number. According to the Missionary Gill, the Mangaians hold that the seven inhabited islands of the Harvey Group are the body or outward presentment of another seven in the spirit-world of Avaiki ("Myths and Songs of the Pacific"). These correspond to the seven sunken islands of the lost Atlantis, and both are a localized earthly form of the Celestial heptanomis which sank down in the course of one great year. The name of Mangaia signifies peace, and Mangaia in Avaiki was the paradise of peace like the Egyptian Hetep. This, therefore, was a form of the paradise lost in the form of seven islands sunk in the Pacific, as well as in the Atlantic Ocean, and other waters which were firmamental from the first.

The heptanomis came to an end with the great deluge of all; and in the Book of Genesis the deluge of Noah is followed by the new kingdom that was reared on a fourfold foundation, the seven cities on the other side of the flood being succeeded by the cities of the four quarters built on this. When Nimrod or Gilgames became "a mighty one in the earth," "the beginning of his kingdom was Babel and Ereck, and Akkad and Kalneh in the land of Shinar," and out of that land he went and built four other cities in Assyria. The heaven of the four quarters had then superseded the heptanomis or heaven founded on the seven stars or astronomes, and this was the figure followed in the building of the four cities on earth. After the great deluge of all had taken place (i.e. the ending of the precession of the seven Stars of Ursa Minor) and the reckoning of time had ceased to be from the observation of these, and the inhabitants of all of the heptanomis were figuratively drowned, it was seen that the seven pole stars kept their place in the circumpolar heaven. Thus the seven gods sat in their circle round the tree of the pole, the fixed and never setting stars for ever safe from all the deluges of time, as the seven lords of eternity. These are the seven that were saved when all the world was drowned.

The Shenin in the Ritual are a group of spirits that surround the seat of the highest. The name denotes the circle of those ministers or officials that surround the throne of the god or the King. In one text this circle is called the shenin of fire. They are the spirits of fire = the saluting apes in the circle of eternals.

The Chinese recognize a Stellar enclosure, or circle of stars in the Northern Heavens in the region of Draco and Ursa Minor. These bear the names of ministers and officers who surround the sovereign, and therefore are identical with the Egyptian circle of the shenin. The circle of the seven lords of eternity was first: the throne of the highest was erected in the centre. Thus the seven as servants (seshu) Khuti, Uræus-gods saluting apes or angels, spirits, or lamps of fire, are depicted around the throne of God according to the mystery of the seven stars in Revelation.

CHAPTER XI

LUNAR CULT

THE Lunar Cult followed the Stellar Cult and was so called because the time was reckoned by the Moon instead of the Stars. Much of the Symbolism of the latter was brought on and merged into the former. The chief difference was a change of names and types, both of the Great God and His Attributes, and the method of reckoning time. Hitherto time had been reckoned by the Stars, Lesser and Great Bears, and Inundation: now it was measured by the phases of the Moon, and Taht was the recorder or measurer.

Taht was the measurer of time by means of the Great Bear, the Inundation, *and the Moon.*

The Inundation was a primary factor in the establishment of time in Egypt and the foundation of the year. The fact is recognized in the "Hymn to the Nile," where it is said: "Stable are thy decrees for Egypt": that is in the fixed periodic return of the waters from their source from "The two Great Lakes" to inundate and fertilize the land of Egypt.

In the Stellar Cult, Apt, the Goddess of the Great Bear, had presided over the birth of Horus in the inundation, but when the Lunar time was established the child became Lunar as well. Khnmu was the name of Horus of the inundation in this Cult, and the child was now depicted as being brought forth by Hathor in Sothis, as the Star of the Annunciation.

The birth took place in Sothis, the birthday being determined by the heliacal rising of the Star, as well as by the tail of the Great Bear. Khebt or Apt, the old first mother, still presided over all, but as if she were a midwife, or Meskhenat, in attendance at the birth, when Hathor, as the Lunar type, had become the Mother.

The Goddess Hathor was termed the mistress of the beginning of the year, in relation to the rising of Sothis. Hathor was thus the Lunar form of the Hippopotamus-headed Mother of the beginnings in the Great Bear, with the Milch-Cow substituted for the Water-Cow, both images, or types, of the wet nurse and giver of liquid life.

There was also an advancement in religious ideas and beliefs according to evolution. As in the Stellar, there were several types or images of the Great Mother. It was bringing on the same divinized elemental powers under different names from those in the former Cult, as well as portraying them in a different phase. The Celestial heptanomis and the division of seven was followed by the enclosure of Am-Khemen, the division of eight, and the eight Great Gods; this was followed by a division of heaven into ten regions of space, but the eight Great Gods were not increased until the time of Ptah (in Solar Cult). The ten was followed by twelve divisions, all of which preceded the formation of the zodiac and twelve signs. Taht, the Moon-God, was not reckoned as the ninth. The eighth was the highest power in the Lunar, as it was in the late Stellar. The group of seven remained intact, with Taht-Khemen (later Smen) as the highest and the eighth, instead of Anup-Horus in the Stellar: but the two were one and the same Great God under different names and phases. Taht-Khemen was the highest in the Lunar Cult and worshipped under this name as "The Only One." Hathor was the Moon Goddess, and the Lunar type of Kept and Apt, the most ancient Hippopotamus Goddess as Mother-Earth, or the Lady of the Tree.

The Sycamore Fig-tree of Hathor and the Palm Tree of Taht were imported into Egypt from the South, as had been the primary representation.

Hathor the Cow, who gave rebirth to the child of Light as her Calf, was propitiated as the Mother of plenty, like the Inoit Sidne, and was imaged by the Cow as the figure of food and fecundity. She was also the goddess of generation, maternity, and child-birth, as well as of music and love. I reproduce Hathor in Zootype form with Horus her Son standing in front, Plate XXX ; and in human form, Plate XXXI.

The Lunar Cult was symbolized and depicted in the building of the first temple of Hathor at Denderah, or Annu : this can be shown by referring to the Ritual. The present remains of the building are not the original temple, as may also be proved by the inscriptions which recount how Thothmes III gave command *to rebuild the temple according to ancient designs.* The previous building had been erected by Pepi of the Sixth Dynasty, who reigned at least nineteen centuries before the time of Thothmes III ; but the temple of Hathor, built by Pepi, was also on a plan of a more ancient temple, the design of which was found in a crypt, or secret chamber, written in ancient Hieroglyphics by Khufu (so stated) of the Fourth Dynasty, and the first temple was long anterior to Khufu. As Professor Dumichen has observed, the religious ceremonies depicted on the walls belong to a very remote period. On one side of the vast entrance-hall, or " Khent," the walls are covered with a representation of the fourteen accents of the Moon, leading up to the throne of Thoth, the Lord of Measurements and corresponding to the number of days between new and full moon. On the opposite side are depicted eighteen boats, each led by a Solar Serpent or spiral representing the eighteen decades. In the area of the same entrance-hall rise eighteen enormous columns, divided into three rows, each containing six columns, corresponding with the number of decades of days. In the Ritual it says that " Horus gave the command : ' Let the pillars be here,' that is, in his own House or Habitation."

In the centre of the temple is the hall of the Altar, with entrances opening east and west ; and beyond it lies the great Hall of the temple, entitled the " Hall of the Child in his Cradle," from whence access is obtained

Drawn by K. Watkins.

THE URÆUS SERPENT OF EGYPT.

PLATE XXIX.

Drawn by K. Watkins.

THE GODDESS HATHOR IN ZOOTYPE
FORM WITH HER SON HORUS DEPICTED
STANDING IN FRONT OF HER.

PLATE XXX.

[*To face p.* 196.

Drawn by K. Watkins.
THE GODDESS HATHOR IN HUMAN FORM.
PLATE XXXI

Drawn by K. Watkins.

HATHOR, THE GREAT MOTHER, AMONGST THE PAPYRUS REEDS IN THE FIELD OF HEAVEN.
A Uranographic type of the Lands of the Reeds on Earth.
PLATE XXXII.

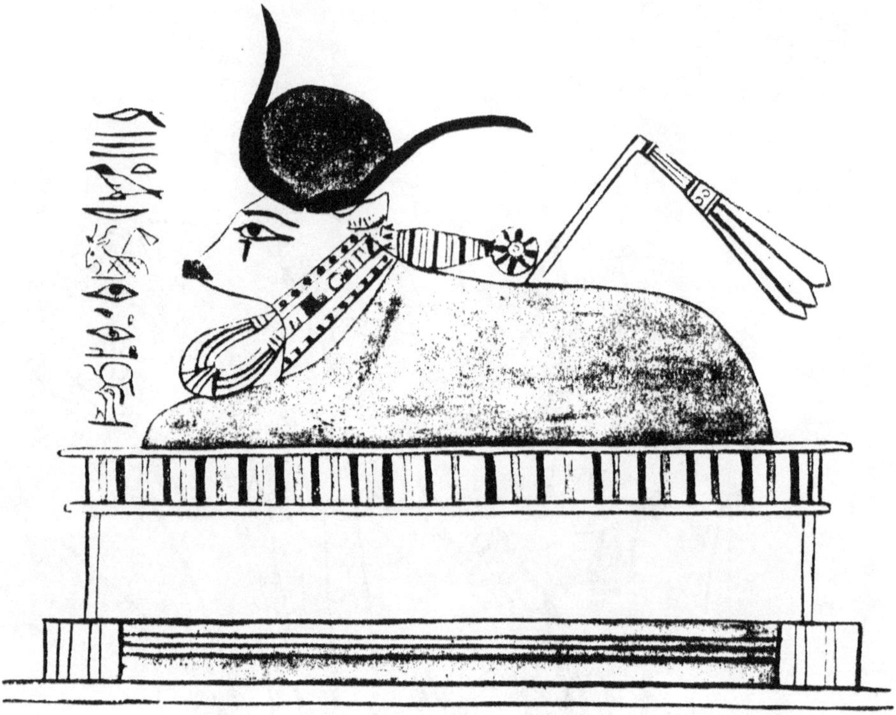

Drawn by K. Watkins.

THE GODDESS MEH-URIT.

PLATE XXXIII.

Drawn by K. Watkins.

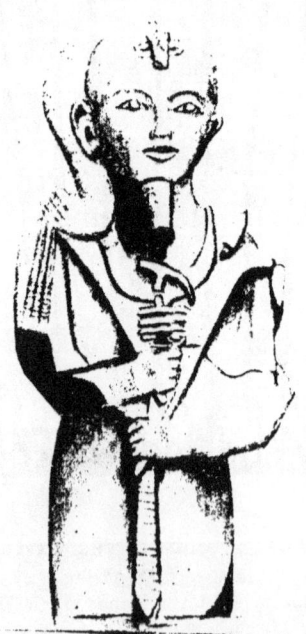

STATUE FOUND IN THE TEMPLE OF KHONSU AT KARNAK. IT HAS THE FEATURES OF TUTANK-AMEN.

PLATE XXXIV.

to the secret and sealed shrine entered once a year by the high-priestess, on the night of midsummer. From that shrine the image of the Holy Mother was on that night conveyed up a secret staircase to an open chamber on the roof. Upon the walls is depicted the figure of the Virgin Mother with the rays of the divine splendour streaming from her womb, " giving birth to Her Child of Light." On the wall painting now in Paris, which was brought bodily from the Temple of Denderah some time since, there is depicted the Divine Horus, the child of Hathor, Queen of the starry universe, and Nut, the mistress who presided over the waters.

In the Babylonian version, the Great Mother as Ishtar descends into the underworld in search of the water of life, otherwise represented as her child Tammuz = Horus or Khnmu.

This descent in search of the vanished water, the lost light, the disappearing child, was made by the goddess in her Lunar character. It was as the Moon that Ishtar passed through seven gates on her downward way when she was stripped of all her glory ("Records of the Past"). The descent of Ishtar is dated in the Aramaic-Akkadian Calendar by the month Ki-Ginger-na, the errand of Ishtar, which was dedicated to the goddess with "Virgo" as its zodiacal sign.

This is the Egyptian Hathor and Horus. As the Mother-Moon she fetched light and the water of life from the lower regions, and gave rebirth to vegetation in the upper world.

Plutarch, in speaking of the Egyptian Mysteries, tells us that " on the eve of the winter solstice " the Egyptians " carry the cow seven times round the Temple," which was a model for " the seeking of Horus," the Child of Light and Saviour by water. Plutarch adds that the goddess who in one character is the Earth-Mother was in great distress from want of water in the winter time.

Another type of the Goddess Hathor as a form, or image, of the Earth-Mother, was as the Mistress of the Mines, precious stones and metals, called Mafket. It was under this type that she gave birth to the blue-eyed golden Horus as her child, her Golden Calf, or Hawk of Gold. Horus as the Hawk standing on the column within the necklace zone, or cestus, was the child of Hathor, and these two, Hathor and Horus, the divine Mother and Child were the Lunar Cult images of " Horus of the Vulture that was the bird of Neith " in the former Stellar Cult.

The Sacred Heifer was the Zootype of the Virgin Mother in this Cult.

As we have seen, at one time the birthplace in the Stellar Cult was in the South, and was uranographically represented when Sothos rose up as an opener of the year, as the herald of the inundation. In the Lunar Cult, Sothos became the star of Hathor and her Messu, or Messianic babe, who came to make war on the great Dragon and " bruise the Serpent's head."

Hathor as the Cow of Heaven, as the Milch-Cow, was portrayed standing, or resting, on the summit of the Mount which was " connected with the Sky," as depicted on the Monuments. This is the Lunar type of the Stellar Virgin Neith as the Milch-Cow of Heaven. She was the typical Mother amongst the reeds, and thus represented first the birthplace on Earth and thence re-birth in Heaven, Plate XXXII. This, in the Persian rendering, was the Cow on the summit of Mount Alborz.

In the Norse mythology it is the Cow Andhumla. The " Prose Edda" describes it : " Immediately after the gelid vapours had been resolved into drops, there was formed out of them the Cow Andhumla. Four streams of milk ran from the teats, and thus she fed Ymir " (" Prose Edda," 6). It is the same as the Egyptian Cow of Hathor which suckled Horus. Heaven as the Cow, is called the Spouse upon the Mountain. She is the Mother of her Lunar Bull, and as Goddess is described as suckling her child Horus and as having " drooping dugs " (Ren., "B. of D.," Ch. 62, note 1). The Milky Way was pictured as the Celestial Water, now called milk, that flowed from the Cow of Heaven standing upon the summit of the

Mount, the apex of which was the Celestial Pole. The Cult of the Great Mother and her child was thus brought on from the Stellar to the Lunar. Hathor as a Cow and Horus as the young calf, as her child on one horizon and her Bull or fecundator on the other.

The passage from West to East was through the Mount of the West that had been imaged as a passage through the Cow of Earth.

The Stellar Serpent type, Tem, was also brought on and depicted in the Lunar Cult.

Tum or Tmu (Plate XXXIII) makes his passage through the Mount by means of the Cow, and is reborn as Tem, the little child from the Kepsh of the Cow Meh-ur. It is recorded of Him in setting forth from the Western Horizon "Earth stretches her arms to receive Thee." He (Tum) is embraced by the Mother whose womb is the Meskhen of rebirth, and at His coming forth to the Eastern Horizon it is said: "Thou hast rested in the Cow, thou hast been immersed in the Cow Meh-ur" (inscript: of Darin, lines 27–8). The Goddess Meh-ur or Meh-urt is mentioned but rarely in the Book of the Dead (XVII, 76–9; LXXI, 13; CXXIV, 17). Meh-urt is the "Cow of Earth and Sky," a Lunar type of the Great Mother Earth and Water. Her name signifies "mighty fullness," indicating that she represented zoomorphically the abundant and unfailing source of the matter of every kind which was fecundated by the male germs of life of every kind. She was a Lunar form of the primeval female creative principle, a form representing the Stellar Neith in the Lunar Cult. In one later form of the representation of the goddess, figured by Signor Lanzone, she is depicted in the form of a pregnant woman with full, protruding breasts, emblems of fertility and food, but originally she was represented by her zootype as a Cow resting and associated with Hathor; it was a type of Hathor, the Mother. The usual titles of the goddess are "Lady of Heaven," "Mistress of the Gods," and "Mistress of the Two Lands," said to have "existed from the beginning " and to have helped Taht to create the first things which appeared in Khemennu (Plate XXXIII). In the Lunar Cult the Godhead consisted of the Mother, the Child, and the Divine Adult.

" Horus of the Dual Power " of the Stellar Cult is imaged as Khensu-Tehuti, the twice great, the Lord of Khemennu. As the Babe he is Khensu-Pa-Khart, i.e. Khensu the Babe. As the child of twelve years he is Khensu-Hunnu, i.e. Khensu the child of twelve years, as shown here (Plate XXXIV).

As Khensu-Pa-Khart he caused to shine upon the earth the beautiful light of the Crescent Moon, and through his agency women conceived, cattle became fertile, the germ grew in the egg, and all nostrils and throats were full with fresh air. P. nb. Ta, Lord of the World, God, Son of Horus, is the earliest representation in Lunar Cult of the Child Horus. In " Bun. Dict." p. 503, Fig. 101, He is represented by a child crowned with a triple crown and Goat's Horns.

" Khensu " signifies to travel, to move about, to run, etc., and as the Moon God, this was so, and very appropriate. He was styled the Great Lord of Heaven. He was Lord of Maat and the Moon by night. As the New Moon he is likened to a mighty or fiery Bull ; as the full Moon he is said to resemble an emasculated Bull.

Thus Horus of the Dual Power of the Stellar Cult is imaged as Khensu or Khennu in the Lunar. I give here (Plate XXXV), the Egyptian portrayal of Khensu of the Lunar Cult standing upon two Crocodiles, which depicts Him as Horus of the Double Horizon, or Double Power—also as the Fish-man, or God. Here he has been given four wings which are equivalent to the wings of the dual Mother in the former Cult as well as in this. He has the Lunar disk in a Crescent above the duplicated head of the Hawk, and the Crook and Flail, emblems of Power and Sovereignty in his hands.

As the man of thirty years he was named " Khensu-Tehuti " " the twice Great," " The Lord of Khemennu," i.e. the Chief of the seven Stellar Gods as the eighth,

THE DUAL GOD KHENSU OF THE LUNA CULT, STANDING UPON TWO CROCODILES.

This is the Lunar portrayal of Horus of the Double Horizon or Double Power of the Stellar Cult. Khensu is depicted here with four wings which are equal to the wings of the dual Mother in the Stellar Cult. This represents Him also as the Fish-Man or God as demonstrated by the two Crocodiles He is standing on.

PLATE XXXV.

Drawn by K. Watkins.

HERU-SMA-TAUI, i.e. HORUS THE UNITER OF THE SOUTH AND NORTH. (*Several forms.*)

PLATE XXXVI.

Drawn by K. Watkins.

AÄH-TEHUTI IN HIS LUNA ARK, OR BARK, RECEIVING ADORATION (see Text).

PLATE XXXVIII.

[To face p. 201.

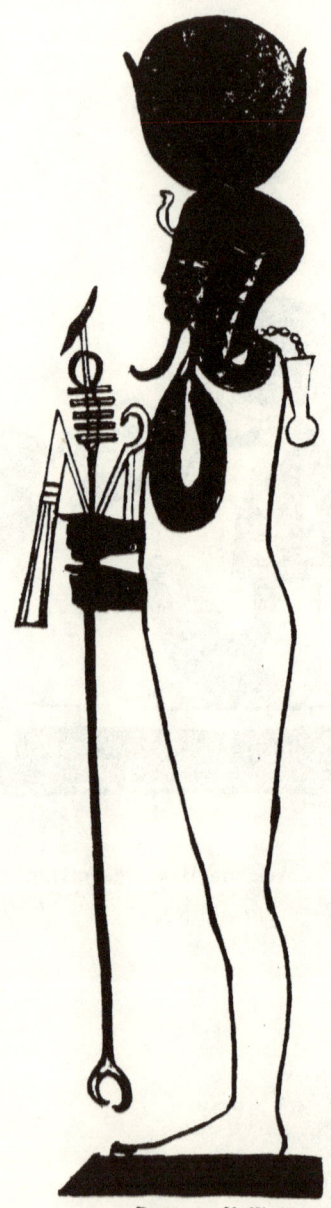

Drawn by K. Watkins.

KHENSU-TEHUTI OR AĀH-TEHUTI. THE MOON GOD RISEN.

(*Spiritual form.*)

The Great God, the Lord of Heaven. The King of the gods, and the maker of eternity, and creator of everlastingness.

PLATE XXXVII.

the 7 + 1 ; here portrayed as the seven Powers, and called the seven Taasu with Taht (or Khensu-Tehuti).

This is also the Lunar image of the Stellar Heru-Sma-Taui, that is Horus of the South and North, " the uniter of the Two Lands " (Plate XXXVI).

Khensu was one of the chief images connecting the Lunar with the Solar Cult. In the later phase the text states that he was the second great light in the Heavens, and was the first great (Son) of Amen, the beautiful youth, who maketh himself young in Thebes in the form of Ra, the son of the Goddess Nubit, a child in the morning and old man in the evening. He was a youth at the beginning of the year, who cometh as a child after he had become infirm and who renewed his birth like the Disk. This expresses Khenu as a god of the Dual Horizon, although part of it is in Solar language the prior was Lunar. It also identifies him with Horus as " Aten " of the Disk, which was the *primary* or first portrayal. Another name for him in this Cult was Aāh son of Hathor, that is the Moon God commonly called Aāh-Tehuti; the Great God, the Lord of Heaven, the King of the Gods and the Maker of Eternity, and Creator of Everlastingness, were his titles (Plate XXXVII).

Under this form he is depicted as a mummy, bearded, standing upon the symbol of Maat or cubit ⌑, and holding in his hands the emblem of life ♀ stability 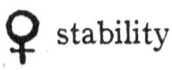 sovereignty and dominion ⧸⫯ and the sceptre ⫯ on his head is the Crescent Moon and by the side of his head he has the Horus lock of hair, symbolic of youth. As a bearded mummy human figure, with the Crescent Moon on his head, and the lock of hair, symbolic of youth, it represents two faces, that of youth of twelve years and the man of thirty years, or in other words, it represents the risen Horus in this Cult as " Aāh-Tehuti " in Spirit form. In some scenes we see Aāh-Tehuti represented in the form of a Disk resting between the horns of the Crescent Moon.

In one interesting scene the God is represented with the head of an Ibis surmounted by the Lunar Disk and Crescent seated in a boat (Plate XXXVIII) and a dog-headed Ape stands before him and presents the Utchat ◉ the "all-seeing Eye" (as the full Moon, or the Eye in the dark in the underworld). The curved end of the boat is notched, like the notched palm branch which symbolizes ⦃ years, like the zootype Frog, as millions of years, or millions of renewals of light.

The zootypes representing Taht or Taht-Aan were:

The Ibis and the Dog-Headed Ape (Figs. 30 & 31).

This was Aan of the Stellar Cult.

Taht Aan in the Lunar Cult was the messenger—*the word*, or logos, and the Lunar portrayal of John.

THE IBIS OR HEBI WITH THE
GODDESS MAAT IN FRONT.

FIG. 30.

The Ape was the worshipper, as an image in Sign-Language, the Saluter of the Gods.

The Ape, Ani, denotes the Saluter, and to salute was an Egyptian gesture of adoration. The Ape or Cynocephalus with its paws uplifted is the typical worshipper or Saluter of the Light.

It was, and still is, looked upon in Africa generally as a pre-human Moon worshipper, who laments the disappearance of its night light and rejoices at the renewal and return of that luminary.

The Cynocephalus also represents a pre-human source of speech, and is personified in Taht-Aan, or Taht-Ani, as the Divine Speaker.

Taht is called the creator of speech; his name, Tehuti, is derived from Tehu, a word for speech and to tell, and he is portrayed in the form of the Kaf-Ape. The Cynocephalus was the "clicking Ape," and he is here recognized

Drawn by K. Watkins.

THE DOG-HEADED APE AS ANI THE SALUTER WAS EMBLEMATICAL OF THE MOON.

In the Egyptian Judgment Scenes the Baboon or the Cynocephalus, who sits upon the Scales as the tongue of the balance and a primitive determinitive of even-handed justice—as an image of the Judge.

FIG. 31.

as the clicker who preceded the speaker, the zootype from whom language originated.

Hanuman in India is, or corresponds to, Taht-Ani. The Jaitwas of Rajputana claim to be descendants of the "Monkey-God"; that means their original Mother-Totem was a Monkey, which was later divinized into Taht-Ani or Hanuman, the Monkey-God, as a Lunar image.

In the " Ritual of the Resurrection," the book of the divine words written down by Taht, are said to be " in the keeping of Horus the Son," who is addressed as " him who sees the father."

The word of God personified in Horus preceded the written word of God, and when the words of Power were written down by Taht, the scribe of Truth, they were assigned to Horus as " the Logia of the Lord," and preserved as the precious records of Him who was the word in person ; first the word of power, as the founder, then the word in truth, or made truth, as the fulfiller.

The divine words when written down constituted the Scriptures, earliest of which are those ascribed to Hermes or Taht, the reputed author of all the sacred writings.

Now, " the word in person " and the " written word," together with the doctrines of the word, according to ancient wisdom, are extant and living (partially at least) in the " Egyptian Book of the Dead," or "Ritual of the Resurrection."

But the Magical words of Power when written down by Taht became the nucleus of the Ritual, which is late in comparison with the Astronomical Mythology and other forms of Sign Language, and belong, according to the later editions at least, to the Osirian Cult which was the latest form, or phase, of the Solar.

The Mystical word of Power from the first was female. The Stellar-Apt at Ombos was worshipped as " the living Word." The thigh or khepsh of Apt is the typical Ur-heka and is a symbol of great magical power, and the Ur-heka or magical sign preceded words, and words preceded writings.

I give here (Plate XXXIX) the Egyptian representation of Tehuti or Thoth, the recorder of the Gods, the Ibis-headed, with Maat the Goddess of Truth (Plate XL), who was associated with him. Taht-Aan was the scribe of Truth who wrote the book of life ; also, as there was a failure in keeping time in the Stellar Cult attributed to Set in Egypt and Bel in Babylonia, the new heaven

(Lunar) followed the Stellar, and Taht was appointed supreme time-keeper. The Ape as Aan, here also portrayed from the Egyptian, in one form is the saluter, in another is imaged as the Judge. Another zootype used as imagery in this Cult was the " Hare " representing " A Springer-up of Light."

The Ibis, or Hebi in Egyptian, is the messenger by name, and the Crescent Moon was the Ark of the Lord of Light upon the waters of the night; thus the Crescent Moon that sailed the sky by night became the image of the Ark of Taht (see Plate XXXVIII).

The typical fight between Horus and Set was continued in this Cult, and was imaged by the two phases of the Moon—light half and dark half, or the waxing and waning of the Moon.

There are two types of evil, or devil, in the Egyptian Mysteries. One in zoomorphic form as the great Apap reptile, the other in anthropomorphic as Set the adversary of Osiris, or the Christian Satan.

In this Cult (Lunar) we have the *first image of the Mother as the slayer of the Great Dragon of evil*, and the Son of the Woman followed as her helper.

The Goddess Heket represented the Moon and its transformation. Heket was also a prophet of rain and, therefore, of the inundation as consort of Khnmu, Lord of the inundation. Heket also represented the resurrection and makes her transformation into Sati the lady of light. As transformation (Plate XLI) in the Mythology it was applied to the renewal of the Moon; in the Eschatology it was the transformation of the mortal into the immortal. Lamps have been found in Egypt with the Frog upon the upper part, and one is known which has the inscription " I am the Resurrection " (Lanzone: "Disionaris," p. 853).

Also the Frog and the Grasshopper, as " leapers," were earlier zootypes of the Moon than the Hare, as figures of the Moon, the light of which leaped up in a fresh place every night. It was the leaping up of the light that was imitated in the dances of the primitive races in Africa who jumped for joy at the appearance of the New Moon, which they celebrated in the monthly dance, and still do. The Leapers were the Dancers who danced the primitive mysteries and dramatized them in their dances. And the Frog, the Grasshopper, the Mantis, and the Hare were amongst the zootypes that were pre-human prototypes.

The Cat was another type adopted for the Moon, because the Cat could see by night; like the Moon that saw by night and kept watch in the dark. So the Eye of Horus which images the Moon is given to the deceased for his night light in the darkness of death. Horus presents the (Solar) eye by day and Taht the (Lunar) eye by night (Rit., Ch. 144, 8).

Hathor "the dark part" of the Moon transforms into Sati, the Lady of Light; Heket, imaged as a Frog, being the power of transformation. Sati, the Lady of Light, exclaims: "I brighten up the darkness and overthrow the devouring monster" (Rit., Ch. 80), that his soul (Khensu) may rise to Heaven in the Ark of the Moon, the same as Indra who slays the Serpent of darkness who was thought of as the swallower of the light, waters of Heaven and the waters of day (as light) rush forth. Heket was also a type of renewals, millions of years, or millions of renewals of the light of the Moon.

The Goddess Maa, or Maat (see Plate XL) Goddess of Truth and Justice, was closely connected with Taht. The Symbol of Maat is the ostrich feather which is always seen fastened to her headdress, and sometimes seen in her hand.

The Goddess was the personification of physical and moral law, order, and truth.

"Taht-Khemen" or "Khensu-Tehuti" was the highest in the Lunar Cult, the highest being worshipped as the "Only One."

The Moon-God "Taht" was not reckoned as the ninth Power. The eighth in the Stellar and the highest was Horus-Anup, or El Elyon; but in this Cult He appears under the name of Taht-Khemen or Khensu-

Drawn by K. Watkins.

THE GODDESS SATI IN HUMAN FORM.

She holds in her hand the Hare-Headed Sceptre and the Ank emblem of Life. She wears on her head the Crown of the South and the Lunar Horns and Vulture's Head.

PLATE XLI.

SED, THE ERPĀ OF THE GODS.

PLATE XLII.

THE GODDESS MAÄ OR MAÄT.

The female counterpart of Tehuti or Thoth in this Cult.

PLATE XL.

Drawn by K. Watkins.

TEHUTI OR THOTH.

The recorder of the gods—Maāt may be considered the female counterpart of Tehuti.

PLATE XXXIX

[To face p. 208.

Tehuti, and under this Cult Anup and Tehuti become the two witnesses to the supremacy of Horus as Taht-Khemen, who later in the Solar becomes witness of His Father under the name of Ra-Unnufer. In the Lunar Cult, Taht " balances the divine pair " (Rit., Ch. 128), and puts a stop to their strife in the circuit of precession (in the later Solar, Seb was the reconciler of the warring twins). Law and order was established by putting bounds to the contention of the Powers of Light and Darkness, and here in the Lunar Cult Taht, one form of the Moon-God, takes the place of Shu in the previous Stellar Cult as reconciler of the warring twins.

Shu in this Cult is represented as standing on a Mount of Pyramid form of seven steps, called the " Ladder of Shu," lifting up the Heavens. The type of ascent was taken from the Moon which fulfilled its four quarters in twenty-eight steps, fourteen up and fourteen down. The Moon in its first quarter took seven steps from the underworld to the summit. In other words, Shu now made use of the Lunar reckoning established by Taht.

The Moon-God Taht also became the opener of the year, he who was the measurer of time, the first month being assigned to him in the place of Tekhi, who was the opener with the Inundation in the Stellar Cult.

The Lunar year was one of twelve months of thirty days each, to which five days were added by Taht.

In this Cult the cubit ⌐⌐ was the measure, four measures or cubits typified an Ark of the four quarters in space. Seven cubits were a fourth of twenty-eight measures in the cycle of twenty-eight Lunar Signs. Thus seven cubits or measures in an Ark, Shrine, or Tabernacle, formed a figure of Heaven in seven divisions, as in the formation of the seven Stellar Celestial Heptanomis. Seven times in the Great Year the statue of the Pole was changed, or raised aloft, as a landmark amid the firmamental waters of space, in the shape of an Island, Mound, or Mount, or Pyramid, or City, or some other type was raised and rested on the seven Mounds, the seven Pillars, the seven Pyramids, the seven great giants, or other types. So the " Human Birthplace " became localized according to the different stations, or positions, of the Pole, and each in turn sank into the waters of space, or were drowned beneath the deluge of firmamental water ; the whole seven deluges ending in the one great Deluge of all when the seventh Polaris-star sank into space, to give place to a recommencement again ; the time taken being one Great Year of 25,827 years. When the Stellar Heptanomis was followed by the Heaven of Taht, the Ark of eight cubits superseded the Ark of seven cubits, and the Ape became the zootype of Taht in the octonery instead of the heptanomis. In the destruction of mankind, Ra says to the Moon-God Taht : " Thou art my abode, behold thou art called Taht the abode of Ra."

The Am Khemen, the Paradise of the eight Great Gods in the Lunar Cult, had its likeness in the Nome of the Hare, the chief town of which was Khemenu, the present Ashmunein, the town of Taht, who as Khensu-Tehuti was an eighth to the seven gods.

The seven wise masters of Art and Science, with Tehuti in the Lunar Cult, are the same as the seven Sahus with Horus in Orion, the seven born of the Great Mother as the seven powers of Earth. They were reborn of Nut, the Mother in Heaven, as the seven Glorious Ones who were called the Khuti, the seven with Anup-Horus or El-Elyon, situated at the Pole, who were the executors for Him as the Great Judge, and the seven rulers of the Celestial Heptanomis in the Stellar Cult.

The ceremony of the seven stations of the Cross, which is supposed to commemorate the seven resting-places of the Cross on the way to Calvary, is similar to a procession celebrated at Abydos and Memphis when the Tat-Cross was carried round the seven resting-places that marked and memorized the seven stations of the Pole. In one of the ancient Chaldean Oracles the seven stations of the Pole are spoken of as seven Poles. "The Chaldeans call the god Dionysius, or Bacchus, Iao in the Phœnician tongue (instead of the intelligible light) and He is often called Sabaoth, signifying that He is above the seven Poles, that is, Demiurgus" (Taylor: "Collection of Chaldean Oracles"). Iamlichus says of the Chaldeans: "They not only preserved the memorials of twenty-seven myriads of years, as Hipparchus tells us they have, but likewise of the whole Apocatastes and periods of the seven rulers of the world" ("Nat. Gen.," Vol. II, p. 321). These are the seven that were uranographic figures in the Stellar Cult as the seven old ones, the seven Patriarchs of enormous age, the seven giants of colossal stature, the seven rulers of the world, the seven Lords and Masters of eternity. Here in the Lunar Cult they represent the seven wise Masters of Arts and Science with Tehuti, the seven, called the first of the stars which in the beginning were in Heaven, and connected with the Great Year according to Enoch, as is shown by their being cast out until the day of the "great consummation" in "the secret year," also called the period of the Great Judgment. These seven that were separated and single as rulers of the Pole, were also grouped together as a pictorial illustration in the planisphere. The names as given by Enoch are: Azazyel, Amazarak, Armers, Barkayel, Akebeel, Tamiel, and Asaradel. The Egyptian divinized seven elemental Powers represented by the seven Pole Stars of the Lesser Bear. They are the seven who are charged with causing the deluge in the Babylonian legend. Their names were:—

(1) Bel, (2) Ea, (3) Rammon, (4) Nebo, (5) Marduk, (6) Ninib, (7) Nerra,

who equal and correspond to the Egyptian

(1) Set, (2) Sebek-Horus, (3) Shu, (4) Hapi, (5) Tuamutef, (6) Kabhsenuf, (7) Amsta,

respectively, who were the original seven children of the Thigh or Meskhen in the Stellar Cult.

The Crescent Moon of Taht equals or represents a bow. It was figured as a bow in Heaven for a Sign that there should be no further deluge of destruction, because the time and season did not now depend upon the setting or non-setting Stars. Time was now reckoned by Tehuti, the teller, by means of the dual lunation.

Thus the deluge in the Stellar Cult being over, and the power of darkness being defeated and destroyed through the agency of the Lunar Goddess Hathor, the bow of Taht was set in heaven with its promise that the waters should not again cover the earth. This as Egyptian was true Mythos, and not a false explanation of natural fact as the tale in the Hebrew text. It does not mean that the Moon was created then and there to give light for the first time; that would be fictitious history and not Mythology. The Egyptian account is Mythological, the Biblical is pretended history. The Lunar Crescent was not only the bow of the deluge and sign of promise for all future time (not the rainbow which was afterwards substituted), it was also the Ark of safety from the waters of the Nun in which the young child of light was bosomed and reborn of the Lunar Virgin Mother.

In the ancient city of Copan in Guatemala, the Ape or Cynocephalus was frequently represented in the sculptures on the Temple walls in an attitude of adoration. There, as at Thebes, those monkeys were buried in stone tombs in which their skeletons have been found in perfect preservation. It was the same in Babylonia; in Japan, also, we find the similar zootype representation.

In this Cult the "Uræus Serpent of Life" that was worn on the frontlets of the gods and the glorified manes was a sign of protection and safety (Rit., Ch. 34) = Renewal of Eternal Life.

The Lunar Cult must have lasted for a considerable period of time, as we find remains of Lunar Cult Temples in South America, Europe, and other places.

Thus we see that although the imagery was different in the Lunar Cult, the religious ideas and beliefs were the same as in the Stellar, i.e. the type of the Godhead was the Mother, the Child, and the Adult Man.

In "Origin and Evolution of Freemasonry" I have given other types, Signs and Symbols of the Great Mother and her Child as depicted in Lunar Cult.

When the Stellar heptanomis was broken up and divided into four quarters, it was multiplied by four, and twenty-eight signs took the place of the primary seven.

It is said that Anup did not keep correct time in the Stellar phase but let the deluge in, as also did Sothis during the course of precession, on the scale of the Great Year. One of the checks upon Sothis, in the lapse and loss of time was furnished by the Moon. So that Anup might retrieve his character as timekeeper by means of the Moon he became the male Lunar Logos under the name of Taht: thus he passed from the earliest star-state to measure the time by the month instead of the year.

Taht becomes Master of Truth; he maketh the truth, the established order of things, that is, as the reckoner and the keeper of the register of time and period. It is said of Taht, the Lunar god in a Turin Papyrus: "He hath made all that the world contains, and hath given it light when all was darkness and there was as yet no Sun," that is, no Sun as a representative of time.

This was a new creation, the first creation of time was Stellar, the second creation was Lunar, and the third creation was Solar, the latter had not yet come into being.

In the Babylonian account of creation the Moon is produced before the Sun, in reverse order to that of Genesis. Which proves that the Lunar Cult had been carried to, and was known in Babylonia before the Hebrew Solar version came into existence.

CHAPTER XII

SOLAR CULT

THE Solar Cult followed the Lunar; it was called Solar because men had changed the mode of reckoning time. The time was now reckoned by the Sun instead of the Moon or Stars, but much of the Symbology of the former Cults were merged into this. It was a new creation.

There were many phases of this Cult, and I have endeavoured to place these in the order of their evolution.

The Solar, with the Eschatology, lasted about 100,000 years. Exodes of the different phases left their old land and went to various countries. We still find traces of this Cult in the different countries to which they migrated.

Remnants of the Solar Cult Temples are found in most parts of Africa, in Europe, some parts of Asia, Central America, and on the west of South America (where the Incas travelled).[1] These Solar Cult Temples are recognized from the Stellar by the absence of the Iconographic figures. Wherever the Solar Cult people travelled they tried to destroy all previous Cults, and if they could not obliterate these entirely, they imposed as much as possible of their own, and absorbed previous phases into their own.

Hitherto, from the first inception of religious doctrines, the Matriarchal type had been the first and primary, founded on the Totemic ceremonies of primitive man, originating with Mother Earth, followed by the Mother of the Tribe, where the Father was not known, or not recognized, and then astronomically depicted in the

[1] See "Origin and Evolution of the Human Race."

Stellar and Lunar Cults, all symbolized in zootype forms and divinized.

The first phase of the Solar Cult was that of Tem and Tum brought on from the Stellar and Lunar Cults under the name of Atum-Iu as the child (Tem) and Atum-Ra as the father (Tum); it was far older than the Osirian Cult, which might be termed a continuation of it under different names. Iu was another name for Tem, who proclaims himself to be the Sayer in the Ritual (Ch. 82). He says: "I have come forth with the tongue of Tum and the throat of Hathor that I may record the words of my father Tum with my mouth, which draweth to itself the spouse of Seb." That is the mother on earth who was represented in this Cult as Hathor-Iusāas. The speaker here is Horus as Iu the coming Su, or son, who in Egyptian is Iu-sa or Iusa the child of Iusāas the consort of Tum or Amen-Ra. The sayer as Tem or Iu, the son in one character, is Tum himself as father in the other. As Ra, the father, he is the author of the sayings; as Iu, the son, Iusu, he is the utterer of the sayings "with his mouth," or in person on earth as the heir of Seb. To the Egyptians "the words of Tum" were the teachings of an everlasting gospel of truth, law, justice, and right, not to be altered in that which Tum hath uttered (Rit., Ch. 78) by the mouth of the sayer Iu, or by the pen of the writer Taht-Aan. Thus we can identify Tum or Atum-Ra as the author of the sayings which are to be spoken on earth by God the Son.

Tum was the author of the sayings in the Ritual which he gave to Horus (Tem) the Iu-su or coming son as Sayer for him to utter to men and manes in the two characters of the infant Horus of twelve years, and Horus the adult of thirty years (see later, Iu-em-hetep).

On a peninsula of the Indus this side of the gulf, and also in Cochin and beyond, there still remains a vestige of the Cult of Tum. The traditions of these people are that "a certain holy man called Mar-Thome, a Syrian or Egyptian, first came to them with a number of beasts from Syria and Egypt" (Calmet Thomas), that is with the hieroglyphic signs. Thome was the Egyptian god Tum. The Mar or Mer, as the surname of the holy man, is an Egyptian title for superintendent of books and also the royal magi in one person. Thus the Mar-Thome was one of the Egyptian Magi or Rekhi, the superintendent of a college or body of priests who went to India from Egypt, via Syria, as missionaries, and who promulgated the worship of Tum as the Father and Tem as the Son, or Iusa, under the Solar form.

The dual character of Tum as the Father and Tem as the Son, equal to Jesus, enables us to identify the child Jesus in the Gospel of Thomas and to that Gospel being copied from the Egyptian. It is one of the most ancient of the Gospels of the Infancy, called Apocryphal; the origin was unknown. Tum is Thomas in Greek, and the Gospel of Thomas in Greek is the Gospel of Tum in Egyptian.

The "sayings" or Logia may be divided and differentiated into two categories, corresponding to the two characters of the double Horus, the child of twelve years and Horus the adult of thirty years. Horus was the afflicted one who suffered and died and was buried, and it was Horus who rose again as the demonstrator of eternal life in his resurrection from the dead. At first, child Horus was the word made flesh as Logos of the mother, who in this Cult was Hathor-Iusāas in relation to Tum or Atum-Ra (Rit., Ch. 82). Next he was the word made truth as sayer of the father and teacher of the greater mysteries. Thus there are two classes of the sayings: those of the childhood and those of the adultship—those that pertain to the earth of Seb (the earth) and those that are uttered in the earth of eternity. It is said in the Ritual that the words of Taht are "written in the two earths," the earth of Seb, or time, and the earth of eternity ("Ren. and Nav.," Ch. 183).

So the sayings were uttered by Horus, as Tem-Iu, or Jesus, in the double earth of time and of eternity. In the "Pistis Sophia" (390 Mead) it is said of "the sayings," "Jesus spake these words unto his disciples in the midst

Drawn by K. Watkins.

THE GOD TEMU IN HUMAN FORM.

The primary form was the Serpent Zootype.

PLATE XLIII.

[To face p. 216.

The God Tem seated in his Boat resting on the Waters of Heaven, as witnessed by the Hieroglyphic Pet=Heaven or Sky. The Four Oars represent the Four Brothers.

Tem-Temu, or Ātem, or Ra-Tem was the first "living" man-god "described" by the Egyptians, represented in human form, i.e. a manifestation of God in human form. He wears the Crown of the North and South.

Plate XLIV.

[To face p. 217.

of Amenta," whence they went forth three by three to the four points of heaven to preach the Gospel of the Kingdom. This was also in the earth of eternity, *versus* the *earth of time*.

Tum, in the Ritual, is pre-eminently "the lord." In one Chapter (79) he is addressed as "the lord of heaven," "the lord of life," "the lord of all creatures," "the lord of all." Thus the Ritual contains "the sayings of the Lord."

In his incarnation Horus, or Iu, the Su, or Son, indicates that he "disrobes himself," to "reveal himself," when he presents himself on the earth (Ch. 71). In his birth he says, "I am the Babe" born as the connecting link betwixt earth and heaven and as one who does not die the second death (Ch. 42). He is pursued by the Herrut-reptile, but as he says, " his egg remains unpierced by the destroyer." He escapes from the slaughter of the innocents (see Herod), and on entering the earth-life Horus knows it to be in accordance with his lot that he should suffer death, or come to an end and be no more (Rit., Ch. 8). He also knows that he is a *living soul*. As such he has that within him which surviveth all overthrow: even if he may be buried in the deep dark grave he will not be annihilated there. He will rise again (Chaps. 10, 30A).

The original legend of the suffering and descent of the Great Spirit on earth in the form of a man was during the Stellar Cult. There can be no doubt of that, for the proof still exists where He is depicted on the two Poles (North and South) and not on the Cross.[1] As Cult succeeded Cult, the evolution of religion gradually assumed a higher type and was symbolized differently in each Cult. The old wise men of Egypt never lost anything; they brought on all the originals and added to them.

The difficulty has been to place the various portrayals of evolution in the correct order, and this has been caused by the latest phase, the Osirian, having been given the most prominent place in the Ritual, which has obscured

[1] See "Arcana of Freemasonry," p. 41.

the former imagery, as these have been brought on, and mixed with the latest development.

The elder Horus came to earth in the body of his humility. It is said of him—Horus, Har-si-Hesi—he was born but not begotten, who issued out of silence as "The Logos" (Rit., Ch. 24). He is called the Kheru in Egyptian, which not only signifies the Word, but also denotes a victim doomed to be sacrificed, whether as the sufferer on the Tat, or on the Cross, or as the victim bound for slaughter. He comes to earth as the one God in the form of a man.

At first in the Stellar Cult all his powers and attributes were represented in zootype forms and mythologically depicted as the son of the virgin Neith. It was in the earliest history of man that the great God came and gave his "Logos" to man.

Har-Ur was one of the earliest names given to the great God : he who came on earth " in the form of a man " to give the message to his people for guidance for future generations. It is said in the Ritual that he instructed his brothers (four brothers or disciples) up to the regions of the primary Mystery, the Mystery within the veil, the veil that was rent in death which is before all Mysteries, because it is the Mystery of the One Eternal God and the son who issues from the father in his likeness, which two were one.

This shows how the people of later generations, after the Great God in Spirit, "in the form of a man" had visited the earth to give his message to men for future generations, had portrayed his coming and going, at the earliest period of the Stellar Cult, and we shall now see how they depicted this in Symbolic imagery and how it has been carried on through the various Cults ever since. There are quite sufficient records still extant to prove this, notwithstanding the different representations and traditions which arose during the various Cults that followed one after the other. Much of the first, or original message, no doubt was lost, especially as all the sacred message given by God to man must have been handed down orally, as until the Stellar Cult there were no writings; even then, up to the time of the Solar Cult, all writings were in glyphs or hieroglyphics only. One of the results of this message was the building of the Great Pyramid, a living book in stone, wherein is portrayed "The Ritual of Ancient Egypt," the oldest sacred writings in the world, written in Sign Language.

In the Solar Mythos Horus was symbolically represented as the Sun God. The pole and equinox are travelling *pari passu*, one in the upper circle of the heavens, the other in the larger lower circle of the ecliptic, and the shifting of the equinox was correlated more or less exactly to the changing of the pole star. The circuit of precession was imaged by the Shennu ring, the symbol of the eternal, or seven eternals; also by the coiled serpent with its Eye in the centre, tail in mouth, the serpent of eternity.

The power that presided over the pole was transferred and given rebirth as Horus in the vernal equinox.

As the Stellar Pole God, he was the earliest maintainer of the equipoise and equilibrium in the revolving system of the heavens. Horus as the Power in the Pole Star symbolized fhe Lord of Eternity. Horus in the equinox (or double equinox) was a traveller of eternity manifesting in the sphere of time.

In the Ritual, Chapter 54, it says: "I am the God who keepeth opposition in equipoise," "As the Egg which circles round." The Egg is the Sun. (What the Sun is at the centre of the Solar System the Pole Star had been at the centre of the Stellar universe.) In one phase the Sun was imaged as a golden egg laid by a goose. The lake of the goose is referred to in the Ritual, Chapter 109, the goose being an image of the Earth, the Ancient Mother who laid her egg every morning in the waters of space.

For some time the Pole Star in the Lesser Bear coincided with the vernal equinox in the sign of Pisces.

Previously the Pole Star, "α *Draconis*," coincided with the vernal equinox in the sign of the Ram.

A seventh of the ecliptic was assigned to one or other

of the seven Pole Star Gods, who became the Lords of Eternity. This explains how the Ram could be the special constellation of the God who was at the same time the ruler of the North Pole Star. This celestial drama is portrayed in the Book of Revelation; the fall of the dragon, or, astronomically, the change of the Pole Star when a *Draconis* was superseded, is followed by the exaltation of the "Lamb" upon "the Mount of Solar Glory."

In the Stellar Cult the Great Bear made a circuit on the outside of the "never-setting stars," and the birthplace in heaven was imaged as the Leg or Haunch (Meskhen) constellated in the circle of perpetual visibility.

In the Stellar Cult, when the tail of the Great Bear pointed South, it pointed to the birthplace in water; now, when the Cult became Solar and the tail of the Great Bear pointed Northwards, the Sun coincided with the sign of Aquarius. There was a rebirth of water from the Abyss that issued from the mouth of Pisces Australes, and the picture, or source in the Abyss, was repeated, the wet nurse or Waterer being constellated in the Zodiac as the multi-mammalian, or Menat, who was thus the Solar and later form of Apt, the Water-Cow of the Stellar Cult. The imagery shows the perennial source of water in the underworld and that which preceded from the mouth of the fish now emanates from the numerous mammæ of the wet nurse of the ecliptic.

Nubti, in this Cult, represented the dual Goddess—the Sun combined with Sothis—a known figure.

When it was discovered that the Moon derived its Light and Glory from the unseen Sun, then there was a change. The Moon was previously a Mother to the Child of Light whom she was unable to affiliate, but now, as mythically rendered, she learned that she was a wife (hemt) as well as Mother, and that her infant was begotten by the Solar God. In the Ritual, Chapter 80, it is portrayed as one of the Mysteries of Amenta.

Heket, who was consort of Khnum the Lord of the

Inundation in the Lunar Cult, was also seer of the Night in the Moon in the Solar Cult. Khnum was brought on

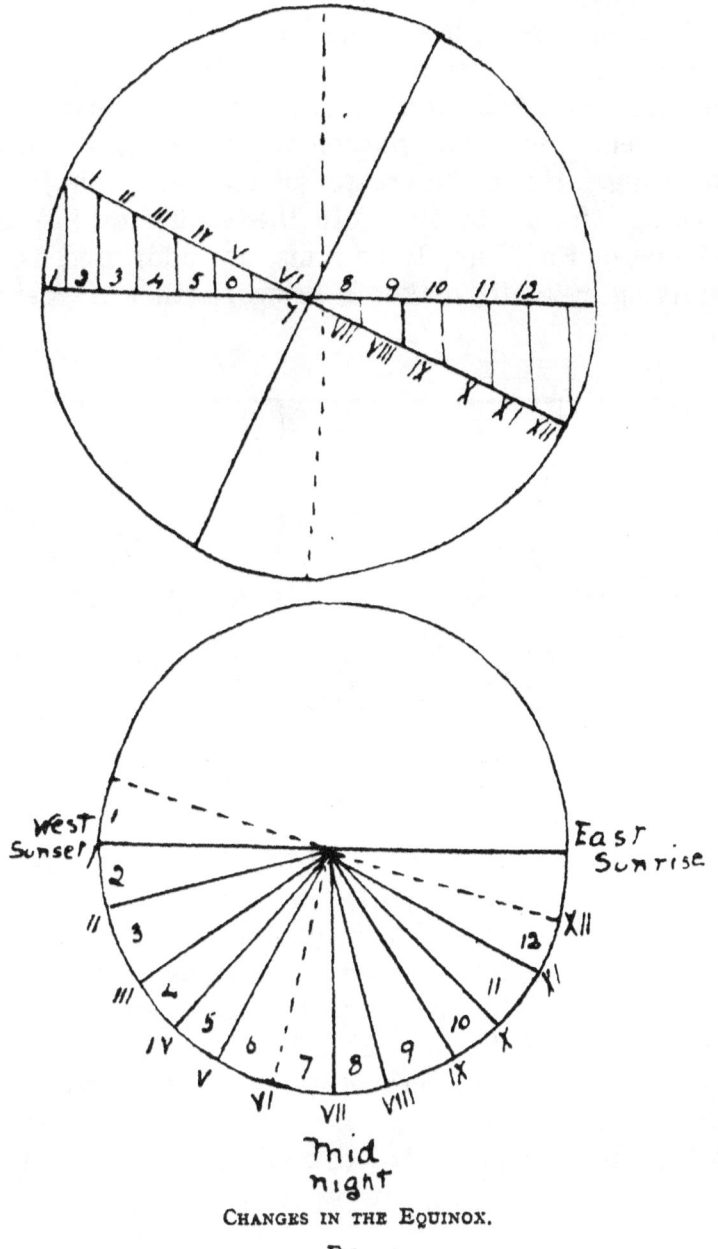

CHANGES IN THE EQUINOX.
FIG. 32.

as Khnum-Ra whose wife was Ank and his two consorts were Heket and Sati.

Tum was brought on as Tum-Ra, the setting Sun, or closer of the Western Gate, and Tem as the opener of the Eastern Gate.

Tum was the earliest name of Atum.

Tum, in the opening verse of Chapter 78, is called the great god, self-produced, and is addressed as Lord of Heaven, who givest motion to all things which came into being. He is the creator of men and things: men proceeded from his eye. In the sepulchral inscription of Panehsi, Ra, Tum, Harmachis, are addressed as " one god living by truth, maker of beings, author of existences,

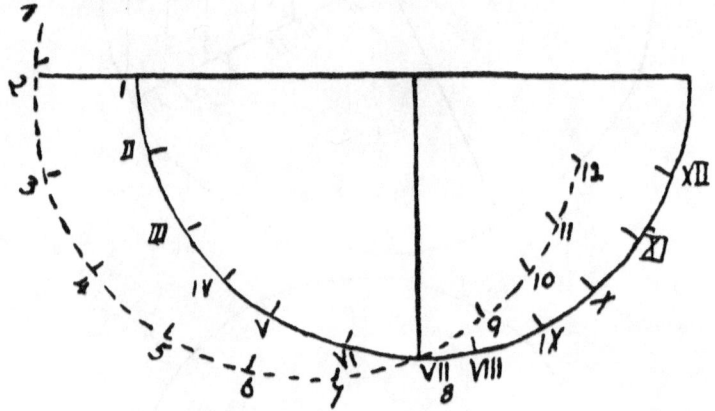

DIAGRAMATIC PORTRAYAL OF THE SHIFTING OF THE EQUINOX.
FIG. 33.

of beasts and men proceeding from the eye" (" Records of the Past," Vol. XII, p. 141).

One form or type of Tum (as the Sun God in Amenta) was the Ass. A vignette in the Ritual shows the Ass being devoured by the serpent of darkness, called " the eater of the Ass " (Rit., Ch. 10).

In the Solar, the birthplace was shifted to the vernal equinox, and as the equinox receded the birthplace went with it from zodiacal sign to zodiacal sign. The time of the Sun parted company with the time of the Great Bear and Ursa Minor and the Inundation for a cycle of 25,827 years.

The point of the birthplace being thus shifting, the point was determined by the position of the vernal

EGYPTIAN SIGNS OF THE ZODIAC.

FIG. 34.

equinox, as it travelled from sign to sign in the circuit of precession, and Khebt, or Apt, the Goddess of the Great Bear, was said " to preside over the birth of the Sun."

In the Stellar Cult she had presided over the birth of Horus in the Inundation. In the Lunar she presided over Khnmu, as Meskenat, but when the Solar time was established the child became Solar as well, and Horus as the Sun God, Horus Har-Makhu superseded Sebek-Horus of the Stellar Cult and Khnmu of the Lunar.

The place of birth being shifted to the vernal equinox,

THE EATER OF THE ASS:

FIG. 35.

the birth itself was, therefore, no longer timed to the Inundation.

The child or Messu of the Inundation on his papyrus was now brought forth as the young Solar God.

The Solar imagery of Horus of the Inundation was imaged as the Sun-God on the Western Horizon in the Autumn equinox, when as Har-Makhu, he was conceived or incorporated as the Virgin's child. It was at this point that Horus entered the earth or matrix of the Mother of the Mount, and thus became the child of Seb (God of the earth), and at first Hathor Iusāas and later Isis, by adoption, but not by begettal.

In the eastern equinox he rose again as Horus of the

double force or double feather, later double crown. When the Sun set at night, or in the autumn season, it sank down below the horizon, which Horus Sebek swam as a fish to cross the Abyss and rise again. The crossing was from equinox to equinox from the western to the eastern side of the mount, from the sign Virgo in the autumn to the sign of Pisces in the vernal equinox.

When the autumn equinox occurred in Virgo, that was the place of conception for Sebek of the Inundation. Six months later, the Sun rose again in the sign of Pisces and in the eastern equinox, where the fish as child and consort, or as the two crocodiles, became the two fishes with Neith as mother on one horizon and Sekhet on the other.

In Sign Language the Virgin Neith conceived her child as Sebek-Horus, which was duplicated to express adult ship. Thus we have portrayed in Sign Language the picture of Child-Horus standing on two crocodiles, or Neith suckling her two crocodiles, to express the power of the Double Horus; that is, Har-Ur, the elder Horus, is described as " the old child who became young." It is the elder Horus who transforms into the younger Horus on the Mount of Glory in the vernal equinox.

The double power was expressed by duplicating the type. In the first place it was the little suffering Sun who went down in the underworld to be buried and to transform and rise again.

In the zodiac of Denderah the sign of the Scales contains a portrait of Har-pi-Khart as Horus the Child who was conceived or incorporated in that sign as Horus of the double equinox called Har-Makhu, also called " the double Harmakhu " (Records, V, 12, p. 53), and this duality was imaged in the Sphinx.

Heru-Pa-Khart (Harpocrates) called Horus the younger (or the child) was so called by many to distinguish him from Heru-ur or Horus the Elder.

In the Egyptian pictures he is represented in the form of a youth wearing a lock of hair, the symbol of youth, on the right side of his head, sometimes he wears the triple crown with feathers and disk and the like, and sometimes a disk with plumes; but usually his crown is formed by the united crowns of the South and North. In one scene he is seated inside a box which rests on the back of a lion.

Heru-Pa-Khart was symbolic of the earliest rays of the rising sun. The Egyptians distinguished seven forms or aspects of the God which may be thus enumerated:

1. Heru-Ra-p-Khart.
2. Heru-Shu-p-Khart the Great.
3. Sma-Taui-p-Khart, son of Hathor.
4. Heru-p-Khart, the dweller in Busiris.
5. Ahi, son of Hathor.
6. Haq-p-Khart, the son of Sekhet.
7. Heru-Hennu, i.e. Horus the Child.

Horus in the zodiac was not simply the Lord of Life as the bringer of food and water. He was also the Solar God, who was the child conceived in Virgo, as Horus of the Inundation, who was Horus of the Resurrection, Lord of the harvest in the sign of Pisces.

In the Kamite zodiacs the fish-mother gives re-birth to her child as a fish in the constellation of the fishes, also in other monuments the Mother, as Hathor-Isis, bears the fish upon her head. Thus the fish-man, or fish-god, was re-born of the fish-mother in the abode of the abyss, or the house of the fish, and the point of emergence for the sun-god in the zodiac was indicated by the sign of the fish or fishes, as Horus of the two crocodiles, with the sign of Pisces.[1]

Thus the symbolical representation of the primary phases of the Solar Cult was that which has been termed the Cult of Atum-Iu or Aiu or Iou (and many other names for the same one). The portrayal was Atum-Iu as the Child of twelve on the one Horizon and Atum-Ra as the Father on the other.

---

[1] This picture is well depicted in "Origin and Evolution of Freemasonry," p. 156.

STELLA OF HORUS FROM MEMPHIS.

Standing on two Crocodiles and strangling serpents, a power of darkness, in his hand.

PLATE XLV.

The portrait of Har-pi-Khart in the zodiac of Denderah in the sign of the "Scales," identifies Him as Horus of the double equinox, called Har-Makhu. The name identifies Child-Horus with the Sign of Scales. In Egyptian the word "Makhu" denotes "scales" and the scales denote the equinox as the point of equipoise. The Greek word "Harmachis" is derived from the Egyptian word "Makhu," for the balance or scales and thence for the level of the equinox, when the balance was erected on the day of weighing words and of reckoning the years. The Horus of the double equinox was also termed "the double Hermakhu" (Records, Vol. XII, p. 53), and this duality was imaged in the two-foldness of the Sphinx with its tail to the west and head to the east, pointing to the Equinox each way.

Drawn by K. Watkin

HERU-PA-KHART. HORUS THE YOUNGER A CHILD (SEVEN FORMS).

In the above image he is seen with the sign of Silence. The Logos issuing out of Silence. In his left hand he carries the two emblems, the Crook and Flail and a Dove—the bird of Hathor, also a sign of the Holy Spirit. On his head is the Crown resting on two Horns—a Lunar symbol of Hathor.

PLATE XLVI.

The sun sinking down every evening into the underworld is described in the Ritual, "The Egg of the great Cackler," "the Egg that Seb hath parted from the earth" (Ch. 54). The soul of the sun in the Egg is the soul of Ra in the underworld, and when the sun issues from the egg (as a Hawk) it is the death of darkness, the evil Apap. Horus the young Solar god is slayer of the evil Dragon by piercing him in the eye. The eye of

Drawn by K. Watkins.

HE IS RELEASING THE LIGHT THAT THE GREAT EVIL SERPENT OF DARKNESS HAD SWALLOWED.

Mexican portrayal of Horus piercing the Serpent of drought and darkness, as God of Heaven in eight divisions above, Stella, and also of Heaven in ten divisions (Solar) depicted below. The whole forms Heaven as a square with the four ideographs for his four Brothers as the four supports at each corner.

FIG. 36.

Apap is the great Dragon, the serpent of darkness who coiled about the tree of Dawn, and Horus slays the Monster with the tree, or stake, or branch as he comes up from the underworld as the Light.

This imagery was brought on and portrayed in Rome; the proof has been recently established by the discovery of an ancient chapel in the catacombs where the above is plainly depicted with other scenes taken from the Egyptian Amenta.

I give here the Mexican portrayal, where Horus is seen slaying the evil Apap by piercing him and slaying him with the light, cutting him in pieces so that he should give up all the light that he had swallowed.

Horus here is depicted as god of "Am-Khemen," or the Paradise of the eight great gods (Stellar symbol above) as well as the Heaven of the ten (Solar) founded on the square. His four brothers, now his children, are depicted in ideographs at the four corners of the square.

The Sun was not considered as human in its nature when the Solar force at dawn was imaged by the Lion-faced Atum, the flame of the furnace by the fiery serpent Uati, the Soul of its life by the Hawk, the Ram, or the Crocodile. Until Har-ur the elder Horus was depicted as the child in the place of the calf or lamb, fish, or shoot of papyrus plant, which now occurred in the Solar Cult, no human figure was personalized in the Mythology of Egypt.

When the Lunar Cult was first changing into the Solar, Khnum Ra takes the place of Khnum, and Isis in this Cult takes the place of Hathor as the Mother-Moon, the reproducer of light in the underworld. The place of conjunction and of re-begettal by the Sun-god was in the underworld, when she became the woman clothed with the sun. At the end of lunation the old Moon died and became a corpse; it is at times portrayed as a mummy in the underworld and there it was revivified by the Sun-god, the Solar fecundation of the Moon representing the Mother, resulting in her bringing forth the child of light the "cripple deity," who was begotten in the dark. Now he was no longer a bastard, because Taht, the recorder of Truth, had demonstrated the Father.[1]

Superhuman nature powers, or elemental souls, which were first represented by the Totems and which are also representative of the Totemic Motherhood, were pre-human and totemic.

The derivation and descent of human souls from these

[1] See Mexican portrayal of this in "Origin and Evolution of Human Race," p. 432.

superhuman elemental nature powers was at first *direct;* afterwards they were represented by Totemic zootypes, but no souls, specialized as human, were derived from pre-human nature souls from which both man and animal derived a soul of life in common.

The progenitor, as male, was not recognized at first as such, although he was now. The bringer forth was female from the first, the descent was first traced by the Totem and afterwards by the name.

The Gods were spirits, or powers, which had never been human. They were forces of nature, divinized as superhuman.

The Ghost, when recognized, was human still, however much he was changed and glorified, he was still " the human."

But Mother-Earth had never been a *human* Mother in any form in which she was imaged ; the Serpent Rannit, Nut the Celestial Waterer, the gods of the Pole, Anup-Horus, the Moon-god Taht, or the Sun-god Ra, these were all divinized elemental superhuman powers, and therefore propitiated or worshipped as such. Powers that were impersonal and non-human were, in the Solar Cult, given human forms, though originally they were all of zootype forms, or images.

When once the *soul of blood born of woman* had been discriminated as a *human* soul, it was no longer possible to postulate a return of that same soul to a pre-human status. Readjustment was made by the wisdom of the Egyptians, but elsewhere it was misunderstood.

In the Buddhist metaphysic the soul (theoretically) continued to pass through the same " cycle of necessity " with the totemic souls, which had been pre-human creatures of the elements.

In the Solar Cult the human soul had been discreted and discriminated from the animistic and totemic souls and personalized in Horus as the Child of the Blood-Mother. This was Horus in the flesh, or matter. A divine soul was then imaged as the Horus who had died and risen again in spirit from the dead. The powers previously extant had been united and continued as the seven souls of Ra. In the Ritual they are the seven elemental powers divinized as the "Ancestors of Ra," those who preceded him in time, but now are "in his following" (Rit., Ch. 178, pp. 22, 34; Ch. 180, p. 36).

Ra is now represented or imaged as the self-originated, invisible, and eternal being, the father in spirit, who is not to be apprehended save through the mediumship of Horus the son: that is, Horus in spirit who bears witness for the father in his resurrection from the dead by testifying to the hidden source of eternal life, the Horus who says in the Ritual, "I am the everlasting One" (Ch. 42), "Witness of Eternity is my name." In him the human Horus divinized in death becomes the spirit-medium of the father-god. Ra, the Holy Spirit, was recognized as the source of a divine descent from human souls, who were higher in status than the earlier gods, who were elemental powers, and higher than the Mother-soul, which had been incarnated in the human Horus. A spirit that lived for ever was now the supreme type of the human soul. The typical seven souls in the one are repeated in the Eschatology as a *type* in the other. The seven elemental souls were continued as the seven souls of Ra and described as the "Ancestors of Ra."

The earliest human soul which followed those that were derived from the elements had not attained the power of reproduction for an after life, on which account the likeness of the elder Horus in the Mythos is an impubescent child (Fig. 37, Mexican). But when he makes his transformation in death, Horus has acquired the reproducing power. In the Eschatology the reproducing power is spiritual. It is the power of resurrection and of reappearing as a spirit, that is the divine double of the human soul, which was considered as the eighth in degree. When Horus rose again from the dead as the divine double of the human Horus, he exclaims: "I am he who cometh forth and proceedeth. I am the everlasting One, I am Horus, who steppeth onwards through eternity" (Rit., Ch. 42, p. 177).

The foundation of Monotheism was laid when the various powers were combined in a single deity to be worshipped as the one true eternal spirit. These were primarily the Great Mother and her elemental powers, the primary imagery being a dual god, or a god with two attributes, represented by Set and Horus, Darkness and Light, which was followed by the conception of a god with three attributes, breathing force, air, or wind, being added to the two previous ones. The primary Trinity was followed by four more elemental powers being

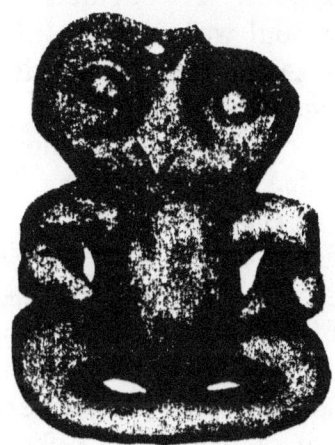

THE ELDER HORUS OR HAR-UR AS AN IMPUBESCENT CHILD. (*Mexican depiction.*)

For others, see "Origin and Evolution of Human Race," pp. 232 and 233.

FIG. 37.

added as attributes to the three, i.e. seven in all. When the goddess was superseded by the god Atum, both sexes were included in the One Supreme Being who was now Lord over all. The fatherhood was established in place of the motherhood.

Atum, the Egyptian Holy Spirit, was the image of the author of that spirit by which totemic man became a living soul. With the Egyptian the soul was of both sexes. The divine being, Atum-Ptah, or later Osiris, was imaged as of a biune nature; hence they are portrayed as male and female in one figure or image. The soul divided in the two halves of sex was united again in establishing an eternal soul. Thus the soul that lived for ever was held to be established for eternity by the female being blended with the male.

When the human soul had been derived from the essence of the male instead of the blood of the female (as Horus had been derived from the blood of the Virgin Isis) the woman was naturally derived from the man, as she is in the second of the Hebrew creations described in the book of Genesis. A soul derived from Atum was dual in sex. This soul was divided into Adam and Eve, the typical two sexes of the Hebrew legend. Adam was Atum in the original Mythos.

The ascent of soul through various elemental phases of existence is alluded to in one of the " sayings of Jesus," when it is said that the fowls of the air, the beasts of the earth, and the fishes of the sea all " draw us " to the Kingdom. These led the way as elemental and pre-human. A soul of the air was imaged by the bird, a soul of the earth was imaged by the beasts, or reptile, a soul of water by the fish, a soul of vegetation by the shoot or branch, etc., all of which are offsprings of the Great Mother. But the highest soul was now derived from God the Father as an effluence of the Holy Spirit. Therefore it is said: "The Kingdom of Heaven is within you: and whosoever shall know himself shall find it." " Know yourselves and you shall be aware that ye are the sons of the Father." Horus in his resurrection, at his second advent, came to proclaim the father as the begetter of a spirit which should attain eternal life. He also came to personate that spirit in the likeness of the father to the Manes in Amenta.

Professor Maspero in his "The Dawn of Civilization" states that Egypt never accepted the idea of the one sole god beside whom there is none other. But Professor Maspero was wrong in making such a statement. Every description applied to the one god in the Hebrew writings was pre-extant in the Egyptian.

Atum-Ra declares that he is the one God, the one just or righteous God, the one living God, the one God living in truth. He is Unicus, the sole and only one (Rit., Chaps. 2, 17) beside whom there is none other; as the Egyptians state he is the only one from whom all other powers in nature were derived in the earlier types of deity.

When Atum is said to be "the Lord of Oneness," that is but a way of calling him the One God, the culmination of all powers in one supreme power; all the various gods and goddesses were but representations of various powers, attributes of the *One* God. In the Ritual, Chapter 62, the Everlasting is described as Neb-Huhi Nuti Terui-f, the eternal Lord, he who is without limit, or who is the god of limitless dilation. Fu-nen-tera is a mode of describing the infinite by means of the illimitable. Without limit is beyond the finite, and consequently equal to the infinite. Teru also signifies time. The name, therefore, conveyed the conception of beyond time.

The Mystery of Horus of the Double Horizon was finally imaged in the great Sphinx of Gizeh, which was cut out of the solid rock by man as a representative image of Horus as the god Har-Makhu. The Sphinx itself informs us of the fact. On the stele of Tahtmes IV it is called "the Sphinx of Khepra, the very mighty, the greatest of the Spirits and the most August." Kheper is a form of Tum-Harmakhis, or Atum-Harmakhis, the solar form of the god of the double horizon in the previous form of the Cult. Now he becomes the god in Spirit, the one god living in truth, the sole power that was worshipped as eternal. This is "the greatest of spirits" represented by the Sphinx of Khepra (the transformer). We learn from the Ritual that the Mystery of the Sphinx originated with the mount of earth as the passage, or place of passage, of burial and re-birth for the solar god. The stele of Tahtmes informs us that the Sphinx was built to commemorate the sacred place of creation, " of the first time," i.e. of a new creation. The fact is that the Sphinx was carved out of the rock at the exact centre of the earth as a lasting witness to "that sacred place of creation," or beginning, which goes back to the domain of Set and to the days of the masters of Ker " or the figure of the primitive Abyss, or Void."

The perfect type is thus represented as dual, as the lion and the lioness combined, only the fore-part, the head, has been rendered anthropomorphically in the likeness of the Pharaoh, who was the lion ruler at the time. The Great Sphinx, as keeper of the secrets, is couched in repose upon the horizon in the eastern equinox, when the gate of the "fair exit" was in the lion sign, and the gate of "fair entrance" was in Aquarius, the water sign that is figured over the abyss of source on the celestial globe. The Sphinx, then, is a monument which was made by these great builders as a figure of the Double Horizon, and of the duality of Har-Makhu. It was erected on the spot where the place of conjunction was at the point of precession in the lion sign and was assigned to Atum-Harmachis or Har-Makhu. Harmachis entered the Sphinx at sunset in the West, or hinder-part, and was born in the East as Horus of the fore-part, lion-faced.

In the Hebrew tradition Adam is associated with the equinox, and the reason was because Adam was the Jews' image of the Egyptian Atum—god of the Double Horizon.

The Sphinx is female in the hinder-part and male in front.

It is a compound image of the Mother-Earth and the young god whom she brought forth upon the horizon of the resurrection. In the picture taken from the tomb of Rameses IV "Aka-Nefer" ("Fair entrance") is written at one end, and "Par-Nefer" ("Fair exit") at the other.

The ancient Egyptian name for the Sphinx is Akar. This was also a name for the hollow of the underworld. Thus the passage through the mount of earth, imaged as the Cow, was followed by the passage through Akar, the Sphinx, which was built for the god Har-Makhu.

The Ritual says, in speaking of the character of the

Drawn by K. Watkins.

THE GREAT SPHINX OF EGYPT.

PLATE XLVII.

Drawn by K. Watkins.

MĀYA PORTRAYAL OF THE SPHINX.

It was found half-buried in the forests of Yucatan near a Solar Temple by my friend the late Dr. Le Plongeon.

PLATE XLVIII.

[*To face p.* 232.

INDIAN PORTRAYAL OF HORUS WITH LUTE.
PLATE XLIX.

Drawn by K. Watkins.
HORUS AS THE GOD OF GAMES, DANCING, AND MUSIC.
(*Mexican Typology.*)

He is here represented as Horus of twelve years and holds the Head of Bes of thirty years in his hand.

PLATE L.

[*To face p.* 233.

newly risen solar god : " I am the offspring of yesterday, the tunnels of the earth have given me birth and I am revealed at my appointed time in the coming forth to-day" (Ren., Ch. 64). It is said that the very bones of the deities quake as the stars go on their triumphant courses through the tunnels of Akar (Pyramid Text, Teta, 319). The speaker is in Akar, which is represented by the goddess Akerit, because it was the place of burial and re-birth.

Renouf says that to understand the nature of Akar we must imagine a tunnel (oblong) starting from the spot where the sun sets extending through the earth as far as the sun rises. Each end of the tunnel has a sphinx-like form.

If we take the signs in the circle of precession, the two Lions correspond to the duality of Atum-Horus, i.e. Atum-Iu and Atum-Ra.

The two Beetles to Kheper-Ptah. The two Gemini to Set and Horus; the Bull and Calf to Osiris and Horus; the Ram and Lamb to Ammon-Ra and Khemsu; the two fishes to the twin crocodiles (as six different illustrations of the sun of the two horizons at six different landing-stages on the other side of the celestial deep). Thus the double Harmachis includes two characters corresponding to the two equinoxes on the double horizon. In one he is the conception of a virgin; in the other he is brought forth by the parturient Mother.

In one he is the calf of time; in the other he is the bull of eternity. In one he is Horus in matter; in the other he is Horus in spirit. In one he is the child of twelve years; in the other he is the adult of thirty years. The first was the founder, the second was the fulfiller. The first was Horus of the incarnation, the second is Horus of the resurrection.

Horus of the resurrection in the Solar Mythos was the prototype of Amsu in the Eschatology, who rose up in spirit from the inert condition of the mummy, as conqueror of death and all the banded powers of evil.

The doctrines of the incarnation and the resurrection

234   THE ORIGIN AND EVOLUTION

were established in the Cult of Har-Makhu anthropomorphically; Horus the child in one equinox, who was Horus the adult in the other, constituted the double Harmachis, one as the founder, the other as the fulfiller; one as Horus of the incarnation, the other as Horus of the resurrection. The doctrine was Solar, symbolically at

MEXICAN PORTRAYAL OF ATUM-IU.   Drawn by K. Watkins.

The young Sun God coming up from "the underworld" with the Egyptian hieroglyphic "Iu" on his feet, that is Atum-Iu of Egypt: two men playing or saluting on conch-shell trumpet; two men offering burnt incense: two men making blood offering by piercing the ears.

FIG. 38.

first; but next it was Eschatological. The doctrine was at least as ancient as the Virgin in the zodiac, who conceived in Virgo and the mother who brought forth in Pisces. The Solar God who united the two horizons was the fulfiller of the annual circle, and came to reign as king for one year, first in the inundation, and then in the zodiac. He also came in the character of the great Judge to see that justice should be periodically administered.

In the Stellar, Anup-Horus had been the great Judge, with the seat of Judgment at the place of equipoise, which was then at the celestial pole. In the Solar this was shifted to the vernal equinox and the mount of glory to the East. An ideal of justice, truth, and righteousness, imaged by the balances or scales, was postulated as established and eternal in the heavens as the reign of Law, and there was an annual attempt to make that justice visible and veritable on earth. Har-Makhu came as the great Judge, accompanied by the seven great spirits who were his executioners, called the seven arms of the balance. The balance was a figure of the equinoctial level, for the weighing of hearts and words. The unjust were punished, wrongs righted, and restitution enforced.

The two Lions expresses the double glory of the double Horus, who was Lord of the Solar force that was double in the vernal equinox. Horus of the double horizon was also Horus of the two Lions.

In the Ritual, Horus rises again, saying: "I am the twin Lions, the heir of Ra" (Ch. 38, 1). He is Horus rising in the strength of the two Lions as the "Lion of the luminous course." Again, he says: "I go out from the dwelling of the two Lions to the house of Isis the divine" (which was in Sothis), "I complete the greatness of Shu the Lion" (Ch. 78, 22, 24).[1]

I reproduce here (Fig. 38) a picture from MS. of Sahagun's work, preserved in Florence, which portrays a life-like picture of Horus as Atum-Iu of Egypt, being worshipped as in Egypt, i.e. with incense-burning and blood offering, accompanied with music.

Horus is depicted as coming up from the underworld. His name, the Egyptian Hieroglyph for Iu, is written on the front of his feet; his head and shoulders depict

[1] For Vignette, see "Origin and Evolution of Freemasonry."

286 THE ORIGIN AND EVOLUTION

the young "rising sun," the typical symbol of Atum-Iu. He is being saluted by the priests. Two men are playing on conch-shell trumpets. Two men are offering burning incense. Two men are making blood offerings by piercing their ears (which was one of the modes of the Mexicans, the same as the Arunta offer blood from their penes).

Drawn by K. Watkins.

BES-HORUS WITH EGYPTIAN HARP, PLAYING. GOD OF GAMES, DANCING, AND MUSIC.

FIG 39.

Horus in the constellation of Lyra, or Horus with the lyre or harp of seven strings (Fig. 39) was the sevenfold one as a divine type of attainment, the octave and the height in music as well as in the building of the heavens. This Horus who imaged the first form of the "All-One" in whom the seven powers were unified in perfect harmony; "Horus who tore out the sinews of Set and, by depriving him of Power, turned the discord of the universe to harmony." He was consequently depicted in the constellation of Lyra as the maker of music which was played upon the harp, the lute, the lyre, or the sevenfold pipes of Pan, as a figure of the "*All One.*" The figures here depicted, one from India (Plate XLIX) and one from Mexico (Plate L) in America, prove how the wisdom of the Ancient Egyptian was carried over the world by the exodes that left that mother-country. The Greek and Roman portrayals were as Apollo with his Lyre, and Orpheus with his Lute.

CHAPTER XIII

SOLAR CULT (*continued*)

THE Mystery of Tem and Tum, or Atum Iu and Atum Ra, and a later evolution of the same under the name of Har-Makhu and the Double Equinox, was known to St. Paul, who was a master of the secret wisdom. The doctrine concerning Tum, or Atum-Harmachis, is well stated by him, only it has been rendered as metaphrastic. The two Atums, or Atum and Nefer-Atum are replaced by the first and second Adam, as the man of earth, and the man from heaven. The second Atum was "he who is our peace," with the title of Iu-em-hetep. This, as the second Horus, was "he who made both one" and "broke down the middle wall of partition" "that he might create in himself of the twain one new man." "The middle wall of partition" is a figure in the eschatology of that which was a fact in the equinoctial mythos. (Eph. ii, 14, 15.)

The doctrine of the incarnation and the resurrection, brought on from the Stellar, was established in the Solar Cult, under the phase of Fatherhood, the Horus of the double equinox. Horus the child in one equinox, who was Horus the adult in the other, constituted the double Harmachis, one as the founder and one as the fulfiller, one as Horus of the incarnation, the other as Horus of the resurrection. The doctrine was at first depicted as Solar, mythologically, and next Eschatological.

We have seen the different portrayals and phases which were evolved of Horus as God of the Double Horizon or the Double Equinox.

Firstly, it was Horus as Horus Behutet, God of the Axe, God of the Hut, or Winged-Disk, when he crossed

ORIGIN AND EVOLUTION OF RELIGION

(first) from the Horizon South to the Horizon North; (secondly) from the Horizon West to the Horizon East on the Vulture's Wings, or on the wings of the Hawk. Another imagery was Horus as Aten.

Secondly.—He crosses from the Horizon West to the Horizon East as Crocodile, or Great Fish, i.e. Sebek-Horus, who swims the waters of space round about the earth, i.e. on the outside of the Earth.

Thirdly.—In the Lunar Cult he makes his passage from West to East through the Cow of Earth imaged as the Cow Meh-ur, an image of the Mount of Earth.

Fourthly.—As Tem, he makes his passage through the underworld from one Horizon (West) to the other (East), typified by the Sun sinking down in the Abyss in the West and rising again in the Eastern Horizon.

Fifthly.—As Atum, as a worm he made the crossing through the Earth.

Sixthly.—The Sphinx was an image created by man symbolical of the Mount of Earth, for the passage of Horus as Har-Makhu, or Atum-Harmachis, for crossing from the Western to the Eastern Horizon, through the body of the Sphinx.

The conception and representation of the Sun as a worm passing through the earth from West to East is proved by the 87th Chapter of the Ritual, where it says: " I am Seta (Earthworm) at the confines of the Earth. I lay myself down (at evening) in the West, I restore myself and I renew myself daily" (Budge: " Book of the Dead," p. 337); and Renouf says there are several pictures at Denderah representing the Sun-God in the form of the worm, rising out of the Lotus of Dawn (see Plate 23, from " Mariette Dend." 1, 47, 48; Renouf: " Book of the Dead," p. 157, and " Proc. Soc. Bib. Arch." XVI, 7, 184, and on Ch. CXXV, note 17). The worm, working its way through the earth, would leave a hollow tract. The hieroglyphic sign for the Earth is a hollow tube, a reed, and it is always used as a determinative of the divine name Seb, in the Pyramid texts. In a picture taken from the tomb of Rameses IV and reproduced in " Proc. Soc. Bib. Arch."

Vol. XV, p. 8, a tunnel extends through the Earth from the place of sunset to the place of sunrise; each end has a sphinx-like form, and it is thus through the Sphinx that the passage was at this time made. At one end is written Fair entrance and at the other Fair exit. That this form of the Solar Cult, i.e. the type of passage being imaged by the Sphinx, was carried to America is proved by the figure, which was found carved in stone (see supra, p. 231). (Plate XLVIII.)

Now follows another creation, or phase, of the Solar Cult, which has been called the Cult of Ptah, who with seven assistants formed "Amenta" (which lasted about 9,000 years).

The eight great gods of Am-Khemen of the Stellar and Lunar Cults were followed by the Put-cycle, or Ennead, of the nine. The word Put denotes the number nine; hence Putah, or Ptah, who was added to the earlier eight great gods as the ninth; Ptah with his seven Ali co-workers tunnelled *through the Mount of Earth* to form "Amenta," and one of his names was "the opener." This formed a group of divinized Elemental Powers.

The foundation of the Fatherhood was laid by combining the eight powers, or spirits, to the one, to be combined into one single Deity, to be worshipped as the one true and eternal spirit. The eight were primarily the Great Mother and her seven elemental Spirits. Now the Goddess was superseded by Ptah, and both sexes were included in the one supreme Being, who was now Lord over All.

Joseph Thomson in his "Travels in Central Africa" states that when the Masai get married, it is the native custom for the bridegroom to dress himself in woman's clothes and wear them for a month after the marriage. This I can personally confirm. He is assuming the phase of parentage in the guise of the mother, and literally following suit to the female, because the maternal type and imagery of parentage are still dominant, and thus the father comes into existence, so to say, as the male-

Drawn by K. Watkins.

PTAH FASHIONING THE EGG OF THE WORLD UPON A POTTER'S WHEEL, WHICH HE IS WORKING WITH HIS FOOT.

PLATE LI.

KHNUM FASHIONING MAN FROM EARTH, AND TROTH MARKING HIS SPAN OF LIFE.

PLATE LII.

mother. The significance is the same as the custom of the couvade. The father was assuming the parentage in the likeness of both sexes.

Thus Ptah, or Atum, presents a form of the same duality, which is the same as the Australian " man with a vulva," who, in his primitive way, was a two-fold figure of the All-One. In the Egyptian Genesis " created man " is Tum, later Atum, or Amen, the original of the first man Adam. Atum was the son of the creator Ptah, the earliest biune parent that was divinized. The seven primordial powers had been previously recognized in nature as the offspring of the Mother. Six of these were pre-human powers or souls developed from the external elements. The seventh was the earliest human soul, born of the blood-mother. This was the blind, imperfect soul in matter that was imaged in Child-Horus, An-ar-ef. The soul of all the seven was matriarchal; they were the children of the mother only. Two other powers were added to make up the total in the Put-cycle. The " double primitive essence " had been assigned to Ptah. Doctrinally this was the soul of blood derived from the maternal source, in combination with the spirit of the male. Thence came the human soul that was constituted in two halves, the soul in matter and the soul in spirit, and the biunity was first personified in Ptah as the mother and father in one divinity, and, as the biune parent, Ptah gave birth to man, or created his son Atum. In the text from Memphis the god is called " Ptah of the Earth. The Mother giving birth to Atum " (line 14). Here Atum-Adam has a mother, an item which is omitted from the Hebrew version.

Thus Atum-Horus is the product of the biune parent; and the seven powers that contributed the seven souls or constituent parts of created man with Ptah and Atum, and the seven associate gods compose the cycle of nine gods, the eighth one having already been added to the primary seven as the highest, because he was the son of god the father, and not merely the product of the mother, like the original seven Ali or Elohim.

Thus we can identify Iu, or Aiu, as the Jewish divinity, and also the name of Iah or Iahu, distinguished from Ihuh. The compound title Iahu-Elohim shows that Iahu is one of the Elohistic group who was continued in the new rôle as the planter of the garden in the second of the two creations in the Book of Genesis. Chapter V announces that " this is the book of the generations of Adam." In this the previous " generation of the heaven and the earth " are represented as the generations of Adam, who meanwhile had been transformed from the divine Atum of Egypt into the human Adam of the Jewish writings, and the genuine mythos transmogrified into a spurious history.

The translators of the Memphian text point out that there were evidently two originally independent texts which have been artificially blended to produce a deceptive appearance of unity which agrees with the fundamental difference betwixt the Elohistic and Jehovistic versions in the Book of Genesis, those of the Elohim and Iahu-Elohim, in which two accounts of the creation have been run into one. This is proved by the two different beginnings in which heaven and earth are formed and man is made twice over. The first chapter contains the generations of heaven and the earth when these were created *by the Elohim*. The second contains the generations of the heaven and the earth when they were created in the day that earth and heaven were made by the Iahu-Elohim. As Egyptian, these are:

(1) The Ali or associate gods with Neb-er-ter; (2) Iu or Aiu, the son of the god who became the one god, both of the Egyptians and the Jews who were worshippers of Iu-Iahu. The first was Totemic man, the second being at the time when Atum the man was created in the likeness of mortal man, or the image of man, instead of being represented by some pre-human and Totemic type. And this latter portrayal was first depicted during the Solar mythos when Atum was first delineated in the form of man. Hence men are mortal or human since

the time of Atum-Ra (Rit., Ch. 17). Previously they were imaged as zootype forms.

This difference betwixt the animal and human types is recognized in the Ritual, Chapter 153a, when the primary imagery in zootype forms are called the "Ancestors of Ra" and the "Ancestors of Seb." They were designated "worms" and were mere reptiles, i.e. zootypes in comparison with the human type. In the Hebrew Genesis, when the man as Adam was created (i. 26), he was to have dominion over all creatures of air, water, and earth. Atum, or Tum, in the Ritual, Chapter 79, is designated the "Lord of all creatures"; that is when he makes his appearance in the figure of man, who is being described as being "in the form of the lord of all creatures" (Rit., Ch. 82).

Atum, who comes as the one god in the form of man, is hailed in the Ritual as the lord of heaven, who " issues forth from the earth and createth whatever is begotten," and " who giveth vigour to the men now living." As Atum he exclaims : " I am a soul, and my soul is divine. It is the self-originating force." The speaker, in the character of Atum-Ra, who makes his advent as a man, explains that the seven Uræus divinities formed his body, but his soul is divine. It is an image of the eternal. These Uræi were a type of the seven primordial powers which were grouped and unified in one, whether as god or man. They are companions, seven in number, who become the associate gods of Ptah in his creative work, and who were afterwards absorbed in Atum as constituents of his body, or the means of his embodiment as man. It was the ascent of soul through various elemental phases of existence—the pre-human souls now blended to form one eternal soul imaged as being derived from god the father instead of the mother alone, as an effluence of the holy Spirit.

Horus in his resurrection, at his second advent, came to proclaim the father as the begetter of a spirit that should attain eternal life, and he came to impersonate that spirit in the likeness of the father to the manes in

Amenta. Thus Atum, the Egyptian holy Spirit, was the author of that spirit by which Totemic man became a living soul, while with the Egyptians the soul was of both sexes.

"*Amenta*" (from *Amen*, secret, and *ta*, land—the secret land) was *not a real place;* it was an "*Ideograph*," symbolically representing a passage, which Ptah and his seven Ali tunnelled through the Mount of Earth for the passage of the Sun and Manes to cross from the West to the East.

Amenta was not supposed to be under the Earth, but deep down through the Earth.

It was fashioned mentally, or as an Ideograph, *as consisting* of a *world of various states,* including an Upper and Lower Egypt, the seven Nomes of the Heptanomes, the fourteen domains that were based upon the lower half of the Lunar Cycle, and the fifteen domains that belonged to the Solar reckoning (Rit., Ch. 142). The forming of Amenta was part of the evolution that was taking place in religious ideas and which included the necessity of repeating and bringing on the representation of the Stellar and Lunar imagery into the Solar, which now required a duplication, thus forming another, or dual Earth.

There was first a duplication of Paradise of the Stellar Cult represented here in the Solar.

The former was the Celestial Paradise configurated as the Paradise of the eight great gods, or Am Khemen, situated on the North Celestial Mount, at the Pole, imaging "Puanta," or the "Land of the Reeds," their primal home on Earth.

The Solar Paradise was sub-terrestrial, founded on the subterranean path of the nocturnal Sun, first opened by Ptah. It was called the Mount of Glory in the East, and named the hill of Bakhu. The Solar Mount in the East was added to the Mount of Glory in the North, but these were two distinct Mounts and were separated by the waters of space.

Paradise in Amenta is said to be "the beautiful

earth of eternity." But the Manes does not stay in it as his place of rest; it is not the eternal Paradise, or eternal dwelling place. It is only a passage for the manes on his journey to the heaven of eternity above, and when the Manes leaves Amenta, he crosses the Celestial waters in the boat to the summit of the North Celestial Mount, or Pole, where the stars are that never set, which always remained the final Paradise through all Cults.

Amenta in one aspect became the world of the dead, the Kasu, or burial-place in the Osirian Cult, which followed the Cult of Amen. In the latest imagery, Osiris became the god of Amenta, or the god of the dead or underworld, or heaven of eternity, where the Sun and the Manes went down in the West to pass through and emerge to rise again on the Mount of Glory in the East. By many writers Osiris has been considered to have been a human living man, but he was, in fact, only the last imagery of the Solar Cult, before the phase of Eschatology.

The Egyptians dramatized this intermediate world, or state, and acted the eschatological drama in accordance with conditions familiar to them in this world. Not that the Egyptians thought the other world a replica of this, but such was the natural plan on which they wrought in making out the unknown by the known.

In Egyptian the Nu, or Nun, or Heaven, is the Celestial water, and this as sky was both above and below the earth. We find in many depictions the name of Nut has the sign ▭, also in the reversed position as ▭. But the Egyptians did not believe in this nether sky *as a fact; they created it as an image or figure in Sign Language to teach the mysteries.*

The Upper and Lower Earth each had a sky represented in the Ritual as supra.

The two earths, or the "double earth," were the upper earth of Seb and the lower earth of Ptah-Tatanan, Lord of Eternity.

Ptah was sometimes called the son of Khnmu, the divine potter. He is portrayed at Philoe in the act of heaping plastic clay upon the potter's table, from which he is about to form the image of man, which he had sketched in the likeness of child Horus. Likewise (as shown in Plate LI) he is forming the Egg of the world upon a potter's wheel which he works with his foot. As a comparison, I have reproduced here (Plate LI) Khnmu (of the Lunar Cult) who is depicted as a potter in the act of forming man from the matter—earth. These are Egyptian types of creation.

Previously the gods and goddesses were shaped in the likeness of zootypes. Khnmu himself was Ram-

Drawn by K. Watkins.
Bes signifies to change from one to the other: signifies a transformation of the elder Horus into the typical younger Horus.

FIG. 40.

headed, and Kheper, the former, or transformer, was Beetle-headed. Up to the time of Ptah, or Bes, the Negroid Pygmy (Fig. 40) the human likeness was not given to any god or goddess, and Atum-Horus, or Amen, the son of Ptah, is the earliest divinity in perfect human form. As I contend that the Egyptian Atum is the original of the Hebrew Adam it follows that we are witnessing the creation of Adam from the earth in a mythical representation, when Ptah shapes the archetypal man as his son, Atum or Amen, from a lump of plastic clay.

In one character, Ptah was portrayed as the god

Ptah-Tanen, the title indicates the land (*ta*) in the Nun or Nnu which engirdled the earth outside. Thus the outer world was below the level of the waters at the same time that it was in the nethermost part of the Mount of Amenta. Hence the land, or Earth in the Nun, is Ta-nen, which is the name of the earth in the waters of the Nun, the lower earth of the Egyptian Tanan. Tanen as a geographical locality was earlier than Amenta, and Ptah-Tanen or Ptah Tatanen was lord of the lower earth as lord of eternity; as here portrayed (Plate LIII), in spiritual form, he is seated on the square which is resting on the Cubit or Maat, and the Sem symbol of the uniter of the two lands, that is the uniter of the earth of time and earth of eternity, or the spirit in death to everlasting life; He also rests on the Maat, the Judgment-seat emblem of truth, justice, and right, also a symbol of a measurer for work and time. On his head the two Maat feathers rest on the two horns, signifying Solar descent. The Solar symbol is between the two feathers of Maat, signifying that he is lord of truth, justice, etc. His beard portrays him as a man of thirty years, and he holds in his hands symbols of sovereignty and dominion. His " white form " denotes that this is a Spiritual depiction.

In the hymn to Ptah-Tenen we find the following address to the god and titles : " Homage to thee, O Ptah-Tanen, thou great god, whose *form* is hidden." " Thou openest thy soul and thou wakest up in peace, O father of the fathers of all the gods, thou disk of heaven! Thou illumest it with thy two eyes and thou lightest up the earth with thy brilliant rays in peace; thou begetter of men and the maker of their lives, the creator of the gods, he who passeth through eternity and everlastingness, of multitudinous forms, the hearer of prayers which men make to him, builder of his own limbs and maker of his body, when as yet heaven and earth were not created and when the waters had not come forth. Thou didst knit together the earth, thou didst gather together thy members, thou didst embrace thy limbs, and thou didst find thyself in the condition of the One who made his seat and who fashioned or moulded the two lands. Thou hast no father to beget thee in thy person and thou hast no mother to give birth unto thee, thou didst fashion thyself without the help of any other being. Fully equipped thou didst come forth fully equipped. Thy feet are upon the earth and thy head is in the heights above in the form of the dweller in the

Drawn by K. Watkins.

THE ANCIENT MAYA PORTRAYAL OF PTAH
FASHIONING MAN OUT OF CLAY.

FIG. 41.

Tuat. Thou bearest up the work which thou hast made, thou supportest thyself by thine own strength, and thou holdest up thyself by the vigour of thine own hands. The upper part of thee is in heaven and the lower part of thee in the Tuat."

This is only a part of the text, but it is sufficient to prove that Ptah-Tanen in the Cult of Ptah was the earlier representation of the Ptah-Seker-Ausar in the later Osirian, with all the attributes of the great god in

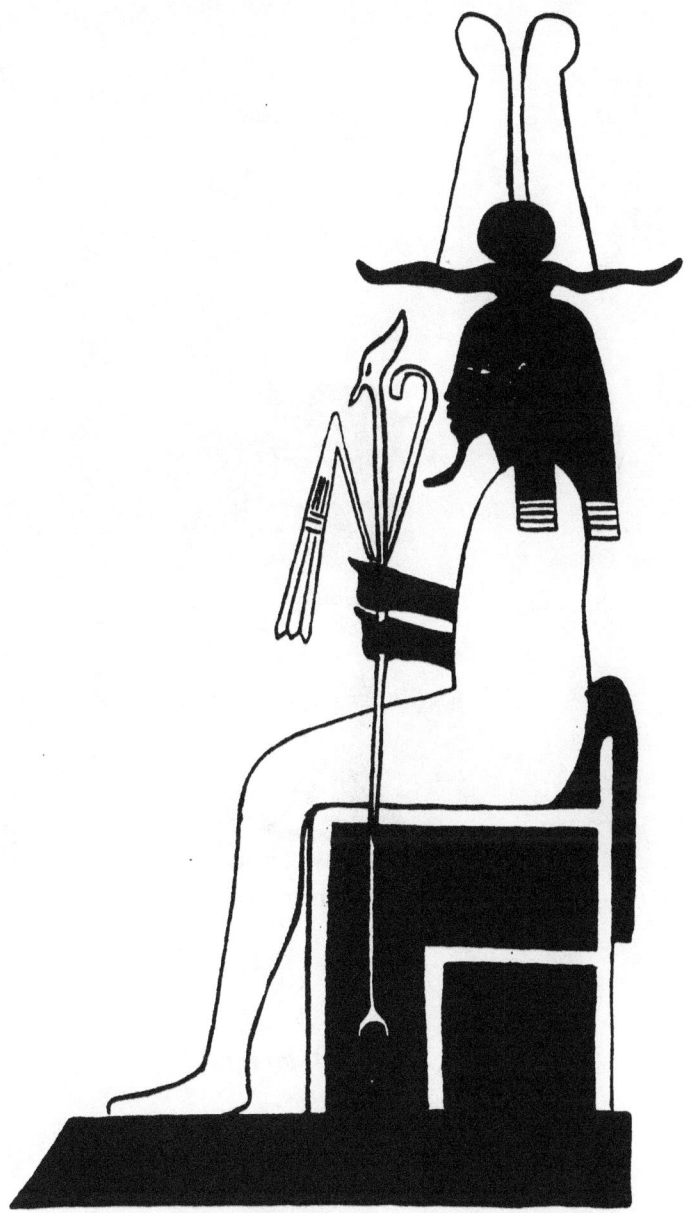

Drawn by R. Watkins.

PTAH-TANEN SEATED ON THE SQUARE OF THE FOURFOLD FOUNDATION ON WHICH IS DEPICTED THE SUN SYMBOL INDICATING THE UNITER OF THE TWO WORLDS—EARTHLY AND SPIRITUAL.

He is depicted as everlasting Spiritual form (white) with the Royal emblems on his head and crowned with the two feathers. Maat, with the Solar emblem at the base resting on the two horns, symbols of Solar descent. His head is symbolic of the man of thirty years.

PLATE LIII.

Drawn by K. Watkins.

THE EGYPTIAN TATT
PILLAR OF PTAH.

PLATE LIV.

[To face p. 249.

Spiritual form, or as the risen Horus of thirty years, who was represented as Iu-em-hetep the child of twelve years, in the Cult of Ptah. I give here the Maya portrayal of Ptah forming a living soul out of clay as the above glyphs prove (Fig. 41.)

Thus Ptah was not only the opener and founder of the new Earth of eternity, or Amenta, but also the fashioner of men from the earth. Ptah was the opener of the nether earth for the Sun to pass through, or for the resurrection of the Manes from Amenta in the coming forth to day. In the chapter by which the mouth of a person is opened for him in the earth of Ptah, the manes pleads: " Let my mouth be loosed by the god of the

THE TWO TATT PILLARS.
FIG. 42.

domain." I refer my readers to Chapters 23-54, 56 of the Ritual, where the Manes says: "*My nostrils are opened in Tattu*, the place of being permanently established," and by these ceremonies performed in mysteries man became a breathing soul after he had passed into the land of life.

The two Primal Pillars of Set and Horus which stood at the entrance of the Temple of Ptah were figuratively placed at the entrance of Tattu, in Amenta, the place of establishing for ever. As this was a new creation established on the fourfold foundation, or a square, four lines were drawn across the top of each pillar to represent a square, thus depicting heaven as a square, and earth as a square, otherwise their then representation of the Terrestrial and Celestial Heavens, and were called the two Tatt Pillars of Set and Horus. I portray here (Fig. 42) the two Tatt Pillars placed at the door or entrance to Tattu in Amenta with the Ankh Symbol of life representing the door of life between the Pillars. Tattu was the place where the Holy Spirit was blended with the Immortal Spirit. This was first depicted symbolically in the Cult of Ptah, later in the Cult of Amen, which followed that of Ptah, and still later and last in the Osirian Cult, where Osiris symbolized the inert and breathless mummy. It was here in Tattu that the Holy Spirit descended to the Spirit of the Mummy of the Manes, and he rose again in Spirit form and was established for ever as an eternal Spirit. In the first Cult he rose again as the divine Ta-Tanen, and in the Osirian Cult it was as the divine Amsu-Horus. The Hebrews and others later depicted the *globes* in place of the *squares*.

I have drawn attention to this portrayal because until the time of Ptah these two Pillars of Set and Horus, which were placed at the entrance of every temple in the world, were without the square, or globes, surmounting the top, but from the inscription at Shabaka (as well as from the Ritual, Chapters 151, 155, 156, and vignette, Plate LVI) we see that these were the primal Pillars of Set and Horus brought on. In Solomon's Temple they were called " Jachin and Boaz," the primal symbolism having become lost. As the two primal Pillars of Set and Horus, they were the supports of Heaven in two divisions, the two Poles.

The Ankh Key between the Pillars represents the door of entrance to eternal life, which could only be used, or opened, through, or by, Horus.

The Tatt Cross or Pillar (Plate LIV) is the Symbol for the support of the heaven of eternity created by Ptah on the fourfold foundation, or square, typified symbolically in Amenta as the Cross on which the God (later Osiris) was raised and overthrown annually, in Tattu, the place of establishing for ever. The Tatt Cross, therefore, had nothing to do with the two Tatt Pillars of Set and Horus, which were placed at the entrance of Tattu (symbolically). These represent two different images of their Mysteries, and as evidence I give (Fig. 43) the vignette in Ch. 18, Pl. 9 of this from the "Book of the Dead" (Renouf), where it states that this has been overthrown and raised again in *Tattu in Amenta, as the Symbol of Salvation.*

The Manes, like the Sun, was imaged to go down in the West to Amenta, through the Tuat, or entrance,

Drawn by K. Watkins.

THE RAISING OF THE TATT CROSS IN TATTU IN AMENTA.

FIG. 43.

traverse through and emerge again in the Eastern Horizon, or Eastern Mount of Glory.

The Sun in Amenta typifies the hidden god, who manifests in the Sun on the horizon and who made, as it were, to undermine all the rest in the endeavour to delve beyond visible phenomena.

Thus the hidden and unborn god becomes the foundation and support of the whole creation, including that of the seven Stars, brought on from the Stellar Cult, and those of the six spheres, or six divisions of time and space in the Lunar Cult.

Iu-em-Hetep is the Egyptian Jesus.

There is no difficulty in tracing him to the beginnings or through all the Cults up to and including the Christian.

The word "Hetep" denotes peace or rest, plenty of food, water, and good luck.

In the earliest form, in the beginning of the Stellar Cult, he comes as a Saviour in the inundation bringing food and water. As Prince and Saviour, he came from the Southern Lakes as giver of rest to the weary, bread to the hungry, water to the thirsty, and wine to the periodic wassail, which was celebrated by the Uaka festival. We have traced Horus through all the Cults, where his attributes have been also the Lord of Light and the Child of great knowledge. Iu- or Iu-em-Hetep is the promised Prince of Peace, whose coming was periodic and æonian, from generation to generation.

Iu-em-Hetep, or Horus as a child of twelve years, Chief of the eight great gods, called the son of Ptah, at Memphis, son of Atum at Annu. Builder of the Temple, Bruiser of the Serpent and Conqueror of the dragon, Prince of Peace and Goodwill. Teacher of twelve years old in the Temple. The Divine healer. He is depicted seated on the Square with the Ankh of life ♀ in one hand and the Hare-headed Sceptre in the other. His Papyrus Roll is in front of Him and the Uræus Serpent (emblem of wisdom) on His forehead.

He wears His necklace, a symbol of truth and justice, virtue and wisdom, etc. In "Signs and Symbols of Primordial Man," 3rd edit., I have given both the Egyptian and Mexican portrayals on pp. 280, 281.

Until the time of Ptah all the types were expressed zoomorphically. There was only the Great Mother in her several characters with her children, the same as in Totemism, but in Ptah the fatherhood is founded in the human type, and his predecessors were called his children, and that is how we can understand the hieroglyphic inscription found in the Temple of Philae, where we read that Iu-em-Hetep was called "the Great One," Son of Ptah the Creative God, made by Tanen (a title of Ptah) begotten by him, "the god of divine forms who giveth light and life to all men."

In the Solar Cult, in one line of development, he becomes the father God as Atum-Ra, on the other he was God the Son, as Atum-Horus, or Iu, and so we trace him from the fish of the inundation to " Jesus teaching in the Temple." He, as we have seen, was chief of the eight great gods—in the Stellar and Lunar Cults, and Builder of the Temple of Heaven.

We have seen the Stellar and Lunar imagery before the anthropomorphic was depicted ; at first it was without dogma or historic personality, except spiritual.

The Messu or the Messianic prince of peace, the wondrous child who is the figure of eternal renewal, the type of everlasting youth, was first imaged as a child in human form at Memphis, under the name of Iu-em-Hetep, although we have seen that as the divine Horus in the Solar Cult he was first imaged as Tum, or Nefer-Atum, or Atum-Iu, or Aten and Kheper. Before this in the Lunar, and previous to that Cult in the Stellar imagery, he has been portrayed in zootype form. His Mother's name at On was Iusāas, she who was great (as) with Iusa, or Iusu the ever-coming child, the Messiah. His father Atum was Ra in his first sovereignty. The Priests of On attributed a new creation of the heavens to Atum-Ra. Atum was born as Horus or Iu, Child of the Mother, and afterwards was depicted as Atum-Ra, as God the Father.

The Cult of Amen [1] was then established at Annu,

[1] The late Lord Carnarvon and Mr. Carter discovered in 1922, near Thebes, a tomb of Tut-ank-Amen, where they found evidence that the King had set up and restored the Cult of Aten at first, and then reverted to the Cult of Amen. It is well known that Amen-Hetep III and IV reintroduced the Aten Cult worship for a time over a limited area of Egypt, but it had no chance of a general revival. The Aten worship, as I have stated above, was first evolved in the Stellar Cult, as is amply proved by the " Book of the Dead of Nesi-Khonsu." It was brought on and revived in the Lunar for a short time, and as we see from the Theban Recession and from the Tomb of Tut-ank-Aten, in the Solar Cult. But the Cult of Amen was also an older Cult revived by Tut-ank-Amen, as the Osirian had first been established 40,000 years earlier at least. Many of the old forms had been revived during the later period of the Solar Cult, when Egypt began to decay. For example, when the Hyksos

where Amen was also imaged as the One God in two characters of Father and Son.

Amen, which was another name for Atum, was the god who followed Ptah. In the Put-cycle he was the tenth, and the god of the ten circles of Ra (Rit., Ch. 18).

He was then called the creator of the nine. This was accomplished by amalgamating all the previous powers and exalting the latest development to the primary position, or the first in status. As stated in the Ritual in an address to Amen: " The gods proceeded from thee. Thou didst create the nine gods at the beginning of all things, and thou wast the Lion-god of the Twin Lion-gods" (Budge: "The Gods of the Egyptians," Vol. II, p. 88). This was in the course of making the latest in development the first in status, which was done in the evolution of their religion.

Thus in the cycle of Ptah the gods were nine in number, with Amen added as Ra the number is ten, and as Ptah was called the father of the eight so Amen is called the father of the ten. In the hymns to Amen-Ra he is adored as one and the same as Atum, which shows that Amen is a later name for Atum; and he is represented as " the hidden god" of Amenta, or " the secret earth."

The word Amen means "what is hidden," "what is not seen," "what cannot be seen." The hymns to Amen often state that he is " hidden to his children," " hidden to the gods and men." Not only is the god himself said to be " hidden," but *his name also is* " *hidden*," and his form is said to be unknown. This shows that

conquered the Egyptians at Memphis, they destroyed all the Solar Cult there, the Cult of Ptah, and re-introduced the old Stellar Cult. This Cult they took with them when they were driven out and founded Jerusalem. Indeed, there was much overlapping of the various Cults in the latter part of the Egyptian Empire. Some were revived after a long period of obscurity. At the later stage of the Osirian Cult (which was the latest phase of the Solar) the old and the new were practised in Egypt at the same time, which has caused Egyptologists to vary in their opinions as to the origins of these different Cults, and has taken the writer very many years to unravel the mystery.

it was not in reference to the hidden Sun that these terms were applied but to the "Great Hidden God in Amenta," "The Eternal God."

The Litany of Ra describes itself as being "the book of the worship of Ra," and identifies Atum or Amen with Ra in Amenta. Amen in Amenta is the hidden soul of life that was imaged by the nocturnal sun. He is the supreme power who dwells in darkness and causes the Principles to arise. He is the "Pillar of Amenta," like the Tat with which Ptah supported the sky of the secret earth. He is manifested or born of his own son, he who was Ra as father, is Horus as the son. Atum in the Western Mount, Horus in the East.

He was worshipped as the supreme Power in seventy-five characters under an equal number of names. Amen is the one god who is always depicted in the human form and who enters Amenta in the shape of a man for the overthrow of Apap the monster and all the powers of evil.

Amen (or Atum-Iu or Atum Ra or Atum-Hui) was the only deity in all Egypt who was expressly worshipped by the title of "Ankhu," or the *ever-living one eternal God*. This is he who is reproduced by name in Revelation, saying: "I am the first and the last, I am he that liveth and was dead, I am alive for evermore" (Rev. i. 17, 18).

"In the coming forth to-day from out the dark of death," which is the resurrection in the Ritual, Atum-Iu is the closer and the opener of Amenta; he carries in his hands the keys that close and open the underworld. These are the Ankh-key of life and the Un-sceptre, with which Amenta is closed and opened.

These are repeated in the Book of Revelation as the keys of death and hell.

The god in spirit was the highest type of deity attained as the "Holy Spirit" in the Cult of Amen or Atum-Ra. In Revelation we have a typical character called "the spirit," but which is not otherwise identified.

"Hear what the Spirit saith." "To him that overcometh to him will I give to eat of the tree of life, which is in the Paradise of God" (Rev. ii. 7). It is this god in spirit who proclaims the "blessedness of the dead who die in the Lord" to "rest from their labours" (xiv. 13), and calls on those who are athirst to come and take of the waters of life freely (xxii. 17). He is also the spirit with the bride, but distinguished from the lamb. "The Spirit and the Bride say ' come '" (xxii. 17).

As Egyptian, "the Spirit," in the Eschatology, was Atum-Ra, the Holy Spirit in the Cult of Annu: Iusāa was the bride, and Iu-em-Hetep, he who comes in peace, was their son, whom we identify as the Egyptian Jesus in the Book of Revelation, in "Pistis Sophia," in the Apocrypha, and in the Book of Taht-Aan. The "entire god" was a mystical title of Amen-Ra as the child, and husband of the mother. According to the gnosis there was a triune being distinct from the male trinity, consisting of the mother, child, and adult male, in one person. The "head" of this triad might be either the mother, the father, or the child according to the Cult, and whereas the initiated worshipped the "entire god," who was three in one, one Cult would exalt the mother. The Jews as monotheists, by eliminating both the mother and the son from the godhead and setting up the father by himself alone as the "entire god," who was the Kamite Neb-er-ter, thus eliminated part of the Symbolism. Irenæus is scornful of the gnostic who assigned but one consort to both the father and son. But it is the same with the spirit (father) and the lamb (son) in connection with the bride in Revelation, as it was in Egypt and as it still remains in Rome. The mystical bride had two characters "which could not be taken away by the Bishop of Lyons." She was the virgin in one, the gestator in the other. As virgin, she was the bride of Horus, the lamb of god. As gestator, she was the consort of the Lion-faced man, who was Atum as god the Father.

The Bride in Revelation was equivalent to the Horus of both sexes and to Jesus as Saint Sophia. This was he whom the gnostics call Pan and Totum, the all-one, who became the manifestor as the ever-coming son. This all-oneness of the son is described in the Ritual

Drawn by K. Watkins.

MEXICAN DEPICTION OF THE FORMING OF "AMENTA."

Ptah is depicted as forming a passage through the earth and raising the Tatt Pillar of Four Quarters to support the new sky and heaven, with the aid of Shu and Amen, the Great God of the Ten Spirits, on the Right. The Stellar Sky and Heaven are above and the Subterrestial Sky represented above Amenta.

FIG. 44.

and proclaimed by Atum the father, when it is said that " Horus is the father ! Horus is the Mother ! Horus is the brother ! Horus is the Kinsman ! Horus is seated upon the Throne, and all that lives is subject to him.

All the gods are in his service. So saith Atum, the sole force of the gods, whose word is not to be altered" (Rit., Ch. 78).

The imagery, as we have seen, was carried to many lands throughout the world wherever the old Mystery Teachers travelled, although the true gnosis later became lost or perverted.

I here produce from the Vienna Codex the Maya portrayal of Ptah forming Amenta (Fig. 44).

Ptah is here depicted making the passage through the earth of eternity or the underworld, i.e. Amenta, and is about to erect the Tatt Cross, or Pillar in Tattu, which he is carrying in his hand, and which is shown to be the Tatt Cross, or Tatt Pillar, of the four quarters. The pathway where he is standing denotes that he has arrived in Tattu. The two figures on the right and left of the pathway (above) at the entrance to Tattu, are Set and Horus; their names are depicted and they have the Symbolic supports. The Symbol on the right below with ten ◯'s denotes the god Amen, and the heaven in ten divisions or the ten circles of Ra.

There are two portrayals on the left, the Holy House of Anup with the six ◯'s and the previous division of five.

Above are the five Houses situated at Am-Khemen with Ra seated on the right speaking to Horus, as the child of twelve years, or Iu-em-Hetep, "sayer of sayings," and Horus as the man of thirty years seated on the left. The sayings being of two kinds, and Horus being the sayer, he is thus given the duality of the child of twelve years, the sayer of the sayings to men on earth, and Horus of thirty, the sayer of the sayings to the manes in Amenta, or earth of eternity, or, as stated in Revelation, to the Spirits in Prison. See also 1 Peter iii. 19.

I also reproduce (Fig. 45) the Maya depiction of Ptah as the opener and closer of the underworld.

Horus as the "grain god," or food of life, is represented in the tomb of Seti as a man wearing two full ears of corn upon his head (Lefeb: La Tom: de Seti:

in the "Memoirs de la Mission Française," Vol. II, Pt. IV, Pl. XXIX, 2nd row, Pl. XXXI, 3rd row).

The Corn God as Horus was also represented at Philae as the god Naprit, i.e. Corn Spirit. He is portrayed with stalks and ears of corn springing from its mummy, near running water. This is Horus represented as a bringer of food in the shape of corn, a type of the eternal, manifested by renewal of food produced from the element of water in inundation. The ear of corn—green wheat-ear of the mysteries, which was held in the hand of Neith and

Drawn by K. Watkins.

CAN (PTAH) FORCING HIS WAY (OPENING AND CLOSING BY HIS IMPLEMENTS) THROUGH THE UNDERWORLD OR AMENTA.

The glyphs read: Can Ahau cimen eb Evanab kan can oc cib ik lamat ix uac ta luumilob umukan can Kak-Mul Timanik.

FIG. 45.

Isis in Virgo, and still survives in the star Spica of this constellation—represents Horus the child as bringer and giver of food by the water of the inundation or rising of the Nile—the food of Egypt being dependent on the periodic overflow of the Nile. The Maya portrayal is shown in "Signs and Symbols of Primordial Man," p. 92.

The Heaven of Amenta [1] was uplifted by Shu.

[1] "Heaven of Eternity" is the Paradise situated at the North Pole or "The Circumpolar Paradise." "The Heaven of Amenta" is "The Earth of Eternity" or "Paradise in Amenta"—a mythical Ideograph: the two must be differentiated and not be mistaken one for the other.

The "upliftings of Shu" are spoken of and portrayed in the Egyptian Ritual. Shu is depicted in three different characters in the Ritual.

The first two are depicted in the Stellar Cult. First, as An-hur, he was the uplifter of heaven—or the Cow of Nut—with his two hands, by pushing up the heavens, assisted by his supporting gods (Plate LVI). Second, as Shu, lifting up the heavens, which shows Nut sleeping in the Arms of Seb (Stellar Cult, Fig. 5). As Kepheus standing on the mound, or mount, with rod in his uplifted hand, is a representation of Shu who stood on the mount to raise the firmament of Am-Khemen, or the Paradise of the eight great gods. This imagery was carried on as Lunar.

In the Solar Mythos he becomes the auxiliary of Ra, and is called his son, Shu-si-Ra. He is the deity who

Mexican Depiction of the Implements for the Opener and Closer of Amenta.

Fig. 46.

kneels upon the horizon to uplift and support the Solar orb or upon the mount of dawn, or as the Egyptians state: "He brings the eye of light to Ra." He is the helper of Horus as the Solar God upon the horizon where the great battle is fought against the Apap of darkness (Rit., Ch. 39). This has been rendered in the Hebrew as "Joshua helping to fight the battle of the Lord."

He also passed into the Eschatology as the typical kneeler (Fig. 47). The keeper of the door in the Hall of Judgment is named after Shu, "the kneeler." The keeper, in the Mysteries, says to the initiate: "I open not to thee, I allow thee not to pass by me unless thou tellest my name." The password given is "the knee of Shu," which he has lent for the support of Osiris (or Horus), that is, as the supporter of the sun-god in the character of the kneeler (Rit., Ch. 125).

Shu-Anhur, in his two characters, was constellated in Kepheus and Leo, partially by means of the double Regulus. As An-hur in Kepheus he stands upon the mount to lift up heaven with his rod or staff. As Shu, or Regulus, in Leo he is the supporter and uplifter of the Solar Orb on the horizon as "the kneeler." Shu upraised the heaven of day in one character and the heaven of night in the other. In the Solar he is the pillar or support of the firmament as founder of the double equinox. It was at the equinoctial level that Shu settled

Drawn by K. Watkins.
SHU THE KNEELER OR UPLIFTER.
FIG. 47.

the quarrel of Set and Horus for the time being. The twins in Gemini and Shu in Sagittarius being three of the first seven powers that were thus imaged in two signs of the zodiac, Tefnut his sister, a form of the Great Mother, is joined with Shu in constituting the sign of Sagittarius.

Shu was the arbitrator in the Stellar Cult between Set and Horus (Rit., Ch. 110).

In the Lunar Cult, Taht "balances the divine pair," and was the judge and reconciler of the warring twins (Rit., Ch. 123).

In the Solar Cult, Seb, the god of the earth, was the adjudicator, as is shown in the text (Mythological) from Memphis. When Ptah had built his mansion in the double earth, the two horizons were united, or, as it is said, the double earth becomes united, "the union is in the house of Ptah," and the two pillars in the gateway in the House of Ptah are Horus and Set. The united ones made peace. They made a treaty. Seb says to Horus and Set: "There shall be an arbitrator between you." Seb said to Horus: "Come from the place where thy father was submerged," that is in the North. Seb said to Set: "Come from the place where thou wast born," that was in the South.

As Anhuri or Har Tesh, I have depicted him in "Origin and Evolution of Freemasonry," p. 188.

A mountain in the midst of the earth united the portion of Horus to the portion of Set, at the division of the earth, and this in the Solar Cult was the mount of the equinox. Horus and Set each stood upon a hillock; they made peace, saying: "The two earths meet in Annu, for it is the border of the two earths." In this there is a shifting of boundaries from South to North, to East and West, in the union that is now established. Henceforth the twin powers, Set and Horus, now called Horus and Set, who had stood as the two pillars South and North, for the two Poles in Apta, are now "the two pillars of the gateway to the house of Ptah," which two pillars are afterwards portrayed as the double Tatt of eternal stability in the making of the Heaven of eternity.

Shu was chief of the sustaining powers of the firmament, who were known in one phase as the seven giants. He then became the elevator of the Heavens that was imaged as the Cow of Nut. Lastly he was the sustaining power with Atum-Horus in the Double Equinox.

Many Egyptologists have believed that the wars of Horus in the Astronomical Mythology were historical in Egypt, but this is a popular delusion. They have converted the Lord of Life and Light who overcame the Powers of

Darkness and Drought into ethnical personages and glorified him as a national hero. The wars of Horus were fought in Heaven and Amenta against the Sebau, the Dragon; the Serpent, and as Horus, Orion was one of the great Stellar figures. This as Egyptian was Horus as Heru.

The word signifies Chief; the one is overlord, the ruler, the mighty one. This hero as Heru, or Horus, was a Stellar image. He was the annual bringer of food and drink before there was a Sun-God imaged, when the Stars were the Annunciators of the coming time and seasons. The character was afterwards made Solar, and then eschatological. Horus the mighty conqueror, the Nimrod, the slayer of the gigantic Apap, and the wars of Apap and Horus, or Ra, also of Set and Osiris in the eschatology, were dramatically rendered in the Astronomical Mythology. This imagery was carried to many lands ; take, for instance, the Mexican portrayal of Shu (illustrated in "Signs and Symbols of Primordial Man," p. 271).

He is there depicted as lifting up or sustaining the *Heaven of Amenta. Above is shown the starry heaven of Am-Khemen with the names and glyphs of the eight great gods* under the ideograph for the Starry firmament. In the centre below is *Shu lifting up the heaven* of *Amenta created by Ptah;* on the left of Shu, Ptah and his Put cycle of nine (nine ◯'s). On the right we see the heaven of Atum or Amen with the ten great Circles or Powers or Spirits, and the double Holy House of Anup. Between this and Shu is portrayed the Ideograph for Horus, God of the North and South and God of the Pole Star or Heaven of Am-Khemen.

I here produce Shu depicted on Pottery from Guatemala (Plate LVII). I give also a figure of Shu from Peru as "He of the gaping mouth" (Fig. 48). I also produce the Mexican portrayal of Shu dividing the North from the South and giving the North to Horus and the South to Set (Plate LVIII). In the upper (No. 1) depiction it is in the Earth of Seb, and the lower (No. 2) it is in the earth of eternity or Amenta. Number 3 is the Mexican portrayal of the fight between Horus and Set in Amenta.

Horus in his resurrection, at his second advent, came to proclaim the father as the begetter of a spirit that should attain eternal life. He also came to personate that spirit in the likeness of the father to the manes in Amenta. Atum, the Egyptian holy spirit, was the author of that spirit by which totemic man became a living soul. With the Egyptian the soul was of both sexes. The divine being Ptah, or Atum, was of a biune nature.

DEPICTION OF SHU.
FIG 48.

Hence they are portrayed as the male and female in one image, and this one soul was discreted as human in the two sexes. In passing through Amenta the human soul is represented as the male accompanied by the female, the wife or sister, or some other female supplemental to the male. This soul, divided into the two halves of sex, was united again in establishing an eternal soul. One form of the dual type is imaged by Shu and his sister Tefnut, who are blended in Tattu. They represented the soul that had been separated in two sexes. Tefnut,

THE CREATION OF HEAVEN—BY "SHU."

"Said by the Majesty of Ra, My son Shu take with thee my daughter Nut, and be the guardian of the multitudes which live in the nocturnal sky. Bear them on thy head and be their fosterer."

This is an allusion to his raising overhead the beautiful creation of the starry firmament which Shu sustains whether in the form of the son of Nut, the water of the Nun, or the ark of Nnu. The Cow of Nut.

PLATE LV.

THE GOD SEB SUPPORTING NUT OR HEAVEN, AND SHU UPLIFTING THE HEAVENS.

PLATE LVI.

DEPICTING "SHU," FROM GUATEMALA.

PLATE LVII.

Drawn by K. Watkins.

III

THE FIGHT BETWEEN HORUS AND SET IN AMENTA.
(*Mexican Portrayal.*)[1]

PLATE LIX.

[1] For many Egyptian Plates I have to thank Messrs. Methuen & Co. for their kind permission to reproduce them from Dr. E. Wallis Budge's "**Gods of the Egyptians.**"

I

Drawn by K. Watkins.

II

SHU DIVIDING THE NORTH FROM THE SOUTH, AND GIVING THE
NORTH TO HORUS AND THE SOUTH TO SET.

One depicted celestially, the other in the earth, of Eternity
or Amenta.

PLATE LVIII.

the sister soul, was absorbed in Shu the brother, who wears her emblem on his head, and who is the twofold type of a dual soul now unified in one. Thus the soul that lived for ever was held to be established for eternity by the female being blended with the male. That this belief was carried out from Egypt to other lands may be seen by studying the different races, African, Melanesian, and others, where the women will volunteer to be strangled at the funeral, or buried alive in the graves of their husbands (or the chiefs), believing it to be solely in company with the male that they can reach the realms of bliss ; and the favourite wife in the abode of the blessed is held to be the one who meets her death with the greatest fortitude. That is, by the female being blended with the male in death, as Tefnut was blended with, or absorbed in, Shu.

The next and latest phase of the Solar Cult was the Osirian, and although it is the last phase of the Solar, it has been given the most prominent place in the Ritual, or Book of the Dead.

Dr. Wallis Budge, in his "Book of the Dead," states that "concerning the form in which Osiris rose from the dead the texts are silent, and nothing is said as to the nature of his body in the underworld." But this is incorrect, for in the Ritual it distinctly states that Osiris in Amenta, or the underworld, is represented "in Mummy form," "without sign of breath or beat of heart," *and he is so represented in several of the vignettes*. When *he rises* again, it *is not as Osiris but as* **Amsu-Horus** *in Spirit form*, which is also stated in the text and shown in the vignettes. Dr. Budge states ("Book of the Dead," Imt., p. 93) "although it is pretty certain that every Egyptian believed that he would be judged after death, there is no definite statement of the fact." How does he justify his assertion in face of the facts found both in the texts and papyri of Ani and other vignettes ?

Osiris was the great god in matter as source or wellspring of life.

He rested as the perfect one in Amenta, without sign

of breath or beat of heart, but as the fount of motion and the fulfiller of existence in the nether earth, where he suffered in his death and burial, though not directly.

Deity could not die or suffer in itself; this part of the character was represented by the human Horus. He was the sufferer in various natural phenomena; and his portrayal in human guise as the mortal led the way to the later euhemerizing of the mythical representation and the reproducing of the drama as human history.

Horus, as the son of Osiris, takes the place of Amen, or Nefer-Horus, of the previous imagery, with his two mothers, Isis and Naphtys.

The darkness difficulties and dangers of the Tuat are fully set forth in the book of " That which is in the Underworld."

The account of Creation in the Book of Genesis was copied from the earth of eternity made by Ptah; it could not have been written " with its waters above the firmament and its waters below the firmament" until the division of these waters of Heaven above the earth, and of Amenta below the earth, was effected when Ptah created the firmament of the lower-earth and raised another heaven in Amenta. Thus, when Ptah had made Amenta, there was a sky above the underworld as well as over the upper earth; this is the nether firmament that was suspended overhead by Ptah, and memorized in the Mysteries, and this duality must be comprehended before the Ritual can be read or its traditions followed over other lands where the old exodes travelled. The most primitive imagery secretly preserved in Amenta makes the Ritual of Ancient Egypt an Eschatological record of the beginnings in Mythology that is unparalleled; and by mastering the Sign Language, and the Wisdom of Egypt, as recorded in Amenta, it becomes possible to read and understand it wherever it has been scattered by the different exodes after they left the old land of Kam. It is the only Truth of the past history of religions of the Human Race that is recorded.

First comes the natural fact, next the mythical

representation, and lastly the eschatological application. All three phases have to be studied, collated, and compared for this purpose.

The "Egyptian Book of the Dead" and Amenta and the Great Pyramid are not only the oldest in the world, but are worth all other sacred writings in the world.

When the Stellar had been added to the Solar, the pathway to Paradise was through the nether-world. The road of the Sun in the Mythos imaged the road of souls in the eschatology.

The road to heaven for the manes began with a pathway through the lower earth from the place of sunset in the West to the gate of sunrise in the East.

There was no passage through the earth or lower world in the Stellar Cult.

The Sun went around the Mount of Earth and not through it. Thus Ptah, "the opener," added earth to earth and heaven to heaven, the Stellar Mythos to the Solar, and the Sky upraised by him is indicated by the figure of heaven reversed, and is called the firmament of Ptah ▰. Hence it is said by the Osiris in Amenta: "Mine is the radiance in which Ptah floated over the firmament" (Rit., Ch. 64). His firmament being that of the nocturnal sun in the lower-world.

The Jackal, or dog, or Ap-Uat, is the guide of the dead through the paths of darkness in the underworld (Plate LX).

Ap-Uat represents a power of salvation from the drowning deep (see Rit., Ch. 44).

In crossing the Gulf of Putrata, into which the helpless dead fall headlong and the sinking souls are swallowed up by the dragon, the manes says: "Ap-Uat lifteth me up." This power is shown to be localized in the region of the Pole by the speaker saying (after being saved by Ap-Uat): "I hide myself among you, O ye stars that never set"—that is, in the circumpolar paradise of the Pole where the Jackal or the Dog was the guide of the ways.

Amenta was partially a Solar copy of the Stellar Great Pyramid, but only partially so, as much more was created, or evolved, and added; also the orientation was changed. The Pyramid is a type of " the Stellar Mount of Glory " in the North with *the door of entrance at the North*. In the Solar Amenta the *entrance is in the West* and the Mount of Glory is at the *Eastern exit*.

In the Stellar, the passage of the manes was from the door of entrance down a passage beset with darkness, difficulties, and dangers to the Tank of Flame at the bottom and centre of the Pyramid.

In the Amenta, the passage is through the Tuat beset with all the difficulties of darkness and danger of " that which is in the Underworld " to the " Field of Flame." At the " Tank of Flame," at " the Field of Flame," the manes are judged.

There was an individual judgment which took place at the " Tank of Flame " in the former, and in the Maat of Amenta, or Field of Flame, called the first judgment, and a second, the last great judgment of all, was on the summit of the North Celestial Pole. Those who were found guilty were condemned in the primary trial and suffered the second death in Amenta; they went no farther, but were annihilated in the " Tank of Flame," into original and separate corpuscles, not to be reformed again as spirits of the human.

This is followed in the Revelation, according to St. John, when the two different resurrections are differentiated the one from the other, when it is said the dead are to come forth; they that have done evil to " the resurrection of judgment " and they have done good to " the resurrection of life." Both are described in the Ritual, one for the judgment in Amenta, the other on the Mount for the last judgment and the resurrection to eternal life, the original writings being the Ritual of Ancient Egypt.

The Eschatology followed the phase of the Osirian Mythos.

Horus, in the Eschatology, was he who died and was

ANUBIS OR ANUP OR AP-UAT.
PLATE LX.

[To face p. 268.

buried and rose again in Spirit at his second advent in human guise.

This time he was imaged in the likeness of his Father as the beloved and only begotten Son of God, who manifested as the fulfiller of His Word and the doer of His Will.

In the Eschatology, Har-Makhu passes into Ra, who becomes the Great God in Spirit as the Holy Spirit Father.

The two types in this way were deposited and made permanent in Horus, the child of twelve years, and as Amsu-Horus, the man of thirty years.

The Solar, in its supremacy, obscured the Stellar.

Anup was merged in Osiris. The Seven Glorious Ones became the servants of Horus and subsidiary souls of Ra. The place of sunrise in the East was figured as the Mount of Glory in relation to Amenta, instead of the Mount of Glory in the Celestial North. Otherwise it was interpolated in the Solar Cult. Paradise was now both terrestrial (or subterrestrial) in Earth, as well as on the summit of the North Celestial Mount, because it was Solar as well as Stellar. But the Am-Khemen, the Paradise of the eight Great Gods, was not obliterated—it still remained *The Paradise.*

One form of this duality was represented in the Ritual by the Mythical two houses, the Great House and the House of Flame. The manes says: "Let my name be given to me in the Great House, let me remember my name in the House of Flame on the night when the years are counted and the months are reckoned one by one" (Ch. 35). The Great House was Stellar in heaven at the Celestial Pole. The House of Flame (Pa Nasrut) was Solar and in the East in Amenta.

The Japanese also have the double Mount Kagu; one is on the earth, that is, *it is the earth*; the other is in Ame or heaven, the divine Mount, that is, *the heaven*, which had the North Pole for its highest peak ("Tran. As. Soc. Jap.," Vol. VII, p. 431). The Japanese, likewise, have the eight great gods of the mount, who are said to have been produced by Kagutsuchi, which are a form of the original eight Kami that correspond to the Kamite Khemenu, the eight great gods in Am-Khemen, the heaven upraised by Shu.

The same duality of the mount is illustrated in the two Chinese Kimentuns. Here the terrestrial paradise is described as being at the centre of the earth. The Queen-Mother dwells there alone in its midst. At the summit there is a resplendent azure hall with lakes enclosed by precious gems. Above the clear ether rules the ever-fixed, the Pole Star ("Chinese Records," Vol. IV, p. 95). This is the Egyptian Mount of Amenta in which Hathor was Queen. The "azure-hall" is the empyrean over the summit of the mundane mount, which is here identified as the Mother Mount.

The other mount is Celestial; on its summit at the North Star is the heavenly palace of Shang-ti. At the centre is the Circumpolar Paradise, with its circle of thirty-six gods or rulers, which answer to the thirty-six decans of the zodiac.

From the above we see that some of the Solar has crept into the old Stellar Cult of these two countries, as it also did into Central and South America.

Here is a proof of the great antiquity of the Great Pyramid, as well as a proof that it was built by the *Stellar Cult* people called in the Ritual "the followers of Horus," that it was built prior to the Sphinx, which is a Solar symbol, and that it has the great antiquity of at least 260,000 years which I have always attributed to it in my previous works.

In the Stellar Cult figuratively the manes enters the door of the Pyramid forty-five feet above the ground, at the *Northern aspect* (a triangular door of stone) and descends a long passage down to the Tank of Flame; the passage is beset with darkness, difficulties, and dangers. Here the judgment takes place by fire. He is judged by *ten judges* and there are *seven Mysteries*. If he is condemned his spirit is annihilated in the Tank of Flame. If he passes his examination, he makes the ascent of the passage to the throne room and is invested with illumination and joins the Stellar boat of souls on its passage to the North Celestial paradise *via* Sothis and the Milky Way.

In the Solar, the entrance is by the passage *of the Tuat*, where *there are twelve doors*, and the entrance is *situated* in the *West*. After travelling through the Tuat, he arrives at the Field of Flame, where he is judged by *forty-two Assessors*, and there are *twelve Mysteries*. His exit is through the *Eastern gate* and *from* the *Eastern Mount of Glory he ascends in the Boat of Ra, then changes to the Sektet boat for the Paradise at the North.*

I think this evidence supports my contention that the Great Pyramid was built by the followers of Horus to depict the astronomical Stellar Cult, and had nothing whatever to do with either the Lunar or later Solar Cult, which did not come into being for thousands of years after. Menes, the first King of the First Dynasty (supposed) built Memphis and the Temple of Ptah. But, as I have shown, the Cult of Ptah and Memphis was later than the Sphinx, and the Sphinx later than the first phase of the Solar Cult.

Moreover, the Pyramid is a figure of the " Mount of Glory at the North," whereas Amenta was a figure of the lower, or nether Earth, in which the figure of the Mount of Glory was imaged in the East.

There is no " Fatherhood " depicted in the Pyramid, it is the " Motherhood." In Amenta it is the Fatherhood that has been portrayed in place of the Motherhood as the Supreme One.

Horus, as the highest of the seven elemental powers in the Stellar Cult, passed into the Solar when the typical virgin and child were reproduced and constellated as repeaters of periodic time and seasons in the zodiac.

In the Stellar Cult there was but one birthplace for the typical child who originated in imagery as Horus of the Inundation, who brought life to Egypt annually. The birthplace was where Sothis rose up as opener of the year and heralded the inundation.

This was the Star of Hathor, also in the **Lunar Cult**,

and the Messu or Messianic child who came to make war on the Dragon and to bruise the Serpent's head.

The child, the birthplace, and the bringer-forth to birth were all continued, or brought on, in the Solar Cult from this the original.

This then was the starting point with Sothis, now as announcer of the inundation and the life of vegetation, figured as Atum-Horus issuing from the Lotus (see Fig. 7), on the day of "Come thou to me," which was the first day of the Egyptian year of the New Creation, i.e. of the Solar Cult.

The fulfilment of the primitive promise of the coming child, as a bringer of life and all good things, was annual in the Stellar Cult, and the time was the old year of the Great Bear and the precession of the seven Pole Stars of the Little Bear.

This had not yet been subject to the changes in precession of the Equinox, but now when the Solar had taken the place of the Stellar and Lunar time, time was reckoned by the precession of the Equinox and was for ever changing during the period of the One Great Year of 25,827 years, and thus, as the result, the old Egyptians of the Solar Cult were ever obliged to fall back on the Urshi of the Stellar Cult to obtain the correct reckoning of time.

The Solar wise men built the Labyrinth to depict the Solar zodiacal Heaven in the Land of Egypt.

Although the Solar Cult gradually overlapped and superseded the older Stellar Cult throughout Egypt, and other parts of the world where it established itself, yet the Priests of the Pyramid, who always practised and believed in their Cult, were never suppressed until the destruction of Egypt took place. They continued in their old faith long after the time of Moses, and rather looked down upon the Priests of the Temple of the Sphinx, established so close to their own great Temple, recognizing that the new Cult was based upon the old, and that the Solar brothers were obliged to consult them to correct the time at the end of every "Great Year"—the Stellar Cult Priests having all details connected with the astro-

I

MEXICAN PORTRAYAL OF SET ATTACKING HORUS IN THE PAPYRUS SWAMP.

II

EGYPTIAN PORTRAYAL.

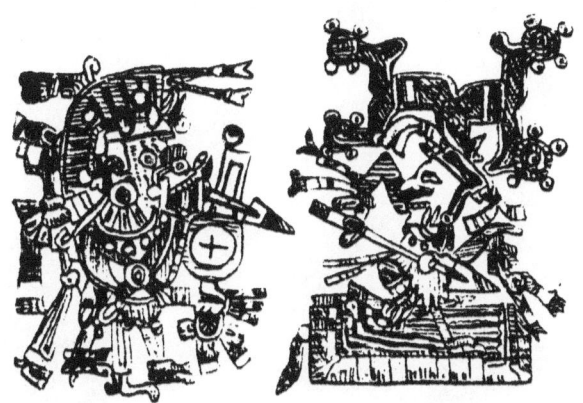

Drawn by K. Watkins.

III

MEXICAN DEPICTION OF HORUS FIGHTING SET.

PLATE LXI.

[To face p. 272.

Drawn by K. Watkins.

HORUS AS "CLEAVER OF THE WAY," (*Mexican representation*).

He is seen cutting His way through the underworld, and Set is shown on the right as opposing his progress, and evil fiends assisting him, below.

PLATE LXII.

[*To face p.* 273.

nomical and mathematical problems, as their knowledge on these matters was far superior in every way than that of the Solar Cult Priests.

There can be no doubt that they were also in communication with China, Korea, and Japan, if not with America, as the great nations in Asia were mostly of the Stellar Cult races and Religion. We know from historical records still extant, that there was trading between these countries.

The old Stellar Cult Priests never changed their faith, or, rather, form of faith ; they had from the first blended all the elemental powers into the One Great Spirit and founded the primary Eschatology on this, but all was written and illustrated in signs and symbols, i.e. Sign Language, and although they had watched through long ages of time the development of Lunar and Solar Cults from their own original, they knew that the fundamental facts of their beliefs had not altered.

From the glyphs still extant, found in old temples in Asia, America, and other parts of the world, and the architecture of the Great Pyramid, written in Sign Language, and from a careful study of the papyri composing the " Ritual of Ancient Egypt," one can arrive at the definite truth of the evolution of religious doctrines.

Some of the Totemic Mysteries survived as Eschatological in the Osirian Cult. As an example, Horus the child who was born of the Mother only, under the divine matriarchate, makes his transformation into Horus the adult, who rises from the dead in Amenta, in the character of the Anointed Son of the Father.

Anointing had then become the mode of showing the glory of the Father in the person of the Son. This was imaged with the holy oil upon the face of Horus. He who had been Horus the mortal in the flesh is now Horus in spirit personalized and established as the Anointed Son. The " original anointing " was done in the Totemic Ceremonies when the boy was made a man at puberty, that was when the Mother's child assumed the likeness of the Father at his Totemic re-birth ; at the end of the ceremonies he was " anointed with the fat of the Totemic animal," which was previously forbidden food.

The difficulty of obtaining entrance to " Amenta " was insuperable to mortals. Hence the need of divine assistance.

The Sun-God, as opener in the Solar Mythology, led up to the God as opener for souls in the Eschatology.

In this character Horus becomes " the door and the way of life " to the manes who followed in his wake of glory through the dark of death. One name of the Western Hill, or entrance to Amenta, is Manu. It is said to Ra, when setting : " Wake up from they rest, thine abode is Manu " (Rit., Ch. 15).

The principal subject of the inscription written on the Sarcophagus of Sati I, now in the Sloane Museum, is the nocturnal passage of the Sun God through Amenta by night, having the blessed on his right hand and the damned upon his left. There are twelve divisions of the passage, corresponding to the twelve hours of the night. The entrance to the first of the divisions is without a door, or it is a " blind doorway," like the Pyramid entrance in the Stellar Cult. The last has a double door in the Solar.

Therefore the entrance consists of a " door," of which the mortal, or manes, could not know the secret, and none but the Solar God could open. Hence the necessity of a deity as opener, or a god who is " the door and the way."

The manes should be properly equipped and in the possession of the magical words of power that secure the opening of every gate, including the hidden entrance. These words he carries in his hand as his " papyrus roll," or he has made them truth in his own life and death. He exclaims : " I am accoutred and equipped with the words of power, O Ra," the god that is, who says of himself: "I am he who closeth and he who openeth, and I am but one " (Rit., Ch. 17, Renouf). Following his burial on earth, the deceased enters as a manes into " Amenta," the land of the living, and seeks to enter the boat of souls; the Priest says: " O, ye seamen of Ra, at the closing of the day let the Osiris (the Manes) live after death as Ra does daily." Here the helmsman " As Ra " is born from yesterday, so he, too, is born from yesterday, and as every god exults in life, so shall the Osiris exult even as they exult in life (Ch. 3, Renouf).

After the manes had passed through darkness, difficulties, and dangers, he enters the paradise, or gardens of Arru, in the eastern part of the passage where he has to perform an allotted task, and finally he emerges upon the Mount of Glory in the East. But his final end of the journey is not yet; his aim is to reach the Circumpolar Paradise, a place amongst the Stars that never set, the abode of the eternals. From the Mount of Glory on the eastern summit he enters the boat of Ra, or Solar bark, in which he makes the voyage from the Mount of Bakhu East to Mount Manu in the West, on his way to the Mount of Glory at the Celestial Pole. Thus was the pathway for the dead from this life to the upper paradise laid down by the Egyptians in their Mysteries. It was the Egyptians who hollowed out Amenta. The Spirit is led by the Jackal Anup, as a guide, through all the places of purgatory, its hells and its paradise of plenty in the Aarru fields, and lighted by Taht the Lunar God, who carries in his hand the lamp of light and eye of Horus, as the Moon of Amenta shining through the night, emerging at length from the nether earth on the Solar Mount of Glory. Then commences his voyage in the Solar bark from the East to the West, where the manes changes boats and passes on his way to the final paradise of the Celestial Pole. We find that in the Book of the Dead they have left the portrayal of all their Mysteries—first as Mythology, and secondly, Eschatology.

The passage of the all-conquering Sun is followed by the soul of the deceased. He enters the Mount in the West by the opening in the rock, in a later stage is carried on the boat. He is accompanied by those who have gone before as guides. He fights with the adversary, and is victorious in the character of Horus. He opens all the doors and paths with his words of power and magic of might. He cleaves open the Earth for resurrection. He is delivered from the devouring demon who lurks invisibly in the lake of fire and feeds upon the damned (Ch. 17). The caverns of Putrata, where the dead fall into darkness, are opened by him. He is supported by the eye of Horus, or the light of the moon. Ap-Uat, the opener of roads or walls or doors, raises him up and carries him across the waters (Ch. 44).

He wanders in the wilderness where nothing grows. He obtains command of the water in the underworld and prevails over the deluge. He escapes the second death (Ch. 58). The double doors of heaven are opened for his coming forth. Still following the course of the Sun, the passage of Amenta endeth with the garden eastward and the ascent by which the manes enter the Bark of Ra.

There is now the voyage through the Nu from East to West by the Maatit bark at dawn, and the passages continue to the region of Manu in the West, and they sang the song, "To the West, to the West," but as the Sun goes down to Amenta again they change from that Maatit boat to the Sektet boat. With the change of boat another voyage begins along the great stream of the Milky Way.

This is described as "that most conspicuous but inaccessible stream," when contemplated from the earth (Rit., Ch. 98).

When the departed reach the starry shore, the seven steps, or ladder, for ascending the mount of heaven is now erected in the boat. This ladder has a dual type. It is called the ladder of Set for the ascent from Amenta, and the ladder of Horus for the ascent to Heaven to the Circumpolar Paradise. On approaching, the manes stands erect in the bark, which the god is piloting and the non-setting stars are open to receive him (Ch. 98). He says: "I arrive at my own City (Ch. 17); I reach the City of those who are in Eternity." That is the Eternal City, the City of the Blessed, the Holy City, the City of the Great King, the Heavenly City, the Eternal City that was the model of Memphis and Annu, Thebes and Abydos, Eridu and Babylon, Jerusalem, Rome, and other sacred Cities of the world.

The Semites would have had no Heaven on the summit of the mount to go to if the Egyptians had not enclosed it and planted it and showed the way in their Astronomy.

They would have had no Sheol if the Egyptians had not excavated the Amenta for the passage of the Sun in their Mythology and for the souls in the Eschatology. And it is only by means of the Egyptian imagery that the restoration of the truth can be restored.

Entrance into the Eternal City was preceded by baptism, with Anup, father of the inundation, as the baptizer and sprinkler both in one. On approaching the two lakes, the manes says: "Lo I come that I may purify this soul of mine in the most high degree. Let me be purified in the lake of propitiation and equipoise. Let me plunge into the divine pool beneath the two divine Sycamores of heaven and earth" (Rit., Ch. 97). This precedes the sacrament. He says: "Let me be made pure by the sacrificial joint, together with the white bread," that is, by partaking of the sacrament (Rit., Ch. 106).

The Solar people built the Labyrinth as an objective image. It has twelve courts enclosed with walls, with doors opposite each other, six facing North and six facing South, to memorize the heaven of the twelve Kings and twelve zodiacal signs, that is, the heaven of Atum-Ra. The starry roof was depicted inside, to glorify the temple of the gods. At the centre is the old first mother of all, the pregnant hippopotamus, Apt or Khebt, with the Jackal Ap-Uat, the guide of the ways in heaven, and the haunch or leg of Nut the Celestial Cow. Anup and Tehuti are figured back to back on the equinoctial colure; Shu and his sister, Tefnut, back to back, constitute the sign of Sagittarius. Child Horus is enthroned on his papyrus plant; he is also portrayed as Har-Makhu in the sign of the scales. Khunsu-Horus offers up the black boar of Set as a sacrifice to the disk of the full moon.

Thus we see: First, that during the Astro-Mythology, or Stellar Cult, the Egyptians built the Great Pyramid as a Symbol, and in written Sign Language, to depict their beliefs in a future life. In it everything was portrayed Symbolically—the whole of the primary Eschatology, as well as the Architectural Universe, proved by mathematical calculations so exact that even our present-day astronomers and mathematicians cannot calculate with the same definite precision. Second, they hewed the Sphinx from the solid rock to depict their Symbology of the phase of one part of the earlier Solar Cult. Third, they built the Labyrinths to portray the latest phase of the Osirian Cult and their final Eschatology.

The orientation of the Solar Temples differed from those of the Lunar in that the latter were orientated at right angles to the Solar. This may still be seen by the Temple of Hathor and the Temple of Isis at Denderah.

The Mysteries of Osiris, Isis, and Horus, though the latest in evolution have taken the primary position in the Ritual and have made the position chronologically of the earlier, or pre-Osirian Cult, at times somewhat obscure. There is ample evidence, however, that after the Cult of Ptah the god Amen, often called " Atum," was the great Judge in Amenta upon the Mount preceding the Osirian Cult, and lasted about 20,000 years.

The Ritual contains the oldest known religious writings in the world; it has been edited several times, and deals principally with the Osirian group, which was the latest phase, but that is no criterion of the original, and the presence of Tum, Sebek-Horus, and Apt, proves that the original was incalculably remote. It contains the eschatology or doctrine of final things, and this was founded or based in the mould of the mythology; the eschatology of the Ritual can only be comprehended by the mythical representation, in which Amenta, the mythical underworld, is the picture gallery.

The mythology repeated in the Ritual is mainly Solar and Osirian, but contains fragments of the Lunar and Stellar from the beginning. For example, Apt, the ancient great Mother, as goddess of the Great Bear Constellation and leader of the Celestial host, was kindler of the starry lights by night in the Stellar and Lunar. In the Eschatology she is continued as the mistress of divine protectors for the soul; thus she who had been the kindler of the lights in the darkness of the night was now propitiated as rekindler of life from the spark in the dark of death (Rit., Ch. 137, B.).

Ra, in the mythos, is the Solar god represented by the Sun in Heaven; in the Eschatology he becomes the god in spirit, who is called the holy spirit and the first person in the trinity, which consisted of Amen or Atum the father god, Amsu-Horus the son, and Ra the holy spirit, the three which were also one in the Osirian Cult, first as three forms of the Solar god, and next as three forms of the god in spirit.

There is no death in the Osirian Cult, only decay and change and periodic renewal, only evolution and transformation in the domain of matter and the transubstantiation into spirit. In the so-called death of Osiris it is rebirth, not death—exactly the same as in the changes of external nature.

At the close of day the solar orb went down and left the Sun God staring blankly in the dark of death. Taht, the Moon God, met him in Amenta with the eye of Horus as the light that illuminated the darkness of the subterranean world. In the annual reckoning on the third day light was generated by the renewal in the moon; thus Osiris as Amsu-Horus rose again, and a doctrine of resurrection on the third day was founded in the eschatology.

The sun, in sinking, was buried as a body (or mummy) in Amenta. When rising again at dawn, it was transformed into a soul, a supreme elemental soul, that preceded god in spirit. This was the mythological representation.

In the Eschatology the same types were re-applied to

the human soul which was imaged in the flesh as the inarticulate, blind, and impubescent Horus, who died bodily, but was preserved in mummy form to make his transformation into the luminous Sahu when he rose again in glory as Horus the divine adult. "I am the resurrection and the life" is the perfect interpretation of an Egyptian picture that was copied by Denon at Philæ ("Egypt," Vol. II, Pl. 40, No. 8, p. 54), (Sundry figures). Divine Horus is depicted in the act of raising the deceased Osiris from the bier by presenting to him the Ank sign of life. He was the life in person who performed the resurrection, and therefore is the "resurrection and the life." As such, he simply stands for a soul considered to be the divine offspring of god the father. Previously he had been imaged as the resurrection and the life as solar vivifier in the physical domain, i.e. in mythology.

From the beginning to the end of the written Ritual we find it based upon the mythical representation, which was primary.

The mythical representation was first applied to the phenomena of external nature, and the mode of representation was continued and re-applied to the human soul in the Eschatology. Totemic representation came first, mythical founded on this secondly, and the Eschatology, thirdly, was continued in the same phase. In the mythology, the Solar God Ptah (Kheper) is the maker of a complete circle for the sun as founder and opener of the nether earth, or Amenta, this solar pathway being a figure of "for ever," a type of the eternal working in time. In the Eschatology the god in spirit, who is Ra the holy spirit, is "the god who has created (or opened out) eternity" (Rit., Ch. 15).

The Ritual is the pre-Christian word of God. This is proved from the account therein written. It is attributed to Ra as the inspiring holy spirit. Ra was the father in heaven, who has the title of "Huhi" the eternal, from which the Hebrews derived the name "Ihuh."

The word was given by God the Father to the ever-coming Son as manifestor from the father. In the Solar depiction this was Horus who, as the coming son, is Iu-sa or Iu-su, and as the prince of peace, Iu-em-Hetep. Horus the son is the "Word in person." "I utter the words—the words of Ra—to the men of the present generation, and I repeat his words to him who is deprived of breath" (Ch. 58), that is, as Horus, the sayer or logos, who utters the words of Ra the father in heaven to the living on earth, and to the breathless manes in Amenta when he descends into Hades, or the later hell, to preach to the spirits in prison. The word or the sayings thus originated with Ra the father in heaven. They were uttered by Horus the son, and were written down in hieroglyphics by Taht-Aan for human guidance, and they supplied the basis for the Book of the Dead.

"It has been ordained by Ra that his words, such as those that bring about the resurrection and the glory, should be written down by the divine scribe Taht-Aan to make the word truth" (Rit., Ch. 1) and to effect "the triumph of Osiris against his adversaries." It is stated in the opening chapter that this mandate has been obeyed by Taht (Aan).

In studying the Egyptians, we must come to the definite conclusion that they are the only chronometers of the history of all the religions in the world—at least, up to the time of the commencement of the decay of that great nation. Menes, his empire, and the religious doctrines at that time, are the culminating point of a long preceding constitutional development of Egyptian Religion and Life, perhaps for a million of years, and whether we trace the records backward or forward, there is always found the truth recorded.

To the first commencement in Egypt belong the earliest form of man. The roots of all language, and the earliest form of religious belief can only be found in Egypt, and from the original we can trace a progressive development and a study of the religious texts of all periods, which proves that the great fundamental religious ideas of the Egyptians remained unchanged from the earliest to the latest historical times. The earliest priests of historical times received the earliest religious creed from their predecessors, and no doubt this was passed on orally, before it was inscribed on papyrus, in the same form as that in which it was handed down from the originals, the original being given to them by the Great Spirit who came in the form of a man. During the Stellar Cult, however, much was engraved on stone monuments and Temples, where we still find the iconographic figures and Sign Language, which we can now read. The doctrine of immortality and everlasting life, and the belief in the resurrection of the Spiritual body, are the brightest and most prominent features of the Egyptian religion ; they have survived all the theological theories and speculations of the later various schools of religious thought. Nothing demonstrates this better than the " Book of the Dead of Nesi-Khonsu," written by a Priestess of Amen, which reads as follows :

"This holy god, the lord of all the gods, Amen-Ra, the lord of the throne of the two lands, the governor of Apt ; the holy soul who came into being in the beginnings ; the great god who lived by (or upon) Maat : the first divine matter which gave birth to subsequent divine matter (or the primeval paut which gave birth unto the (other) two pautti, the being through whom every (other) god hath existence. The One who hath made everything which hath come into existence since primeval times when the world was created ; the being whose births are hidden, whose evolutions are manifold and whose growths are unknown : the Holy Form, beloved, terrible, and mighty in his risings : the lord of wealth, the power Khepera who createth every evolution of his existence, except whom at the beginning none other existed : who at the dawn in the primeval time was Atennu (Aten or Horus) the prince of rays and beams of light : who having made himself (to be seen) caused all men to live : who saileth over the celestial regions and faileth not, for at dawn on the morrow his ordinances are made permanent; who though an old man shineth in the form of one that is young, and having brought (or led) the uttermost parts of eternity goeth round about the celestial regions and journeyeth through the Tuat to illume the two lands which he hath created: the God who acteth as God, who moulded himself, who made the heavens and earth by his will (or heart), the greatest of the great, the mightiest of the mighty, the prince who is mightier than the gods, the young Bull with sharp horns, the protector of the two lands in his mighty home of the everlasting one who cometh and hath his might, who bringeth the remotest limit of eternity, the god-prince who hath been prince from the time that he came into being, the conqueror of the two lands by reason of his might, the terrible one of the double divine face, the divine aged one, the divine form who dwelleth in the forms of all the gods, the Lion-god with awesome eye, the sovereign who casteth forth the two eyes, the lord of flame (which goeth) against his enemies; the god Nu, the prince who advanceth at his hour to vivify that which cometh forth upon his potter's wheel, the disk of the Moon-god who openeth a way both in heaven and upon earth for thy beautiful form: the beneficent (or operative) god, who is untiring, and who is vigorous of heart both in rising and in setting, from whose divine eyes come forth men and women: at whose utterance the gods come into being, and food is created, and *tchefau* food is made, and all things which are come into being: the traverser of eternity, the old man who maketh himself young (again) with myriads of pairs of eyes, and numberless pairs of ears, whose light is the guide of the god of millions of years; the lord of life, who giveth unto whom he pleaseth the circuit of the earth along with the seat of his divine face, who setteth out upon his journey and suffereth no mishap by the way, whose work none can destroy; the lord of delight whose name is sweet and beloved, at dawn mankind make supplication unto him the Mighty one of victory, the Mighty one of two-fold strength, the possessor of fear, the young Bull who maketh an end of the hostile ones, the Mighty one who doeth battle with his foes, through whose divine plans the earth came into being ; the Soul who giveth light from his two Utchats (Eyes), the god Baiti who created the divine transformations ; the holy one who is unknown ; the King who maketh kings to rule, and who girdeth up the earth in its courses, and to whose soul the gods and the goddesses pay homage by reason of the might of his terror ; since he hath gone before that which followeth endureth ; the Creator of the World by his secret counsels ; the god Khepera who is unknown and who is more hidden than the (other) gods, whose substitute is the Divine Disk : the unknown one who hideth himself from that which cometh forth from him : he is the flame which sendeth forth rays of light with mighty splendour, but though he can be seen in form and observation can be made of him at his appearance yet he cannot be understood, and at dawn mankind makes supplication unto him ; his risings are of crystal among the company of the gods, and he is the beloved object of every god : the god Nu cometh forward with the North Wind in this god who is hidden ; who maketh decrees for millions of double millions of years, whose ordinances are fixed and are not destroyed, whose utterances are gracious, and whose statutes fail not in his appointed time ; who giveth duration of life and doubleth the years of those unto whom he hath a favour ; who graciously protecteth him whom he hath set in his heart ; who have formed eternity and everlastingness, the King of the South and of the North, Amen-Ra the king of the gods, the lord of heaven and of earth and of the deep, and of the two mountains, in whose form the earth began to exist, He the mighty one, who is more distinguished than all the gods of the first and foremost Company."

This remarkable document proves my contention. Note the reference to Apt, the old Mother Earth divinized in the Stellar Cult—" The principal paut," which gave birth unto the two other pautti, which were imaged as

Set and Horus, the two primary attributes, depicted as gods of Darkness and Light; " every other god that existed." These were the seven elemental powers divinized in the Stellar Cult, the seven primary gods. The next was Aten or Horus.

From the "Negative Confession" we see that the Egyptian code of morals was the grandest and most comprehensive of those known to have existed amongst any nation, past or present. I have given these in " Origin and Evolution of Freemasonry."

Maspero, in his " Egyptian Archæology " (p. 149) states that " the deeds which the deceased had done here on earth in no wise influenced the fate that awaited the man after death." I do not agree with Maspero in this; how could it be so when the new heart which was given to the deceased in Amenta, where he or she was reconstituted, is said *to be fashioned in accordance with what he has done in his human life*; and the speaker pleads that *his new heart may not be fashioned according to all the evil things that may be said against him?* (Rit., Ch. 27).

He is anxious that the ministrants of Osiris in the Neter-Kar, "*who deal with a man according to the course of his life*" may not give a bad odour to his name (Ch. 30). And again he pleads: " Let me be glorified through my attributes; let me be estimated according to my merits " (Ch. 72).

This proves that the future state of the soul was dependent on the deeds which the body had done, and the character of the deceased was judged according to his conduct in the life on earth.

In the Eschatology, Osiris represents, in Amenta, the dead man who was torn in pieces by the machinations of Set. As a mummy he enters the Tuat in Amenta, and then he rises from the tomb in spiritual form as Amsu-Horus, who has burst the bonds asunder and is regenerated as the Sahu of Osiris. He was transformed and transfigured from the Osirian dead, or sleeping mummy, into the luminous body, which still retained the mummy form, i.e. Amsu-Horus at his rising from the sepulchre. Osiris, the hidden god in the earth of Amenta, does not come forth at all, except in the form of the risen Horus, who is the Manifestor for the ever-hidden father.

To issue thus, he makes his transformation which constitutes the Mystery. The Mummy, as Corpus, is transubstantiated into the Sahu. The mortal Horus, by the descent and union of the Holy Spirit Ra, into the Immortal, the physical mummy of the mortal Horus disappears instantly. The Ritual says: " He is renewed in an instant in his second birth " (Ch. 181). The above prove how incorrect are the statements of Dr. Wallis Budge in his " Book of the Dead."

Some human souls, after death of the body-matter on

MEXICAN PORTRAYAL OF AMSU-
HORUS WITH ONE ARM FREE
AND ONE STILL BOUND DOWN.
FIG. 49.

this Earth, are admitted to Paradise direct. " They have made truth their words and actions " in their earthly life and they join " the Glorified " at once. Others have to go through an " Amenta " to work out their salvation to become " perfect manes " or the " Ka-Soul " before being admitted to the Eternal Paradise. A fragment of this gnosis is seen in the Hebrew writings when Elijah is " taken up to heaven," but the Hebrews here again have rendered the Ritual exoterically instead of in the true representation.

Mummies were made on purpose to preserve the physical likeness of the mortal. The mummy was a primitive form of the effigy in which the body was preserved as its own portrait.

The Ka was intended for a likeness of the Spirit, or immortal, the likeness in which the just spirit made perfect was to see God in its glory.

Both the mummy and the Ka were represented in the Egyptian tomb, each with a chamber to itself. From the earliest beginning of the Nilotic Totemic Ceremonies there had been a visible endeavour to preserve some likeness or memento of the earthly body, even when the bones alone could be preserved as extant at the present day amongst these people.

Mummy-making in the Ritual begins with collecting the bones and piecing them together, if only in the likeness of the skeleton. It is at this stage that Horus is said to collect the bones of his father Osiris for the resurrection in a future life by means of transubstantiation. The same imagery of preparing the mummy is indicated when it is said to the Solar god on entering the underworld: " Reckon thou thy bones, and set thy limbs and turn thy face to the beautiful Amenta " (Ch. 133, Renouf). Teta, deceased, is thus addressed: " O, Teta, thou hast raised up thy head from thy bones, and thou hast raised up thy bones from thy head." Thus the foundation was laid for building the mummy-type on a present image of the person who had passed.

One title of the first chapter in the Ritual is "The chapter of introducing the mummy into the Tuat on the day of burial." This applies to the mummy interred on earth; and also to the Osiris, or manes, in Amenta, who was figured in the mummy form. The Tuat is a place of entrance to and egress from the underworld.

The Egyptian Ritual is written in the Language of Animals, and never was it read in the past, never will it be in the future unless the thinking can be done in the Ideographic type of thought. Merely reading the hieroglyphics as phonetics is but a primary lesson in Sign Language.

The zootypes were continued in the religious mysteries

to denote, visibly and audibly, the characters assumed in this primitive drama.

The manes exclaims I am the Beetle, I am the Jackal, I am the Crocodile, I am the god in Lion form. These express his powers. They are superhuman forms taken by superhuman powers—Power of transformation, Power of resurrection, Power of seeing in the dark of death, Power over water, etc., all of which are assumed because superhuman. In assuming the types he personates the powers, as examples. When surrounded by enemies of the soul, he exclaims: " I am the Crocodile-God in all his terrors." This has to be read by the Osirian Cult. Osiris had been thus environed by the Sebu and the associates of the evil Set when he lay dismembered in Sekhem. But he rose again as Horus. In this case the crocodile type of terror was employed; and down went the adversaries before the Almighty Lord, thus imaged in Sign Language as the Crocodile God.

This phase of teaching, continued in later Mysteries with the transformation of the performers in the guise of birds, reptiles, and animals, had been practised in the Mysteries of Amenta, where the human soul in passing through the nether-world assumed shape after shape, and made his transformation from one to the other in a series of new births according to the Egyptian doctrine of metempsychosis, which was afterwards perverted and turned into foolishness in India and in Greece. In this divine drama the Soul from earth is assimilated to the zootypes or is inverted in their forms and endowed with their forces which have figured from the very earliest nature powers in the Mythology.

The Egyptian Ritual is the book of life: life now, life hereafter, everlasting life. It is, indeed, the book of life and salvation, because it contains the things to be done in the life hereafter and here, to ensure eternal continuity (Rit., Ch. 15, Hymn 3).

The departing soul, when setting into the land of life, clasps and clings to his roll of papyrus for very life. As the book of life, or word of salvation, it was buried in the coffin with the dead when done with on earth. It shows the way to Paradise objectively, as well as subjectively, as Heaven was mapped out in their Astro-Mythology. The manes enters on his journey (Amenta) with a papyrus roll in his hand corresponding to the one that was buried in his coffin. This contains the written word of truth, the word of magical power, the word of life. The great question now for him is how far he has made the word of God truth and established it against the powers of evil in his lifetime on earth. The word that he carries with him was written by Taht Aan, the scribe of truth. Another word has been written in his lifetime by himself, and the record will meet him in the Hall of Justice on the day of weighing words, when Taht will read the record of the life to see how far it tallies with the written word and how far he has fulfilled the word in truth to earn eternal life. The sense of sin and abhorrence of injustice must have been peculiarly keen when it was taught that every word as well as deed was weighed in the balance of truth on the day of reckoning, called the Judgment Day.

The "Egyptian Book of the Dead" is based upon a resurrection of the soul and its possible return to earth at times, for some particular purpose, as the double or ghost. He prays that he may revisit the earth (Rit., Ch. 71). The persistence of the human soul in death and its transformation into a living and enduring spirit is a fundamental postulator of the Egyptian Ritual and of the religious mysteries. It will be sufficient to show how profound the belief in the Spirit must have been when the prayers and invocations are made, and the oblations and the sacrifices are offered to the Ka-image of his eternal soul, which was set up in the funeral chamber as the likeness of the Spiritual self to whose consciousness they made their religious and affectionate appeal.

We learn from the Ritual that the soul might revisit the earth when it had attained the status of the Ba, which is imaged as the Hawk with a human head. In

Ritual, Chapter 126, it says: "Enter those in and come forth at thy pleasure like the Glorified Ones."

The Ritual, Chapter 123, gives us the ideas of the Egyptian Religion, as when the manes arrives at the Judgment Hall he says: "I have propitiated the great god with that which he loveth, I have given bread to the hungry, water to the thirsty, clothes to the naked, a boat to the shipwrecked. I have made oblations to the gods and funeral offerings to the departed," or to the Ancestral Spirits (Rit., Ch. 125). This statement shows that he recognized and made oblations to the Elemental Forces, or Animistic nature powers, divinized as the gods; that he had made funeral offerings to the Ancestral Spirits; that he had been charitable to his fellow-beings, and that he worshipped the One Great God only, who was over all. In the late Osirian Cult, the Trinity was Asar-Isis in matter, Horus in soul, and Ra in spirit, which three were blended in the One Great God. This shows also that the Egyptians always discriminated the three, i.e. the Ancestral Spirits from the divinized elemental powers, and that "The One Great God" governed all. "The Glorified" are identifiable as spirits that once were human who have risen from the dead in a glorified body as Sahus (Corpuscular, or body in the likeness of the man in a beautiful corpuscular form).

In the Solar Cult "the place of coming forth" had been given to Horus (as typified by the Sun) in the East, and the East therefore became "The Holy Land" of the Solar Cult people, in place of the earliest "Ta-Neter," or "Holy Land," of the earlier Egyptians, which was Puanta the ever-golden, or the Land of the Reeds, and which was sacred on account of its being the primeval home, *not in Asia*, but in the Land of the Lakes in Africa.

CHAPTER XIV

THE JEWS AND ISRAELITES

HEBREWS

THERE should be a distinction made with regard to these terms, i.e. "Jews" and "Israelites." The term "Hebrews" would be more correct.

The Jews strictly are of the Tribe, or Totemic Clan of Judah. The Israelites are not Jews, although some Jews may be Israelites. Moses and his followers have been termed Israelites, but there is no evidence that the "Israelites" were ever in Egypt except once when they made a raid, and were driven back with great slaughter. The Israelites, a mythological name, were a number of Totemic Tribes who originally left Egypt and went to the East during the Stellar Cult. But a large body of Egyptians left Egypt and went to the East under Moses, or Mosheh or Amosis or Osarsiph (various names for the same man). The Jews never had any ethnology as a nation, but only as a religious sect.

Manetho states that Moses received his priestly education and learned all the wisdom of the Egyptians in the city of Heliopolis, in the Delta, the Biblical City of On, or Beth-Shemish, the House of the Sun. Manetho also states that *Moses was one of the priests* and was learned in all the Osirian and Amen Ra doctrines, and that he changed his religion twice (i.e. forms of religion), which means that at one time he professed the old Stellar Cult and then changed to the Solar Cult : this is proved by several records.

According to Volney, Moses tried vainly to proscribe the worship of the Symbols which prevailed in Lower

Egypt and Phœnicia, and to blot out from his religion everything which had relation to the Stars, i.e. the old Stellar Cult doctrines.

Again, when his followers revolted from the Solar doctrines that he tried to impose on them in the wilderness, he was obliged to have recourse to the old Stellar Cult symbols, when he lifted up the serpent in the wilderness (a symbol of the God Tem in Stellar Cult), his followers understood (Numbers xxi. 9). The God Tem they knew was a Saviour under the old Stellar Cult. Moses fell back upon a symbol of the former Cult, of which he knew the meaning, and which he, no doubt, knew his followers would recognize as part of the old doctrine. Compare also John xiv. 14.

Tem, symbolized by a serpent in the Stellar Cult, was the older form, but he was brought on in the Solar Cult as Tem-Ra. Tem, therefore, was symbolized by the "Holy Serpent," the "other serpents" represented the spawn of Apap.

Only one mention of the people of Israel occurs by name on all the monuments of Egypt. This was discovered a few years ago by Professor Flinders Petrie on a stele erected by the King Merenptah II. There is no possibility of identifying this with the Biblical Israelites.

The "people of Ysiraal" on the monuments belong to the confederated "Nine Bows," the marauders who were subdued by the King Merenptah. It is said "the people of Ysiraal is spoiled; it hath no seed."

The people of Ysiraal in this inscription are identified by the Pharaoh with the nomads of the Edomite Shasu or shepherds, and are classed by him with the confederate marauders who invaded Egypt with the Libu and were defeated with huge slaughter in the battle of Pa-ar-shep, which is recorded on the monuments. They were a tribe, or totemic community, of cattle-keepers. One of the "tribes of the Shasu from the land of Aduma," went down into Egypt in search of grazing ground to find food for their herds in the eastern region of the Delta, at the very time when the people of Ysiraal and their seed were being annihilated as the Israelites in Syria. There was an exodus of the Edomite Shasu, which has been put forward in documents on behalf of "Biblical History," but these tribes had considered the eastern region of the Delta as far as Zoan to be their own possession until they were driven out by Seti I.

Now they bestirred themselves anew under Merenptah, but in a manner alike "peaceful and loyal." As faithful subjects of Egypt they asked for a passage through the border fortress of Khetam in the land of Thuku (Heb. Succoth) in order that they might find food for themselves and their herds in the rich pasturelands of the lake districts about the city of Pa-Tum (Pithom) (Brugsch: "Egypt under Pharaoh," Vol. I, p. 317). An Egyptian official makes the following report on the subject. He says: "Another matter for the satisfaction of my master's heart; we have carried into effect the passage of the tribes of the Shasu from the land of Aduma (Edom) from the fortress (Khelam) of Merenptah-Hetephima, which is situated in Thuku, to the lakes of the City Pa-Tem in order to feed themselves and their herds on the possessions of Pharaoh, who is their beneficent sun for all peoples. In the year 8 —— Sat I caused them to be conducted (according to the list of the days on which the fortress was opened for their passage)" (Brugsch: cit. Pop. Anast. 6).

Here we have the field of Zoan and the store-cities of Pithom and Rameses, which have been introduced into the second book of Moses with futile efforts to show that this record confirmed the Biblical version. But in this exodus we see that the Shasu or shepherds are peaceful and loyal people, faithful subjects of Pharaoh, who are carefully conducted from the land of Edom through the fortress of Khetam to the lake country of Thuku (or Succoth), the first encampment assigned to the Israelites, where they would find abundance of food for themselves and flocks instead of wandering in the wilderness for 40 years, according to the Biblical story, at the same time the people of Ysiraal in Syria were exterminated root and branch by Merenptah. Here we find that the Hebrew translators have converted the "coming forth" from Amenta into the Biblical exodus from Egypt, and have tried to affiliate the cattle-keepers in the land of Goshen to the nomadic tribes of the Edomite Shasu (Genesis xlvi. 32).

The defeat of the Libyans and their confederate invaders, the people of Ysiraal, in the time of Merenptah, is a matter of historic fact (see Monuments). That they were vanquished and driven back is equally historical. They could not make an exodus from Egypt as 600,000 fighting men, for they never got there, but were defeated on the borders of the land ; therefore, to elucidate the Biblical story, we must return to the "Ritual of Ancient Egypt." Israel in Egypt is not an ethnical entity—the story represents the children of Ra in the Lower Egypt of Amenta, built or founded by Ptah, and entirely mythical. The Egyptian exodus is a mystery of Amenta. It is described in the Ritual as the Peri-em-heru or coming forth to-day from the Hades of Egypt and the desert (Records, Vol. X, p. 109).

The Books of Genesis, Exodus, and Joshua are not intentional forgeries ; the subject-matter was already extant in the Egyptian Mysteries, and an exoteric version of the ancient wisdom has been rendered in the form of historic narrative and ethnically applied to the Jews. The most learned of the Rabbis have, however, most truthfully maintained that the books attributed to Moses do but contain an exoteric explanation of the secret wisdom. We see that fragments of the original mythos crop up in the Haggadoth, the Kabalah, the Talmud, and other Hebrew writings, which tend to show that in the earlier times the same matter had been known to the Jews themselves as non-historical. The chief teachers have always insisted on the allegorical nature of the Pentateuch. Thus it is seen that "Biblical History" has been mainly derived from misappropriated and misinterpreted wisdom of Egypt contained in their mythological and eschatological representation as witnessed by the " Ritual of Ancient Egypt." The proof can be found in the Books ascribed to Moses, where an esoteric rendering of the same mystical matter is also presented exoterically.

As amongst the Egyptians, there were two versions of the dark sayings and the hidden wisdom, the esoteric and the exoteric, and these have doubled the confusion.

As regards the Patriarchs and the number of years they lived, it ought, strictly speaking, to be unnecessary to adduce any proof that if there be historic truth in this tradition, it never can have meant that individual men lived six, seven, eight, or nine centuries. Had this been the case the statement ought to have been declared intrinsically impossible. But the original account meant no such thing. If we study the question and the oldest documents, we find it cannot have been the original intention and purport of the tradition to *indicate persons* by the Biblical names, and still less the length of life of individuals by the dates assigned to them. They were originally meant to designate, not persons, but epochs. Thus having not one tradition, but two (in the Hebrew) *we have no historical account;* that is, documents which are originals; but what we have is the misunderstood and perverted earliest records these forefathers brought from Egypt, or Egyptian records obtained from *some other* source.

The Samaritan, as well as the Septuagint, version had already made alterations in the dates of the patriarchs, but Eusebius, for the sake of these dates, which are not only unintelligible in the letter but confused and misunderstood, altered the traditions of the rest of the old world. Then came two Brazantine monks, Anianus and Panodorus, with their scheme for reducing the dates to years of single months, or even days; they were not deterred even by the absurdity of the result, which was that their Patriarchs begot children when they were four years old. Philo, the learned Jew, states, that the Logos or word of God is pre-eminent over the

Messengers, but he makes the mistake in assigning to the Divine Being the Male gender exclusively.

Tablionos, the very first of the hierophants of Phœnicia, gave a sensuous meaning to most of his works, and jumbled it all up together with what befel the earth and heavenly bodies.

He then communicated it to the prophets. These again did all they could to increase the obscurity as much as possible, and transmitted the traditions to their successors and the foreigners who were initiated (Philo's translation of Sankhumathon's writings).

The oldest Hebrew Pentateuch, the oldest known of any part of the Bible was probably written in the ninth century. *The Samaritan Pentateuch*, the earliest known extant, dates from the tenth century. The Samaritans have kept the old form of writing which was in use among the Hebrews before their adoption of the square characters, and is more nearly connected with the Phœnician, from which most authorities believe it was copied. It contains the old Hebrew text of the Pentateuch with an Arabic version in Samasiha character. *The Hebrew Pentateuch*, imperfect, beginning with the last words of Leviticus xii. 8, was written in Babylonia or Persia in the twelfth century; the text is accompanied by the Aramaic (Chaldee) Targum or translation attributed to Onkelos. Both of these, as I shall prove, originated from the Egyptian. The " Hebrew Scriptures," no doubt, were written in *the Phœnician characters* for many centuries, *although they have not survived in this form*, and the Phœnicians were first Stellar Cult and later Solar Cult Egyptians.

Dean Inge considers that the Hebrews borrowed " their legends " from the Babylonians. I disagree with this view, for, as already stated, I believe that both obtained their " legends " from the Egyptians. There was a common origin for each, but they did not borrow from each other. One fact in itself will show that the Biblical Eden was not derived from the Assyrian or Babylonian *Edin*, because in this garden there is but a *single tree*, which is apparently the tree of life. The divine lady of Edin is the goddess of the tree of life, and there is no mention of a tree of knowledge. Again, the serpent, as a type of evil in the Book of Genesis, is not the Babylonian dragon Tiamat. The Biblical dragon is of neither sex, whereas Tiamat is female. The Hebrew dragon, or evil serpent, is the Apap of Egypt, from Genesis to Revelation. Apap is a water-reptile, whose dwelling is at the bottom of the dark waters, called the void of Apap, from which it rises in rebellion as the representative of drought. This is the serpent described by Amos : " Though they be hid from my sight in the bottom of the sea, thence will I command the serpent, and he shall bite them" (Amos ix. 3). Another reason. The Hebrew Eden is in a land that was watered by a mist which went up from the ground, and where no rain fell on the earth (Gen. ii. 5. 6). That land above all earthly prototypes was Egypt, which assuredly did not suffer like Babylon from the " curse of rain," from which the Akkadin month " As-an " was named. The Babylonian Edin was the Stellar Cult image and was pre-Solar ; the Hebrew Eden was the Egyptian Solar Cult type or portrayal. The Stellar Cult was the Egyptian Am-Khemen, which Shu uplifted with his two-pronged prop imaging the Pole, when he divided earth from heaven and raised the upper circumpolar paradise.

Paradise, says Ibn Ezra, is the place of one tree. Mount Hetep, in the northern heaven, is represented as a one-tree-hill. In some of the Mexican drawings there is a point of departure by water from the mount, which has a single tree upon its summit (Stellar Cult portrayal). It is a legend that is universal in this Cult. This typical one-tree-hill is also to be found at Sakapu in Manchuria, where it is represented by a mountain designated, " lone-tree-hill." The Norse tree, Yggdrasil, is also single. Nor is there more than one tree, or stalk, in the garden of Eridu, where the Great Mother is the lady of the eternal tree. The eternal tree is the Pole. The seven branches show it to have been a numerical type of the Heptanomis.

In the Stellar Cult circumpolar paradise there was but one tree as a figure of the northern Pole of heaven, also in this Stellar Cult the Chinese Fu-tree, the self-supporting, is likewise a figure of the Pole. Hence it is said to grow " on the summit of a mountain in mid-ocean at the north" (Schlegel, Prof. G. Fou-Sang Kono).

The two trees in the Garden of Eden can be accounted for upon Egyptian ground, but on no other, one being the tree of the Pole in Stellar Cult, the other the tree of life, or of dawn, in the garden eastward in the Egyptian Solar Cult. The two typical trees are recognizable as Egyptian in the " Book of the Dead." In one chapter (97th) they are called the two divine sycamores of heaven and earth. The sycamore of heaven is identified as the tree of Nut; it stands in " the lake of equipoise," which is the Celestial Pole.

The tree of earth is the tree of Hathor and of dawn. The tree of earth, or Hathor, and the tree of heaven, or Nut, were brought on together and united in the tree of burial for the mummy. Wherever it was possible the Egyptian coffin was made from the wood of the sycamore tree, the Khat-an-ankhu, or tree of life, so that the dead might be taken in the embrace of the mother of life, who was in one form represented by the tree. This was Hathor as bringer of birth in the Mythology, and Nut the bringer of souls to their rebirth in the Eschatology. Hathor, the tree-form of Mother Earth, is portrayed inside the coffin upon the board upon which the mummy rested, taking the dead to her embrace as the mother of life. Nut, the mother of heaven, was represented on the inner part of the coffin-lid, arching over the mummy, as bringer of the manes to new life above. This symbolized a resurrection of the spirit from the tree of life as Horus rose again from out the tree of dawn.

In the Solar Cult, when the Egyptians formed Amenta, they brought on the circumpolar paradise and duplicated it. The primal Stellar Cult paradise was the place of one tree. The paradise or garden in Amenta (Solar Cult)

OF RELIGION

is the place of two trees, because the ground-rootage had been doubled in phenomena. These two trees appear in the Ritual as the tree of Hathor and the tree of Nut; the tree of Earth and the tree of Heaven; the tree of the North and the tree of the East. The tree of Hathor was the tree of life. It was the sycamore fig-tree, from the fruit of which a divine drink of the mysteries was made. It was the tree to make one wise, which became a tree of wisdom or abnormal knowledge. The tree of Nut was the tree of heaven and eternal life, hence it was designated the eternal tree. Hence they are called the tree of knowledge and the tree of life.

The whole of the imagery of the Hebrew writings can be read and understood by the original Egyptian, but not from any other source.

The secret of the sanctity of the Hebrew writings is that they were originally Egyptian.

The wisdom of old, the myths, parables, and dark sayings that were preserved, have been presented to us dreadfully deformed in the course of being converted into history.

An exoteric rendering has taken the place of the true esoteric representation, originally written in Sign Language, which contained the only true interpretation. The past was known to Philo, who, when speaking of the Mosaic writings, told his co-religionists that "the literal statement is a fabulous one, and it is in the Mythical that we shall find the true." There is ample proof that the same fundamental matter belonging to the wisdom of Egypt, in which Osarsiph (Moses) of On was an adept, appears thrice over in the Hebrew writings.

It is Mythological in the Books of Genesis, Exodus, and Joshua.

It is Eschatological in the Psalms.

In the later Books it is converted into matter of prophecy.

All three phases are Egyptian, with this difference, that the sole possible fulfilment of prophecy was astronomical, not human, history. These three phases in the Hebrew writings must be followed if we wish to gain the truth.

In the first part we see that the older religion of the patriarchs was that of the Stellar Cult of the Egyptians. They worshipped God under the name of Baal or El-Shadda, sacrificed in high places, adored in groves, planted oaks, intermarried with their immediate relations, all of which was afterwards forbidden by Moses, who substituted the Solar Cult of Egypt. Their two creations were: first, that of the Stellar; second, that of the Solar Cult.

The exodus, or "coming out of Egypt," first celebrated by the festival of the Passover, or the transit at the Vernal Equinox, occurred in the heavens before it was made historical in the migrations of the Jews. The 600,000 men who came up out of Egypt as Hebrew warriors in the Book of Exodus are the 600,000 inhabitants of Israel in the Heavens according to the Jewish Kabalah, and the same scenes, events, and personages that appear as mundane in the Pentateuch are celestial in the Book of Enoch.

Clement of Alexandria fixed the date of the exodus amongst other enumerations by the statement: "That it occurred 345 years before the Sothic Cycle." The Sothic Cycle was in existence before the time of Mena over 4000 B.C., is borne out by "Manetho and the Monuments," and was a cycle of 1,460 years with four years as intercalary.

The Hyksos period of "Shepherd Kings," and their reign at Memphis and Lower Egypt, was 2554 B.C., and when they were driven out of Egypt they went East and built Jerusalem. This occurred in the reign of Tuthmoses, and Moses lived after this and was driven out with his followers.

Josephus is supposed to be the most authentic writer on the Jewish antiquities, but he wrote his work in the beginning of Trajan's reign, and there is a great discrepancy in the traditions and variation in the Hebrew and Greek text which no power can reconcile. Josephus wrote 2,000 years after Moses lived. These traditions were derived from " Rabbinical Comments," and none of the chronology by the most able writers will agree. Josephus leaves out the time of the leadership of Tola and Abdon altogether, and never mentions them.

The ancient sacred records of Phœnicia state that the worship of the Kabu or Pataikoi, i.e. the Stellar Cult, was brought to the coast of Phœnicia from Egypt. The Phœnician Sadda, the Almighty or El Sadda, " God the Almighty," was Stellar Cult. Set, as the primary God and, later, El Esmun=Horus, or the God of Healing, Iu-em-Hetep. The Kabiri were the old " Elohim," or Ari, as elsewhere stated.

Josephus knew from the works of Berosus, or at all events, of Polyhistor, the names of the eighty-seven kings of which the Babylonian dynasty consisted, and who are said to have reigned 30,000 years. The Temple of Belus or Bel (Set) was in the centre of the town of Babylon, and not $9\frac{1}{2}$ miles away. Philo of Byblus, in his work about celebrated cities, " His. Gr.," Frag. III, 575, as stated by Stephanus of Byzantium, who made the following statement about it: " Babylon was built not by Semiramis, as Herodotus says, but by Babylon, a wise man, the son of the All-wise-Belus, who, as Herennius states, lived 2,000 years before Semiramis." We find the same account coming from Herennius (Philo) in Eustathius ("Coms. to Dionys" Vol. V, p. 1005), and this agrees with the Egyptian account or statement. Although " Nimrod " is mentioned several times in the Hebrew writings, his name is not among the first Chaldean dynasty; therefore, if such a man lived, he must have preceded this.

In the Hebrew text Tubal-Cain, who is there called the son of Lamekh, was said to be the first " Artificer in Metals." But in the Phœnician, which is much older, we find the truth. Here he is called " Tubal-Qayin," which means smith, or a maker of tools. The brother, the sisters, and mother of this same Tubal-Cain or Qayin, are all mentioned in the Theogony of Uranos-Kronos as being Kosmological deities of Phœnicia (3rd fragment of the 2nd Kosmogony of Philo) and the original was Horus Behutet of the Egyptians.

(Tekai=Hadah or Na'Hamah. Hadah is mentioned in the Hebrew text as the wife of Lamekh, and again as the wife of Esau, who was the Phœnician Usov.)

(The Kabiri, or Pataikoi, belong to Phœnicia, both as the 7 and the 8. These Pataikoi were called "The mighty Kabiri in Phœnicia, in Samothrace, and Lemnos" = the divinized elemental Powers of Egypt.

Sadda, the Almighty.

El-Sadda, God the Almighty.

Esmun, the God of Healing=Iu-em-Hetep of Egypt.

Kronos, called El, whence Elohim is derived.)

We see that under the old Stellar Cult the Israelites were accustomed to adore God under the title of Bel or Baal or El Sadda (Phœnician), "The God of the Highest Star," or "Pole Star." Hu was an epithet of Bel, signifying the self-existing Being—"He that is."

The change from the Stellar Cult to the Solar Cult in Israel, i.e. from the worship of Bal or El Shaddai to the worship of Ihuh-Hu or Iu Egyptian—that is, from the Elohistic to the Jehovistic—is plainly portrayed.

Bel or Baali, who was Set as primary God of the Pole Star South, afterwards Horus of the Pole Star North, was no longer to be considered "the One God." "Thou shalt call me Ishi and shall call me no more Baali." Hosea ii. 16; also see Exodus xxxiv. 13.

The first Deity, as God of Israel, was Jashar-El, the god of Jashar—Jeshurum or Baali (El Elyoun, Phœnician) the god of the Pole Star in the Stellar Cult. Elim was a general name of god in Phœnicia (Gessnic Thesaurus, 3, v), El in the highest being the Star God on the summit of the Mount or the Pole. In the Book of 1 Chronicles xii. 5, we find that Baal-Jah, as divinity, supplied a personal name. Thus the Baali as Jah was one of the Baalim, who were the primary seven elemental powers, divinized in the Stellar Cult.

In the Solar Cult the One God in Israel was known by the two names of Ihuh and Iah.

Turning to the Egyptian original, the One God Amen or Atum-Ra was Huhi the Eternal in the character of God the Father and Iu in the character of God the Son, which two were one.

Gesenius derives the name Ihuh from the root Huh, which root does not exist in Hebrew, but it does exist in the Egyptian 𓎛𓅱.

Huh or Heh signifies everlastingness, eternity, the eternal, and was a title which was applied to Ptah, Atum-Ra, and Osiris, as Neb-Hui the everlasting Lord or Supreme One, Self-existing and Eternal God.

Ptah was in one phase the father of Amen or Atum-Ra (see supra).

Memphis was a much older foundation than On, the Northern Annu.

The wisdom of Ptah-Iu was indefinitely older than the writings of the Jews, or Aiu, which had been preserved in the library at On and brought forth thence by Osarsiph (or Moses) as the basis of the Pentateuch.

They (the Jews or Aiu) held to their one God Ihuh the eternal, and left out Iu, or the ever-coming Son, except as a prophecy, although the Phœnicians brought on the Son under the name of El Elsmun, the God of healing, who was Iu-em-Hetep of the Egyptians. They made their God, like the Mohammedan Deity, a Father without a Son, and disposed of the Mother as well, whether in Astronomical or Eschatological phase.

We also see from Exodus xxxiv. 13, how Moses changed the Cults. "Ye shall destroy their altars, break their images, and cut down their groves." Also Moses said unto the Judges of Israel: "Slay ye every one his men that were joined unto Baal-Peor" (Numbers xxv. 5).

Thus we see how they begin to root out the old Stellar Cult faith wherever they found it, although at first "Grove Worship" was equally prevalent amongst the Israelites as amongst the Druids, who also were an exodus of Solar Cult people from Egypt. Moses was learned in both Cults, and he brought the seven candlesticks with seven lighted candles on to represent as types the powers, or spirits, or glorious ones of the seven stars in Ursa Minor.

Moreover, Ptah is represented in the form of a Pygmy, and his Ari are seven little Pygmies, the Egyptians having taken the type from the primordial, or first human evolved from the Anthropoid Ape in Africa.

We have it in Philo's "Cosmogony," called the Materialistic, or Mokh, doctrine of the beginning of the world and of men—taken from the Sankhuniathon—that the first were "little men and little women." Another proof that these documents (Philo's) were a copy of the Egyptians at the time of the Solar Cult, is that the little men and little women are distinguished from the "Giants" (Mythological Stellar Cult), which were types of the seven stars of the Little Bear, or at least of the gods which were associated with each star, and which at a later time became the Hebrew seven Archangels.

The "Laws of Moses" were the old Egyptian Laws, and brought out of Egypt by him; this the stele or "Code of Hammurabi" conclusively proves. Moses lived 1,000 years after this stone was engraved.

Philo derived most of his knowledge from the book of Sankhuniathon, who was a learned scholar, held in high estimation by King Abibaal, and by men of learning at his court; he lived in the time of Semiramis, and wrote the history of Phœnicia in eight or nine books (accounts differ as to the number) which gives an acount of the oldest Phœnician, Babylonian, and Chaldean cosmogonical systems. This is a critical proof that these books were copies of Taht Hermes and Toth of the Egyptians, but show how little the copyists comprehended the true esoteric rendering of the Sign Language therein. Since the Armenian version of Eusebius has been published, the works of Berosus have been accepted as regards the theogony and cosmogony of Babylonia, and they show how perverted was the true rendering of the wisdom of Egypt. Philo, in his three books " On Paradoxical History," clearly shows that the Greeks had misunderstood the old Myths from ignorance of the names which occur in them, the Greeks having adopted names and the Myths without knowing the original meaning.

The " Sacred historical documents " of the Hebrews are not historical at all, only traditions and copies from some other documents much older, which can only be traced to Egypt. The copies of the older documents are Metaphrastically rendered as " human history," whereas the original were the esoteric rendering in Sign Language of the original beliefs of the ancient Egyptians.

Modern research sees in ancient Hebrew literature nothing but a succession of editorial scribes, including Ezra and Nehemiah, who exercised free discretion in correcting, interpolating, and transposing the contents of ancient Egyptian records which they could not understand, and in even canonizing the recent compositions of anonymous authors in the name of ancient prophets.

In 2 Esdras xiv, we read that the law, having been burnt, was reproduced by Ezra under the inspiration of the Holy Spirit.

Clement of Alexandria stated : " The Scriptures, having been destroyed, Ezra, the Levite, inspired as a prophet, reproduced the whole of the Sacred Scriptures in the time of Artaxerxes, the King of the Persians " (Strom, I. 22). This pious fiction obviously originated in the desire to invest these compositions with the authority of true ancient records. Theologians have exhausted the resources of criticism in the vain attempt to unravel the enigma of authorship, dates, and veritable texts, with no more satisfactory results than the development of interminable controversies, establishing nothing more clearly than universal ignorance on the subject, because the originals, the " Ritual of Ancient Egypt," has been a closed book to them which they have been unable to read. Even the evidence of Jeremiah condemns them : " How do ye say, We are wise and the law of the Lord is with us ? Lo, certainly in vain made he it : the pen of the Scribes is in vain " (Jer. viii. 8).

The original of the Hebrew collection consisted of " the precepts of the Pentateuch," which may be said to be the Jewish Torah, which signifies, or denotes, the whole law, and in the Egyptian Teruu signifies all—entirely the whole laws.

Shu-Anhur was the giver of laws to man as revealed by Ra, and is mentioned in the Ritual as the author of writings called " His rules and laws and his papyrus." Shu is said to work in the abode of the Book of Seb, i.e. of earth (Rit., Ch. 17). This can be identified with the great Library at Annu. " The papyrus Mahit of Shu " is mentioned in the Ritual—" I am in unison with his successive changes and his laws (or rules) and his writings " (Rit., Ch. 110).

The writings of Shu-Anhur were preserved at Annu amongst the 36,000 books traditionally ascribed to Taht. He wrote them at dictation from Ra or Atum-Huhi, the father of Iu, who was carried into Judea as Ihuh, and brought on the sacred writings that had been placed in the Temple of Atum-Ra-Har-Makhu to be transmitted from generation to generation.

Modern research discovers in the Hebrew writings a composite work, not as the autogram of the Hebrew legislator, but as the editorial patchwork of mingling Semitic legends with cosmopolitan myths, which were copied from the Egyptians, either directly or indirectly, but without the gnosis. Take the second creation for an example, and see how it reads in the Hebrew.

" Let us imagine the sudden awakening of primeval man to startled consciousness of the external world according to the second or Jehovistic creation (which knew nothing of humanity fashioned in the image of God). Adam being simply vitalized dust, and Eve a mere after-thought devised for his comfort and convenience, confused by sensation, alarmed by sound, dazzled by light, absorbed in the mysterious sympathy of sex, and yet unconsciously entrusted, in this condition of

OF RELIGION

mental imbecility, with the future destinies of all Humanity, staked on his unintelligent obedience to an arbitrary command sustained by a death penalty conveying no meaning to his infantine ignorance, and at this supreme crisis Jehovah retires from the scene. Then a mysterious Serpent, detected by later theologians as Satan, or the Devil, in masquerade, tempts Eve with the fruit from the tree of knowledge. As no divine assistance is there, 'the Fall' is a foregone conclusion. Poor Eve has tasted the fruit and held it to the lips of Adam in her simplicity, knowing no difference between the command of a god and the advice of a serpent, and yields inevitable victory to the wiles of the snake. Later Jehovah walks through the garden of Eden in the cool of the evening, discovers man's disobedience, curses the serpent with the bodily motion, evolved by ages; condemns Adam to the labour by which prehistoric man had existed for millions of years; decrees the degradation of humanity through the domestic bondage of woman, henceforth dependent for her social position on the prejudice, caprice, and passion of her lord and master, and finally pronounces the sentence of death, in apparent unconsciousness that mortality had reigned supreme on earth throughout millions of ages remote from the chronology of Eden. Then the Lord God said, Behold this man is become as one of us to know good and evil, and now lest he put forth his hand, and take also of the tree of life and eat and live for ever (Gen. iii. 22). These are the words of Jehovah. If Eve had chanced to pluck an apple from the other tree, Adam, contrary to the design of his Creator, would have been enrolled among the gods, and this little earth would have long since failed to hold the countless multitudes of his immortal descendants."[1] That is the rendering exoterically, but I have here set forth the true esoteric rendering from the original Egyptian.

Let us see the origin of Adam and Eve in the Garden of Eden. Nothing portrays it better than the papyrus of Ani published by the British Museum.

[1] From "Evolution of Christianity," by Charles Gill.

In this happy garden they are portrayed as the pair of souls, once human, passing through the various scenes which are depicted in the Ritual.

The Soul, or manes, makes the journey through Amenta in the two halves of sex: "male and female created he them." Thus Ani is accompanied in the picture by his wife Tutu, who had died eight years before him, and now comes to meet him at the entrance to Amenta, to protect him on the way she travelled first, and to scare away all evil spirits with the shaking of her sistrum as she guides him to the heaven of the glorified elect. As gods, the divine pair in the garden of this late beginning, called Gan-Eden, were Atum and Iusāas. As human, they may be any pair of manes like Ani and his wife, to whom an allotment in Sekhet Aarru was given for them to cultivate. In the Hebrew version the divine pair have been humanized in Adam and Eve, as being *on this earth*, and thus the mystery of Amenta loses all the meaning, which has to be restored by reading the original once more in the Ritual. The male and female pair are portrayed together in the vignettes to Chapters 15, 15a, 2; 15a, 3; 15a, 4; 156, 1; 156, 2, all of which scenes belong to the earth of eternity (Naville: Das Egypt, Todt, pp. 14, 15, 16, 17, 18, 19). The primal pair of human beings, who are Adam and Eve in the Semitic version of the legend, had been represented in the Papyri as Ani and his wife Tutu, the man and woman that once were mortal on the earth, but have passed into the state of manes, who are on their way to or in the terrestrial paradise. They enter the Aarru garden; they drink the water of life at its secret source in the Tuat: they eat the fruit of the tree of life which is offered to Ani, the man, by the divine woman in the tree, Hathor of the Sycamore fig-tree (whose primal type and image was Rannut, see "Origin and Evolution of the Human Race," p. 150). Iusāas, the wife of Atum=Adam and Mother of Iu at Annu, was a form of Hathor. So that Hathor Iusāas offering the fruit of the Sycamore fig to Atum in the Sekhet Aarru is equivalent to Eve, who offers the fruit

Drawn by K. Watkins.

THE MANES, OR SPIRIT, DRINKING THE CELESTIAL WATER OF LIFE, BEING POURED OUT BY NUT FROM THE TREE OF LIFE.

PLATE LXIII.

[To face p. 308.

Drawn by K. Watkins

THE DECEASED AND HIS WIFE BEFORE THE SYCAMORE OF NÛT RECEIVING THE BREAD AND WATER OF THE NEXT WORLD.

PLATE LXIV.

… of the tree of knowledge to Aham in the Garden of Eden which, as shown by the apron of fig leaves, was a fig-tree.

When Ani and his spirit consort, who had been his wife on earth, appear together in the happy garden, they drink the water of life and eat the fruit of the tree as spirits amongst spirits. In one scene the pair are portrayed hard by the tree of life, both of them drinking the water of life that flows from beneath the tree (Plate LXIII).

In the next vignette the man is kneeling alone before the tree, which is a sycamore fig-tree. A woman in the tree is offering some fruit to Ani (Plate LXIV). This is the goddess Nut, the lady of heaven, who presents the fruit of the tree to the man in the garden of the earthly paradise (Pap. of Ani, Pl. 16), whose earliest zootype form was a Serpent, and who has been converted into the woman who tempted Adam to eat of the tree as the cause of the fallacious fall. The Biblical rendering of this representation is impious and profane against the Ritual, against womankind, against nature, and against knowledge and the truth.

The goddess Nut, who offers the fruit of the tree of knowledge to the kneeling man, is in shape a woman, and the meaning has been misread, as it has been in the legend of the first woman who tempted the first man to eat of the forbidden fruit and to cause the loss of paradise.

According to the Ritual, the manes who receive food in the garden of Aarru (Ch. 99, 32, 38), or who eat of the fruit of the sycamore fig-tree of Hathor (Ch. 52) are empowered to make what transformation they please, and go out of it as spirits. The manes says: " Let me eat under the sycamore of Hathor ! Let me see the forms of my father and mother " (Ch. 52), as he would when the spirit sight was open for him to perceive with the beatific vision. This is sufficient as text for the Serpent when he says : " Ye shall not surely die ; for·God doth know that in the day ye eat thereof, then your eyes shall be opened and ye shall be as gods, knowing good and evil" (Gen. iii. 4, 5). Instead of being damned eternally, through eating the fruit of the tree, the manes in Amenta are divinized as the result of eating it (Ch. 82, 2, 5).

The subject of the Hebrew beginnings is fundamentally the same as in the legends of the aborigines the whole world over, as will be seen when traced to its origin. Sociologically the "Creation of Man," *qua* man, was a birth of Totemism. It is the evolution of the human race from the pre-human conditions that were actual in nature and not, as alleged, the abortions of a false belief. It was the subject dramatized, danced and taught in all the mysteries of gesture-language and totemic ceremonies by means of which the unwritten past was commemorated by repetition of the acted drama, and is so acted by the Nilotic Negroes in whatever part of the world we find them. The Totemic people were known to the Semites as pre-Adamic people: the Admu, the Kings of Edom, and the origin can only be found in the Egyptian. But as a Semite tradition, it came to us in the latest and least genuine form, with no clue to any true interpretation.

In a Maori myth, Man was created by the god Tiki from red clay. This he kneaded with his own blood, or with red water from the swamps. The same legend of a later origin for mankind is also Mexican. When there were no human beings on the earth, certain of the lower powers solicited help from the supreme gods in the work of creation, or of a re-beginning. They were instructed to collect the remains of the former race, who would be vivified by the *blood of the gods*. In this version the god who plays the part of Atum, Adam, or Belus procures a bone from the burial place, and on this the gods drop the blood drawn from their own bodies. Whereupon there is a new creation—namely, that of mankind (Mendieta: "Hist. Ecl. Ind.," p. 77). Here, as elsewhere, the human soul of blood is derived from source as male instead of from the earlier motherhood. So in the Book of Genesis the second creation of Adam is based upon the bone called the rib, which is extracted from the male. In the Egyptian creation (the original) it was in Atum, the son of Ptah, that man was symbolically perfected. In him the Matriarchate is completely superseded by the Father-Right, or derivation from the Fatherhood. The beginning of the change in the human descent from the Mother-blood to the Father-blood can be traced so far back as the mysteries or ceremonial rites of the Arunta, and inner African races at the present time.

The man created by the Elohim, or Ali, was totemic man, like the legendary Adam, with the tail of an ape, a lion, or other zootype. It was thus the elemental powers were represented:

Set, by the Hippopotamus.
Sebek, by the Crocodile.
Atum, by the Lion.
Iu, by the Ass.
Seb, by the Goose.
Taht, by the Ibis.
Anup, by the Jackal.
Kabhsenuf, by the Hawk.

The first man who failed, the totemic Adam, fell from not possessing individual fatherhood; he was only born of the group in communal marriage under the matriarchate, which accounts for the Rabbinical tradition in which it is related that previous to the creation of Eve the man Adam entered into sexual intercourse with the animals, which is a statement made by ignorant theologians who could not read or understand Totemic Sign Language.

Jehovah—" I appeared unto Abraham, and unto Isaac, and unto Jacob by the name of God Almighty," but " by my name Jehovah was I not known to them."

Shadda signifies he who is self-sufficient. Jehovah, he who subsists of himself and gives being and existence to others.

The Patriarchs of old before Moses did not know the name Jehovah. Moses afterwards uses this name in Genesis; for example, he says that the sons of Seth called themselves by the name of Jehovah, and that Abraham sware and lift up his hands to Jehovah (Gen. xiv. 22); and, again, "the Lord said to Abraham I am the Lord that brought thee out of Ur of the Chaldees" (Gen. xv. 7). The reason of this is that Genesis was written after God had revealed this name to Moses; or, in other words, part of the Solar Cult was mixed with the Stellar by Moses on purpose to blot out the Stellar.

It was not until Amen or Atum was born as Horus or Iu, child of the Mother, and afterwards developed into Atum-Ra as God the Father, that he became the maker or creator of gods and men as the *begetter*; previously, up to and including Kheper-Ptah, the type was depicted as *transformers*.

The seven primordial powers had been recognized and divinized as offspring of the old first Mother. With Ptah the great Mother was combined and Atum, or *created* man, was formed as an evolution from the seven elemental Powers, which became the seven souls of Atum-Ra, otherwise called the seven souls of man, as elemental powers that went to the making of the manes in Amenta, or the human being when the rendering was literalized. The evolution of man was therefore from the seven powers of the elements on which the doctrine of the seven souls was founded according to the Egyptian wisdom. Six of these had been pre-human souls and the seventh alone attained the human type.

These souls of life had been identified and divinized as early as the commencement of the Stellar Cult; three, at least, during the Hero Cult.

The tradition that prevailed among the nations of antiquity depicted their ancestors as men of "gigantic stature," and grotesque legends (Gen. vi. 1, 4) are found in full detail in the Book of Enoch (Enoch x. 16) as follows: "Two hundred sons of heaven, or angels descended upon Ardis, the top of Mount Armon, under the leadership of Samyaza, and selected wives among the most beautiful daughters of men, who became the

THE MEXICAN DEPICTION OF THE TREE OF NUT OR THE TREE OF HEAVEN.
PLATE LXV.

mothers of monstrous giants, of appetites so destructive that they not only devoured birds, beasts, reptiles, and fishes, but even lived as cannibals, on human flesh. This appalling reign of violence and cruelty on earth at length aroused Michael, Gabriel, and Raphael, and other loyal members of the Heavenly Host, and on their appeal for retribution to the throne of God, the giant offspring of the apostate angels were superhumanly excited to destroy each other; and Samyaza, with his companions in crime, were hurled in fetters beneath the earth, to await in darkness the day of judgment, in which they shall be taken away in the lowest depths of the fire in torments and in confinement shall they be shut up for ever." The credibility of this legend is attested by Peter. " For if God spared not the angels that sinned, but cast them down to hell, and delivered them into chains of darkness to be reserved unto judgment" (2 Pet. ii. 4). Also Jude—"And the angels which kept not their first estate but left their own habitation he hath reserved in everlasting chains under darkness unto the judgment of the great day" (Jude iv). The authors of these epistles were therefore well acquainted with the Book of Enoch and Genesis, but not with the true Egyptian gnosis, which was the precession of the seven "stellar gods," or the Pole Stars of Ursa Minor. The divinized elemental powers in one image were giants. This is also portrayed by the Mexicans, and refers to the change from the Stellar to the Solar Cult.

There was a judgment annually in the Solar Mythos. This is still celebrated yearly by the Jews: the same assizes that were held each year, or periodically, in the Egyptian great hall of dual justice. The drama appears as tremendous in the Book of Revelation, because the period ending is on the scale of one Great Year. It *is not the ending of the world, but of a great year of the world.* The great judgment of all, like the great " deluge of all," was held at the end of the great year of all, in the Cycle of Precession.

The fable of " the giants," who were seven, in relation to the stations of the Pole, are identified with the mountains themselves as places of birth by Sanchoniathon. He says that they were beings of vast bulk and stature, "whose names were given to the mountains which they occupied." He also states that children were begotten through intercourse with their mothers, "the women of those times without shame having intercourse with any man they might choose to meet." Here the giant and mountain, as human birthplace are identical as figures of the Pole (Cory: "Ancient Fragments," 1876, p. 6). These are a form of those giants called the Sons of God who "Came into the daughters of men" (Book of Genesis; also Book of Enoch). Thus were the seven divinized mythical powers, sons of Apt, and all "bulls of their mother," rendered in the Hebrew marchen, the original gnosis of the Astronomical Cult being perverted, and the original imagery lost.

The seven old ones who were the primordial powers, the seven wise masters, watchers, judges, rishis, manus, moulders, masi, Ali, Elohim, or Kabari, are the seven patriarchs of Genesis who lived for such an enormous length of time. They are the typical old ones in the Ritual, the fathers in the first and highest circle of gods, but, in the Hebrew, it is only the patriarchs who have been humanized.

The Rabbis relate that Moses was born circumcised. So the Kaf-Ape is said to be born in the same condition, "It is born circumcised, which circumcision the priests adopt" (Hor-Apollo, B.I, 14). Shu, in one of his divers characters, is said to have taken the form of a Kaf-Ape ("Magic Papyrus," p. 8; Records, Vol. X, p. 152).

Shu, or Ma-Shu, as the Ape in the Mythos, becomes the man Moses or Mosheh, who is said in the marchen to have been born circumcised when the anthropomorphic type had taken the place of the zootype, showing how fragments of the ancient wisdom got mixed up in the Hebrew legend, and adopted as exoteric, whereas the true reason of the rite is as stated above.

The earliest Egyptians imaged a creator as the

moulder or potter; one of the earliest forms of this is seen where the god Khnum is portrayed as the potter in the act of forming man from the matter of earth. Ptah, called the son of Khnum sometimes, is seen occupied in a like act, forming the child Horus. All previously were depicted in zootype forms, and until "Bes" was portrayed in the likeness of a Pygmy by Ptah no perfect human form was depicted. As Atum, or Amen, is the original of the Hebrew Adam, we have the picture in a mythical representation when Ptah, as the potter, shapes the archetypal man as his son Atum from a lump of clay, or from the matter of earth, or the dust of the ground (Gen. ii. 7).

Dr. Kuenan and Sir Le Page Renouf rejected the theory of the Egyptian origins of the Hebrew creed—mistakenly, in my view. The important points of resemblance between the theology and ritualism of Ancient Egypt and of Israel are too analogous for such a supposition, and the explanation of the Books of the Old Testament can only find sense in the light of the Egyptian original.

In the Hebrew Genesis it says: "In the beginning Elohim created the heaven and the earth." This in the Egyptian original was Nut and Seb, who were divided from each other, not created, and were separated permanently by Shu and the supporting powers, or Elohim.

But instead of a cosmogonical creation, the Egyptian portrayal proves that this was a mode of representation in Astronomical Mythology, and therefore uranographic. The Hebrews literalized the figures of the Constellations that represented the elemental forces of water, air, earth, etc., whereas these elements were as much figures in the Astronomical Mythology as were the two firmaments and the abyss in the constellated lights, formed by the old Urshi wise men. In the Hebrew legends the earth and firmament were already extant, but "the earth was waste and void," and "darkness was over the face of the deep." Therefore the beginning in the Hebrew is without form, nothing but a void. Darkness existed,

Light came. Light was then divided from the darkness as a mode of describing "day" and "night." Next the upper firmament was separated from the lower, or, as stated, the waters above were divided from the waters below; whereas, in the original Mythos, the upper and lower waters were the upper and lower firmaments, because the water was a figure of the firmament.

Then followed the formation of the Abyss, "the waters under heaven" being gathered together in one place. The dry land is made to appear; and the Elohim called the dry land earth and "the gathering together of the waters they called seas."

According to Esdras (2 Es. vi. 41, 42) the waters were gathered "in the seventh part of the earth." In this seventh part the two monsters of the deep were figured, which are here called "Enoch and Leviathan," who represent the water and the dry land as do Leviathan and Behemoth in the Book of Enoch, which images are, as we have seen, still surviving in the "Southern Fish" and the monster "Ketos." The water of the firmament was without form or void before the type was constellated, or before a uranographic depiction was brought into being, which was accomplished by the ancient Egyptians during their Astro-Mythology, or Stellar Cult.

The word Elohim in Hebrew is employed both as a singular and plural noun for God and Gods, or Spirits, with no origin in phenomena by which the plurality could be explained except through the Egyptian wisdom.

In "The Despatches from Palestine" there is a perfect parallel to the twofold use of "Elohim" in the plural and singular forms employed in the Hebrew books. The scribe addressing the Egyptian Pharaoh says: "To the king, my lord, my gods, my sun-god" ("Records of the Past," Vol. II, p. 62, 2nd series).

Here "the gods" were the powers gathered into "one God" as supreme. These when seven were called the souls of Ra. They became the eight in the Paradise of Am-Khemen. They are nine in the Put-cycle of Ptah. They were ten as the sepheroth of the Kabalists. They are twelve in the final heaven of Atum-Ra. They are the Elohim as a form of the Egyptian Ali, or Ari, as companions of workers and, later, creators. There are at least three different groups of the Elohim—that is, the Ali or Lli with the plural ending of the name as Semitic. The first group of these Creators was seven in number, with Set-Anup at the head.

The second was that of the eight in Am-Khemen, with Horus as Anup added to the seven.

The third is the Company of Ptah, who formed the Put-cycle of the nine.

These preceded Amen, who was Ra in his first sovereignty. The Cult of Ptah lasted about 9,000 years; before this Horus of the Double Horizon and the Double Equinox symbolized by the passage through the Sphinx, existed for about 10,000 years; before this Tum, as Atum Iu, made the passage for about 20,000 years. Before this the Lunar Cult lasted for about 50,000 years, and previous to the Lunar was the Astro-Mythology, or Stellar Cult, which existed for about 300,000 years. As the Astronomical or Stellar Cult proves, the primary seven marked out one Great Year at least in the cycle of precession before they could become those Lords of Eternity at the North Celestial Pole, represented by the group of the seven non-setting stars, or the stars that never set, and records prove at least ten such cycles of time were marked out and recorded by the old Urshi. Under the title of Elohim, both the one god and the company of gods are present, though concealed, just as Ptah and his associates, the Ari, were included in the Put-cycle as Ptah the God, Iu the Son, and the Put as the group of the gods.

The Put-cycle of the Ari are the originals of the Phœnician and Hebrew Elohim; therefore it follows that the deity Ptah is the one god of the group in Genesis as well as in the original Cult.

Although the name of Ptah is not plainly given, yet the creator, as the worker in the secret earth, the potter, the moulder, etc., is plainly depicted in the Hebrew.

Also the Hebrew word " puth or peth " for the opening is identical with Put in the Egyptian " to open," and the Ptah or Putah was named from this root as " the opener," both as opener of Amenta or the secret earth for the passage of the Sun as well as for the resurrection of the manes " in coming forth to day " in Amenta.

There is a biblical name—that of Puthahiah—which shows that Iau (Iu) is the opener, or that he is identical with Ptah (1 Chron. xxiv. 16 ; Ezra x. 23 ; Neh. ix. 5, and xi. 24). The same root enters into the name Pethuel, which is equivalent to Ptah-El, or the divine opener, who was the Egyptian Ptah (Joel i. 1). In Egyptian, Ptah is God the Father in one character and Iu the Son in the other. Iu in the character of the Son is also a representative of the Put-cycle ; that is, of the Elohim or company of Creators.

Thus the Elohim are represented in the first creation of man by the maker, Ptah, and in the second by Iu, the son of Ptah ; and Iu, the son of Ptah, is Iahu-Elohim, who becomes the creator of the second Adam in the second chapter of the Hebrew Genesis.

In the first of two creations Ptah and the Ari, who are his associated gods, the Ali, or Ari, or Elohim, are the creators of Atum or Amen, the Hebrew Adam, who in the first phase was created male and female, man and woman, in one. The associated gods, or Elohim, are said to become his members, i.e. the lips, the limbs, the joints, the hands, etc. of Atum, or Amen, the son of Ptah. In another version they are the seven souls of man.

In the second creation it is Atum or Amen and his associate gods who are the creators of man, the same as Iahu-Eloh in the Genesis. The parallel is perfect ; only in the Hebrew rendering the gnosis is omitted. There are two Adams, man the mortal on earth and man the manes in Amenta.

The Elohim in the plural are the Ari or associate gods of Ptah, and Iahu-Elohim is the deity. Iu, who was a form of Ptah as god the son, afterwards became the father god in Israel under the name of Ihuh or Jehovah. Iu or Iu-em-Hetep, he who comes with peace, is the Egyptian original of the promised prince of peace, whose coming was periodic and æonian, for ever and ever, and from generation to generation.

Thus the Creation in the first chapter of Genesis is the creation of Kheper-Ptah and his Ari, and the creation of Ihuh in the second chapter is identical with that of Iu or Atum or Amen and his associate gods.

The Garden of Eden is the Aarru garden which Ptah and his Ali or Ari or Elohim created for Atum or Amen, the son, to cultivate in the earthly paradise in the eastern part of the secret earth or Amenta.

There were two Atums corresponding to the two types of Adam, one human, one divine. One was the Atum who died—the Adam in whom all men die, as Paul expresses the doctrine. The other is the second Atum called Nefer-Atum or Iu the son, who rose again to change the earthly man into the heavenly man in whom the dead were to be made alive again in Amenta.

Thus we see in the Hebrew version Atum-Iu has been divided and brought on in two characters which correspond to the two Adams, human and divine; the first Adam a man of earth, the second Adam or man who is of heaven—the life-giving spirit who became Atum-Ra—the Holy Spirit in the Egyptian Eschatology.

It is the making of the secret earth or Amenta by Ptah and his associate gods that has been converted into a creation of the heavens and the earth in the Book of Genesis. That the Hebrew Creation was cosmical is fixed for ever as an impossibility inasmuch as the heaven and earth are made twice over. In the second chapter of Genesis there is a second creation of heaven and earth, and the first creation is followed by the making of a second man. In the first—the Mythology—Atum was Solar. In the Eschatology the second Atum is Spiritual. Amen or Atum not only passed into the Hebrew legends as the earthly father in the Book of Genesis, but also as the Adam-Kadmon of the Kabalah, who is the primordial archetypal man, the heavenly man, or man from heaven.

The first man Adam, like the first Horus, was finite and imperfect; the second was infinite and perfect. These are the first and second Adam according to the doctrine of St. Paul, who tells us that "the first man is of the earth, earthy, the second man is of heaven heavenly."

The first man, Adam, became a living soul, the second man, Adam, became a life-giving Spirit: "Howbeit that is not first which is spiritual, but that which is natural."

The Circumpolar Paradise upraised by Shu in Am-Khemen was repeated with improvements and additions in the earthly Paradise of Amenta, the Stellar imagery being repeated in the Solar Cult. The Garden of Eden in the Hebrew Genesis is called the garden eastward. This was the position of the Aarru garden in Amenta, a secret earth, and the Hebrew was taken from this; *whereas the original Paradise on Earth* was situated at the Great Lakes, or Papyrus Field in the South. This imagery was depicted in the Circumpolar Paradise in the Stellar Cult and in the Solar the Paradise was again depicted in the earth of eternity, or Amenta.

There is no garden of Eden created in the first chapter of Genesis. No tree of life or knowledge was planted, nor is there any prohibition against eating the fruit of the tree. On the contrary, the primal pair, the male and female, are told that every herb and *every* tree are given to them for food. The theology of the Elohim differs from that of Iahu-Elohim. This agrees with a non-Semitic version of the Creation (Records, New Series, Vol. VI) in which there is no garden created, no mention of man being placed in the garden to tend it, no tree of life nor tree of knowledge, and no temptation by the serpent or story of the Fall.

The Primal Paradise or Circumpolar Paradise is thus differentiated from the garden in Amenta made by Ptah in the secondary representation. Thus from the older documents we see how the Stellar and Solar Cults have been mixed up together by the Elohistic and Jehovistic narratives in the Book of Genesis.

According to the Hebrew, the deluge was provoked by the sins of men. " The Lord saw that the wickedness of man was great in the earth," and he determined to blot out and obliterate the race: "but Noah found grace in the eyes of the Lord" (Gen. vi. 5, 8).

The Chaldean and Hindu legends know nothing of *human* sin as a cause of the deluge.

The sin against the gods, however, is described as the cause of a deluge in the so-called " destruction of men " in the Egyptian. Ra says to Nun and others of the elder pre-Solar gods, " Behold the beings who are born of myself ; they utter words against me." That is they are in rebellion against the one true God. But these beings in this case were elemental, and not mortal, and the sin was not human.

When the deluge or destruction is over and past, Ra swears that he will not again destroy man. Said by Ra : " I now raise my hand that I shall no more destroy men. I shall now protect men on account of this." So the Hebrew deity promises that He " will not again curse the ground any more for the sake of men : neither will I again smite any more any living thing," as in the " deluge of destruction."

The Hebrews have written this as *human* history, whereas the original is Mythological and relates to the superseding of the Stellar and Lunar Cults by the Solar wherein Ra establishes a new heaven for the keeping of Solar time.

Further, for the true story of the Exodus, we have to go as far back as the Stellar Cult, at least. In the Ritual, Chapter 110, heaven is described as the mansions of Shu, " the mansions of his stars," which was nightly renewed as " the beautiful creation which he raised up." Here was the origin of the Exodus in the Stellar Cult. Shu was the uplifter of the sky under his name of Anhur with his rod. As a raiser of the firmament, he uplifts the starry host or multitude of beings known as the offspring of Nut.

These were previously the dwellers in the Lower Egypt of the mythos, who are to be set free from the realm of darkness and gathered together in the land of light, the starry heaven of Nut on high. Their deliverer was Shu-Anhur, the leader up to heaven, with his rod as "repeller" of the dragon coming out of the Abyss (pp. 2, 5, 6). Traditions of the Exodus are found in various parts of the world and amongst people in different states of evolution, and these traditions can be explained by the Kamite rendering only. They prove one common origin and how widespread the old religious Cults radiated from the centre; also that from the first imagery of Shu, as Shu-Anhur, must derive all the traditions of the Exodus wherever found and under whatever Cult.

The Quiche "Popul Vuh" portrays the ancestors of the race as wanderers in the wilderness upon their way to the place where the sun was to rise. They also crossed the water, which divided whilst they passed, and which they went through just as if there had been no sea. They passed on the scattered rocks rolled on the sands, that served for stepping stones. This is why the place was called "ranged stones and torn up sands," the name that was given to it on their passage through the waters that divided as they went. At last they came to a mountain where, as they had been told, they were to see the sun rise for the first time (Bancroft, Vol. III, p. 51).

This was the mount of glory in the Solar mythos and the waters which were crossed were those of the celestial Nun. The "ranged stones" in the waters correspond to the twelve stones that were set up by Joshua to mark the spot where the waters were held up for the Israelites to pass dry-footed through the river Jordan. In the Hawaiian tradition the king of the country, named Honua-i-lalo, was the oppressor of the Manchune people. Their god Kane sent Kane-Apua and Kanaloa, the elder brother, to bring away the oppressed people and take them to the land which Kane their god had given them. The legend tells how they came to the Red Sea of Kane, Kai-ula-a Kane, and were pursued by Ke-Alii Wahanui. Thereupon Kane-Apua and Kanaloa prayed to Lono, and then they passed safely through the sea, and wandered in the desolate wilderness until at last they reached the promised land of Kane called " Aina-Lauena-a-Kane." This, says Fornander, is an ancient legend, which also contains the story of water being made to gush forth from a rock (Fornander: " An Account of the Polynesian Race ").

The passage of the Red Sea and the destruction of those who follow the fugitives are also found in Hottentot fable (which they obtained by mixing with the Hero Cult people who returned to South Africa after the development in the North—i.e. Egypt) as also did the Stellar and Solar Cult afterwards.

Heitsi-Eibib was once travelling with a great number of his people when they were pursued by the enemy. On arriving at the water, which had to be crossed as the only way of escape, the leader said : " My grandfather's father, open thyself that I may pass through and close thyself afterwards." So it took place, as he said, and they crossed the water safely. Then the pursuing enemy tried to pass through the opening likewise, but when they were in the midst of the divided water, it closed upon them and they perished (Bleek : " Hottentot Fables," p. 75).

In this personification of the water as the first father, God, the grandfather, is in accordance with the Egyptian Nun or celestial water, who is represented as the primordial male divinity, the father of the fathers in which we must include Ra the Solar God. The Nun, or Nnu, identifies the water as celestial, and it is that which divides —in the Solar—to let the sun-god and his followers pass through dryshod. These in the Ritual are pursued by the Apap and the Sebu to the edge of the horizon and the waters of day overwhelm the powers of darkness, and Apap the dragon with all his evil host are overthrown, submerged, and drowned in the waters of the Lower Nun (Rit., Ch. 39).

They are described in the "Magic Papyrus" as the "immerged," who do not "pass" or go along, "but remain floating on the waters like dead bodies drifting on the inundation; with their mouths for ever shut and sealed" (Records, Vol. X, 151).

Amenta is spoken of at least once in the Ritual as the place wherein the living are destroyed. It is also the Kasu or burial-place. One of the twelve divisions was "the sandy realm of Sekari," the place of interment. The dead were buried underneath their mounds in this domain of Sakari, which was a wilderness of sand. It is the origin of the wilderness full of buried corpses in the Book of Numbers. "Your little ones I will bring in, but as for you, your carcases shall fall in the wilderness," said the Lord (Num. xiv. 31, 32). The carcases that were to rot in the wilderness are the mummies buried in the sandy realm of Osiris-Sekari, god of the coffin and the desert sand.

In the Egyptian eschatology those who made the exodus from Amenta to the world of day are those who rise from the dead "in the sandy realm of Sekari or the wilderness." They rise again as children, who are called "the younglings of Shu." And Shu was the leader and forerunner of this new generation of divine beings, called his "younglings," from "Sekari," where their redemption from that land of bondage dawned (Rit., Ch. 55).

The Egyptian exodus is from the desert of Amenta in the Solar Cult. It is in the Solar that the seed of Ra, or, later still, the children of Ra, when the Peri-em-hur, or coming forth to day, takes place, according to the Ritual. In the later phase the resurrection of souls has taken the place of the Stars in the Stellar Cult, and of the Sun in the Solar mythos. The exodus was now the coming forth of the manes from "Egypt and the desert," as localities in the mysteries of Amenta.

If we wish to show that the Jews' version was a fable, we can obtain the proofs in Egypt, and nowhere else.

The sufferings of the Chosen People in Egypt, and their miraculous exodus out of it, belong to the celestial allegory; we have seen that it originated in the Stellar Cult, but that there was a new creation and new imagery in the Solar, and that the drama was greatly expanded and enlarged. The allegory of the Solar drama was performed in the mysteries of the divine nether-world, and had been performed by symbolical representations ages before it was converted into a history of the Jews by the literalizers of the Ancient Symbolism.

The tale of the ten plagues of Egypt contains an esoteric version of the tortures inflicted on the guilty in the ten hells of the underworld.

In the Stellar Cult we have seen the imagery of man's *descent* from a celestial birthplace that was constellated as an enclosure on the mountain of the Pole. In this new creation, the Solar, we have to trace man's *ascent* from the regions of the nether-earth, which, as Egyptian, is an exodus from Lower Egypt and the "desert" of Amenta.

Amenta is described in the Ritual as consisting of two parts called "Egypt and the desert land or wilderness." The latter was the domain of Set in the Osirian mysteries, which were very late. In one part of the domain of Set, named Anrutef, is a desert of fruitless, leafless, rootless sand, where nothing grows, in which there was no water for the people (the children of Ra) to drink, or if any, it was made salt and bitter by the adversary Set, or the Apap dragon. The Struggle of Set and Horus in the desert lasted forty days, as commemorated in the forty days of the Egyptian Lent, during which time Set, as the power of drought and sterility, made war on Horus in the water and the buried germinating grain. Meanwhile "the flocks of Ra" were famishing for want of pasture and for want of water in the wilderness. These forty days have been extended into forty years, and confessedly so by the Jews. They were the forty days of suffering in the wilderness of the underworld which lay betwixt the autumn and the vernal equinox. And when it is threatened by Ihuh that only the children shall go forth with Joshua, it is said, " your children shall be wanderers in the wilderness even forty days, for every day a year " (Num. xiv. 33, 34).

The Lower Egypt of Amenta was a land of dearth and darkness to the manes. It was the domain of Set at the entrance to Amenta in the West. This was the typical wilderness founded on the sands that environed the Egyptian Aarru, or the Garden of Eden, or the promised land that was far to the East, as an oasis in the desert, and it was there for the manes if able to reach it.

The domain of Set was a place where all the terrors and plagues in nature congregated, including drought and famine, fiery flying serpents, and monsters. There were the hells of heat in which the waters were on fire, the slime-pits, the blazing bitumen, and brimstone flames of Sodom and Gomorrah. All these had to be crossed and all the powers of death and hell opposed the glorified elect, the chosen people of the Lord, who were bound for bliss in the land where their redemption dawned upon the summit of the mount, a land of bondage where the manes was in need of a deliverer. The typical tyrant and taskmaster in the *Hebrew history* has never been identified on earth, and it is only in the Egyptian that this can be done.

The devourer of the people in that land takes several forms. The Apap reptile lies in wait at the entrance to the valley of the shadow of death. There is one typical devourer. The Red Sea is his dwelling place, and " eternal devourer is his name." Another of his names is Mates, the hard, cruel, flinty-hearted, and he is described as having the skin of a man and the face of a hound. His dwelling is in the red lake of fire, where he lives upon the shades of the damned and eats the livers of princes. As he comes from the Red Sea his overthrowal is in the Red Sea, like the overwhelming of Pharaoh and his host. The same typical devourer has another figure in the Judgment Hall, where it is named Amemit. Here it has the head of a crocodile (see " Papyrus of Ani Judgment Scenes ").

When we speak of the jaws of death and hell, or destruction, the Egyptians spoke in Sign Language by showing the head and jaws of a crocodile. Those who are condemned to be devoured pass into the jaws of the devourer; thus depicting the typical tyrant, the cruel, hard-hearted monster who bars the gate of exit and will not let the suffering people go up from the land of bondage.

When the manes seeks his place of refuge in Amenta or in the Ammah (Rit., Ch. 72) he prays for deliverance from the crocodile in the land of bondage. He also says: "Let not the powers of darkness (the Sebu) have the mastery over me," and prays that he may reach the divine dwelling which has been prepared for him in the fields of peace and plenty, where there is corn of untold quantity in that land towards which his face is set (Aarru fields).

This is the chapter "by which one cometh forth to-day and passeth through Ammah or the Ammah," in seeking deliverance from the "dragon" in the land of bondage. Protection is sought in Ammah, because the god who dwells there in everlasting light is the overthrower of the dragon. The crocodile is the dragon of Egypt to the Hebrew scribes, who use it as an image of the Pharaoh. Ezekiel writes: "Thus saith the Lord God: Behold, I am against thee, Pharaoh King of Egypt, the great dragon that lieth in the midst of his rivers," the imagery was derived from the Egypt of Amenta. The great dragon, as typified devourer in the land of bondage, is here identified with the Pharaoh of Egypt, as it also has been in the Book of Exodus.

CHAPTER XV

BABYLONIAN CULT

In the first Tablet of the Chaldean account of creation it is said of the Creator: "He fixed up Constellations whose figures were like animals" ("Records of the Past," Vol. IX, p. 117). It is also said on the seventh Tablet: "At that time the gods in their assembly created (the beasts), they made perfect the mighty (Monsters)." These were figures of the Constellation.

The Chaldean account of creation also describes the construction of "dwellings for the great gods." There were celestial habitations, or, as we say, "houses" of the Sun, Moon, and seven Stars or the Khuti. In the Kamite creation by Ptah they are called the shrines of the gods. "He formed the gods, he made the towns, he designed the nomes, he placed the gods in the shrines which he had prepared for them" (Inscription of Shabaka, lines 6, 7), which was a mode of representation of the heavens in the phase of "Creation."

As we have seen, it began with the Abyss and the water, the Creatures of the Abyss, as the Southern fish and Ketos, the water serpent and other Constellations imaged by animals, and the habitations of the seven Polar gods that were built upon a "glorious foundation."

When the Abyss had not been made and Eridu had not yet been constructed, it is said that the whole of the lands were water. But when a stream was figured within the firmament, "in that day Eridu was made; E-Sagila was constructed," which the god Lugal-Du-Azaza had founded within the Abyss. Two earthly cities were built upon a heavenly model, and the earthly Eridu corresponds to the celestial or divine original. Thus the earliest cities in Babylonia were modelled on cities that were already celestial, and therefore considered to be of divine origin, and the original were first founded in the Astronomical Cult of the Egyptians. That, however, was not the genesis of the universe—the firmament was there from the time that the earth was thrown off by the sun, but it remained for man to distinguish the upper and lower and divide it into the domains of night and day. Heaven and Earth existed when these were nameless, and did not come into existence on account of being named. (I have already explained other phases of the Babylonian Cult on pages 58, 114, 115, 128, and in other parts of this book.)

CHAPTER XVI

BUDDHISM

MODERN students of Buddhism, who are also Masons, have found the most striking likeness between the rites of Buddhism and Masonry, not because Masonry is a direct survival of Indian Buddhism, but on account of their common Kamite origin. "Who knows not Adi-Buddha" knows nothing of the beginning of Buddhism in India.

The Buddhists designate God by the name of Buddha, or wisdom, and Adi-Buddha, which means "Ancient" or First Wisdom, literally Grandfather Wisdom, to indicate him as Eternity. He is before all, and is not created, but is the Creator. The names of Adi-Buddha are very many. The Valentinians, or Western Buddhists, call God Buthos, which means the Abyss, or first Mother. In the Pali, God is called Lok-utaro, which signifies the Supreme of the Universe. Yin means Mother-Creator, or the Holy Spirit, the everlasting of the Heavens (Apt of the Egyptians). In the Sadhaya Mala we read that Yoni, from which the universe was made manifest, is the Trikonagar Yantra; in the midst of that Trikona or Triangle is a point, and from that point Adi-Prajna revealed herself by her own will. Yin has also been translated as Mother-Earth (Ta-Urt), but the true Chinese word for Mother-Earth is Te-Mo, which also means the word of God.

In the Rig Veda we have the Mata Prithivi, which means Mother Nature.

The Buddhist God is Tri-une. God made the Spirit first when the universe consisted of two—God and the Holy Spirit. After this the Spirits were formed when the universe consisted of three Gods (in the Egyptian, Set, Horus, and Shu).

Kal or Kali, the invisible Queen of Heaven of the Buddhists, the voice or logos of God, in its primary phase, was represented by Apt of Egypt.

Phra and Buddha are two expressions, which, though not having the same meaning, are now used indiscriminately for designating the divine Messenger. Buddha, or the Messiah, descends to the earth from the heaven, which is called Az-Ara (e.g. Horus).

The word belongs also to the Zend, in which it signifies " A Messenger from God to Man."

It is taught that he is thus enabled to see and fathom the misery and wants of beings. The laws that he preaches are the " parables," like Horus in his first advent. Like Horus and Jesus, he commissions his chosen disciples to carry on the same benevolent undertaking, and then he arrives at the state of Nibau.

The word Phra is a word to express the idea of God the Supreme Being, according to Buddhistic notions. He labours during his mortal career for the benefit of of all living beings and brings them finally to the " never troubled," or Paradise, or Nirvana.

Their belief in Palingenesis is because they believe that the elemental divinized gods were once men, which is entirely an erroneous doctrine. They were only the Simulacrum.

The first Buddha was called Hermias, and can be traced back to Set of the Egyptians; he originated in the Stellar Cult. Later, however, the Solar Cult was carried to India, and the Buddha is there the representative of Ptah of the Egyptians, by name and number. The Consort of Ptah is Ma (the earlier Maka or Menka, the measurer with the Vase), and the Consort or Mother of Buddha is Maya. Ptah is the opener, and Buddha was expressly worshipped as the opener: the open flower, the lotus of his eyes, being one of his types. In Buddhism this opening has passed into later and less material phases of phenomena. Nevertheless, the opening is at the root of all the awakening, expanding, unfolding of the mind.

In the peculiar system of Buddhism existing in Thibet it is said: "He who does not know the first Buddha knows not the circle of time." This identifies the Buddha with the circle and the Stellar Cult originally. Buddha also wears the nine-headed Naga serpent, and one of his types is the tree with nine branches rising out of water, as depicted by a gilt bronze Buddha from a Burmese Temple, which represents Buddha beneath a tree, which has three branches, and these three divisions are subdivided so that the tree has nine branches in all. The Buddha is seated on a bell, the pattern upon which is the yoni. Thus the bell is feminine and identical with the well or abyss of waters in which the tree of the three quarters and the nine branches stands.

The Hindu Golden City of the Gods, also called the eight-leaved Lotus, has eight circles and nine gates in agreement with the eightfold Amamen and Sesennu of the Egyptian, which was followed by the Put-cycle of the nine.

It is said the initiates know that living Being which resides in the Lotus with nine gates, with three spokes, and triple supports. Thus the Lotus of nine gates rests on a threefold rootage in the Waters, which is equivalent to the three water-signs. In another Hindu representation of paradise there is a silver bell with nine precious stones surrounding the square of the four quarters.

The four quarters represented by the Put-cycle, the tree and well, or tree and bell, are identical with the Ank Cross ♀ in a reversed position—thus ☿, with the feminine Ru below, the masculine Tau above. The legend relates that Gautama Buddha was reborn under the tree in the ninth incarnation of Vishnu, and that it was by means of the tree that he attained Nirvana, or passed into the divine circle of the gods, called the Put pleroma in the Egyptian originals. Here also the number identifies the name of Buddha with the Egyptian Put for number nine, and the circle of the nine, and with Putah, the founder of the circle of the nine gods.

Buddha in China is Yo, Fo, Fot, or Boud, whose great work was the dividing of the land into nine parts after the deluge, which is identical with the work of Ptah, who founded the Put-cycle of nine gods upon the waters which were thus limited to one quarter of the four. The Put pleroma of nine gods was likewise extant in China. In the third of the divine dynasties there was a company of nine Brothers, who were the ruling powers, and during their reign, as in the time of Yu, the earth, the mountains, and the waters were separated into nine divisions. This proves that some of the earlier Solar Cult had found its way into the old Stellar Cult empire of China, as the Put-circle established by Ptah must be looked upon as a "primary zodiac" of nine signs, imaged by the nine stones, nine brothers, nine branches, nine bridges, or other forms of the nine, representing nine numbers, which, together with the inundation, made up the earliest Solar year, the four quarters being typified by the Abyss (or three water signs), that the Sun travelled in the passage mythically created by Ptah.

In the legendary life of Gautama, Buddha is described as having to pass over the celestial water to reach Nirvana, which is the land of the bodhi-tree of life and knowledge. He was unable to cross from one bank to the other, but the spirit of the bodhi-tree stretched out its arms and helped him over in safety.

By the aid of this tree he attained the summit of wisdom and immortal life.

It is the same tree of the Pole and of Paradise— the tree of the guarani garden, the Hebrew Eden; the Hindu Jambudvipa is likewise the tree of Nirvana. Nirvana was not the conception of Buddha; it is not identifiable as anyone's idea or doctrine, but belongs to the Egyptian mythical origins, and is an ultimate deposit from the Egyptian prehistoric development of primitive thought. The Great Mother in her primordial phase was the Abyss in space, or Mother Earth, and became the divinized goddess of the seven stars, in time representing all the seven portrayed in many phases afterwards. The incarnations of Buddha were dated astronomically. His coming was indicated by the Messianic Star of Announcement, or prophetic Star of an incarnation, and the birthplace is known by astronomical signs. It belongs to the cycles of time, the ends of which were foreknown and prophesied from the beginning.

The last of the Buddhas, who is designated "All the Buddhas," is called, like the gnostic Christ, "All things," or Totum; he was the final flower of the whole pleroma perfected, and is described as having advanced hitherward by "making seven steps" towards each of the four cardinal points of the zodiac. Therefore he had travelled the circle measured by the twenty-eight lunar asterisms. This, as we have seen, was the course of the seven Rishis and the seven Manus (who are also known as the seven Buddhas) in fulfilling the cycle and following the path of precession. They are represented as voyaging round in the Ark that makes the circle and the cycle of the Great Year, and Buddha is the manifestor of the pleroma of seven primary forces, faculties, spirits, or gods, which is shown by his symbol of the eight-rayed star, the sign of Assur in Assyria and of the Christ in Rome, and the original Horus in Egypt.

Agni also had been the manifestor of the seven ever since the entrance of the vernal equinox into the sign of the Ram. This is shown by the god being portrayed upon the Ram with the sign of the Ram on a banner in front of him, which identifies him with Aries in the zodiac. Agni also embodies the seven powers, typified by his figure with seven arms. The Hindu Agni was at times portrayed with two faces, three legs, seven arms, as a form of the one total God of a duplicative nature, twin in sex, triadic in form, and manifestor of the seven primary powers corresponding to the Egyptian Har-Khuti or Iu=to the $3 + 7 = 10$ the one great god of Egypt. "In an address to the god it is said, Agni! seven

HUNIMAN (INDIAN) GREAT GOD OF THE HAMMER OR AXE. SHIVA.

PLATE LXVI.

Drawn by K. Watkins.

KRISHNA INDIAN TYPE OF HORUS STRANGLING SERPENTS, OR "BRUISING THE SERPENT'S HEAD," AND INCARNATE OF VISHNU.

PLATE LXVII.

STORY OF THE ANNUNCIATION.

PLATE LXVIII.

are thy fuels ; seven thy tongues ; seven thy holy sages ; seven thy beloved abodes ; seven ways do seven sacrifices worship thee: thy sources are seven " (" Dabistan," Vol. I, p. 218, Shea and Taylor).

These are the seven which began as Elementary Powers or Spirits in external nature and were afterwards uranographically depicted, first as stars of Ursa Minor, and other Planetary and Zodiacal types, and finally Eschatologically. The six-leaved Lotus springs from the navel of Vishnu as the flower of breath and of reproduction out of the water.

Horus the child is called " the soul rising out of the lotus flower."

In all the Manvantara classes of Rishis they appear seven by seven and pass and are repeated in the same order. If we reckon by the twenty-six signs, the time would be 1,000 years in each and this would correspond with the Egyptian—" The celestial house of the 1,000 years," " Pa-pe-Kha-Renpat."

Huniman is the Egyptian Atum-Iu, God of the Axe and God of the Hammer. He is here (Plate LXVI) depicted with the great Hammer in his right hand and the " food of life " in his left hand, ascending from the underworld.

In the Indian Mythology it is said " that he built the bridge for Rama, the Preserver," by which he crossed to Lanka (Ceylon) and was able to defeat Ravena the Demon King.

After the great battle had raged long and fiercely most of Rama's supporters were either wounded or slain. Then Huniman sped to the sacred Himalaya Mountains and there he plucked the fruit of the Tree of Life and gave it to the dead and dying, who were preserved and restored to life and health and so enabled to renew the battle through another night and day.

Huniman is the uniter or bridger of the two Horizons, in his twofold character, and the uniter of the soul of death with the soul of life in the Eschatology. The great battle that raged long and fiercely was the battle of Set and his Sami and Horus in the passage of the desert of Amenta, where Horus was wounded. His crossing to Lanka (Ceylon) proves that Adam's Peak was not only considered one of the terrestrial stations of the Pole in their former Cult, but had also been brought on and associated with their Solar-Baku ; also that the Himalaya Mountain was the earthly representation of these people with that of the Egyptian Mount Hetep in Amenta, where the Arru garden with the tree of Life was situated. The whole representation is taken from the Egyptian Amenta, and is mythical.

Another Egyptian imagery is found in the goddess " Tari-Pennu," a form of the Earth-Mother who was worshipped by the Kolarians of Bengal and made fecund periodically by oblations of blood at her festival of reproduction, when the human doctrines were repeated and re-applied to external nature and she was fertilized with blood. Sometimes the offering was the flesh and blood of a virgin. A young girl, called the Meriah, was stripped naked and bound with cords to a maypole crowned with flowers, and ultimately put to death with horrible tortures, being torn to pieces and partially eaten (Reclus: " Primitive Folk," pp. 311–15), a rite which was brought on from the totemic mysteries. In the Khond sacrifices of the Meriah we have another imagery of the Great Mother.

The girl was fastened to the stake by her hair and forced to become a figure of the Crucified, for her arms were extended crosswise by four priests, who pulled her legs apart to complete the figure. This was the earliest type of the Crucified, as she was the cross, the crucified and the Charis in one.

The Khonds of Orissa have a divinized form of the primal pair in the ancient goddess Tari-Pennu, and her son Buri-Pennu, who answer to the Pole Star god, inasmuch as he was called " The Light." These are identical with the Egyptian Set and his Mother Apt, because he is credited with creating a Primal Paradise, and she was charged with having maliciously caused its destruction—or a fall from heaven—which occurred when the Southern Pole Star dipped below the horizon and disappeared as these original people travelled up from the Equatorial regions to the North. In Egypt, Horus became primary god, and the paradise at the North Celestial Pole was founded. As the Ritual states, the two gods Set and Horus were one, and when the Hero Cult people arrived in Egypt the attributes of the two were merged into one. One name of Horus then was "Khuti," "The Light"; it is also one of the names of the Great Pyramid.

I give in Plate LXVII a drawing of "Krishna." It is the Indian type of Horus "strangling serpents," or bruising the serpent's head. As the eighth incarnation of Vishnu, he represents Horus of Am-Khemen, i.e. the Paradise of the eight great gods—the seven with Horus, as the head and the eighth, which was prior to the Put-cycle of Ptah. Horus as the eighth and highest of the seven elemental powers in the Stellar Cult passed into the Solar when the typical virgin and child were reproduced and constellated as repeaters of periodic time in the zodiac. Thus we see him depicted in various characters in India as in Egypt.

The Buddhists and Brahmins in many of their religious ceremonies make use of words that are not Sanskrit, but are said to belong to a very ancient form of speech now dead. These words can be traced back to their Egyptian origin.

In the Hindu deluge of Manu we find some of the old Stellar Cult still surviving, for the Manu, whose vessel was made fast to a stupendous horn, i.e. the Pole, was Vaivasvata, the seventh Manu, and the seventh. Manu corresponds to the great deluge of all as the latest of seven cataclysms in the world's Great Years (i.e. of 25,827 years according to the Stellar Cult reckoning of one precessional epoch of the seven Pole Stars of Ursa Minor, called by the Stellar Cult people "one Great Year").

As there were seven stations of the Pole in measuring

the circuit of precession, each type or symbol of the Pole may be represented seven times, or is finally a figure of the number seven.

Dhruva was said to be the god who maintained himself upon one foot motionless as a statue—in other words, was a God of the Pole Star, until the earth inclined with its weight, or the station of the Pole leaned over and sank down with the declination of the Star that was Polaris at the time. Thus the sustainer of the Pole, as a person, was able to stand on one foot for the period of 3,690 years on end ("Bagavata-Purane," Ch. VIII).

These Hindu people talk of "seven mountain peaks" and "seven footprints." A footprint on the peak is a symbol "of a station" in precession. The seven footprints of Buddha also denote the seven Steps in precession which are co-types equivalent to the seven stations of the Pole.

Thus the footprint of Buddha upon Adam's Peak in Ceylon shows that this was one of the seven Annular Mountains in the sevenfold system of Mount Meru. Also when the Buddhist footprint is represented by the sacred horse shoe, it has seven gems, or nails, which still preserve a figure of the seven prints in one image.

In his visions Enoch sees the seven splendid mountains which were all different from each other. They are described as six, with the seventh mountain in the midst of them.

Seven footprints were assigned to Abraham. These are depicted on the south side of the Sakhra rock at Jerusalem, and were shown to Nasir-i-Khunan in the year A.D. 1047 ("Pal. Pilgrin. Text Socty.," p. 47, 1888) (which goes to prove that all the "old men" in the first part of the Hebrew writings in the Book of Genesis were astronomical figures). No one would ever believe that any man lived for 900 years. There is no record of any such except in the Hebrew myths. But if we "translate" them as "the typical old ones in the Ritual," "the fathers in the first and highest circle of the gods," then the seven patriarchs can be identified with the seven

OF RELIGION

rishis in the Lunar Mythos of the Hindu astronomy, who were in both cases the seven primordial powers of the Egyptians.

When the Stellar Cult was founded, the seven Pole Stars of Ursa Minor had been identified and established in the circle of precession; six of these were ever moving with the sphere, but there was always one remaining fixed at the centre. These were the origins of the seven Manus or Buddhas, and it is evident how the condition of the motionless, or sleeping Buddha, was attainable by all the six, as each in turn moved round the stationary one; in the seventh stage of precession the true Buddha, the Prince, the Rishi or Manu, was reborn, and his birth was indicated by the stationary star that showed the new position of the changing Pole.

In the Hindu astronomy, where the group of manes travel round the zodiac, the seventh is a divine man, or a Buddha. The seventh Buddha is always the man who is held to be divine. The seven Buddhas are often portrayed in the temples and monasteries of Thibet, where they are better known as the seven Sang-gye, meaning increase of purity, who are named :

1. He who saw through and through.
2. He who had a crest of fire.
3. The preserver of all.
4. The dissolver of the round life.
5. Golden might.
6. The guardian of light.
7. The Mighty Shakya.

The seventh is that pre-eminent personage known as Sakya-Muni or Gautama, whose life and history were evolved from the pre-extant mythos, the true Buddha, who could become no more historical than the Christ of the gnosis.

If Buddhism could but explicate its own origins, it would become apparent that it is both natural and scientific, i.e. the old Stellar Cult of Egypt. But the blind attempt to make the Buddha historical in one personality will place it ultimately at the bottom of a dark hole.

The seventh Buddha that comes once in a phœnix cycle of 500 years is the divine man who can only be repeated as an astronomical figure—a measurer for the eternal in the cycle of time. But the manifestation of the seventh, the man of the group, has been made exoteric as an incarnation of the seventh Buddha in the human form on earth.

The divine man as the seventh of a series is still extant in many folklore tales, where the seventh son of a seventh son is always the great leader.

The Totemic soul was twin.

The human soul was singly born as the soul of the man or woman. It was not as the Hebrew Adam that man was made, but as the Egyptian Amen or Atum or, even earlier, Tum. Tum in Egyptian means created man. Adam is a later rendering of the name. And this "created man" was made as Atum, son of Ptah, with the aid of the Ari or Co-Creators. It was they who created the senses of man, the breathing of the nostrils, the sight of the eyes, the hearing of the ears, the thought of the heart, and utterance by the tongue—according to the religious sense.

Of all the seven elementary powers which were divinized and given stars in Ursa Minor only the seventh was "a man," and the cycle of precession must have been marked down and recorded for at least over 50,000 years before they could form this uranographic picture.

Thus we see that the seven Manu of the Hindu are identical with the seven Elohim of the Hebrews and the Babylonians, and the Egyptian originals.

I reproduce in Fig. 50 the Hindu Goddess Maya, which is a very late type as here portrayed, because it is humanized; but she represents the old Ancient Egyptian Great Mother, who is portrayed as the pregnant Water Cow in front and the Crocodile behind, thus representing the two primal elements of water and breath, or the breathing life which she produced from the water.

OF RELIGION

Here she is seen hovering over the waters of Source and pressing her two breasts with both hands, the feminine fount that streams with liquid life, the flowing and the fixed, as the un-girt and the up-bound are depicted. The face and upper part of her body lighten with radiance of the fire that vivifies the Spiritual life. Within the *cincture* of her scarf she is seen to be the bearing Mother;

Drawn by K. Watkins.

HINDU GODDESS MAYA.
Portrayal in human form of the Great
Mother Apt of Egypt.

FIG. 50.

it is also seen that her figure and aureole of glory form the Cross symbol corresponding to the Ru and the three-quarter Cross of the Ankh-sign. Her scarf also represents the Tie.

In the second phase the genetrix, as a personification of space below and above, of Darkness and Light, of Water and Air, of Blood and Breath, divides in twain.

and she is thus portrayed in *two* characters precisely as in the Egyptian.

The Hindu Aditi is the Great Mother of the Gods who becomes twain. As the Mother who yielded milk for them, she is identical with the Cow of Heaven in Egypt.

Aditi was the primeval form of Dyaus, the sky divinity who appears as such in the Rig-Veda, however rarely. She alternates with Diti as mother of the embryo *that was divided into seven parts*. The seven who were called the Seven Adityas (Muir: "Sanskrit Text," Vol. IV, p. 145; Vol. V, pp. 39 n., 147 n.). She is the Mother who brought forth the seven primal elemental powers which became divinized as in Egypt.

She became Diti in her second character, and is identical in both with the one original genetrix of Egypt, the Great Mother who at first was the All One in space, and then became divided, or dual in character, into the two sisters above and below, or North and South, and who was also the goddess of the four quarters.

In the Avesta it says: "The wise have manifested this universe as a Duality." The word used to render duality is Dum, identifiable with the Sanskrit Dvam (dvamdam, a pair), a word that is not found elsewhere in the Avesta, but was taken from the Egyptian Tem or Tem-t, the hieroglyphic for the double heaven ⩗, and also the sign of the Twin-total. (The Chinese goddess Thima is the dual equivalent.)

The One God of the Avesta, Ahura-Mazda, is made up of the seven spirits, or Amshaspands, who preceded his supremacy, the same as the Egyptian Atum-Ra. One title of the Sun-God Amen Ra is "Teb-Temt," and temt means totalled, from tem, the total. His total as Teb-temt consists of seventy-five characters. These seventy-five manifestations of Atum or Amen Ra are repeated in number in the Ormazad-yasht of the Avesta, where the divinity gives to Zarathushtra his seventy-five names. The Parsees say the number should be seventy-two, correlating them with the seventy-two

Decans, but the seventy-five correlate with the original Egyptian unknown to them ("Litany of Ra of Bluck," Vol. III, p. 23).

The same imagery was carried across to America. In the Chimalpopoca MS. it states that the Creator produced his work in successive epochs, man being made from the dust of the earth on the *seventh day*.

Here again man is created, or comes into existence, on the last of the seven periods, which is one day in the Book of Genesis, and 3,690 in the Astronomical or Stellar Cult, or 25,827 years as the one great Day. In all versions of the seven creations, the creation of man was last; and this is repeated in the seven stations of the celestial heptanomis, because the first seven "ending of times" were totemic, or of zootype forms, and therefore prehuman man had not been imaged until the compounding of the seven into one, which in the Egyptian was the eighth. How many cycles of 25,827 years had elapsed before the one when man was "created" is impossible to calculate. It may have been observed through seven cycles first, and as we know that the Stellar Cult was in existence 600,000 years ago, it is possible that the date would be about 800,000 years ago, when the old Stellar Cult people commenced to reckon time by the observing and recording the precession of the Pole Stars. Man must have been in existence 2,000,000 years before that to attain the evolution that we find. Two cycles of 25,827 years at least must have been observed and recorded before the old Urshi could formulate and blend all the powers of the divinized totemic souls into one of "Man."

I give here (Fig. 51) some drawings of the so-called "Makara" from the Buddhist Rails at Buddha Gaya and Mathura (after Cunningham: "Archæological Survey of India," Vol. III, 1873), which prove how the representative constellations of the Solar Cult of Egypt was brought on into India after the Stellar and Lunar. The fauna in some cases have been changed, but that occurred in almost every country to which the various exodes travelled, as when they did not find the original image they adopted another which they thought would be the nearest approach to the symbol of the attribute, but they still retained all the old symbolism as far as possible. Thus in the original Kamite zodiac the Fish-Mother gives

MAKARAS.

FIG. 51.

Drawn by K. Watkins.

re-birth to her child as the fish in the constellation of the fishes, to image the fish-man or fish-god, as being re-born of the fish-mother in the abode of the abyss of the fish, and that is the reason why all the portrayals of the so-called "Makari" here depicted have fishes' tails; but the different heads show which representation was intended. We have here:

C. The sign of Taurus=Osiris as the Bull of Eternity.

D. The Ram-headed=Amen with the Constellation of Aries.

E. The Sign of Leo, here represented by a tiger's head=The Lion-faced Atum.

F. An Elephant's head, which was a very old image for Horus in Egypt. The Egyptian name for Elephant is "Abu." "Abu" is also the name of a Numidian Goat,

L

THE MAKARA OF VARUNA.

The Elephant type was a very early type of Horus in Egypt. Cunningham, "Archæological Survey of India," Vol. III, 1873, gives many plates of the "Makara" of Varuna, amongst them the Head=Hathor as the great Mother.

FIG. 52.

and is intended to represent Num, who presided over the Abyss with the Sign of Capricornis.

G. Head of Horse=Shu.

H. Horus as Sebek-Horus } = Horus of the two Croco-
I. Crocodile of the South }   diles.

K. Anubis or Ap-Uat. The conductor of the ways represented here by a Dog's Head in place of the original Egyptian Jackal.

L. The Hippopotamus=Set. The so-called Makara as the vehicle of Varuna (after Sir George Birdwood).

CHAPTER XVII

THE DRUIDS

MUCH confliction of opinion has hitherto arisen in the minds of those historians who have written on the subject of the Druids, mainly on account of their having " mixed up " one Cult with another in the evolution of the Solar from the Lunar and Stellar Cults, imputing all under one term " Druids," whereas it was only the " Priests " of the Solar Cult who should have that terminology applied to them. Cæsar and other Roman writers, as well as the Greeks, knew nothing of the esoteric wisdom of Ancient Egypt, and therefore of the Druids. They perverted all that had been told them by the Her-Seshta.

The Druids were not Pagans, and did not worship the Sun, as most writers have stated, any more than the Stellar Cult people worshipped the Stars.

As we have seen, the Solar Orb was a Symbol of the Great God, and also a means by which time was recorded, as likewise were the Stars of the Little Bear in the Stellar Cult, with Horus supreme symbolically. Obviously, therefore, it was not the Symbol that was worshipped but the Great God. The Druids were no more Pagan than are present-day Christians who have a Lamb and Fish as symbols, and it would be just as truthful to say that the Christians were " Sheep-worshippers," or " Fish-worshippers " ; these are only types or images of the attributes of the Great God.

The Druids were an exodus of Solar Cult people who left Egypt at the time the Egyptians worshipped Iu, or Hu, the son of Atum, or Amen or Huhi, corresponding to the gnostic Iou and Iao—Iu-Iahu. We can see the change of Cults here as also with the Hebrews. The change from the worship of El Shaddi to the worship of Ihuh (Egypt, Iu) from the Elohistic to the Jehovistic God corresponds to the change from the Stellar to the Solar Cult.

In the primary Solar Cult it is Atum-Iu in whom the Father becomes the Son on the Eastern Horizon and the Son transforms into the Father on the Western Horizon. The Mystery was deepened in the later eschatology. In the Osirian drama they superadded a more spiritual form of Fatherhood in Ra, the Holy Spirit, and when Horus in his second advent comes to establish the kingdom of his Father, who is Ra in the Solar Mythos and the Holy Spirit in the Eschatology, he has in the Egyptian two witnesses who testify that he is verily the Son of God the Father in Heaven and the true Light of the World. These are the two Osirian Johns—Anup and Aan, who were the originals in the Canonical Gospels.

That many names were given and associated with "the Original" only implies different Attributes to the One Great God, and not a multiplicity of Gods, as many suppose. As an example, we take Horus of the Double Horizon—in the Solar Cult, some of the names by which He was known were:

Hu, or Iu or Iau, The Light of the World.
Haru-Khuti was another name for the same.
Atum-Ra, The Holy Spirit.
Huhi was another name for the same.
Neb-Huhi, The Everlasting Lord, or Supreme One, Self-existing and Eternal God.
Har-Tema, The Revealer of Justice.
Har-Makheru, The Word made Truth.
Kha-su-meri-f, The Spirit of my beloved Son.

And one hundred others, too long a list to enter here, but all given in the "Ritual of Ancient Egypt."

The Signs and Symbols used by the Druids were the same as used by the Hebrews, Persians, Hindoos, and all other Solar Cult people, and are copies from the Ancient Egyptian "Solar Cult" people. For example, this

Symbol , with or without the circle, is a Sign of Horus of the Double Horizon; the Triangle with the Swastika in the centre, is a Symbol of Horus as God of the four quarters, or as the God of Heaven, which was built on the four quarters, i.e. as a Square. This

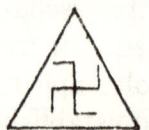 was one of the Druids' Sacred Symbols.

The Druids and Israelites wore similar Priestly dresses with breast-plates, because these were copied from the Egyptian Priests; and for the same reason the twelve stones had engraved on them the twelve signs of the Zodiac. Later the Israelites substituted the names of twelve Tribes, or Totems. The different colours of their vestments can be traced to two causes, or for two reasons, viz., firstly:

White denoted pure Spirit and Spiritual World, at all times.

Blue at all times depicted heaven and Celestial objects.

Red depicted the Sun, the Earth and Egyptian Sky.

Yellow depicted the Moon.

The Thibetans and many other Solar Cult people still pray in accordance with a scheme of colour.

Secondly, different colours denote different Spirits, or forces in nature that were representatives of the seven elemental powers and seven localities of Spirits.

Thus the Spirits prayed to are identified by their Colours, and at others by their Totemic Zootype.

1. The Spirit of Darkness was Black=Black-man=Set or Osiris, the Black God.

2. The Spirit of Light was White=White-man= Horus the White God.

3. The Spirit of Water or Vegetation was Green= Green-man=the God Num.

4. The Spirit of Air was Blue=Blue-man or the God Amen.

5. The Spirit of Fire was Red = the Red-man or God Shu.

6 and 7. The Spirit of the Highest God on the Summit is Golden = Ra = the Grey Man = the Golden Man, the divine Holy Spirit in the Eschatology.

According to Cæsar, the Druids taught the Gauls that they were all descended from *Dis Pater* the Demiarge—that is, from the god of Hades, or Amenta, who is Tanan as consort of the goddess, and whose name was taken by Ptah-Tanan, the better known *Dis Pater*, who was earlier than Osiris in the Egyptian Cult and from whom the Solar race *ascended*, whether from Puanta or from the Tuat. Thus interpreted, the Tuatha, or tribes who brought the ancient wisdom out of Lower Egypt or the Tuat may be called genuine Egyptians, as the traditions of the Keltæ and the Kymry yet strenuously maintain.

The birthplace of the Stellar race was in the Celestial North; the Solar race were they who came from the East—that is, from the exit of Amenta (and the Druids were these). As going down to Amenta as manes, they were the Westerners; in coming forth they are the Easterners. The course of the sun god by day is reckoned to run from Ta-Ur to Am-Ua, that is, from the east to the west; and the manes from Am-Ua to Ta-Ur.

Cæsar tells us that Manannian, son of Lir, was patron of roads and journeys and was worshipped by the Druids above all other gods. This is the Egyptian Ap-Uat, a form of Anup—the guide through the earth of eternity, or Amenta. Whatever the Egyptians portrayed celestially and in the earth of Eternity in their religious doctrines was mapped out geographically; thus Manannian, who was Ap-Uat, was guide to the manes in the road of the underworld, which Cæsar could not comprehend.

The remains of three stone circles of the Druids, or a depiction of heaven in three divisions, are found in many parts of these Islands and other countries where the Druids went, and must not be confounded with the two circles of the old Stellar Cult people.

The Druids (High Priests from Egypt) carried the Solar doctrines with them to whatever country they went, and when mixing with the old Stellar Cult people, who had left Egypt as an exodus years before, if they could not convert them, merged much of the ancient doctrines of the Stellar Cult with their own, being well acquainted with each.

The tonsure was one of the visible signs and symbols adopted to distinguish the Solar Cult Priests, who called themselves the Priests of Ra. The hieroglyphic sign for Ra is ☉ and the tonsure was the symbolic mode for depicting it.

That the tonsure was referred to as " the diabolical mark " can readily be accounted for, because the Cult had changed. During the Stellar Cult, which preceded the Solar, the custom was to shave the head of the Priests entirely ; but at the change to the Solar Cult the tonsure was adopted as one of the distinguishing Signs of the Priests of the new Cult (not the only change), and this was naturally abhorrent to the Stellar Cult people, and probably would continue to be so during the whole time of the overlapping. It must not be forgotten that before the Druids came to these Islands and Europe the Stellar Cult Priests had preceded them by many thousands of years. The latter have not only left their Osteo-remains, but remains of these Temples and implements of Arts, Signs and Symbols, and writings in Glyphs, which are still extant and are easily distinguished from those of the Solar Cult people.

The reason why the initiate in their Mysteries is marched around the central Altar nine times instead of the former seven was because the original attributes of God had been increased.

As a company of associated gods, they originated in the primordial powers, which were seven in number, under various types. That was in the Stellar Cult, and in the circumambulation of the Stellar Cult the initiate was marched round the central altar *seven* times to represent these powers—*and only seven times.*

But when these powers were grouped in the Put-cycle, with Ptah and Atum-Horus added, as father and son, the associated gods are nine in number, sometimes called the ennead of Memphis, or of Annu. Before this, in the Stellar Cult, the Priests marched around the Temple seven times, carrying the Ark; now the Put-cycle was completed they marched around nine times, and as the Druids were Solar Cult, it becomes obvious why they made nine circles in their perambulation instead of the original seven.

The whole ceremony of initiation of the Druids was performed after the manner of the Solar Cult initiation of the Egyptians, in which is portrayed dramatically and in Sign Language the passages of the manes through Amenta from West to East. The manes entered Amenta in the West in the boat or ark of Ra, and if found justified before his Judges, passed through to Mount Hetep in the East, when he continued with the course of the Sun until the setting in the West; he then entered the sacred boat or Ark of Nnu, or the Ark of the Celestial waters and was conveyed to the Khui Land or the Land of the Spirits—Paradise in the North—the Eternal City at the Pole of Heaven, or the Grand House above situated in the waters of space. The manes in Amenta began his course when he left off on earth, when his eyes and mouth were closed in death; it is now in Amenta that these are open once more for him by Ptah and Tum, and Taht supplies him with great magical words of power that open every gate or door.

Amongst the Druids the Cave in the earth was a sign or symbol for the Womb of the Bringer-forth; like the hole in a stone, it was the uterine symbol of the Genetrix. The earth itself as a producer of food and drink was looked upon as the Mother of Life. The Mother in Mythology is the abode. The sign of the female signifies the place of birth; the birthplace was the Cave. The Cave, the Cavern, or Cleft in the rock was an actual place of birth for primitive man and beast and, therefore, a figure of the uterus of the Mother Earth. A symbolism of Motherhood and birth was the earliest type identified throughout external nature. The Yao of Central Africa affirm that Man, together with the animals, sprang from a hole in the rock. This birthplace, with the Arunta of Australia, is represented by the stone with a hole in it, from which the children emanate as from the womb of Creation (N.T., p. 550).

These are universal *symbols* of the female as the dwelling and the door of life under whatsoever type. These symbols were her image " in all the Earth." The likeness was also continued as a *sign and symbol of re-birth*, and, lastly, as the Vesica in Freemasonry in the oval form, it was not only a prototype of the tomb or temple, but also represented the house of the living. Thus the Cave and the Dolmen were used symbolically and dramatically as a place of re-birth, from the material to the spiritual, to instruct the novitiate as to his future life.

In the " Ritual of Egypt," Chapter 182, it states : " I give Ra to enter the mysterious Cave in order that he may revive the heart of him whose heart is motionless," which explains the mystery.

That the initiation took place in a cave " because of the legend which existed that Enoch had deposited certain invaluable secrets in a consecrated cavern deep in the bowels of the Earth, etc." is a false and futile explanation founded on the above without the gnosis.

Other ceremonies typified the confinement of Noah in the Ark and the Druidesses passing over the arm of the sea in the Ark of the Deluge in the dead of night to certain isles, etc. These ceremonies were not a representation of the exoteric Biblical portrayal of Noah and the Flood, nor was there any connection except as an esoteric representation of the wisdom of the Egyptians as written in their Ritual. The Druids were teachers of the wisdom of Egypt in Gaul and the British Isles ages before the Bible was heard of in Europe. The Solar Cult Priests possessed the Ark in two forms ; first, as the boat of Ra ; secondly, as the Ark or boat of Nnu (or Noah), the Ark of the Celestial waters. The earlier Stellar Cult Priests possessed the Ark of Nnu only, which was an Ark with the Ali or Ari, with the seven on board, who were rulers in the heptanomis. Nnu was the master, or Lord of the Celestial waters, and these Arks with Ari are equivalent to Horus with the seven great spirits. Under the name of Num, in the Solar Cult he was represented as the Lord of the inundation. There was never any *one Great Deluge* as in the Biblical rendering. There were seven deluges—one at the change of each Pole Star, when it fell down in the Celestial waters and another took its place, once in about every 3,600 years, and one Great Deluge at the end of 25,827 years, when the seventh Pole Star fell and was drowned in the waters of space—all to recommence again. Also at least ten Great Deluges have taken place at each glacial epoch, when the snow and ice have melted. This is the explanation of the part of the Ritual where the compilers of present doctrines have gone wrong from the want of the gnosis, and the reason why the story of the Deluge is universal wherever the Stellar Cult people travelled. There was also a great inundation once a year—when the Nile came down in flood. There is a portrayal on the monuments where Num is in his boat or Ark waiting for this flood.

Much more could be written to prove how the Ancient Wisdom of Egypt was carried out from the Mother Land to all parts of the world, and that the original Cults are still extant in many countries. Names and fauna have been altered by time and circumstances, and the descendants of the original exodes have in some places mixed up the different Cults together, but in all cases the knowledge of the true original Egyptian renders the unravelling of the Mysteries quite easy, and this is the only way to obtain the truth of the various religious doctrines now scattered over the face of the earth and all their origins and interpretations.

One of the Ideographic Symbols the Druids used was \|/ (the three feathers, or rods, or rays of light), which signified amongst them the Eyes of Light, or radiating light of intelligence shed upon the Druidical circle. It is also the name of their God, the Egyptian Iu or Iau, the son of Ptah, or the Egyptian Jesus—"The Light of the World." Another Symbol used by the Druids was ▽ the triangle of Horus.

They divided the Heavens into three parts, represented by three circles, or three triangles, one for the North, one for the South, and one for the Centre, the latter bisecting the other two. Each of these three were divided into twelve, making thirty-six divisions in all, just as did the Egyptians; the Druids must have brought this imagery with them from Egypt, because they could not see the Southern heaven here to so divide it, and that they did so we still have distinct evidence in the three stone circles in this form found in many places, not only in England and Ireland, but still further north, in Scotland. A very good example was found at Rough Tor in Cornwall (see illustration in "Signs and Symbols of Primordial Man"). The thirty-six divisions represented originally the thirty-six "Nomes" of Egypt, and, as depicted in the Heavens, the thirty-six gates of "the Great House of Him Who is on the Hill," based upon the thirty-six gates, duodecous of the Zodiac. "Him who is on the Hill" is Horus on the Mount of Glory, depicted as Iu or Atum-Iu rising on the Solar Mount of Glory in the Eastern Horizon.

Canute, during his reign 1015-36, issued an edict against the Druids, whom he calls "Gentiles," prohibiting the following of their religious Cult. Many of the Priests retired to the remotest parts of the Islands and some few joined the Christian Church and Cult which was now being spread over the Isles, and called themselves Culdees, and so the old Solar Cult religion gradually died out in these Isles and the Christian Cult has since occupied its place.

CHAPTER XVIII

MOHAMMEDISM

THE Arabs, sometimes spoken of under the appellation of Saracens, occupied the whole of the land of Arabia bounded by the river Euphrates and Persian Gulf, the Sindian, Indian, and Red Seas and part of the Mediterranean; although there is some difference of opinion on this subject. They were originally Stellar Cult people; some of the Solar Cult people tried unsuccessfully to convert them through the Prophet Hûd or Heber. They were divided up into several tribes under the old Totemic Banners although originally there were only two Kingdoms. One comprised the followers of Horus while the other possessed the Cult of Set. Later, however, several Tribes of Solar Cult people (the Jews) inhabited part of the country. At the decay of the Greek and Persian nations, the Arabs were not only a populous nation but were unacquainted with the luxury and delicacies of the Greeks and Persians, and inured to hardships of all sorts. Their political government was also such as favoured the designs of Mohammed, for the division and independency of their tribes were so necessary to the first propagation of his religion and the foundation of his power that it would scarcely have been possible for him to have effected either had the Arabs been united into one great Kingdom. But as soon as they had embraced his religion, the consequent union of their tribes was necessary for future conquests.

Mohammed was a merchant in his younger days and travelled much, so he was thus enabled to inform himself of all those particulars.

His father, Abd'Allah, a younger son of Abd'almotalleb, died while he was young, and he was then adopted by his grandfather who introduced him to a rich widow, which enabled him to assume an independent position and to carry on his propaganda.

Although the Jews were an inconsiderable and despised people in other parts of the world, yet in Arabia, whither many of them fled from the destruction of Jerusalem, they grew very powerful—many of the Arabian tribes and their princes embracing their religion. This made Mohammed show great regard to them; he adopted many of their opinions, doctrines, and customs, thereby to draw them if possible into his interests. But the Jews, agreeably to their wonted obstinacy, were so far from being his proselytes that they were later some of the bitterest enemies he had, waging continual war with him, so that their reduction cost him infinite trouble and danger, and at last his life, and it is for this reason that his followers treat them to this day as the most abject and contemptible people on earth.

The Roman Empire declined after Constantine; the Western half of the Empire was overrun by the Goths, and the Eastern reduced and threatened by the Huns. The Persians also had been declining for some time before Mohammed, on account of the socialistic doctrine of Mazdak. Thus as the principal empires were weak and declining through the socialistic doctrines set up, Arabia under Mohammed became strong and flourishing, and the difficulty of imposing his doctrines was much less than if these nations had remained strong and powerful.

Mohammed professed to establish a new religion, or, rather, of re-planting the only true and ancient one professed by Adam, Noah, Abraham, Moses, the Jews, Jesus, and all other prophets (Stellar, Lunar, and Solar Cults), which had all been mixed up, and corruptions and superstitions introduced. His religion was the worship of one God only, of whom he (Mohammed) professed to be the true prophet, receiving instructions direct from Him. Mohammed took the character of the ever-coming son of the Jews under the title of the last and greatest Prophet. Whether this was the effect of enthusiasm or only a desire to raise himself to the supreme government of his country may be a question, but one must not forget that his mother was left a widow with a son in very mean circumstances, his whole substance consisting but of five camels and one Ethiopian she-slave, and it was not until after he married a rich widow that he commenced his propaganda to attain a still higher status for himself.

The terrible destruction wrought by the spreading of Mohammedism, and the great successes of its professors against all the older Cults, inspired a horror of that religion in all those to whom it was so fatal. It must be also a question if Mohammed acted through malice or ignorance of the real and pure doctrines of his predecessors, which were then so abominably corrupted, and resolved to abolish what he might think incapable of reformation. He certainly had no acquired learning, having had no other education than what was necessary to his tribe, who neglected and despised what we call literature. The scheme of religion which Mohammed framed was a pretended revelation which he induced his followers to believe, but which, however, were copies and extracts from various documents written by different authors, and these copies and extracts were the basis on which he composed his Koran.

He commenced by retiring to his cave in Mount Hara with his wife Khadijah and family, and acquainted her that the angel Gabriel had just before appeared to him and told him that he was appointed the apostle of God; he also repeated to her a passage which he pretended had been revealed to him by the ministry of the angel. Khadijah was overjoyed, and immediately communicated all to her cousin Warakah Ebn Nawfal, who, being a Christian, could write in the Hebrew character, and was fairly well versed in the scriptures, and he agreed with her opinion, assuring her that the same angel who had formerly appeared unto Moses was now sent to Mohammed. This first overture the Prophet made in the month of Ramadan in the fortieth year of his age. He soon made proselytes of those under his own roof, viz., his wife Khadijah, his servant Zeid Hâretha, his cousin Ali the son of Abu Taleb, then Abdallah Eban Ali Kohâfa surnamed Abu Beer, a man of great authority among the Koreish, who gained over for him Orthmān Ebu Affan Abd'alrahmân Ebn Awf, Saad Ebn Abiwakkâs al Zoben Ebn-all-awan and Telha Ebn Obeid'allah, all principal men in Mecca. These were his six chief companions who, with a few more, were converted in the space of three years, at the end of which time Mohammed made his mission no longer a secret, believing he had sufficient interest to support him. Mohammed had a competitor for a time, Moseilama, who set up for a prophet in the province of Yamâma, had a great party, and was not reduced till the time of the Khalifat of Abu Beer, after which the Arabs, being then united under one prince, Mohammed, and one faith, found themselves strong enough to make those conquests which extended the Mohammedan faith over so great a part of the world.

The "Koran"—the book of the Mohammedan faith—signifies "that which ought to be read." It was written part at Medina and part at Mecca. There are several principal editions or ancient copies of this book differing in many particulars, and there is great copying and imitation of the Jews and Persian Magi. It is written in the dialect of the tribe of Koreish, with a small amount of mixture of other tribes.

The great doctrine of the Koran is the unity of one God, to restore which point Mohammed pretended was the chief end of his mission, it being laid down by him as a fundamental truth that there never was, nor ever can be, more than one true orthodox religion. For though the particular laws or ceremonies are only temporary, and subject to alteration according to the divine direction, yet the substance of it being eternal truth, is not likely to change, but will continue immutably the same. He taught that whenever this religion became neglected or corrupted in essentials, God had the goodness to reinform and re-admonish mankind thereof by several prophets, of whom Moses and Jesus were the most distinguished, till the appearance of Mohammed, who is their seal, and no other being to be expected after him. Much of Mohammed's works are taken from the Old and New Testament, but much more from the Apocryphal Books and traditions of the Jews and Christians of those ages, set up in the Koran as truths, in opposition to the Scriptures which the Jews and Christians are charged with having altered. I believe that few or none of the relations or circumstances of the Koran were invented by Mohammed, as is generally supposed, it being easy to trace the greater part of them to perverted copies of the Egyptian Ritual. Probably there were more of those books extant at that time, as the Arabs were all Stellar Cult people before Mohammed's time, but the " the old true faith " had been almost lost by being so perverted; moreover, the Lunar and Solar Cult had become mixed up with the original. Part of the Koran is taken up in giving laws and directions to his followers.

Although monasticism was explicitly forbidden by Mohammed, yet quite early in the history of this religion societies were formed for the purpose of mystic meditation. But while the earlier members of these fraternities swore a formal vow of fidelity to the doctrines of the Prophet and continued to perform their duty as citizens of the world, their successors by degrees abandoned this original rule and, withdrawing themselves from mundane affairs, founded in course of time a variety of new fraternities frankly monastic in character.

In the thirteenth century twelve distinct Dervish Orders were recognized, the founders of which were men of learning and culture. Under Orchar, the first Turkish Emir, Dervish mystics spread themselves over Asia Minor, and, after the conquest of Brossa, this prince founded and endowed for them convents and colleges throughout his dominions, at the head of which he placed the most distinguished of the Sheikhs, as the Priors of these communities are termed. And in every succeeding century the influence of the Dervishes was made use of by the Sultans and the Generals to excite the courage and zeal of the troops against the Christian foes.

In every part of the Near East inhabited by Moslems, European as well as Asiatic, one may still find at the present day the monasteries and shrines of these mystics. At Salonica and Smyrna they are well represented. In Constantinople and its suburbs many of the Order possess several establishments, and in every provincial town will be found the *tekkeh* and *turbéh* as Dervish convents and shrines are respectively termed, of one or more of their communities.

The Arabs claim descent from Kathen or Kaften the Adite, and Kaften in Egyptian is a name of the great Ape who was one of the giants of the seven Pole Star Constellations, and a zootype of Shu, which is identified with the Constellation of Kephus.

Commentators of the Koran repeat the ancient traditions concerning the Adite ancestors of the Arab race, proving that originally they were old Stellar Cult people.

These Adite were the seven giants of prodigious size and stature, like the monstrous figures imaged of the primitive constellations of the heptanomis, which after the Deluge were said to have changed into monkeys.

The human birthplace of the past generations who left Egypt during the Stellar Cult had been localized according to the seven different stations of the pole, and each race or exodus claimed a particular place for a starting point in their migrations " from the Mount "; all the various races have preserved some fragments of the stories told about their origin, and wanderings from one land to another. Moreover, " the Mount of migration," from which the various races claim to have descended, is finally the Pole which had seven starting points and stations in circuit of precession, and all the mythical birthplaces of the various races can, without exception, be critically assigned to one of these.

The same tradition is extant in the " Codex Chimalpopoca, " that men were transformed into monkeys as the result of a deluge, or great hurricane."

According to reckoning, " Kephus" was the "fourth station" of the Pole, and Kephus was the Constellation of Shu, whose zootype in one imagery was the great Ape ; therefore, when the third Pole Star " had fallen," the deluge would take place and all those of the " third world" would be drowned, or changed into the zootype which represented the " fourth world," or fourth station of the Pole, which as Shu, or Kephus, would be as zootypes —monkeys. This will enable one to reckon the time of the exodus of the Arabs and other races from Egypt, which in these cases must have been 17,000 years ago plus the cycles of time of 25,827 years that accord from the latest position during the Stellar Cult.

CHAPTER XIX

CULT OF CHRISTIANITY

A RELIGION of the Cross was first of all established in the Mysteries of Memphis as the Cult of Ptah and his son Iu-em-Hetep, otherwise Atum-Horus, who passed into Atum-Ra or Amen-Ra the father in spirit with Iusa son of Iusāas as the ever-coming Messianic son. The evidence left on the Pyramid of Medum proves that the dead in Egypt were buried in a faith which was founded on the Mystery of the Cross and scientifically so founded, the Cross being a figure of the fourfold foundation on which heaven itself was built. The Tat Cross is a type of the eternal in Tattu; it was a figure of all-sustaining, all-revivifying power that was re-erected and religiously besought for hope, encouragement, and succour, when the day was at the darkest and things were at the worst in physical nature. The sun was apparently going out. The life of Egypt in the Nile was running low towards the desert drought. The spirit of vegetation died within itself. The evil elemental powers led by Set and the Sebu were gaining the upper hand in the great fight. At this point began the ten Mysteries grouped together in the Ritual (Ch. 18). The Tat, or Cross, for the time was overthrown. The deity suffered, as was represented, unto death. The heart of life that bled in every wound was pulseless. The god in matter was inert and breathless. Then came the word: " Make the word of Osiris truth against his enemies. Raise up the Tat *which imaged the resurrection of the god*, let the mummy type of the eternal be once more erected as the mainstay and divine support of all."

It was thus that the power of salvation through Osiris-Tat was represented in the Mysteries.

ORIGIN AND EVOLUTION OF RELIGION 363

Fundamentally the Cross was astronomical.

A Cross with equal arms —|— denotes the time of equal day and equal night, and is a figure of the equinox.

Another Cross † is a figure of time in the winter solstice, and is a modified form of the Tat of Ptah on which the four quarters are portrayed in the four arms of the pedestal. This was re-erected annually in the depths of the solstice when the darkness lasts longest and the daylight least; the measure of time is imaged by this Tat figure. These two are now known as the Greek and Roman Crosses, and their origin has been lost. The first was a type of time in the equinox and the other a symbol of the winter solstice, and the two were scientific figures of the Astro-Mythology and symbols of mystical significance in the Egyptian Eschatology. They formed the ground plan of the Ka chamber of King Rahetep and his wife Nefermat in the pyramid of Medum (Petrie: "Medum"), and also of the tomb of Ollamh Fodhla in Ireland (See "Signs and Symbols of Primordial Man," p. 168).

As a first form of imagery, "as sustainer," was the Great Mother Earth, imaged as a tree, and one of the first human figures on the Cross, or as the Cross, we see in the Khond sacrifice of Meriah.

In the Stellar Cult the uranographic depiction in the starry vast was in the form of the female Great-Mother, as the meskhen, as bringer-forth of life, and the elements of life, or as the Light of Nut.

This in the Solar Cult was superseded by the image of the man, in the Cult of Amen or Atum-Ra, the divine man described by Plato, who bicursated and was stamped upon the universe in the likeness of the Cross. In the Book of Revelation the New Heaven (Amenta) was formed according to the measure of a man—that is, of the angel (Rev. xxi. 17).

This was the Heaven founded on the four cardinal

points which was imaged by the Cross of four quarters. The Cross of the four quarters or the earlier Tatt pillar was a figure of the power that sustained the universe as the Osiris-Tat, or as the later man upon the Cross. Thus the divine man as the Tat, or Cross, support of all, and Ptah-Seker, or Osiris, was the prototype of the Crucified. The god of the four quarters was portrayed as Amen-Ra or Atum-Ra in the Ritual (Ch. 82); as the Ritual states: " My head is that of Ra and I am summed up as Atum four times the arm's length of Ra, four times the width of the world."

Thus Atum or Amen, the divine man, was imaged as a quadrangular figure of the four quarters in the heaven founded in the earlier Stellar and brought on in the Solar Cult, "according to the measure of a man," which is reproduced in Revelation. Osiris-Tat typified the power that sustained the human soul in death. The Cult was founded many thousand years ago. The Christian doctrine of the crucifixion with the victim raised aloft as the sin-offering for all the world is but a metaphrastic rendering of the primitive meaning, a shadow of the original which, as we have seen, went back to the Stellar Cult when one of the Symbols for the divine Horus was a Serpent; and so when Moses' followers revolted he made use of it by lifting up, or sustaining, on a rod, symbolic of a divine Saviour, a sustainer or saviour of a human soul in death.

The Hindu figure of Witoba is portrayed in space as the Crucified without the Cross (Moor's " Hindu Panth."). The Mexican name is Zipe Totec, the meaning of which is " Our Lord the flayed One," as Ptah-Seker is portrayed in the Egyptian original.

But as stated above, the original was the Stellar Cult Amsu or the Risen Horus as the " Symbolic Cross " proves.

The name " Bible " was taken from the Greek " Biblos," which signifies a book. The Hebrews call it " Mikra," which signifies " Lecture " or Scripture.

The Apocryphal Books of the Old Testament are the Books of Enoch, the 3rd and 4th Books of Ezras,

OF RELIGION

the 3rd and 4th Books of Maccabees, the Prayer of Manasseh, the Testament of the twelve Patriarchs, and the Battle of Solomon. In the Roman Canon, according to the Decree at the Council of Trent, they are more numerous.

The oldest writings are in Hebrew-Chaldee, in Syriac, and later Greek. The oldest Testament was the Coptic, from which the Ethiopic and Greek were taken about A.D. 160.

The Coptic version was taken from the Egyptian, and is the oldest. St. Matthew's Gospel was said to be originally written in Syriac. Latin translations were later. There are also two Arabic versions which are very much later. The Gospel of St. John had no historical existence until the last quarter of the second century, except that taken from Taht-Aan of the " Ritual of Ancient Egypt."

Present historical opinions differ as to whether St. John's Gospel was first heard of through Irænœus, Bishop of Lyons, and Theophilus of Antioch (A.D. 175, 188) —Tatian, or Apollinaris and the Author of Clement. The work of Theophilus was, in fact, the production of a philosophic gnostic.

Tatian, an Assyrian, said to have been a native of Mesopotamia who flourished A.D. 160-80, was the founder of the Gnostic sect of the Encratites which, according to Irænœus and Hippolytus, combined the heresy of Marcion with that of Valentinus. His only extant work is his " Address to the Greeks," the obvious production of a Gnostic Christian, but Dr. Lightfoot (Bishop of Durham) writing in the "Contemporary Review," Vol. XXIX, 1877, affirms that when Tatian wrote his " Address to the Greeks," he was "regarded as strictly orthodox." We may therefore infer from its contents that orthodoxy, at that age, consisted of Christianity minus all its important dogmas, as they are not found in its pages.

The " Cortex Vaticanus " (B), which is the oldest of the three great Uncial MSS. of the Bible in Greek, cannot be earlier than the fourth century A.D.

The Armenian Gospels and version of the Bible was made at the close of the fourth century A.D. from the Greek and Syriac.

The "Codex Alexandrinus" (A) is of the fifth century. There are others of much later date.

It has been commonly assumed that the Book of Revelation attributed to St. John the Divine constituted an historical link between the Old Testament and the New; but the Sarkolatroe, or worshippers of the word made flesh in *one* historic form of personality, the carnalizers of the Egypto-gnostic Christ, have never yet discovered what the revelation was intended to reveal. The book is and always has been inexplicable, because it was based upon the symbolism of the Egyptian Astronomical Mythology without the gnosis, or "meaning which hath wisdom" that is absolutely necessary for an explanation of its subject-matter; and because the debris of the ancient wisdom has been turned to account as data for pre-Christian prophecy that was supposed to have its fulfilment in Christian history. The Palaeoanthorpic has never been taken into account.

The gnostic Jesus is the Egyptian Horus, who was continued by the various sects of gnostics under both the names of Horus and of Jesus. In the gnostic iconography of the Roman Catacombs the child Horus reappears as the mummy babe who wears the solar disc.

The Royal Horus is represented in the cloak of royalty, and the phallic emblem found there witnesses to Jesus being Horus of the Resurrection.

Amongst the numerous types of Horus repeated at Rome as symbols of the alleged "historic" Jesus are "Horus on his papyrus," as the Messianic shoot or natzar; Horus the branch of endless ages, as the vine; Horus as Ichthus, the fish; Horus as the bennu or phœnix; Horus as the dove; Horus as the eight-rayed Star of the Pleroma; Horus the Scarabœus; Horus as the child-mummy with the head; of Ra; Horus as the Bambino; Horus of the triangle (reversed) ▽ ("Lapidarian Gallery of the Vatican," Lundy, p. 92); Horus in his resurrection between two trees; Horus attended by two divine sisters, or two women; Horus as the lion of the double force; Horus as the Serapis. The Catacombs of Rome are crowded with illustrations which were reproduced as Egypto-gnostic tenets, doctrines, and dogmas which had served to Persian, Greek, Roman, and Jew as evidence of the non-historic origins of Christianity.

In the transition from the old Egyptian religion to the new Cult of Christianity there was no factor of profounder importance than the worship of Serapis. As the Emperor Hadrian relates, in his letter to Servianus, " Those who worship Serapis are likewise Christians: even those who style themselves the Bishops of Christ are devoted to Serapis."

According to inscriptions at the Serapeum of Memphis the Ancient Egyptian Serapis was born of the Virgin Mother when she was represented by the sacred heifer, that was Horus, son of Hathor during the Lunar Cult, which was a type thousands of years older than the type of the Mystical *human Virgin*.

Prehistoric Christianity was founded, as Egyptian, on the resurrection of the human soul, issuing from the body of the Corpus imaged in death, and its coming forth to-day as demonstrated by the reappearance of the eidolon or double of the dead. It was a belief of the true Palingenesis.

The Egypto-gnostic Christ only existed in the Spirit as a Spirit or a god, and was represented by the super-human type of the risen mummy. The legend of the voluntary victim, who in a passion of divinest pity became incarnate, and was clothed in human form and feature for the salvation of the world, did not originate in a belief that God had manifested once for all as an historic personage. It has its roots in the remotest past. The same legend was repeated in many lands with a change of name, and at times of sex, for the sufferer, but none of the initiated in the esoteric wisdom ever looked upon the Kamite Iusa, a gnostic Horus, Jesus, Tammuz, Krishna, Buddha Witoba, or any other of the many saviours as historic in personality for the simple reason that they had been more truly taught.

Horus came as a Spirit in the form of a Man, but was not a Human-Man, and the whole of the tale can be traced back for at least 600,000 years ago, when Horus came in Spirit in the form of a Man to give His message to the men on Earth.

The story outlined in the canonical Gospels can be traced to " The Annunciation, Conception, Birth and Adoration of the Child " of the Ancient Egyptians.

The story of the Annunciation, the miraculous conception (or incarnation), the birth and the adoration had already been engraved in stone and represented in four consecutive scenes upon the innermost walls of the holy of the holies (the Meskhen) in the Temple of Luxor, which was built by Amen-hetep III, 1700, or 1800 B.C. (Plate LXIX).

In these scenes the maiden queen Mut-em-Ua the Mother of Amen-hetep, her future child, impersonates the virgin-mother, who conceived and brought forth without the fatherhood.

The first scene on the left hand shows the god Taht, as divine word or logos, in the act of hailing the virgin queen and announcing to her that she is to give birth to the coming son (that is, to bring forth the royal Repa in the character of Horus the divine heir).

In the second scene the ram-headed god Kneph, in conjunction with Hathor, gives life to her. This is the Holy Ghost or Spirit that causes conception, Kneph being the Spirit by nature and by name. Impregnation and conception are apparent in the virgin's fuller form.

Next the mother is seated on the midwife's chair and the child is supported in the hands of one of the nurses.

The fourth scene is that of the Adoration. Here the infant is enthroned receiving homage from the gods and gifts from men.

Behind the deity, who represents the Holy Spirit, on the right, three men are kneeling, offering gifts with the right hand, and life with the left. The child thus announced, incarnated, born, and worshipped was the

Pharaonic representative of Áten, or Child-Christ, of the Aten-Cult, the miraculous conception of the ever-virgin mother, which had existed from the primary Stellar Cult, here imaged by Mut-em-Ua.

(The scenes were copied by Sharpe from the temple at Luxor.)

This proves that a dogma of "historic personality" had existed in Egypt at least 1700 B.C.

We must now trace when this was first established. The earliest Kings of Egypt did not assume the vesture of divinity; they were "Horus Kings," except a few earlier ones who were "Set Kings." According to a record of the Twelfth Dynasty, it had become historical in Usertsen First. In this the King says of his god, the Double Har-Makhu: "I am a king of his own making, a monarch long living, *not by the Father*. He exalted me as lord of both parts; as an infant not yet gone forth, as a youth not yet come from my mother's womb." This was in the character of the unbegotten Horus, the Virgin's child who had no father (Records, Vol. XII, pp. 53–4). Har-Makhu was earlier than God the Father as Amen Ra. The title of "Son of Ra" was assumed when "Ra" was representative of God the Father and the Repa was a type of God the Son, as heir-apparent for the eternal. The Father was the ever-living, and the Son the ever-coming one, and *this* portrayal was first depicted in *human form* in the Cult of Ptah at Memphis, as a type of an eternal Father manifesting in the person of an ever-coming Son who was Iu-em-Hetep, he who comes with peace; in the Cult that followed, Amen-Ra was the Father, and Iusa the Egyptian Jesus, the coming Son. The eternal existence of the Father was thus demonstrated by the ever-coming of the Son. This was brought on in Rome under Cæsar Augustus, whose birthday was hailed in Rome as that of the Messianic Prince of Peace. (This is given in a well-preserved Greek inscription of eighty-four lines.) But the doctrine in the Christian phase, where the Holy Spirit makes its descent on Mary and insufflates her with the dove, and also where the Virgin Mary is portrayed in the act of inhaling the fragrance of the lily to procure the mystical conception of the Holy Child, is only a survival of one of the most primitive doctrines of the human race, which is still found amongst the Nilotic Negroes all over the world, and originated before the Hero Cult. It is the belief of the earliest humans who had evolved totemic ceremonies with the elements as totems. The insufflation of the female by the spirit of air, or the animistic soul of air, is still believed in by the Arunta tribes in Australia and is extant in the earliest tribes before the Hero Cult. Spencer and Gillen state " that the Arunta believe a spirit child was *incarnated* in the Mother's womb by the Spirit of Air." But it is an Egyptian doctrine from the first. In Egypt, from the earliest period, the female was represented mythically as the Great Mother Neith whose Totem, as we may call it, was the White Vulture, and the bird of maternity was said to be impregnated by the wind. "Gignuntur autem nunc in modum. Cum amore concipiendi vultur exarserit, vulvam ad Boream apericus, ab es velut comprimitur per dies quinque" ("Hor Apollo" B. I, II).

The only difference is that the Holy Spirit takes the place of the spirit of air in the later doctrine, or, as Egyptian, Ra, as source of soul, has superseded Shu, or Kneph, the breathing force or soul or spirit of air. It is the custom for the Mother amongst the Arunta to affiliate her child thus *incorporated* (not incarnated) to the particular elemental power, as spirit of air or water, tree or earth, supposed to haunt the spot where she conceived or may have quickened (N.T., pp. 124, 128). Thus the spirit child is, or may be, a reincorporation of an Alcheringa Ancestor who, as Egyptian, is the elementary power divinized in the eschatology, and who is to be identified by the animal or plant which is the totemic type of either. Not that the animal or plant was supposed to be transformed directly into a human being, but that the elemental power, or superhuman spirit, entered like the gust that insufflated the vulture of Neith, or caused conception whether in the Arunta female or the Virgin Mary. The element of life incorporated as the source of breath, or the spirit of air, would have the same natural origin whether it entered the female in her human form, or into that of the bird, beast, fish, or reptile. It was the incorporation of an elemental spirit, whether of air or earth, water, fish, or vegetation. Air was the breath of life, and therefore a soul of life was in the breeze. It was the same doctrine with the running water, not still, or so-called "dead" water, where there is no motion, force, or spirit: but the running spring or flowing inundation, the living water, which is the force and the soul of life in the element. These were two of the elemental powers that were brought forth as nature powers by Mother Earth, the original Mother of life and all living things. Birth from the element of water was represented in the mysteries by the rebirth in spirit from the water of baptism. It is as a birth of water that Horus calls himself the primary power of motion. The "Children of Horus" who stand on the papyrus plant or lotus are born of water in the New Kingdom that was founded for the Father by Horus the Son.

Hence, two of Horus's children, Tuamutef and Kabhsenuf, are called the two Fishers (Rit., Ch. 113), and elsewhere the followers of Horus are the fishers. The transformation is a symbolic mode of deriving the totemic people from the pre-totemic humans and pre-totemic powers which were elemental. It was the elemental powers that supplied pre-human souls in the primitive sociology. These may be termed totemic souls, souls that were common to the totemic group of persons, plants, animals, or stones when there was no one soul yet individualized or distinguished from the rest as the human soul. They could not be "the souls of men" that were supposed to inhabit the bodies of animals, birds, reptiles, plants, and stones, when there were no souls of men yet discreted from the pre-human souls in old totemic times. The human lives, or souls, are bound up with the totemic animal, bird, reptile, or tree, because these represented the same animistic nature power from which the soul that is imaged by the totem was derived.

It is because the sun was looked upon at one stage as the elemental source of a soul that its power could be, as it was, represented by a Phallus. Thence arose the belief that the sun could impregnate young women.

Blood was the latest element of seven from which a soul of life was derived. This *followed* the soul of air, water, heat, vegetation, or other force of the elements, and a soul derived from blood was the *earliest human soul*, derived from the blood of the female. Not any blood, not ordinary menstrual blood, but the blood of the pubescent virgin who was personalized in the divine virgin Neith, or Isis or in the later Christian Mary.

The sacred books of the Hebrews and Egyptian gnostic writings were the only Scriptures of primitive Christianity.

The Apostolic Fathers freely quote the Hebrew Scriptures, but there are also traces of references in their works which indicate some knowledge of the wisdom of Ancient Egypt outside these Hebrew documents. The first reliable traces of the existence of Evangelists are found in the writings of the Fathers succeeding the Apostolic Age, who, however, adopt a freedom of expression irreconcilable with the theory of an infallible New Testament.

Justin Martyr (A.D. 150) was acquainted with some of the Egypto-gnostic gospels. He was ignorant of, or rejected Pauline literature, spoke of Revelation as the work of a man named John (Taht-Aan) and assigned to Books, which we now call Apocryphal, the same authority as to works now deemed infallible.

In those early days, no supreme Pontiff or infallible Council held the pretensions, or claimed the right to select and authenticate Sacred Scripture. The old wise men of Egypt had been killed or scattered over the face of the earth, and the true gnosis had been lost. The downfall of Egypt had been accomplished by her enemies, internal and external, and the divine laws given to her had mostly been destroyed or became unreadable ; her enemies had destroyed the most precious gift that man had ever possessed, the only true religion the world had ever evolved, and left themselves groping in ignorance through a dark and degenerate age for 5,000 years.

The task, therefore, was unconsciously undertaken by a small body or group of zealous but credulous men, known to us as the early Fathers of the Christian Church. Clement, Irænœus, and Tertullian, who lived at the close of the second and beginning of the third century, stand out prominently in ecclesiastical history as the canon-makers of the New Testament. The successors of Irænœus closely followed in the footsteps of their teacher ; the work was practically accomplished by a man so credulous that he declares that there should be neither more nor less than four Gospels, because there are four universal winds, and four quarters of the globe (Heressis, III, 9).

Irænœus, writing in the last quarter of the second century, adopted the four Gospels, thirteen Epistles of St. Paul, 1 St. John and Revelation, and assigned a secondary place to 2 St. John, 1 St. Peter, and the Shepherd of Hermas. He knew nothing of the Epistle to the Hebrews, St. Jude, St. James, or second and third St. Peter. Clement added to this collection the Epistle to the Hebrews, St. Jude, the Revelations of Peter, the Epistle of Clement of Rome and Barnabas, both of whom he accepts as Apostles, and the Shepherd of Hermas, viewed by modern orthodoxy as a pious fiction, he declares to be divine.

The child Jesus in Egypt is the child Horus in Egypt. Jesus is described in " Pistis Sophia " as passing through the twelve signs of the Zodiac, all mentioned by name—the Ram, Bull, Twins, Crab, Lion, Balance, Scorpion, Bowman, Goat, and Waterer (B. of the S., in "Pistis Sophia," 266–372, Mead).

In Philo, St. Paul, St. John, and the Gnostics, the doctrinal identity is indisputable. Philo and the others knew no more of a Christ that could be made flesh than they knew of a Jesus as a human man.

The gnostics declared it was not possible that he should suffer who was both incomprehensible and invisible (Irænœus B. I, Ch. VII, 2).

According to the gnostics, says Irænœus, "neither the Word, nor the Christ, nor the Saviour was made flesh." And Manetho states that no god ever became a man through all the ages that the Egyptians had reckoned and kept the time. In the earlier Stellar Cult, as we have seen, the earlier Horus came in the "form of a man," i.e. in Spiritual form, but was not a "human man." Moreover, if we wish to learn one of the reasons why this form of the Solar Eschatological Cult was changed we must read the general Epistle of Barnabas, who was a companion and fellow-preacher with Paul, as this Epistle lays a greater claim to canonical authority than most others. It has been cited by Clement, Alexandrinus, Origen, Eusebius, Jerome, and many other ancient Fathers. Certainly there were different opinions as regards the author by others, but the MS. was written to do away with some of the rites and ceremonies which were so tenaciously held by the earlier Christians, who had brought this on from the old Egyptians. In establishing the new Cult, as in all previous ones, what they could not make use of they blotted out. The Apostles' Creed, before or at the time of A.D. 600, was very different from what it is now; there is no "He descended into Hell" before A.D. 600, but, like the Egyptian, "He was buried," that is like Osiris. He was buried in "Mummy form," and rose again from the dead (mummy) on the third day, as Amsu-Horus, in Spiritual form. Neither was Jesus depicted on the Cross as a man until the eighth century. He was always before that portrayed in the Totemic type of a *Lamb on the Cross*, as may be still seen in the Vatican and Catacombs of Rome.

Of all the ante-Nicene Fathers, Origen (A.D. 254) studied the Christian literature with the greatest ability and in a spirit of rational criticism to find the truth.

His evidence established general corruption in the text of the Evangelists. He states: " It is obvious that the difference between the copies is considerable, partly from the carelessness of individual scribes, partly from the impious audacity of some in correcting what is written, partly also from those who added or removed what seems good to them in the work of correction" (Orig., M., Matt. xv. 14).

It was not until the Emperor Constantine (about A.D. 330) applied to the ecclesiastical historian Eusebius that a collection was made.

Thus when Christianity was taken in hand by the temporal powers in the fourth century with a view of establishing a Catholic Church, its primitive literature was dependent for attestation on a Roman philosopher who had never heard of the Gospel of St. John or the Epistle of St. Paul; and although "orthodoxy" dates the first three or Synoptical Gospels A.D. 60-3, the *historical* existence only begins in the second century (except in the Eschatology of the Egyptians).

The Acts of the Apostles, purporting to be written by the author of the third Gospel, is first heard of late in the second century, and its contents disclose the idea of constructing history at that date from legendary materials which assumed, in credulous and in a dark and degenerate age, the form of attested facts without the gnosis of truth.

As far as the Gospel of St. John is concerned, it was not identified with the Christian Church until Irænœus, Bishop of Lyons, wrote about it A.D. 185, when the Gnostic Gospel was brought forward, which was founded on the Egyptian Mysteries, John being the Egyptian Taht-Aan.

One of the connecting links of the Jesus legend was brought on to Rome from Egypt by the later Mystery teachers, who may be termed Egypto-gnostics, and one of the most important of all the written gnostic remains is the " Pistis Sophia " ; whoever the writer, he continues the Jesus legend from the Egyptian source. These books of Ieou are the books of Jesus, like the "Wisdom of Jesus" in the Apocrypha and the later-discovered "Sayings of Jesus," that is, the real Jesus, otherwise Iusa the son of Iusāas, whose Jewish name is Ieou, Ieo, or Iah, as derivatives from Iu, in Egyptian. The two books of Ieou are said to contain the Mysteries, the first being the lesser, the second the greater mysteries.

"Pistis Sophia" proves the Egyptian origin of the Jewish Ieou and calls "Ieou the first man, the legate of the first order."

In the Egyptian, Atum, or Amen, was the first man, i.e. the created man, who under one of his names was Iu, who was the Egyptian Jesus, and this also identifies the Egypto-gnostic Ieou with Iu-em-Hetep, the author of the sayings and the Books of Wisdom which included these books of Ieou. One of the two books had the general title of "The Book of the Great Logos," according to the Mystery which is equivalent for "The Logi" or "Sayings of Jesus," which were Christianized as the Logia Kuriaka or "Sayings of the Lord," and on which the canonical Gospels were eventually founded.

"Pistis Sophia," like the Ritual, is mostly post-resurrectional with the shortest allusion to the earth-life. It begins with the after-life, in which Jesus has risen from the dead like Amsu the good shepherd. It opens with the Resurrection on the Mount of Glory, the same as we find in the Ritual.

The localities, like those of the Egyptian book, are not of this world. They are in "the earth of eternity" or "Amenta," not in the earth of time. Jesus rises in the Mount of Olives, but not on the Mount that was localized to the east of Jerusalem. The Mount of Olives as Egyptian was the mountain of Amenta. It is termed "Mount Bakhu," "the mount of the olive-tree," where the green dawn was represented by this tree instead of by the Sycamore. Mount Bakhu, the mount of the olive-tree, was the way of ascent to the risen Saviour as he issued forth from Amenta to the land of the spirits in heaven (Rit., Ch. 17).

So when the Egypto-gnostic Jesus takes his seat upon the Mount of Olives, he is said to have " ascended into the heavens " (" Pistis Sophia," Mead's version).

Jesus " descended into hell " according to the Christian Cult but not until A.D. 600. This forms no part of the Gospel legend, but we find it in the Book of the Dead ; also in " Pistis Sophia " Hell or Hades is the Amenta, as Egyptian.

Horus descends into Amenta, or rather rises there from the tomb, as the teacher of the Mysteries concerning the father, who is Ra the father in spirit and in truth.

This descent into the underworld is spoken of by Horus in the Ritual, Chapter 38. He goes to visit the spirits—to utter the words of the father in heaven to the breathless ones, or the spirits in prison. The character shows the divine teacher in two characters on earth and in Amenta. Speaking of Ra, his father in the spirit, Horus says, " I utter his words to the men of the present generation," or to the living. He also utters them to those who have been deprived of breath, or the dead in Amenta.

So in the " Pistis Sophia " the gnostic Jesus passes into Amenta as the teacher of the Great Mysteries. As it is said of his teaching in this Spirit-World, " Jesus spake these words unto his disciples in the midst of Amenta " (" Pistis Sophia," 394). Moreover, a special title is assigned to Jesus in Amenta. He is called Aber-Amentho. " Jesus, that is to say, Aber-Amentho," is a formula several times repeated in " Pistis Sophia."

According to the Ritual, a " glorious vesture " is put on in the place where the human soul is made immortal. This is represented in the Mystery of Tattu, when the body-soul in matter (Osiris) is blended with the holy spirit Ra—the female with the male—Horus the child of twelve years with Horus the adult of thirty years. It takes place on the day that was termed " Come thou to me " (Rit., Ch. 17). This call is reproduced in the " Pistis Sophia " as " Come on to us " on the day of Investiture, when Jesus puts on the divine vesture in his character of Aber-Amentho, or Lord over Amenta, a title which identifies the Egyptian-gnostic Jesus with Horus in Amenta. The "Pistis Sophia" is a book of those Egypto-gnostics with whom the Father God is Ieou-Ihuh and God the Son is Iao-Iah. It contains an Egypto-gnostic version of the Mysteries, Astronomical and Eschatological.

Now, if we turn to St. Paul's beliefs of the Christian resurrection, 1 Cor. xv. 4, he tells us that Jesus died, was buried, and raised again on the third day *according to the Scriptures;* and declares that *if there is no resurrection of the dead, neither hath Christ been raised*—yea, and we are found false witnesses of God; because we witnessed of God that he raised up Christ, whom he raised not up if so be that the dead are not raised. For if the dead are not raised, neither hath Christ been raised (1 Cor. xv. 13, 16).

I have already explained the origin and meaning of rising up on the third day and how overwhelming is the proof that primitive faith in the resurrection of the Christian Jesus originated from reading some ancient document, the full gnosis of which St. Paul did not understand. In all the language of St. Paul we inevitably detect that he had never heard of Lazarus coming forth from his tomb, or of the apostles raising the dead, and therefore rested all his hopes of immortality on some ancient religious documents containing the Egyptian gnosis. That this must have been so we see from his enthusiastic faith when he exclaims: "Behold I tell you a Mystery: we shall not all sleep, but we shall be changed, in a moment, in the twinkling of an eye, at the last trump: for the trumpet shall sound, and the dead shall be raised incorruptible, and we shall be changed. For this corruption must put on incorruption, and this mortal must put on immortality. But when the corruptible shall have put on incorruption and this mortal shall have put on immortality then shall come to pass the saying that is written, ' Death is swallowed up in victory ' " (1 Cor. xv. 51, 54.)

St. Paul must have been well acquainted with some

ancient copy of the Ritual of Egypt, as expressed here in the almost identical words as found there—where in Amenta the mummied Osiris in a moment was changed, in the twinkling of an eye, into Amsu-Horus, the triumphant one, when the spirit of the Holy Father Ra descends and he rises triumphant over all his enemies, the mortal Horus risen as the immortal—with one hand held aloft with the sceptre of dominion and sovereignty raised above. Death indeed is swallowed up in victory. That St. Paul possessed an equally enthusiastic faith in the immediate return of Jesus (Phil. iv, 4, 5) may be attributed to the prophecy contained in the Hebrew writings, where Horus has been introduced as the ever-coming Messiah. The Hebrew writer had not understood the Stellar Cult imagery of Horus as " the ever-coming Saviour annually " in " the inundation " and other types.

St. Paul also affirms that " flesh and blood cannot inherit the kingdom of God," and teaches that the soul is a spiritual essence, which was first taught and demonstrated by the ancient Egyptians 300,000 years before.

The " Ritual of Ancient Egypt " commences with the Resurrection when Osiris in mummy form, in Amenta, is transformed by the descent of the Holy Spirit Ra into Amsu-Horus, the risen Jesus of the Gnostics.

The history of Christianity begins with the Resurrection, as recorded in the conflicting narratives of the Evangelists. Thus in St. Mark xvi. 8. The last twelve verses of this Gospel are absent from the oldest Greek MSS., which are interpolations of a later writer. Also in the Gospel according to St. Luke we read : " Yea, certain women of our company made us astonished, which were early at the sepulchre, and when they found not his body, they came saying that they had also seen a vision of angels which said that he was alive" (St. Luke xxiv. 22, 23). This passage, read in connection with St. Mark's version, amounts to nothing more than hearsay evidence, and obviously reproduces one of the earliest legends of the Resurrection brought on from the Egyptian originals.

These conflicting accounts agree in one essential point, that it was women, or a woman, who proclaimed the Resurrection, and this *is as it should be according to the* " Ritual of Ancient Egypt " *data.*

Rekhet, the place in Amenta where the two divine sisters, Isis and Nephthys, waited and wept for the lost Osiris, was a locality in the earth of eternity.

Mary Magdalene, who comes to the tomb "early while it was yet dark," and finds the stone moved away "*and light enough to see by* light of Horus kindled in the tomb" is the representation of Isis, who was also a form of the great Mother alone. She is mentioned singly as watching in tears over her brother Osiris by night in Rekhet (Rit., Ch. 18). So Mary Magdalene is described as "standing without the tomb weeping" alone as one woman.

According to St. Matthew there were two women at the tomb, "Mary Magdalene and there was the other Mary sitting over against the sepulchre" (Ch. xxvii. 61).

In the Osirian representation Isis and Nephthys are the two women called the "two mourners who weep and wail over Osiris in Rekhet (Ch. 1). Isis and Nephthys, the two divine sisters, are the two women at the sepulchre of Osiris. They are portrayed, one at the head, the other at the feet of the mummy.

Horus rises in his Ithyphallic form with the sign of virility erect, which is the only reason to account for the Phallus found in the Roman Catacombs as a figure of the Resurrection. If the Gospel story had not been taken from the Egyptian original, it would denote the Phallus of a supposed historic Jew instead of the typical member of Horus, whose word was thus manifested with pubescent power in the person of the risen Amsu—in Sign Language.

The Ritual states that when the deceased Osiris comes forth from the tomb, as Amsu-Horus, and reaches the Horizon of the Resurrection, " I rise as a god amongst men. The *goddesses and the women proclaim me when they see me.*"

OF RELIGION

It is the goddesses and the women who see the risen Horus first and proclaim him to the others.

The women and the female deities are identical as the two divine sisters who are represented in the Gospels by the two Marys; but in some of the scenes in the Egyptian there are other women in attendance as well as the two sisters, Mertæ.

Now, as the two Marys are originally goddesses (in Egypt) we have the same group of goddesses, and "the women" (in St. Luke xxiv. 10) as in the Ritual (79,11), and both agree in proclaiming the resurrection and hailing the risen Lord with jubilation. St. Paul's doctrine of the resurrection is founded on the mystery of the double Horus.

As taught by the Egyptian wisdom, continuity was conditional, and the power of resurrection was personally secured by living the life of a human Horus, in fellowship with his sufferings, as the bearer of his cross by which the power of his resurrection in the after-life was attained through becoming Horus the divinized adult. St. Paul's resurrection is obtainable on the same conditions. As a struggling mortal he hopes "by any means" to attain "unto the resurrection from the dead," and says: "Not that I have already attained or am already made perfect, but I press on."

In St. Paul's Epistles Christ takes the place of Horus the anointed, by whom the power of resurrection was made manifest in the mysteries; and the doctrine is the same in the Ritual.

In his own body and sufferings St. Paul was living the life and trying to emulate the character of Horus the mortal, whilst looking forward to the future fulfilment as it was portrayed in Horus the glorified, whose second coming in Tattu as representative of Ra the Holy Spirit and the power of resurrection is perfectly described by St. Paul.

The manes in the Ritual says: "My enclosure is in Heaven," as it was imaged on the mountain summit in the eternal city.

St. Paul writes: "Our own citizenship is in Heaven,

from whence also we wait for a Saviour, the Lord Jesus Christ, who shall fashion anew the body of our humiliation " (which was one with the maimed, deformed, and suffering human Horus changed and glorified in the resurrection) " that it may be conformed to the body of his glory."

The reason why the Virgin's child should make his change and pass away when twelve years old, and why the divinized adult should not take up the story until thirty years of age, to leave no record during eighteen years is to be explicated by the Egyptian wisdom, and no other. It is because the two as double Horus, or as the dual Jesus Christ, are no more than types and have no relation to an individual human history—either Kamite, Hebrew, Persian, Gnostic, or Christian ; and in this unity the different versions all agree.

" Pistis Sophia " tells us more about the double Horus, the twofold Messiah, or twin Saviour, than all the Records outside the Ritual put together.

The gnostic Jesus represents the double Horus, human and divine, more fully and definitely than does the Jesus of the canonical Gospels and independently of any personal history.

The first and second advents are both fulfilled by the Jesus of "Pistis Sophia." As the youth of twelve years, who was Horus the word, he instructs the disciples " up to the regions of the first statutes only " and is the teacher by means of parables. In his second advent he says : " I will speak with you face to face without parable." He then unveils and expounds the greater mysteries from the centre to circumference—from the first to the last. In the same gnostic Scripture, Mary, the Mother of Jesus, describes her son in accordance with the Egyptian gnosis of the double Horus, which was not derived from the canonical Gospels, but from the divine writings of the divine scribe Taht, and has been preserved sufficiently intact to prove the origin to be pre-historical and non-historical as witnessed by the once more living Egypt's Ancient Ritual.

The Book of Revelation was derived from the wisdom of Egypt, and can easily be understood by the Kamite Mysteries, but not otherwise. In the Stellar Cult, heaven is the Celestial heptanomis that was formed in seven astronomes, on seven hills or seven islands, which sank and passed away.

In Revelation the most ancient genetrix is reproduced as the great harlot. She is the beast that sat upon the waters as a pregnant hippopotamus. Her seven " sons of the thigh " are here as seven kings who were made drunken with the cup of her fornications or promiscuous sexual intercourse. These, as powers, are the seven heads of the scarlet-coloured beast, or solar dragon upon which the woman rode. By a change of type the scarlet-coloured beast becomes the " Scarlet Lady " of later theology : the woman in red being substituted for the red water-cow (great Hippopotamus). The Great Mother is now denounced as the great whore living in adultery with her own children, who originated in the seven elemental powers, to pass through several phases of phenomena as the seven with Anup, with Ptah, with Horus, or with Jesus and with Ra.

In Revelation the Mother of Mystery is called " Babylon the Great," the mother of harlots and of abominations of the earth who has the name of mystery written on her forehead (Ch. xvii. 5). (But there was an earlier Babylon in Egypt known to the secret wisdom and identified with the locality of Coptos nominally the seat of Kep, the Kamite Mother of Mysteries.) The Mother of Mysteries did not originate with the scarlet woman of Babylon, nor as the " Scarlet Woman " of the Protestants, although the title of the great harlot was applied to her also, who was the mother of harlots and to whom the maiden tributes were religiously furnished in that city. Here is a figure of the greatest antiquity in the Stellar Cult which was uranographically represented as the red hippopotamus that preceded the Great Bear. The red Hippopotamus (Apt) had already become the scarlet lady in the Ritual. Hence the Great Mother as

Seket-Bast, who is higher than all the gods and is the only one who stands above her father, is called "the lady of the scarlet-coloured garment" (Rit., Ch. 164, Naville). The Egyptian constellation of the birthplace serves to show cause why the "great harlot" should have been abused so badly in the Book of Revelation.

The creatory of the great mother was depicted in the sign of the meskhen to indicate the birthplace of or bringer forth by the cow of heaven, whose "thigh" is the emblem of great magical power in the hieroglyphics. The Mother of Mystery also carries "in her hand a golden cup full of abominations, even the unclean things of her fornication" (Ch. xvii. 4), such as the mystery of fecundation by water, which was the primitive mystery of Kep. This was symbolized in Egypt by the water-vase and constellated in the sign of Krater, the urn of the inundation. It has been shown that the gods of the Egyptian Mythology originated in the seven elemental forces that were born of the earth the mother of life, and who were then continued in a variety of characters as the primordial seven powers. These are reproduced as the progeny of the mother earth; they were called the "Kings of the earth," over whom the "firstborn of the dead" is to become the ruler (Ch. i. 5) as Jesus in the Book of Revelation, the same as Horus (or Iu) in the Ritual, the god "who giveth light by means of his own body" (Ch. 85). The Stellar Cult was taught in mysteries by the mystery teachers of the heavens. One of the chief of these were the mystery of the seven stars, the seven who are described in the Ritual as "the seven glorious ones," the seven spirits of fire, the seven great spirits, who are also termed the lords of eternity "as never-setting stars"; the seven were beyond the bounds of time; hence they become the witnesses for eternal continuity. Thus the seven stars that never set were made a group of witnesses for the eternal in the eschatology. These, in the Book of Revelation, are the seven Spirits of God. The seven spirits of fire, the seven eyes, the seven golden lamps or lampstands, as variously

OF RELIGION

typified "before the throne" on the celestial summit. The writer, John, follows far later in the wake of Taht-Aan and makes an attempt at showing in the Book of Revelation some of the Ancient Mysteries of Egypt. Amongst the most prominent are the mystery of the seven stars, the mystery of the woman and the beast with seven heads, the mystery of the two witnesses and the four living creatures (the four children of Horus). The mystery of the war in heaven, the mystery of God. The mystery of renewal in the ancient heaven, where every isle and mountain vanish and the heptanomis pass away. All of which can only be rightly interpreted and understood by the ancient Egyptian wisdom, and the explanation is still extant in the Ritual of Egypt written in Sign Language for anyone to read if he so desires.

Taht-Aan was the teacher of the Mysteries in Amenta, the Egyptian Psalmist. The Apocalypse of St. John might be described as "scenes and characters from the mysteries of Taht-Aan," who was the pre-Christian John the divine.

"Revelation" was derived from the Egyptian Stellar Cult and Eschatology ; Jesus of this Book is one with Iu, the son of Atum-Ra, who was portrayed as the divine man and bringer of peace to earth over 20,000 years ago. The prototype of Patmos is to be seen in the Ritual (Ch. 175). John is in the Isle of Patmos, "for the Word of God and the testimony of Jesus." He writes of the God who died and is alive again, saying: "Behold he cometh with clouds ; and every eye shall see him, and they which pierced him" are to mourn (Ch. i. 7). To see how ancient this is, we must turn to the 175th Chapter of the "Ritual of the Resurrection." It is "the chapter of not dying the second death." The divine sufferer is thus addressed : "Decree this, O Tum, that if *I behold thy face, I shall not be pained by thy sufferings.*" This Tum decrees. The great gods have given him the supremacy and he will reign "on his Throne in the isle of flame for eternities of eternities" (Naville : Rit.,·Ch. 175).

The mission of Taht-Aan, the saluter of Horus, could

not be better expressed than in the words of John the divine concerning the Christ of the gnosis called the Word. "That which was from the beginning, that which we have heard, that which we beheld, and our hands handled, concerning the Word of Life (and the life was manifested, and we have seen, and bear witness, and declare unto you the life eternal which was with the Father, and was manifested unto us): yea and our fellowship is with the Father, and with His Son Jesus Christ: and these things we write that our joy may be fulfilled" (John i. 1-14).

Taht-Aan had beheld and heard and handled "the Word of eternal life" manifested in Horus or Jesus, for, as bearer of the symbolic Utat, he carried Horus in his hand and held him aloft as the true light of the world, and as the symbolic likeness of a Soul in human nature that was begotten of Ra the Holy Spirit and the Father in Heaven. This was the revelation of Tehuti-Aan or Taht-Hermes, and the position of Aan, the divine scribe, in relation to Horus the only begotten son of God, is repeated on behalf of John in the Gospel.

It is in the character of Taht-Aan that "there came a man, sent from God whose name was John." He came for witness of the light. He was not the light, but came that he might bear witness of the light (Ch. i.) as did Taht-Aan, who carries the Eye of Horus in his hands and testifies that Horus is the true light of the world as son of his Father Ra, the Holy Spirit. He carried in his hands the eye of light, the talismanic maatkheru and the papyrus-roll or the book of life.

"The Cross of Palanque" at Copan gives the symbolic depiction of the above, and the Indians and Mexicans portrayed the same, proving how widespread the old religious doctrines of Egypt had spread.

From the first Horus was Lord of Light, and Set, or Satan, the adversary of Darkness and Drought. There is no Horus without Set in the Egyptian.

There are two types of evil, or the devil, in the Egyptian. One is zoomorphic as the Apap-reptile, the other anthropomorphic as Set the personal adversary of Osiris. Apap is the evil one in the early Cults, Set is Satan in the eschatology.

(Set—Satan in Egyptian—is a name of "the evil one," Budge: Vocab., p. 268.)

The Gospel story of the Devil taking Jesus up into an exceeding high mountain from which all the kingdoms of the world and the glory of them could be seen, and of the contention on the summit is originally a legend of the Astronomical Cult, which has been converted into history in the Gospels.

In the Ritual (Ch. 110) the struggle is described as taking place upon the mount, i.e. "the mountain in the midst of the Earth, or the mountain of Amenta which reaches up to the sky," and which in the Solar Cult stood at the point of the equinox, where the conflict was continued and the twins were reconciled year after year. The equinox was figured at the summit of the mount on the ecliptic and the scene of strife was finally configurated as a fixture in the constellation of the Gemini, the sign of the twin-brothers, who for ever fought and wrestled "up and down the garden," first one, then the other, being uppermost during the two halves of the year, or of night and day. The mountain of the equinox "in the midst of the earth" joined the portion of Set to the portion of Horus at this point midway betwixt North and South, and it was there that the twins were reconciled for the time being by the Star-God Shu (Rit., Ch. 1, 10), or by the earth-god Seb (text from Memphis). Set is described as seizing Horus in the desert of Amenta and carrying him to the top of the mount called Mount Hetep, the place of peace where the two contending powers are reconciled by Shu according to the treaty made by Seb.

Set is the representation of evil, of darkness, drought, sterility, negation, and non-existence. It is his devilry to undo the good work that Horus does, like Satan sowing tares amongst the wheat. It was Set who paralysed the left arm of Horus and held it bound in Sekhem (Rit.,

Ch. 1). The power of resurrection was imaged by the lifting of the arm from the mummy bandages. Horus in Sekhem is the lifter of the arm. Whilst the arm is fastened in death Set is triumphant over Horus in the dark. When Horus frees his arm, he raises the hand that was motionless (Rit., Ch. 5). He strikes down Set, or stabs him to the heart. The power of darkness, one form of which was Set, is designated the "eater of the arm" (Rit., Ch. 11).

In the Gospel of pseudo-Matthew (Ch. 29) the bad boy is called a son of Satan and the worker of iniquity; he runs at Jesus and thrusts himself against his shoulder with the intention of paralysing his arm; also again in the Gospel of Thomas the boy throws a stone and hits him on the shoulder (Gospel of Thomas, B. 2 Ch. 4). When this occurs, the bad boy is smitten dead by Jesus, just as Set is pierced to the heart by Horus.

When Jesus was "led up of the Spirit into the wilderness to be tempted of the Devil," he is said to have fasted forty days and forty nights.

This contention in the wilderness was one of the great battles of Set and Horus. As Egyptian the wilderness is the desert of Anrutef, a desolate, stony place where nothing grew. Horus in Amenta has to make his way through the barren desert in the domain of Set as sower of the seed from which the bread of life was made, much of which must have fallen on stony ground in the region of Anrutef. Forty days was the length of time in Egypt that was reckoned for the grain in the earth before it sprouted visibly from the ground. It was a time of scarcity and fasting in Egypt, the season of Lent, with its mourning for the dead Osiris and its rejoicing over the child of promise, the germinating green shoot springing from the earth. This is represented in the Gospel as a fast of forty days and forty nights during which Jesus wrestled with the devil and was hungry. The original was the conflict between Horus and Set in the desert of Amenta. During the forty days that Osiris was typically buried in the nether earth as seed from which the bread of heaven was made, the struggle was continued by Set and Horus on the mount. The conflict is between the powers of light and darkness, of fertility and sterility, betwixt Horus the giver of bread, and *Set, whose symbol of the desert was a stone.* The fasting of Jesus in the desert represents the absence of food that is caused by Set in the wilderness during the forty days' burial for the corn, and Satan asking Jesus to turn the stones into bread is a play on the symbol of Set, which in one representation was rendered as " a stone." The Indian representation is Huniman's conflict with Ravena.

The contest of the personal Christ with a personal Satan in the New Testament is no more historical fact than the contest between the seed of the woman and the serpent of evil in the Old. Both are mythical and both are Egyptian Mysteries.

In the earlier narrative we have the struggle between Horus and the Apap-serpent of evil reproduced as truth by a writer in Aramic, in the later we have Set in his Anthropomorphic guise as Christian history.

As Egyptian Cult Mysteries, it explains both and disproves their right to be considered historical.

The evil Apap who drinks up the waters of light, cubit by cubit, at each gulp as the sun goes down, is slain by Horus at daybreak, when he once more sets free the waters of Light, which are designated the waters of dawn.

In like manner the waters of day rush forth when Indra slays the serpent of darkness who was thought of as the swallower of the light = the water of heaven.

The Cat was another image continued in the Christian Church as a living type of the historical Christ.

The vignette to Chapter XVII portrays a Cat bruising the Serpent's Head.

The Ritual states : " I am the great Cat who frequents the Persea Tree (the tree of dawn) in Heliopolis ; on the night of the battle wherein is effected the defeat of the Sebu, and that day upon which the adversaries of the Inviolate God are exterminated." Here is depicted Horus imaged as "The Great Cat," "Seer in the Night," slaying the great serpent of evil, who is swallowing up all the light.

At Aix, in Provence, the great cat was a representative of the newly born Jesus. On the solemn festival of Corpus Christi the finest tom-cat to be found in the canton was exhibited in this character. It was wrapped up like a child in swaddling-clothes and shown in a gorgeous shrine. Every knee was bowed in adoration to this effigy, who was Iu in Egypt and Iahu ("Hampson Medii AE vi Kalendarium": Mill: "History of the Crusades"). The original is depicted in the Egyptian as Horus bruising the serpent's head (Picture: Pap. of Ani, Pl. 10), there we see Iu is imaged in the form of a cat, the seer in the dark, and

GREAT CAT.
FIG. 53.

is grappling with the serpent and cutting off or bruising its head; Ra, his father, is intently gazing at his son whilst the battle is raging. The scene is in the garden of Aarru, where he delivers Ra from Apap in the third domain. The group of gods looking on are watching the struggle betwixt the great Cat and the serpent Apap. The god in conflict with the serpent is Iu, the son of Atum, otherwise Atum in the person of his son. Iu the su-Iusu or Iusa, the son of Iusāas, is the original of Iusu or Jesus.

The war betwixt the serpent and the son who came to save went on for ever, every night, every year, and every other period of time; hence the bruiser of the serpent's head was the saviour who for ever came as the lord of light, the giver of life, protector of the tree of life at its rootage in Amenta. But if we turn back to the Lunar Cult, we see the personification was that of the woman who wars against the serpent, who was Sekhet, otherwise Pasht. The goddess is sometimes depicted standing at the prow of the boat in the act of spearing the serpent as he raises his head and tries to hypnotize the passengers with his evil eyes (Ch. 108, 3, 4). This is Sekhet, who is mistress of the water in which the Apap lurks by night (Ch. 57, line 1) because she was the Lunar goddess, the seer by night, and who was imaged as the cat who killed the serpent abominated by the light. Thus there are two versions, Lunar and Solar. In one the woman or goddess is the slayer of the serpent, in the other and later version it is the son of the woman who bruises the serpent's head. The Roman Church has perpetuated the one and the Protestant world the other; as here shown both are Egyptian.

According to St. John, when Jesus reappears to the seven fishers on board the boat to cause the miraculous draught of fishes, it is *after his resurrection from the dead*. Consequently, this took place in a region beyond the tomb, therefore in spirit world, not in the life on earth. Whereas in St. Luke's version his reappearance was in the earth life, and is not a reappearance after death. Yet the miraculous draught of fishes is the same in both books; and therefore either the transaction is historical in Luke and has been relegated to the after life in another world by John, or else the mythical version was first and has been converted into an historical event by Luke. But for the origin and truth we must turn to the Ritual of Egypt, where the fisher, the seven fishers, the fishing and the fish belong not to this earth but to the earth of eternity and to the mysteries of Amenta as set forth in the Ritual, Chapter 113.

The *Christian miracles* are nothing more than a mode of symbolical representation *literalized* from the *Kamite Mysteries*, all of which can be explained by the latter, but never can be comprehended by the former.

The Mysteries were a dramatic mode of representing

the gnosis of the Egyptian beliefs (both as mythology and eschatology).

The Mysteries of Amenta portray all the phases. It was in these the dead were raised, the blind were made to see, the dumb to speak, the deaf to hear, the lame to walk, and the manes to become bird-headed or as spiritual forms. These depict the scenes when the manes make their transformation visibly, and the mortal puts on immortality—and were founded on the resurrection from the dead, with the Ka or the bird-headed Horus as the representative of a survival in Spirit. In " Pistis Sophia " Jesus tells the disciples that " the mystery of the resurrection of the dead healeth from demoniacal possessions, from sufferings, and all diseases. It also healeth the blind, the dumb, the maimed, the halt," and he promises that whosoever shall achieve the gnosis of this wisdom shall have the power of performing these mysteries of the resurrection, which became metaphrastic miracles in the canonical Gospels (P.S., B., 2, 279). Amenta is the spirit world in which the dead become once more living, attaining their continuity by being proved and passed as true for all eternity.

If they failed, it was there they died the second death and never rose again as Spirits (they were destroyed and returned to original and separate corpuscles).

In the canonical Gospels not only is it represented that Jesus raised the dead, but that he also conferred power on the disciples to do likewise. They are to preach and proclaim that the kingdom of heaven is at hand, to " heal the sick and raise the dead " (St. Matt. x. 5, 8).

So the followers, called the children of Horus, had the power given them previously by their Lord " to raise the dead." In the Pyramid texts of Teta (line 270) it is said : " Horus had given his children power that they may raise thee up " ; that is, from the funeral couch. But this resurrection was in Amenta, the earth of eternity, not on this earth of time, and those who are raised up are manes, not mortal beings in the human world. Christians talk about the mysteries of revealed religion, but these never were revealed except to those who had been duly initiated. They were mysteries to the Christians because they had not been revealed to them, but they were only the mysteries of ancient knowledge reproduced as miracles of modern ignorance. Such mysteries as the Trinity, the Incarnation, and the Virgin Birth, the Transfiguration on the Mount, the Passion, Death, Burial, Resurrection and Ascension, Transubstantiation and Baptismal Regeneration, were all extant in the mysteries of Amenta with Horus or Iu-em-Hetep as the Egyptian Jesus.

The Gospel doctrine of the Holy Spirit is true enough according to the Egyptian wisdom, when properly applied, but only as Egyptian is it to be understood. Certain manifestations of the Holy Spirit in the Gospels are strictly in keeping with the mysteries of the Egyptian Ritual or Book of the Dead.

In the words of St. John, " the Holy Spirit was not given " at the time when Jesus " was not yet glorified " (Ch. vii. 39). The glorifying was by descent of the Holy Spirit, the Spirit that was given to Horus and by Him to the disciples in the mystery of Tattu upon the resurrection day, when the God in Heaven called to the mummy Osiris in Amenta, " Come thou to Me," when the two halves of the soul were blended in the eternal oneness, and Human Horus, the soul in matter, was transformed to rise again as Horus divinized. This was in the resurrection after death, in baptismal regeneration, or in the Christifying of the Osiris Mummy. The canonical Gospels can be shown to be a collection of sayings from the Egyptian Mythos and Eschatology. The original likeness is somewhat defeatured at times in the process of comparison. When the narratives in the canonical Scriptures had taken the place of the primitive drama, certain mysteries of Amenta were made portable in parables, and ·thenceforth the Gospels repeat the same things in parables and logoi that were represented dramatically in the mysteries. We also see the reflection of the foundation in the Totemic Ceremonies in the Eucharist.

The mutilation of Osiris in his coffin, the stripping of his corpse and tearing it asunder by Set, who scattered it piecemeal, has its equivalent by the stripping of the dead body of Jesus whilst it still hung upon the Cross, and parting the garments amongst the spoilers.

In St. John's account the crucifixion takes place at the time of the Passover, and the victim of sacrifice in human form is substituted for, and identified with, the Paschal Lamb. But, as this version further shows, the death assigned is in keeping with that of the non-human victim. Not a bone of the sufferer was to be broken. This is supposed to be in fulfilment of prophecy. It is said by the Psalmist (xxxiv. 20) : " He keepeth all His bones : not one of them is broken." But this was in strict accordance with the original law of Tabu. No matter what the type, from bear to lamb, no bone of the sacrificial victim was ever permitted to be broken ; and the only change was in the substitution of the human type for the animal, which had been made already when human Horus became the type of sacrifice instead of the calf or lamb.

When the Australian natives sacrificed their little bear not a bone of it was ever broken : when the Iroquois sacrificed the white dog, not a bone was broken. This was a common custom, on account of the resurrection as conceived by the primitive races, and the same is applied to Osiris-Horus. Every bone of the skeleton was to remain intact as a basis for the future building.

It is an utterance of the Truth that is eternal to say that Horus as the Son of God had previously been all the Gospel Jesus is made to say he is, or is to become.

Horus and the Father were one.

Jesus says I and My Father are one. " He that seeth Me, seeth Him that sent Me " (St. John xii. 45).

Horus is the Father seen in the Son (Rit., Ch. 115).

Jesus claims to be the Son in whom the Father is revealed.

Horus was the light of the world, the light that is represented by the symbolical eye, the sign of salvation.

OF RELIGION

Jesus is made to declare that He is the light of the world.

Horus was the way, the truth, the life by name and in person.

Jesus is made to assert that he is the way, the truth, and the life.

Horus was the plant, the shoot, the natzar.

Jesus is made to say: "I am the true vine."

The deceased says: "I spring up as a plant" (Rit., Ch. 83, 1).

The deceased, in the character of Horus, or one with him by assimilation, also makes these claims for himself. Hence the sayings—the sayings that were repeated in the Gospels, more especially in the Gospel according to John—the Egyptian or Taht-Aan. In the Gospel according to St. John, Jesus says of himself: "I am the bread of life" (vi. 35). "I am the light of the world (viii. 12). I am the door of the sheep (x. 7). I am the good Shepherd (x. 11). I am the resurrection and the life (xi. 25). I am the way, the truth, and the life (xiv. 6). I am the true vine (xv. 1)." And Horus was the original in all seven characters. Horus was the bread of life, also the divine corn from which the bread of life was made (Rit., Ch. 83). Horus was the good shepherd who carries the crook upon his shoulder. Horus was the door of entrance into Amenta, which none but he could open. Horus was the resurrection and the life. He carries the two symbols of resurrection and of life eternal, the hare-headed sceptre, and the Ankh-key in his hands. Horus was the way. His name is with the sign of the road (Heru). Horus was the true vine, as the branch of Osiris, who is himself the vine in person.

Horus says: "It is I who traverse the heaven; I go round the Sekhet-Arru (the Elysian Fields), Eternity has been assigned to me without end. Lo! I am heir of endless time and my attribute is eternity" (Rit., Ch. 62).

Jesus says: "I am come down from Heaven. For this is the will of the Father that everyone who beholdeth the Son and believeth in Him should have eternal life, and I will raise him up at the last day." He, too, claims to be the lord of eternity. When Horus is " lifted up " to become glorified and is " Horus in his glory " (Ch. 78), " Master of his diadem," he says, " I raise myself up." Then he adds : " I stoop upon the Atit-bark that I may reach and raise to me those who are in their circles and who bow down before me " as his worshippers (Ch. 77). "And I," says Jesus," if I be lifted up from the earth (as Horus was lifted up out of the nether-world) will draw all men unto me " (John xii. 32, 33).

Horus says : " I open the Tuat that I may drive away the darkness."

Jesus says : " I am come a light unto the world."

Horus says : " I am equipped with thy words O Ra (the father in heaven) (Ch. 32) and repeat them to those who are deprived of breath " (Ch. 38). These were the words of the father in heaven.

Jesus says : " The Father which sent me, he hath given me a commandment, what I should say and what I should speak. Whatsoever I speak, therefore, even as the Father said unto me, so I speak " (St. John xii. 49, 50). " The word which ye hear is not mine, but the Father's which sent me " (John xiv. 24). Horus repeated to his followers that which his father in heaven has said to him in the early time (Rit., Ch. 78).

Jesus says : " As the Father hath taught me, I speak these things " (St. John viii. 28). "All things that I have heard of my Father I have made known unto you " (St. John xv. 15). Horus comes on earth to report what he has known and heard and seen and handled with the Father. " I have touched with my two hands the heart of Osiris." " That which I went to ascertain I have come to tell." " I know the mysterious parts and the gates of Aarru (or Paradise) from whence I come. Here am I and I come that I may overthrow mine adversaries on earth though my dead body be buried" (Rit., Ch. 86, Renouf). Horus, who comes from heaven says : " I am the food which perisheth not, in my name of the self-governing force" (Rit., Ch. 85). Jesus says : " I am the bread of life," "This is the bread which cometh down from heaven that a man may eat thereof and not die." "I am the living bread which came down from heaven" (John vi, 48–51).

A comparative list of some *pre-existing types* to Christianity shows further how these types were brought on in the canonical Gospels and the Book of Revelation.

Horus baptized with water by Anup=Jesus baptized with water by John.

Anup the Baptizer=John the Baptist.

Aan, a name of the divine scribe=John the divine scribe.

Horus born in Annu, the place of bread=Jesus born in Bethlehem, the house of bread.

Horus the Good Shepherd with the crook upon his shoulders=Jesus the Good Shepherd with the lamb or kid upon his shoulder.

The Seven on board the bark with Horus=The seven fishers on board the bark with Jesus.

The wonderful net of the fishers=The miraculous draught of fishes in the net.

Horus as the Lamb=Jesus as the Lamb.

Horus as the Lion=Jesus as the Lion.

Horus as the black child=Jesus as the little black bambino.

Horus identified with the Tat or Cross=Jesus identified with the Cross.

Horus of twelve years=Jesus of twelve years.

Horus made a man of thirty years in his baptism =Jesus made a man of thirty years in his baptism.

Horus the Krst=Jesus the Christ.

Horus the manifesting Son of God=Jesus the manifesting Son of God.

The trinity of Atum the Father, Horus the Son, and Ra the Holy Spirit=The trinity of the Father, Son, and Holy Spirit.

The first Horus as child of the Virgin, the second as Son of Ra=Jesus as the Virgin's child, the Christ as Son of the Father.

Two mothers of child Horus who were two sisters = Two mothers of child Jesus who were sisters.

Set and Horus the twin opponents = Satan and Jesus the twin opponents.

Horus the sower and Set the destroyer in the harvest-field = Jesus the sower of the good seed and Satan the sower of tares.

Horus carried off by Set to the summit of Mount Hetep = Jesus spirited away by Satan into an exceedingly high mountain.

Set and Horus contending on the Mount = Jesus and Satan contending on the Mount.

The Star, as announcer of the child Horus = The Star in the East that indicated the birthplace of Jesus.

Horus the avenger = Jesus who brings the sword.

Horus as Iu-em-Hetep who comes with peace = Jesus the bringer of peace.

Horus the afflicted one = Jesus the afflicted one.

Horus as the type of life eternal = Jesus the type of eternal life.

Horus as Iu-em-Hetep the child teacher in the Temple = The child Jesus as teacher in the Temple.

Horus who comes to fulfil the law = Jesus who comes to fulfil the Law.

Horus who came by the water, the blood, and the Spirit = Jesus, who came by the water, the blood, and the Spirit.

Horus of the two horizons = Jesus of the two lands.

Horus as teacher of the Spirits in Amenta = Jesus as preacher to the Spirits in prison.

Horus walking the water = Jesus walking the water.

The blind-mummy made to see by Horus = The blind man given sight by Jesus.

The children of Horus = the children of Jesus.

Horus entering the Mount at sunset to hold converse with his Father = Jesus entering the mount at sunset to hold converse with his Father.

Horus transfigured on the Mount = Jesus transfigured on the Mount.

The mummy bandage that was woven without seam = The vesture of the Christ without a seam.

The seven souls of Ra the Holy Spirit = The seven gifts of the Holy Spirit.

The seven loaves of Horus for feeding the multitude reposing in the green fields of Annu = The seven loaves of Jesus for feeding the multitude reclining on the grass.

Twelve followers of Horus as Har-Khutti = Twelve followers of Jesus as the twelve disciples.

The binding of Apap in chains and casting the beast into the Abyss = The binding of the dragon, the old serpent and casting him into the pit.

Apap and Set bound in chains and cast into the Abyss = The Devil and Satan bound in a great chain and cast into the Pit.

The Ankh-key of life and the Un Symbol of resurrection = The keys of death and Hades in the hands of the opener.

The first resurrection and the second death in Amenta = The first resurrection and the second death.

The revelation of Horus, given by Ra his Father to make known the mysteries of divine things to his followers = The revelation of Jesus Christ which God gave him to show unto his servants.

The revelation written down by Aan (Tehuti) the scribe of divine words = The revelation by John the divine.

The saluter Aani, who bears witness to the word of Ra and to the testimony of Horus = John who bears witness to the Word of God and the testimony of Jesus Christ.

The secret of the Mysteries revealed by Taht-Aan = The secret of the Mysteries made known by John.

The books in Annu = The book of doom and the book of life in Patmos.

Anup and Aan the two witnesses for Horus = The two Johns as witnesses for Jesus.

Horus the Morning Star = Jesus the Morning Star.

Horus who gives the Morning Star to his followers = Jesus who gives the Morning Star to his followers.

The name of Ra on the head of the deceased = The name of the Father written on the forehead.

The water of life as lake or river = The river of the water of life.

The two divine Sycamores over the water of life = The tree of life on either side of the water of life.

The great white lake of Sa = The sea of crystal.

The Ba enclosure of Aarru in twelve measures = The walled enclosure of the New Jerusalem in twelve measures.

Heaven according to the measure of a man = Heaven according to the measure of a man.

The Paradise of the Pole Star—Am-Khemen = The Holy City lighted by one luminary, that is neither the Sun or the Moon = the Pole Star.

The Crocodile as the great Mother = The dragon as the great Mother.

Seven dungeon-seals = The book with seven seals.

The Har-Seshu, or servants of Horus = The servants of Jesus Christ.

The seven spirits of fire around the throne of Ra = The seven spirits of fire before the Throne.

The fathers, or the Ancient ones = The four and twenty elders.

The Four-corner keepers = The four living creatures at the four corners.

Horus as Iu the son of man (or Atum) = Jesus the son of man.

Horus as the firstborn from the dead = Jesus the Christ as the firstborn of those that slept.

Horus in the house of a thousand years = The Millennial reign of Jesus.

The Celestial Heptanomis = The seven mountains of Earth or islands in the sea.

The seven children of the old Earth Mother = The seven kings of the earth.

Horus at the head of the seven = Jesus at the head of the seven.

The Calf (later lamb) of Horus standing on the Mount

with Hathor the bride=The lamb standing on Mount Zion with the bride.

The Lunar goddess Hathor bearing the solar orb =The woman arrayed with the sun and the moon at her feet.

The glorified in Hetep stoled and girdled and crowned =The Angels girt about the breasts with golden girdles.

The Ritual shows how the apostles were established beginning with the two brothers, who were followed by the four brethren, the cycle being completed by the twelve in the fields of divine harvest.

The four as brothers of Horus had been figures in the earlier Stellar Cult. The four as his children are figures in the eschatology: the four who are "foremost among the spirits of Annu," with the aid of whom "the fold" was constructed for him, as for one victorious against all "adversaries" (Rit., Ch. 97). The two fours are thus equated in the Gospels. The four brothers of Horus=the four brothers of Jesus. Amsta, Hapi, Tuamutef, Kabhsenuf=James, Joseph, Simon, Judas. The same four in the character of his children with Horus=the four brethren Simon, Andrew, James and John whom Jesus addresses as his children. At a later stage the followers in the train of Horus are the twelve who are his harvesters in the cornfields of Amenta. "Pistis Sophia," in the agreement with the "Book of Hades," shows us how the twelve as followers of Horus were constituted a company that consisted at first of seven then of eight to which the four were added in forming the group of twelve.

The disciples of Jesus likewise became the twelve who reap the harvest. "Then saith He unto his disciples, the harvest truly is plenteous but the labourers are few. Pray ye, therefore, the Lord of the harvest that he send forth labourers into his harvest. And he called unto him his twelve disciples"—who were previously but four (St. Matt. iv. 18-21)—" and gave them authority over unclean spirits, to cast them out, and to heal all manner of disease and all manner of sickness." At this point the names of the twelve are for the first time given (St. Matt. x. 1-5).

The same words are uttered in Luke concerning the harvest and its reapers, but now the number of disciples appointed and sent forth for the ingathering of harvest home is seventy or seventy-and-two—one for each subdivision of the decans in the twelve signs, both the seventy and seventy-two being identifiable astronomical numbers. The twelve with Horus in Amenta are they who labour at the harvest and collect the corn, otherwise souls, for Horus. When the harvest is ready, " the bearers of sickles reap the grain in these fields. Ra says to them, on earth as bearers of sickles in the fields of Amenta," " take your sickles, reap your grain " (" Book of Hades," " Records," Vol. X, 119). Here the labourers who reap the harvest in Amenta are the object of propitiatory offerings and of adoration on earth, as twelve disciples of Horus, son of Ra, the heavenly father. Here the Harvest is identical with the last Judgment. Atum-Ra says at the same time " Guard the enemies, punish the wicked. Let them not escape from your hands. Watch over the executions, according to the orders you have received from the Founder, who has marked you out to strike," as executioners. So it is in the Gospels, where the harvest is one with the judgment at the end of the world.

The originals of all these identifiable characters (and many more might be cited) could occur but once, and that it was Horus of the Egyptians who was the original, the primary and the only one, and that Christianity was founded on the Eschatology of Ancient Egypt there can be no doubt. The proof is extant—for those who wish for the truth.

I take this opportunity of stating that in all my works I have kept to the old Egyptian original in using the ancient words and lettering. I have never understood, and do not understand, why present-day Egyptologists should have altered the originals, for example, T for D, and S to G in Tat and Seb—as well as others. The letter G, which present-day Egyptologists substitute for S, did not originate until the middle of the third century B.C. There is no D or G in the Egyptian Alphabet, and substituting the Y for the I, in my opinion, does not improve the language; many other examples might be mentioned. We know that the Greeks and others used the Egyptian A very often for every other vowel, and the present Germans have followed the same erroneous rendering.

CHAPTER XX

CONCLUSION

It is only by studying the records of the past, which are still extant and a living truth to those who can read the old Sign Language, in which the past records remain as a living witness, that we can trace how the human race has ascended in the evolution of his religious ideas and beliefs *pari passu* with the development of his brain and to a higher type of man.

Like the human bodily or political development, Religion can be studied and followed in its evolution from the lowest Pygmy to the present Christian, the highest Cult so far attained, just as from the lowest Pygmy to the present highest type of white man. From the first dawn of religious ideas in the little Pygmy, how many millions of years ago I cannot say, we trace it to the Nilotic Negro with their religious totemic ceremonies; thence a further development in the Hero-Cult Nilotic Negroes to be followed by the Stellar Cult. Then through Lunar and Solar to the final Eschatology, where the first check in a progressive form of evolution took place. The country in which the humans had from the first continued to progress in bodily and brain evolution continued also to develop the highest type of religious and moral doctrine.

At first all was oral, then written, illustrated, and demonstrated, by Signs and Symbols, and zootype forms, to express ideas and meaning, men not having yet developed the language to portray their beliefs otherwise.

Then, as their brains grew, they developed their language from a primitive mono-syllabic to an agglutinated, and from this to an alphabetical reflected language;

so also their religious ideas became depicted in the human form and a higher type of the doctrinal evolution took place. At this stage socialism and disagreement amongst the priests occurred, and the result was destruction of the nation and its religion, its wise men murdered or dispersed, and its unpurchasable libraries containing the written records of the past burnt or destroyed; and so we have been groping in the dark for 5,000 years. Now we are able to read the records of the past written by our forefathers, which have given light unto the world again and the truth of the evolution of religious doctrines. From the first we see homo believing in a Great Spirit which he could not see or comprehend, but to Whom he made offerings and propitiations. Then as he understood and comprehended the elemental powers, he attributed these as attributes of the Great Spirit. He could see the spirits of his ancestors, and therefore knew that there was really no death, but an after or Spiritual life, and he made offerings and propitiations to these to assist him in all his undertakings. He observed nature and all nature's laws, saw that " life came with water," with " new branches of trees," and fruit for food. All these beliefs he first depicted in his Totemic Ceremonies; that was the foundation and basis on which he built. The next point he noted was that as the seasons of new life came round, so certain groups of stars always appeared in the same place in the heavens, and he then formed a " picture gallery of the stars," each picture representing either one of the elemental powers, or a cycle of a Saviour, as applied to life, not necessarily human at first, but becoming so afterwards. He observed that when certain Stars appeared at a given place, then the inundation of the great water came down to give life and food to himself and the parched dry land of Egypt—a " very saviour " to him, and so he associated this with the " Great Spirit."

During the long ages that the Stellar Cult lasted his brain expanded and grew, and he commenced to build Temples to the Great Spirit, which he invested with further attributes. His knowledge of Astronomy and Mathematics attained the highest record, and during this period he built the great Pyramid to portray all that he believed his spirit had to pass through before it was enabled to gain the Paradise at the North Celestial Pole that he had uranographically configurated there. He had also learnt to write in glyphs, i.e. Signs and Symbols primarily, followed by the most ancient hieroglyphic writings.

It was during the Stellar Cult that we have the first record of the Great Spirit descending to communicate direct with man—it may have been a million years ago. There is one thing, however, very definite and clear, and that is that " the first history of," and the portrayal of Horus being crucified, occurred during the old Stellar Cult, and that the depiction was not on the Cross, but on the " two Poles " (see " Arcana of Freemasonry," p. 41).

In the Solar Cult it was portrayed as on the Tatt Cross and in the Eschatology on the " Christian Cross." But the proof remains that the first was on the " two Poles."

We have seen how they first measured time by the stars, and that all the attributes of the Great Spirit were portrayed in iconographic or zootype forms. Also that although they had " formed a great God " as a trinity, it was expressed only by the combination of three of the elemental powers. There was no " father God " until the Solar Cult came into existence, when they evolved a higher conception of the Great Spirit. We have seen how the old Stellar Cult was spread over most parts of the world and in some places remains there to the present time. The old Stellar Cult was followed, as we have seen, by the Lunar and then the Solar.

Great developments to a higher type of man had taken place, as well as in religious conceptions; and although at first they were all symbolical and taught by symbols and types, in their final eschatology the human form and human soul was represented by the human body and not by iconographic pictures.

Thus we see how the human race has ascended in evolution in religious ideas through the millions of years that have passed from the first appearance of man on earth. We see also how man, by destroying the most enlightened nation, has set himself back in the true knowledge of that one great subject which most concerns him. He destroyed all the Great Book of Truth and degenerated so much that he was unable to read what God had given to man as a guide to him in this world. Fragments of the ancient wisdom remained here and there and have been found and pieced together to form Holy Scripture, but without the true gnosis. Christianity (without the dogmas which have been added by the various sects) may be looked upon as a step to a higher phase than the older Eschatology of the wise men of Egypt, from the ashes of which the foundation was built. That a higher phase must be evolved I have no doubt; but until the priests, who are supposed to be our guides on this great question, have discarded the dogmas their ignorant predecessors introduced there will be no higher type formed. They must also learn to read the written Sign Language of the past, which is still extant and which will give then the true gnosis, but which at present is a closed and secret book to the majority.

One only has to turn back for a few years to see what dense ignorance the people in this country suffered from. In England, during the Long Parliament, 3,000 persons were executed for "witchcraft," and it is truly pitiful to read on what evidence these unfortunate persons were condemned. When the Jesuits in 1649 introduced Peruvian bark into Europe, its use was prohibited on the ground that its cures were "too rapid," and that it possessed no virtue but what it derived from "A compact made by the Indians with the Devil."

Evolution, anatomic and physiologic, and Religions advance hand in hand, *pari passu*. Therefore it is inconceivable that God will allow the human race to relapse into the mire of death and destruction generally. Rather will He continue to evolve it in the future as He has done in the past, i.e. when a nation has risen to a higher type in evolution and then forgotten, or destroyed or disobeyed His Periodic Laws, He will destroy that nation and cause another branch of the human family to progress to a higher type.

Much controversy has occurred within the last few years as to the truth and teachings of the Bible and the most ancient documents extant of that Book. For the original we have to go back to the Egyptian; when Egypt was destroyed, her religion became debased, not being understood.

Coptic versions were made from extant fragments. All words of the Coptic, not Greek, are Egyptian and belong to the language of the people of the country, which had flourished for centuries by the side of the priestly, or Hieratic, language (which came into existence after the Hieroglyphic. (From the time of Psammetici the Hieratic language had been the written language of daily life.) The Coptic is nothing but the Christian arrangement of the Demotic alloyed with Greek words under the Ptolomies, and which must have continued side by side with the Coptic in the second century. The early Christian wrote the same language with an enlarged Greek Alphabet, but for civil transactions the Demotic writing was used partially with old forms, and continued deep into the third century.

Religion cannot advance in evolution without science, and true science will not advance without religion.

I believe at the present day that there are many who are striving and working to know the truth, and these will increase in number until they find it; then all the dogmas that have been introduced into the Christian religion will be swept away and we shall have a higher religion than that which has yet been evolved, and obtain a truer conception of God in all His great manifestations, and of a future Spiritual life to be attained by all who believe in Him.

How far the old wise men of Egypt obtained their great knowledge through "spirit mediumship" I am unable to say, but undoubtedly a very great deal. Seership was a divine gift ; a few possess it at the present day, but not many. These are allowed (their spirits) to enter in and come out of Paradise, and much information is imparted to them ; the old wise men of Egypt used to cultivate this faculty, which the later priests of the Christian Church denounced as a work of the devil, and burnt many : which shows to what a dark and degraded condition the brains of these Christian priests had degenerated.

The old Her-Seshta, or wise men, of Egypt indicated that man may become co-workers with both nature and Divinity on higher planes if he will. He may sit in the Councils of Destiny and help to shape the progress of the race, or he may crawl like a worm and be trodden under foot till, through misery and pain, he struggles to the Light.

The ethics of true Christianity teach the gnosis to obtain the everlasting Spiritual Life, which ethics were first promulgated in the Ritual of Resurrection of the Egyptian Book of Life, which has been brought on in the true Christian doctrines, and still stands good to-day as it did 300,000 years ago or more, altered only in name and in its chronology.

> Death is but a temporary sleep ;
> An interruption, not an end of existence.
> In a future we shall live again,
> According to the nature of our terrestrial lives.
> How little do men heed spiritual things !
> How slight is their knowledge of God !
> They pass from earth as ignorant as children,
> They have no true insight into the Divine.
> All their religion is taken on trust from others,
> They are too indolent to examine it for themselves :
> Therefore the majority live and die in darkness.
> He has imposed transcendent laws*
> Upon all the elemental forces :
> How few know or study them,
> Yet they are the keys of life.

---

* The Periodic Laws of the Corpuscles.

GLOSSARY OF SOME TERMS USED IN TEXT

ABUSKHAW.—The doorkeeper.

ANDROPHAGI.—Man-eating, a cannibal or anthropophagous.

ANIMISM.—The belief in the existence of spirit, or soul, as distinct from matter; of spiritual beings, as souls and of a spiritual world as distinguished from the natural world; spiritism as opposed to materialism—but not human, or in human form—or spirits from human ancestors.

ANTHROPOMORPHIC.—Having human form or human characteristics—man-shaped.

ESCHATOLOGY.—The branch that treats of the final issue and result of redemption in ending human history, including death, resurrection, immortality; the end of the world, final judgment, and the future state. The doctrine of " last things."

EUHEMERIZING.—The nationalistic system of Euhemerus, a Greek philosopher (fourth century B.C.) who explained Mythology as the deification of earth-born Kings and Heroes and denied the existence of a Divine Being.

GNOSIS.—Cognition, especially the higher knowledge of Mysteries; philosophic insight—possessing knowledge, claiming esoteric insight, or wisdom.

HIEROPHANTS.—The Chief Priests or expositors of the Mysteries relating to religion as the Reki or Her-Seshta.

ICONOGRAPHIC.—An image or likeness of anything, more especially the Zootype forms depicted during Stellar Cult, produced by the graphic or plastic arts or sculptured.

PALINGENESIS.—A new or second birth into a higher or better being—a regeneration.

PALEOANTHORPIC.—Of or pertaining to great antiquity as regards the earliest race of men.

PALIMPSEST.—A parchment or other writing material written upon twice, the original writing having been erased wholly or in part to make room for the second.

POLYTHEISM.—The doctrine or belief that there are more Gods than one, used by some as including the forms of fetishism and divinized elemental powers, usually implying anthropomorphism.

GLOSSARY

POLYDÆMONISM.—The supposed lowest form of primitive religion in which innumerable separate demons or spirits control the phenomena of nature.

PSYCHOTHEISTIC.—The tenet that God is absolute Spirit.

SIMULACRUM.—That which is made in the likeness of a thing or being, an image, an imaginary visionary, or shadowy representation, a representation of something.

THERIANTHROPISM.—Representation of preternatural beings in combined forms of man and beast, especially in primitive polytheistic worship.

THEISM.—Belief in God. Belief in the personality and sovereignty of one righteous and eternal deity who has revealed himself superhumanly to man.

URANOGRAPHY.—Stellar astronomy. Descriptive astronomy, especially that branch of the science which treats of the constellations of the stars. Picture writing in the heavens by means of stars.

INDEX

Aāh-Tehuti, 201
Abdallatif, 155
Aber-Amentho, 377
Abraham, 312
Abyss, the, 27, 51
Acts of the Apostles, 375
Adam, 230, 246, 320
African—
    Beliefs, 31, 32
    Folk tales, 49
    Original habitat, 32
    Spiritualism, 11
Agape, the, 45
Agni, 334
Ainus, the, 52
Ak, the, 175
Akar, 232
Akhemu-Seki, the, 153
Akkadians, the, 182
Amatonga, 4
Amazula, 22
Amen, 254, 255
    Cult of, 253, 312
Amenta, 57, 137, 244
    Entrance, 274
    Mysteries of, 29
    Opening and closing, 258
    Passage through, 264, 266, 268, 274, 276, 319, 325-6
    Primitive form, 26
    Ptah forming, 258
America—
    Stellar and Solar Cult people, 142
Am-Khemen, 154, 195, 208
Ammah, 327
Amsu-Horus, 44, 59, 265, 285
Amsu Cross, 155, 158
An-ar-ef, 236
Ancestors—
    Belief in, 31, 32
    of Ra, 228, 243
    of Seb, 243
    Spirits of, 3, 9, 36, 290

Ancestral—
    the foundation of, 124
    Worship, 3, 9, 32
Ancestresses, the Two, 17
Andhumla the Cow, 198
Ani, papyrus, 133
Anianus, 295
Anima, 3
Animism, 4
Animistic, native powers, 4
Ank-Cross, the, 39
Annunciation, the, 368
    the star of, 194
Anointing, 274
Anthropoid ape, 7
Anu, in Babylonia, 132
Anup, 269
Apap—
    Monster, the, 55, 56, 75
    Sebu, spawn of, 58, 138, 139, 263
Ape, the Dog-headed, 275
Apera-Okilchya, the, 25
Apostles, the Creed of the, 374
Apt—
    the Great Mother, 33, 48, 189, 194
    the living word, 204, 287
    of Nubia, 124
Apta, 137
Apt-Uat, 132, 349
Archangels, 5
Ari, the Put Cycle of, 317
Arieltha, 21
Armenian, Gospels, 365
Arunta, the, 38, 370
    Ceremonial rites, 21, 22, 23, 24
    Name of Great Spirit, 32
Assyrian—
    Deluge, 131-2
    Hymns, 189
    Tablet, 186
Astarte, the Goddess, 43
Astromythology, the, 19
Astronomers, the seven rulers, 119
Aten, 201

INDEX

Atnatu, 32
Atum, 229, 231, 243, 246, 319, 364
    Iu, cult of, 224
    Mexican depiction, 319
    Ra, 23, 48, 214, 231
    the two sons of, 56
Australia, 21, 25, 32
    Natives, 394
Avaiki, the, 191
Avathor or Zivo in Mesopotamia, 132
Aztec—
    Cycle of time, 144
    Writings, 141

Baali, 302
Babel, the Tower of, 186
Babylonians, 58, 132, 189, 196
    Bel-Marduk, 59
    Belus, 130
    Colonization, 130
    Creation, 211
    Cult, 328
    Dual God, 49, 50
    Dynasty, 301
    Edin, 297
    Great Mother type, 138
    Legends, 184
    Seven evil powers, 138
    Talmud, 165
Baiame, 32
Bancroft, 131
Beetle, the Egyptian, 34, 37
Belindi-Yaka, 36
Bes, 246
Bible, the, 364
Biblical exodus, 294, 300
Bird, symbol of divinity, 60
Birthplace—
    of Horus, 123, 124, 222
    Solar Cult, 212, 220
    Stellar Cult, 271
Bi-une God, 51
Black Boar of Set, 59
Bora, the ceremony, 26
Book—
    according to St. John, 314
    of Genesis, 242, 294
    of Revelation, the bride in, 218, 255, 256
    of the Dead of Nesi-Khonsu, 282-5
Brotherhoods, the origin of the, 18
Brothers, of Horus, 134-7
Brugsch, 153, 174
Buddha, in China, 333

Buddhist—
    Metaphysics, 227
    Seven footprints, 338
Buddhism, 330, 334, 339
Budge, Dr. Wallis, 178, 265
Buri-Pennu, 53, 336
Bushmen, Creator, 32

Cæsar Augustus, 369
Cæsar, J., 349
Carnarvon, the late Lord, 180
Carter, Mr., 180
Cat, the Great, 390
Cave, in the Earth, 351
Ceremonial—
    of Circumcision, 21, 23
    of Subincision, 22
    of the Arunta, 21
    of the Bora, 26
    of the Kanana, 26
    Rites established, 20
Cetewayo, 30
Ceylon, 335
Chaldea, 209
    God of the Axe, 177
    Stations of the Pole, 209
    Tablets, 59
Chepra tribe, 25
Chichen, 60
Chimalpopoca, the MS., 151, 343
Chinese, the, 192,
    Tai-Yik, 132
    Triad of, 125
    Yin and Yangi, 50
Cholula, the Pyramid of, 141
Christianity, prehistoric, 367
Christians, 45
    Beliefs, 159, 362-94
    Corpus, 3
    Cult of the, 11, 362
    Eucharist, 45
    Portrayal of Divinity, 128
    Sacrament, 45
    Writings, 365
Churinga, the, 38
Circle—
    of Sidi, 153
    of the Great Bear, division of, 118
    of the Shennu, 30, 39, 193
    of twelve, 133
Circumcision, 21, 23
City, the Eternal, 276
Clairvoyance, 12
Clement of Alexandria, 300, 305

INDEX

"Codex Alexandrinus," 366
Conclusion, 404
Constantine, 375
Coptic, the, 365
Corpus, the, 3
Corpuscles, the, 3, 22
Couvade, the, 22
Cow of Heaven—
    Egyptian, 198
    Norse, 198
    Persian, 198
Creation, the, 50, 90
    Chaldean, 59, 328
    Cosmogonical, 184
    Egyptian, 307
    Genesis (Hebrew), 266, 306, 319
Cross, the, 362, 363
    of Palangue, 386
    the Tatt, 362
Cults—
    Christian, 11, 364
    of Har-Makhu, 234
    the earliest form, 54
    of Ptah, 240, 241, 248
    the Hero, 47, 52, 53
    the Lunar, 194
    the Osirian, 265-79
    the Stellar, 212, 271
Cups and Rings, symbols, 160, 161
Cynocephalus, the, 202, 210

Daramulun, 32
Decle, Lionel, 27
Deluge, the Great, 110, 131, 321
Denderah—
    the Temple of, 133, 196, 197
    Zodiac, 223
Devil, the, 387
Dhruva, 175, 338
Diodorus, 130, 155
Disk-worship, 178
Divine-speaker, the, 203
Draconis 56, 188
Dragon story, 55, 56
Druids, the, 346-54
Drummond, Dr., 125
Dual gods, 48, 50, 60
Dunicher, 174

Eades, Mr. W. I., 177, 178
Easter Island, 29
    Imagery of dual god, 49, 50, 60
    of Egg, 59, 60
    Ka-Image, 26

Eden, the Hebrew, 297, 319-20
Edfu, 77
Edin—
    the Babylonian, 297
    other types, 297
Egg, the, imagery of, 54, 60
Egyptian—
    Alphabetic phonetics, 33
    Conceptions, 246
    Creation, 50
    Gods, 57
    Great Mother Apt, 124
    Great Mother Nut, 120, 309
    Great Pyramid, 141, 145-60
    Great Year, 52
    the building of, 139
    Hero Cult development, 52
    Her-Seshta, the, 117, 153
    Ka, 27, 29, 83, 286
    Ka statue, origin of, 26
    Khui Land, 128
    Khuti, 129, 133
    Lord's Table, 156
    Mummy types, 58
    Mysteries, 138
    Mystery teachers, 11, 153, 154
    Mythology, 54
    Origin of the, 40
    Originals, 134
    Paradise, 136, 138
    Primitive form of Amenta, 26
    Rekki, the, 30
    Sacred year, 124
    Solar Cult birthplace, 123
    Stellar Cult birthplace, 123
    Stellar Gods, the seven, 137
    Trinity, first form of the, 51
    Twelve great spirits, 133
    Zootypes images of primary gods, 51
    Zootypology, 33
Egyptians, the, 8, 30, 31
Elemental—
    Powers, 19, 38, 48
    Souls or spirits, 21-31
    represented, 311
Ellis, 60
Elohim, the, 318
    the word, 316-17
Engwurna Mysteries, 26
Enoch, Book of, 131, 313-14, 338, 352
Erech, the Ark City, 128
Esdras, 316

INDEX

Esquimaux, the, 41
Eternity, witness for, 29
Eucharist—
    the Christian, 45
    the Hebrew, 18
    the primary, 16, 17, 45, 393
Euphrateans, the, 182
Eusebius, 295, 374
Exodus—
    in the "Quicke Popul Vuh," 322
    Traditions, 322
    the Hawaiian, 322
Ezekiel, 327

Fatherhood, superseded motherhood, 21
Fathers, of the Christian Church, 373
Fetishism, 36, 39
Finnic triad, 53
Flame, tank of, 268, 269
Foot-prints, the seven, 338
Forty years, days, 325
Four quarters, the, 129
Frazer, Sir James, 15, 36, 38
Frog, the, 22

Gala, Yaka, 36
Gautama, 339
    Buddha, 332-3
Gemare, the, 166
Genesis, 51, 186, 192
Gesenius, 303, 315
Ghosts, belief in the, 31, 32, 227
Gilgames, 128
Gill, Mr., 191
Glorified, the, 290
Glorious Ones, the, 269
God—
    of the Earth, 42, 48
    Bi-une, the, 48, 50, 51
        the sons of, 21
    Horus and Set, 205
    Mythical, the, 16, 21
    Triune, the, 47, 51
Goddesses, 6, 8
    Hathor, 43, 45, 196, 198, 206
    Heket, 205
    Iusâas, 213
    Maāt, 204
    Meh-ur, 199
    Sati, 205
    Tari-Pennu, 53
    Tekhi, 123

Gospel—
    of St. John, 365, 386, 391, 393, 394
    of St. Luke, 379, 391
    of St. Matthew, 380
    of St. Paul, 378, 379, 381
Great Bear—
    as Clock, 123
    as Coffin of Osiris, 133
    as Mother, 52
    Stars of, 130, 218, 220
Great Deluge, 110, 353
Great Dragon-slayer, 205
Great Judge, the, 235
Great Mother, 8, 16, 17, 19, 43, 47, 52, 54, 197, 336
    Apt, 124, 138
    Apt as the living word, 204
    Apt giving birth to her son (Scottish depiction), 126
    Apt, her first two children, 49
    superhuman types of, 42, 119, 120
    Gale Yaka, 53
    Hathor, 194, 195, 197
    Hathor as the Cow of Heaven, 198
    Meh-Ur, the Cow, Lunar type, 199
    Rannut, 58
    Rerit, 59
    Sinde, 41
    Tari-Pennu, 53
    Tekhi, 123
Great Pyramid, of Egypt, 145-6
    of Cholula, 141
Great Spirit, the one, 18, 24, 255
    Kataragan, 36
Great Spirits, the Four, 6, 129
    the Seven, 88, 129, 133, 137
    the Twelve, 133
Great Year, 52, 139, 150-1
Green, Colonel A. O., 147
Green Jade Stone, the, 37
Greenlander, the, 32

Hadrin, 367
Hannuman, 203
Har-Makhu, the Cult of, 234
Har-Ur, 216
Hathor, 43, 45, 196, 206
Haunch, the, 147
Hawaiians, the, 53
Hawk of Light, 51
Heaven, the divisions of, 162, 195

INDEX

Hebrew—
  Angles of, 6
  Creation, 18, 23, 306
  Eden, 297
  Eucharist, 18
  the rendering, 44, 139, 158
  Traditions, 232
  Word, 318
  Writings, 294, 296, 299, 300, 305, 306, 307
Hebrews, the, 291
Herakles, as the seventh Polar Star, 148, 151
Hero Cult, 47, 52–3
Herod the Great, 168
Herodotus, 39, 42, 146
Heroes—
  of the Veddas, 36
  the Two, 36, 37, 48
  the Three, 48
Heru, 33
Heru-Pa-Khart, 224
Heru-Seshu, the, 86
Heru-Seshta, 117, 153
Hetep, 156
Hippopotamus, the, 188
  Female as the Cow of the Waters, 32
  Figured in the Tree of the Pole, 117
Horus, 159, 160, 228, 243, 269, 275, 367, 377, 380
  and Jesus, comparison, 394–402
  as Amsu-Horus, 59
  as Anup, 131
  as Aten, 178–9
  as Crocodile, the Great Fish, 56, 121
  as Har-Ur, 121
  as Hawk of Light, 51
  as Heru-Sma-Taui, 201
  as Horus-Sebek, 222
  as Iu-em-Hetep, 251–2
  as Khensu, 200
  as Natzar, 176
  as one of the Three Heroes, 36, 47–8
  as Presider over the Pole of Heaven, 184
  as Red Calf, 17
  as Saviour of the world, Indian depiction, 177
  as Sebek, 56, 188
  as Serpent-type symbol, 183

Horus (*continued*)
  as Slayer of the Dragon, 225
  as the Corn God, 258
  as Utterer of Words of Ra, 281
  Birthplace of, 123–4
    Scottish depiction of, 125
  Brothers of, 129, 134, 137
  Child of Light, 181
  Children of, 371
  Eternity witness of, 28
  Eye of, 132
  Forms of, 224
  God of Am-Khemen, 226
  God of Light, 48
  God of the Axe, 77, 135, 174, 177
    Mexican representation, 224
  God of the North, 19
  Golden Hawk, 60
  Immortality, as revealer of, 159, 162
  in Spirit, 28, 78
  in the Dark (An-ar-ef), 25
  in the Equinox, 217
  Lord of Resurrection, 28
  Mysteries, 24
    as represented by the Mexican and Zapotec, 143
    as " word made truth," 87
    teacher of the, 134
    teacher of the greater and lesser, 134
    Mexican portrayals, 122
  of the Double Horizon, 135 (*note*), 230
  of the Inundation, 48
  of the Triangle, 354
  the Crucified Victim, 135
  the Great God, 78, 184
  with the Lyre, 237
    Indian portrayal, 237
    Mexican portrayal, 237
Hosea, 44
Huniman, 335
Huxley, 32
Hydra, 56
Hyksos, the, 164, 181, 190, 300

Ibis, the, 202, 204
Ideographs, 32
  primitive, 33
Ilmarinen, 53
Incas, the, 143
Inge, Dean, 296
Inundation, the, 194

INDEX

Irænœus, 157, 256, 373, 374, 375
Iroquois, the, 52
Isaiah, 157
Israelites, the, 291, 348
    twelve banners of, 134
Isthar, 189, 197,
Iusāa, 256
Izanagi and Izanami, 50
Izedin, the, 189

Jackal, the, 132
Jaitwas, the, 203
Jambechus, 200
Japanese, the, 269
    Ame-no-Foko-Tachi-Kam, 132
    Kami, 50, 126
    Kojiki and Yasumaro, 50
Jeremiah, 305
Jerusalem—
    the Talmud of, 165
    Temples of, 164–70
Jesus, 377, 388, 389
    and Horus, comparisons, 394–402
    as Saint Sophia, 263
    the Child, 373
    the gnostic, 366
Jewish Divinity, 242
Jews, the, 166, 325, 356
    yearly celebration, of, 313
Josephus, 167, 168, 300, 301
Joshua, 360, 222
Judah, the Rabbi, 166
Judgment, the first, 268
Justin, Martyr, 407

Ka, the, 26, 28, 29, 83,
    chamber, 27
Kagan, 32
Kali, 331
Kan de Yaka, 36
Kanana, sacred ceremony, 26
Karens, the, 31
Khemennu, 200
Khensu as Horus, 200
Khensu-Hennu, 200
Khensu-Tehuti, 200, 201
Kheper, creator or transformer, 22, 37
Kheru, 216
Khnmu, 194
Khnum, fashioning man out of clay, 246
Khond, sacrifices, 336
Khonds, of Orissa, 53
Khui Land, 128

Khuti, the seven, 129, 132
King Solomon, 164
Kolarians, of Bengal, 336
Koran, the, 358
    system of angles, 5
Krishna, 337
Kuenan, Dr., 315
Kurungal, the Mystery of, 25

Labyrinth, the, 277
Lanzone, Signor, 199
Lartna, 21
Lefebure, 163
Lenormant, 184
Lightfoot, Dr., 365
Livingstone, 27
Lizard, the, 21, 22
Logia, the sayings, 214
Lord's Table, the first, 157
Lot, 185
Lunar—
    Change to Solar, 226
    Types, 206
    Year, 207

Maa, the Goddess, 206
Magic, 36, 37, 39
Makara, the, 343, 344
Malay representatives, 126
Manava-Dharma-Sastra, 60
Manavatara, classes of Rishis, 335
Manes, the, 251
Manetho, 146,
Mangaia, 192
Manu, the, 337
Maori, the myths of the, 310
Mar-Thome, 214
Mary—
    Magdalene, 380
    the Virgin, 370
Marys, the two, 381
Maspero, Professor, 230,
Max Müller, Professor, 33
Maya, mother of Buddha, 321, 340, 341
Mayas, the, 143
    portrayals, 249
Me-Ko-Ma-ro, 23
Merenptah, 293
Meriah, 336
Mesenti, the, 86
Mesken, the, 136, 162
Mesket, the, 174
Mesopotamia, 132

INDEX 419

Mexican—
   Dual God, 49, 50
   Depictions, 127, 226, 237
   Stellar Cult representations, 126, 142, 143
   Triad, 53
   Writings, 143
Milky Way, the, 198
Mishna, the, 166
Miztec, Indian tale of deluge, 130
Moai-Miro, the, 29
Mohammedan doctrines, 5, 355–61
Monotheism, 229
Monstrance, the, 29
Moses, 291
   Laws of, 308, 314
Mother—
   cast off, 21
   the Great, 55
Motherhoods, 16, 17
Mozel, the Priests' records, 130
Mummy, the, 29
   types, 58, 286
Mysteries, the, 392
   established, 20, 24
   Fight between Horus and the Sebu, 25
   of Amenta, 28, 29, 264, 326
   of Tem or Tmu, 238–9
   of the Blindman, 25
   of the Engwurna, 26
   of the Kurugal, 25
   of the Resurrection (primitive), 23
   the Seven, 152
   Totemic, 40
Mythology—
   Egyptian characters, 17
   Founded on, 19, 51
   the Norse, 198
   Origin of, 34
   Primary, 19, 47, 48, 50, 54

Nac Yaku, 36
Navajio Indians, 53
Neith, the Virgin Mother, 223, 370
Nergal, 189
Neter-Kar, 158
New Guinea—
   ceremonies, 59
   Triad, 54
New Zealand triad, 53
Nilotic Negroes, 21, 27
   Hero Cult, 19
   Religious cults, 14, 23, 28

Nimrod, 192, 301
Nirvana, 333
Noah, 131
Nouchian deluge, 131
Nubti, 218
Nut, the Goddess, 309
   the Leg of, 120

Oblations, offered, 28
Omecuiatl, 142
Ometecutli, 142
Onoatoa, 191
Origen's teachings, 11, 374
Osarsiph, 303
Osiris, 57, 59, 185, 245, 265, 285
   Coffin of, 133
   Cult, 215, 265
   in the monstrance, 29

Palingenesis, belief in, 331
Pandorus, 295
Papias, 157
Paradise, 136–8
   the Circumpolar, 320
   the Solar, 244
   the Stellar, 298
Patriarchs, the, 295–311
Paul, 45
Pentateuch, the, 303
Persians, the, 198
Petrie, Sir Flinders, 292
Phallic, worship, 41, 43
Phallus, the, 42, 44
Philo, 295, 301, 304, 373
Phœnicia—
   Sydik, 132
   Records, 301
Pije-Tao, Pije-Zoo—
   American representations of Shu— 143
Pistis Sophia, 214, 376, 382
Plagues, the ten, 325
Plato, 149
Plutarch, 29, 197
Pole Star, the, 7, 150, 151
   Axis, 162
   Changes, 130, 132, 136
   the shifting, 162, 163
Polyhistor, 301
Polynesia, 191
Pre-totemic people, 12
Priesthood—
   the Aztec and Toltec, 142
   of Sais, 149

INDEX

Priesthood (*continued*)
    Solar-Cult, 273
Primitive—
    Eucharist, 16
    Language, 12
    Man, 7
Propitiation, 2, 8
Prose Edda, the, 198
Ptah, 56, 303, 330
    Cult of, 240, 241, 248–9
    Forming Egg, 246
    Put-Cycle, of, 240
    Seker, 364
Ptah-Tanen, 247
Purgatory, primitive form, 27
Pygmies, the, 2, 7, 9
Pyramid—
    of Cholula, 141, 271
    the Great, 141, 145, 160,

Quetzalcoatl Talaloc Tlamacazpui, 142
Quetzalcoatl Totec Tlamacacazui, 142
Quiche "Popul Vuh," 322

Rannut, the Goddess, 113
Red Sea, the, 326
Reeves-Brown, Mr., 177
Reki, the, 30
Religion—
    Beginning of, 13
    Definitions, 1–3
    of Totemic people, 14
Renen, the Goddess, 34
Renouf, 120, 233, 239, 315
Rerit, 59
Resurrection—
    First, 135
    the Mysteries of, 23, 42
Revelation, the Book of, 87, 366, 383, 384
Ritual, the, 28, 29, 215, 217, 278, 279, 287, 288, 289, 309, 327, 361, 362, 364, 377, 389
Rome, 225, 256
    Ritual of, 29
Roth, Dr., 23

Sacred Year, 124
Sais, Priests of, 149
St. John, 386, 391, 393, 394
St. Luke, 379, 391
St. Matthew, 389

St. Paul, 378, 379, 381
Samoans, the, 53
Samyaza, 312, 313
Sanghalese, the, 37
Sandwich Islanders, traditions of, 60
Sati, the Lady, 206
Scotland, symbols found there, 181
Seb, God of the Earth, 42, 48
Sebau, progeny of Apap, 138, 139
Semite legends, 55, 184
Serapis, 367
Serpent type of Tem, 183, 199
Sesheta, foundress of the Heptanomis, 141
Set—
    as Black Boar, 59, 131, 133
    as First in Glory, 188, 189, 190
    as God of Darkness, 48, 51
    and Horus struggle, 325
    Bi-une God with Horus, 51
    God of the South, 19, 51, 75, 326, 387
Seti, 163
Seven, the, 152, 208, 335, 336
    Chaldean stations of the Pole, 209
    Footprints, 338
    Great Spirits, types of, 139, 140
    Mystery Teachers, 153, 154
    Names, 209
    Old Ones, 314
    Pole Stars as eternal types, 132
    Sang-gye, 339
    Stations of the Cross, 208
    Stellar Gods, 137
    Sunken Islands, 191
    Uræi divinities, 58, 243
Shennu ring, 30, 39, 192
Shu, the God, 19, 41, 50, 55, 143, 207, 259, 260, 262, 263
Shu-Anhur, 261, 262, 306
Sign Language, 7, 20, 22
Signs, in circle of precession, 233
Smith, Professor Elliot, 55, 57, 5
Solar Cult, 143, 154, 303–13
    Imagery, 222
Solomon, King, 164
Solon, 149
Sothos, 198
Souls, or Spirits, 21
    making, 25
Spencer and Gillen, 40, 41, 42

INDEX

Spencer, Herbert, 10
Sphinx, the, 180, 231, 232
Spirit—
 of Ancestors, 36
 of Elements, 9
 the Great One, 3
Spiritualists, 9
Stellar Cult, 22, 124, 126, 135, 141, 163, 164, 173, 339
Stonehenge, 153
Subincision, the rite of, 22
Sun, the, 226
 Imaged as a worm, 239
Superhuman powers, 2
Swastika, 126, 129
Sydik, 132
Syrian, system of angles, 5

Tabernacles and Temples of the Hebrews, 164-9
Table, the Lord's, 156
Tablets of Creation, 59
Tablionos, 296
Taht, 194
 Bow of, 210
Taht-Aan, 202, 386
Taht-Khemen, 206
Tahtmes, 231
Tamils, the, 36
Tanganyika, 55, 136, 137
Tari-Pennu, the Goddess, 53, 336
Tatt-Cross, 250
Tattu, 250
Ta-Urt, the Great Goddess Mother Earth, 48
Taylor, 335
Tefnut, 50
Tehuti, 204
Tekhi, the Goddess, 123
Tem—
 the God, 199, 213, 220, 292
 Mysteries of, 238, 239
 Serpent-type of, 182, 199
Temples—
 of Hathor, 175, 196
 of India, 176
 of Jerusalem, 164-72
Tepeyoltotl, Mexican form of Apt, 144
Thalmud, the, 165
Theoponphus, 130
Thibet, 332
 the Seven Sang-gye of, 339
Thompson, J., 240

Three—
 Feathers, 353
 Heroes, 48
Tiamat, 59, 182
Titian, 365
Toltecs, the, 141-2
Tonga Islanders, 31
Tory, Professor, 81
Totem and Totemism, 15, 16, 40, 47
Totemic—
 Creation, 15
 Mother, 54
 People, 12, 46
 Religious Cults, 14
 Sociology, 14
 Souls, 371
Transmigration of Souls, 3, 8, 21
Tree-worship, 45
Triad—
 the Finnic, 53
 the Hawaiian, 53
 the Khons of Orissa, 53
 the Mexican, 53
 the New Zealand, 53
 the South American, 53
Triangle, the, 128-9
 of Horus, 353
Trinity, the primary, 47-51
Tuat, the, 55, 73, 186
Tubal Cain, 301
Tut-Ank-Amen, 180
Tuthmoses, 164
Twanyirika, great spirit, 32
Twelve Great Spirits, the, 133
Two—
 Heroes, 48
 Lions, 235
 Marys, 381
 Merti, 136, 298, 299
 Pillars, 136, 298, 299
 Pillars of Solomon's Temple, 250
 Primal Pillars, 249, 250, 338
 Trees, 136, 298, 299

Uijo-Tao, the great seer, 142
Ukko, the, 53
Ulthauna, the, 24
Uræi, the seven, 58
 Gods, 193
 Serpent of Life, 210
Ursa Minor stars, 130
Uthlanga, the, 137

Vallalpandus, 171
Veddas, 9, 36
Volney, 291

Wainamoinen, the, 53
Wamyamwezi, the, 27
Winged Disks, the, 179
Witoba, 364
Worship—
    of Ancestral Spirits, 9
    of pre-Totemic people, 13
    of the Pygmies, 7

Worship (*continued*)
    of Tree, 45
    Phallic, 41, 43
    Serpent, 43
    the earliest, 2
    Totemic, 46

Yucatan, 141

Zipe-Totec, 364
Zodiac, the twelve signs, 373
Zootypes, 8, 13, 18, 19, 32, 1.
Zunis, the, 39

ORDER FROM YOUR FAVORITE BOOKSELLER OR CALL FOR OUR FREE CATALOG

Of Heaven and Earth: Essays Presented at the First Sitchin Studies Day, edited by Zecharia Sitchin. ISBN 1-885395-17-5 • 164 pages • 5 1/2 x 8 1/2 • trade paper • illustrated • $14.95
God Games: What Do You Do Forever?, by Neil Freer. ISBN 1-885395-39-6 • 312 pages • 6 x 9 • trade paper • $19.95
Space Travelers and the Genesis of the Human Form: Evidence of Intelligent Contact in the Solar System, by Joan d'Arc. ISBN 1-58509-127-8 • 208 pages • 6 x 9 • trade paper • illustrated • $18.95
Humanity's Extraterrestrial Origins: ET Influences on Humankind's Biological and Cultural Evolution, by Dr. Arthur David Horn with Lynette Mallory-Horn. ISBN 3-931652-31-9 • 373 pages • 6 x 9 • trade paper • $17.00
Past Shock: The Origin of Religion and Its Impact on the Human Soul, by Jack Barranger. ISBN 1-885395-08-6 • 126 pages • 6 x 9 • trade paper • illustrated • $12.95
Flying Serpents and Dragons: The Story of Mankind's Reptilian Past, by R.A. Boulay. ISBN 1-885395-38-8 • 276 pages • 6 x 9 • trade paper • illustrated • $19.95
Triumph of the Human Spirit: The Greatest Achievements of the Human Soul and How Its Power Can Change Your Life, by Paul Tice. ISBN 1-885395-57-4 • 295 pages • 6 x 9 • trade paper • illustrated • $19.95
Mysteries Explored: The Search for Human Origins, UFOs, and Religious Beginnings, by Jack Barranger and Paul Tice. ISBN 1-58509-101-4 • 104 pages • 6 x 9 • trade paper • $12.95
Mushrooms and Mankind: The Impact of Mushrooms on Human Consciousness and Religion, by James Arthur. ISBN 1-58509-151-0 • 180 pages • 6 x 9 • trade paper • $16.95
Vril or Vital Magnetism, with an Introduction by Paul Tice. ISBN 1-58509-030-1 • 124 pages • 5 1/2 x 8 1/2 • trade paper • $12.95
The Odic Force: Letters on Od and Magnetism, by Karl von Reichenbach. ISBN 1-58509-001-8 • 192 pages • 6 x 9 • trade paper • $15.95
The New Revelation: The Coming of a New Spiritual Paradigm, by Arthur Conan Doyle. ISBN 1-58509-220-7 • 124 pages • 6 x 9 • trade paper • $12.95
The Astral World: Its Scenes, Dwellers, and Phenomena, by Swami Panchadasi. ISBN 1-58509-071-9 • 104 pages • 6 x 9 • trade paper • $11.95
Reason and Belief: The Impact of Scientific Discovery on Religious and Spiritual Faith, by Sir Oliver Lodge. ISBN 1-58509-226-6 • 180 pages • 6 x 9 • trade paper • $17.95
William Blake: A Biography, by Basil De Selincourt. ISBN 1-58509-225-8 • 384 pages • 6 x 9 • trade paper • $28.95
The Divine Pymander: And Other Writings of Hermes Trismegistus, translated by John D. Chambers. ISBN 1-58509-046-8 • 196 pages • 6 x 9 • trade paper • $16.95
Theosophy and The Secret Doctrine, by Harriet L. Henderson. Includes **H.P. Blavatsky: An Outline of Her Life,** by Herbert Whyte, ISBN 1-58509-075-1 • 132 pages • 6 x 9 • trade paper • $13.95
The Light of Egypt, Volume One: The Science of the Soul and the Stars, by Thomas H. Burgoyne. ISBN 1-58509-051-4 • 320 pages • 6 x 9 • trade paper • illustrated • $24.95
The Light of Egypt, Volume Two: The Science of the Soul and the Stars, by Thomas H. Burgoyne. ISBN 1-58509-052-2 • 224 pages • 6 x 9 • trade paper • illustrated • $17.95
The Jumping Frog and 18 Other Stories: 19 Unforgettable Mark Twain Stories, by Mark Twain. ISBN 1-58509-200-2 • 128 pages • 6 x 9 • trade paper • $12.95
The Devil's Dictionary: A Guidebook for Cynics, by Ambrose Bierce. ISBN 1-58509-016-6 • 144 pages • 6 x 9 • trade paper • $12.95
The Smoky God: Or The Voyage to the Inner World, by Willis George Emerson. ISBN 1-58509-067-0 • 184 pages • 6 x 9 • trade paper • illustrated • $15.95
A Short History of the World, by H.G. Wells. ISBN 1-58509-211-8 • 320 pages • 6 x 9 • trade paper • $24.95
The Voyages and Discoveries of the Companions of Columbus, by Washington Irving. ISBN 1-58509-500-1 • 352 pages • 6 x 9 • hard cover • $39.95
History of Baalbek, by Michel Alouf. ISBN 1-58509-063-8 • 196 pages • 5 x 8 • trade paper • illustrated • $15.95
Ancient Egyptian Masonry: The Building Craft, by Sommers Clarke and R. Engelback. ISBN 1-58509-059-X • 350 pages • 6 x 9 • trade paper • illustrated • $26.95
That Old Time Religion: The Story of Religious Foundations, by Jordan Maxwell and Paul Tice. ISBN 1-58509-100-6 • 220 pages • 6 x 9 • trade paper • $19.95
Jumpin' Jehovah: Exposing the Atrocities of the Old Testament God, by Paul Tice. ISBN 1-58509-102-2 • 104 pages • 6 x 9 • trade paper • $12.95
The Book of Enoch: A Work of Visionary Revelation and Prophecy, Revealing Divine Secrets and Fantastic Information about Creation, Salvation, Heaven and Hell, translated by R. H. Charles. ISBN 1-58509-019-0 • 152 pages • 5 1/2 x 8 1/2 • trade paper • $13.95
The Book of Enoch: Translated from the Editor's Ethiopic Text and Edited with an Enlarged Introduction, Notes and Indexes, Together with a Reprint of the Greek Fragments, edited by R. H. Charles. ISBN 1-58509-080-8 • 448 pages • 6 x 9 • trade paper • $34.95
The Book of the Secrets of Enoch, translated from the Slavonic by W. R. Morfill. Edited, with Introduction and Notes by R. H. Charles. ISBN 1-58509-020-4 • 148 pages • 5 1/2 x 8 1/2 • trade paper • $13.95

ORDER FROM YOUR FAVORITE BOOKSELLER OR CALL FOR OUR FREE CATALOG

Enuma Elish: The Seven Tablets of Creation, Volume One, by L. W. King. ISBN 1-58509-041-7 • 236 pages • 6 x 9 • trade paper • illustrated • $18.95

Enuma Elish: The Seven Tablets of Creation, Volume Two, by L. W. King. ISBN 1-58509-042-5 • 260 pages • 6 x 9 • trade paper • illustrated • $19.95

Enuma Elish, Volumes One and Two: The Seven Tablets of Creation, by L. W. King. Two volumes from above bound as one. ISBN 1-58509-043-3 • 496 pages • 6 x 9 • trade paper • illustrated • $38.90

The Archko Volume: Documents that Claim Proof to the Life, Death, and Resurrection of Christ, by Drs. McIntosh and Twyman. ISBN 1-58509-082-4 • 248 pages • 6 x 9 • trade paper • $20.95

The Lost Language of Symbolism: An Inquiry into the Origin of Certain Letters, Words, Names, Fairy-Tales, Folklore, and Mythologies, by Harold Bayley. ISBN 1-58509-070-0 • 384 pages • 6 x 9 • trade paper • $27.95

The Book of Jasher: A Suppressed Book that was Removed from the Bible, Referred to in Joshua and Second Samuel, translated by Albinus Alcuin (800 AD). ISBN 1-58509-081-6 • 304 pages • 6 x 9 • trade paper • $24.95

The Bible's Most Embarrassing Moments, with an Introduction by Paul Tice. ISBN 1-58509-025-5 • 172 pages • 5 x 8 • trade paper • $14.95

History of the Cross: The Pagan Origin and Idolatrous Adoption and Worship of the Image, by Henry Dana Ward. ISBN 1-58509-056-5 • 104 pages • 6 x 9 • trade paper • illustrated • $11.95

Was Jesus Influenced by Buddhism? A Comparative Study of the Lives and Thoughts of Gautama and Jesus, by Dwight Goddard. ISBN 1-58509-027-1 • 252 pages • 6 x 9 • trade paper • $19.95

History of the Christian Religion to the Year Two Hundred, by Charles B. Waite. ISBN 1-885395-15-9 • 556 pages. • 6 x 9 • hard cover • $25.00

Symbols, Sex, and the Stars, by Ernest Busenbark. ISBN 1-885395-19-1 • 396 pages • 5 1/2 x 8 1/2 • trade paper • $22.95

History of the First Council of Nice: A World's Christian Convention, A.D. 325, by Dean Dudley. ISBN 1-58509-023-9 • 132 pages • 5 1/2 x 8 1/2 • trade paper • $12.95

The World's Sixteen Crucified Saviors, by Kersey Graves. ISBN 1-58509-018-2 • 436 pages • 5 1/2 x 8 1/2 • trade paper • $29.95

Babylonian Influence on the Bible and Popular Beliefs: A Comparative Study of Genesis I.2, by A. Smythe Palmer. ISBN 1-58509-000-X • 124 pages • 6 x 9 • trade paper • $12.95

Biography of Satan: Exposing the Origins of the Devil, by Kersey Graves. ISBN 1-885395-11-6 • 168 pages • 5 1/2 x 8 1/2 • trade paper • $13.95

The Malleus Maleficarum: The Notorious Handbook Once Used to Condemn and Punish "Witches", by Heinrich Kramer and James Sprenger. ISBN 1-58509-098-0 • 332 pages • 6 x 9 • trade paper • $25.95

Crux Ansata: An Indictment of the Roman Catholic Church, by H. G. Wells. ISBN 1-58509-210-X • 160 pages • 6 x 9 • trade paper • $14.95

Emanuel Swedenborg: The Spiritual Columbus, by U.S.E. (William Spear). ISBN 1-58509-096-4 • 208 pages • 6 x 9 • trade paper • $17.95

Dragons and Dragon Lore, by Ernest Ingersoll. ISBN 1-58509-021-2 • 228 pages • 6 x 9 • trade paper • illustrated • $17.95

The Vision of God, by Nicholas of Cusa. ISBN 1-58509-004-2 • 160 pages • 5 x 8 • trade paper • $13.95

The Historical Jesus and the Mythical Christ: Separating Fact From Fiction, by Gerald Massey. ISBN 1-58509-073-5 • 244 pages • 6 x 9 • trade paper • $18.95

Gog and Magog: The Giants in Guildhall; Their Real and Legendary History, with an Account of Other Giants at Home and Abroad, by F.W. Fairholt. ISBN 1-58509-084-0 • 172 pages • 6 x 9 • trade paper • $16.95

The Origin and Evolution of Religion, by Albert Churchward. ISBN 1-58509-078-6 • 504 pages • 6 x 9 • trade paper • $39.95

The Origin of Biblical Traditions, by Albert T. Clay. ISBN 1-58509-065-4 • 220 pages • 5 1/2 x 8 1/2 • trade paper • $17.95

Aryan Sun Myths, by Sarah Elizabeth Titcomb, Introduction by Charles Morris. ISBN 1-58509-069-7 • 192 pages • 6 x 9 • trade paper • $15.95

The Social Record of Christianity, by Joseph McCabe. Includes *The Lies and Fallacies of the Encyclopedia Britannica,* ISBN 1-58509-215-0 • 204 pages • 6 x 9 • trade paper • $17.95

The History of the Christian Religion and Church During the First Three Centuries, by Dr. Augustus Neander. ISBN 1-58509-077-8 • 112 pages • 6 x 9 • trade paper • $12.95

Ancient Symbol Worship: Influence of the Phallic Idea in the Religions of Antiquity, by Hodder M. Westropp and C. Staniland Wake. ISBN 1-58509-048-4 • 120 pages • 6 x 9 • trade paper • illustrated • $12.95

The Gnosis: Or Ancient Wisdom in the Christian Scriptures, by William Kingsland. ISBN 1-58509-047-6 • 232 pages • 6 x 9 • trade paper • $18.95

The Evolution of the Idea of God: An Inquiry into the Origin of Religions, by Grant Allen. ISBN 1-58509-074-3 • 160 pages • 6 x 9 • trade paper • $14.95

ORDER FROM YOUR FAVORITE BOOKSELLER OR CALL FOR OUR FREE CATALOG

Sun Lore of All Ages: A Survey of Solar Mythology, Folklore, Customs, Worship, Festivals, and Superstition, by William Tyler Olcott. ISBN 1-58509-044-1 • 316 pages • 6 x 9 • trade paper • $24.95

Nature Worship: An Account of Phallic Faiths and Practices Ancient and Modern, by the Author of Phallicism with an Introduction by Tedd St. Rain. ISBN 1-58509-049-2 • 112 pages • 6 x 9 • trade paper • illustrated • $12.95

Life and Religion, by Max Muller. ISBN 1-885395-10-8 • 237 pages • 5 1/2 x 8 1/2 • trade paper • $14.95

Jesus: God, Man, or Myth? An Examination of the Evidence, by Herbert Cutner. ISBN 1-58509-072-7 • 304 pages • 6 x 9 • trade paper • $23.95

Pagan and Christian Creeds: Their Origin and Meaning, by Edward Carpenter. ISBN 1-58509-024-7 • 316 pages • 5 1/2 x 8 1/2 • trade paper • $24.95

The Christ Myth: A Study, by Elizabeth Evans. ISBN 1-58509-037-9 • 136 pages • 6 x 9 • trade paper • $13.95

Popery: Foe of the Church and the Republic, by Joseph F. Van Dyke. ISBN 1-58509-058-1 • 336 pages • 6 x 9 • trade paper • illustrated • $25.95

Career of Religious Ideas, by Hudson Tuttle. ISBN 1-58509-066-2 • 172 pages • 5 x 8 • trade paper • $15.95

Buddhist Suttas: Major Scriptural Writings from Early Buddhism, by T.W. Rhys Davids. ISBN 1-58509-079-4 • 376 pages • 6 x 9 • trade paper • $27.95

Early Buddhism, by T. W. Rhys Davids. Includes ***Buddhist Ethics: The Way to Salvation?,*** by Paul Tice. ISBN 1-58509-076-X • 112 pages • 6 x 9 • trade paper • $12.95

The Fountain-Head of Religion: A Comparative Study of the Principal Religions of the World and a Manifestation of their Common Origin from the Vedas, by Ganga Prasad. ISBN 1-58509-054-9 • 276 pages • 6 x 9 • trade paper • $22.95

India: What Can It Teach Us?, by Max Muller. ISBN 1-58509-064-6 • 284 pages • 5 1/2 x 8 1/2 • trade paper • $22.95

Matrix of Power: How the World has Been Controlled by Powerful People Without Your Knowledge, by Jordan Maxwell. ISBN 1-58509-120-0 • 104 pages • 6 x 9 • trade paper • $12.95

Cyberculture Counterconspiracy: A Steamshovel Web Reader, Volume One, edited by Kenn Thomas. ISBN 1-58509-125-1 • 180 pages • 6 x 9 • trade paper • illustrated • $16.95

Cyberculture Counterconspiracy: A Steamshovel Web Reader, Volume Two, edited by Kenn Thomas. ISBN 1-58509-126-X • 132 pages • 6 x 9 • trade paper • illustrated • $13.95

Oklahoma City Bombing: The Suppressed Truth, by Jon Rappoport. ISBN 1-885395-22-1 • 112 pages • 5 1/2 x 8 1/2 • trade paper • $12.95

The Protocols of the Learned Elders of Zion, by Victor Marsden. ISBN 1-58509-015-8 • 312 pages • 6 x 9 • trade paper • $24.95

Secret Societies and Subversive Movements, by Nesta H. Webster. ISBN 1-58509-092-1 • 432 pages • 6 x 9 • trade paper • $29.95

The Secret Doctrine of the Rosicrucians, by Magus Incognito. ISBN 1-58509-091-3 • 256 pages • 6 x 9 • trade paper • $20.95

The Origin and Evolution of Freemasonry: Connected with the Origin and Evolution of the Human Race, by Albert Churchward. ISBN 1-58509-029-8 • 240 pages • 6 x 9 • trade paper • $18.95

The Lost Key: An Explanation and Application of Masonic Symbols, by Prentiss Tucker. ISBN 1-58509-050-6 • 192 pages • 6 x 9 • trade paper • illustrated • $15.95

The Character, Claims, and Practical Workings of Freemasonry, by Rev. C.G. Finney. ISBN 1-58509-094-8 • 288 pages • 6 x 9 • trade paper • $22.95

The Secret World Government or "The Hidden Hand": The Unrevealed in History, by Maj.-Gen., Count Cherep-Spiridovich. ISBN 1-58509-093-X • 270 pages • 6 x 9 • trade paper • $21.95

The Magus, Book One: A Complete System of Occult Philosophy, by Francis Barrett. ISBN 1-58509-031-X • 200 pages • 6 x 9 • trade paper • illustrated • $16.95

The Magus, Book Two: A Complete System of Occult Philosophy, by Francis Barrett. ISBN 1-58509-032-8 • 220 pages • 6 x 9 • trade paper • illustrated • $17.95

The Magus, Book One and Two: A Complete System of Occult Philosophy, by Francis Barrett. ISBN 1-58509-033-6 • 420 pages • 6 x 9 • trade paper • illustrated • $34.90

The Key of Solomon The King, by S. Liddell MacGregor Mathers. ISBN 1-58509-022-0 • 152 pages • 6 x 9 • trade paper • illustrated • $12.95

Magic and Mystery in Tibet, by Alexandra David-Neel. ISBN 1-58509-097-2 • 352 pages • 6 x 9 • trade paper • $26.95

The Comte de St. Germain, by I. Cooper Oakley. ISBN 1-58509-068-9 • 280 pages • 6 x 9 • trade paper • illustrated • $22.95

Alchemy Rediscovered and Restored, by A. Cockren. ISBN 1-58509-028-X • 156 pages • 5 1/2 x 8 1/2 • trade paper • $13.95

The 6th and 7th Books of Moses, with an Introduction by Paul Tice. ISBN 1-58509-045-X • 188 pages • 6 x 9 • trade paper • illustrated • $16.95